FROM PASTURE TO POLIS

MUSEUM OF ART AND ARCHAEOLOGY 🔲 UNIVERSITY OF MISSOURI–COLUMBIA

FROM PASTURE TO POLIS

ART IN THE AGE OF HOMER

EDITED BY SUSAN LANGDON 🔲 *WITH AN ESSAY BY* JEFFREY M. HURWIT

UNIVERSITY OF MISSOURI PRESS 🔲 COLUMBIA AND LONDON

The Exhibition *From Pasture to Polis: Art in the Age of Homer* has been organized by The Museum of Art and Archaeology, University of Missouri–Columbia, and is made possible by generous grants from the National Endowment for the Humanities and the National Endowment for the Arts. Funding for the exhibition in Columbia was provided in part by the Museum Associates, Inc.

EXHIBITION DATES:
Museum of Art and Archaeology, University of Missouri–Columbia
  October 9–December 5, 1993
University Art Museum, University of California, Berkeley
  January 20–March 20, 1994
Arthur M. Sackler Museum, Harvard University, Cambridge
  April 23–June 19, 1994

Library of Congress Cataloging-in-Publication Data

From pasture to polis : art in the age of Homer / Museum of Art and
  Archaeology, University of Missouri–Columbia ; edited by Susan
  Langdon ; with an essay by Jeffrey M. Hurwit.
      p. cm.
    "Exhibition dates: Museum of Art and Archaeology, University of
  Missouri–Columbia, October 9–December 5, 1993; University Art
  Museum, University of California, Berkeley, January 20–March 20,
  1994; Arthur M. Sackler Museum, Harvard University, Cambridge, April
  23–June 19, 1994"—T.p. verso.
    Includes bibliographical references and index.
    ISBN 0-8262-0928-9
    1. Decorative arts, Ancient—Greece—Exhibitions. 2. Greece—
  History—Geometric period, ca. 900–700 B.C.—Exhibitions.
  I. Langdon, Susan Helen, 1952- . II. University of Missouri–
  Columbia. Museum of Art and Archaeology. III. University of
  California, Berkeley. University Art Museum. IV. Arthur M. Sackler
  Museum.
  NK670.F76   1993
  709′.38′07473—dc20   93-24787
                                                        CIP

Designer: Rhonda Miller
Typesetter: Reporter Typographics
Printer and binder: Walsworth Publishing Company
Typefaces: Albertus, Weiss, and Elante.

CONTENTS

LIST OF FIGURES

LENDERS
TO THE EXHIBITION

Baltimore, MD, *Walters Art Gallery*

Berkeley, CA, *Phoebe Appeson Hearst Museum of Anthropology, University of California*

Bloomington, IN, *Indiana University Art Museum*

Boston, MA, *Museum of Fine Arts*

Brunswick, ME, *Bowdoin College Museum of Art*

Buffalo, NY, *Buffalo Museum of Science*

Cambridge, MA, *Arthur M. Sackler Museum, Harvard University Art Museums*

Cleveland, OH, *The Cleveland Museum of Art*

Columbia, MO, *Museum of Art and Archaeology, University of Missouri–Columbia*

Detroit, MI, *The Detroit Institute of Arts*

Houston, TX, *The Menil Collection*

Houston, TX, *The Museum of Fine Arts*

Los Angeles, CA, *Los Angeles County Museum of Art*

Los Angeles, CA, *Sol Rabin Collection*

Malibu, CA, *The J. Paul Getty Museum*

New Haven, CT, *Yale University Art Gallery*

New York, NY, *The Metropolitan Museum of Art*

New York, NY, *Shelby White and Leon Levy Collection*

Philadelphia, PA, *University Museum, University of Pennsylvania*

Princeton, NJ, *The Art Museum, Princeton University*

Providence, RI, *Museum of Art, Rhode Island School of Design*

Richmond, VA, *Virginia Museum of Fine Arts*

Rochester, NY, *Memorial Art Gallery of the University of Rochester*

South Hadley, MA, *Mount Holyoke College Art Museum*

Tampa, FL, *Tampa Museum of Art*

Toronto, Ontario, *Royal Ontario Museum*

CONTRIBUTORS
TO THE CATALOGUE

T. A.	Tamsey Andrews
M. J. B.	Michael J. Bennett
M. H. F	Marian H. Feldman
S. L.	Susan Langdon
D. G. M.	David Gordon Mitten
J. M. P.	J. Michael Padgett
A. J. P.	Aaron J. Paul

ACKNOWLEDGMENTS

It is only in the last fifty years that a proper appraisal of the significance and the subtlety of Geometric culture and art has been made, and the objects studied with the same attention to detail that had only accompanied studies of the Archaic period. As an exhibition concept, the art of the Geometric period has just once been featured in an American museum, and that was more than twenty years ago and unaccompanied by a catalogue. *From Pasture to Polis: Art in the Age of Homer* is the first comprehensive exhibition of Geometric art in this country or abroad to synthesize recent scholarly research and discoveries made in the art, literature, and life of this period. The occasion for the exhibition is especially appropriate in Columbia, given the Museum of Art and Archaeology's collection of Geometric art, the Department of Art History and Archaeology's long-standing interest in Greek art, and the history of the Center for Studies in Oral Tradition here at the university.

We are most grateful for the generous financial assistance of the National Endowment for the Humanities and the National Endowment for the Arts, which provided funding for the planning and implementation of the exhibition and its various accompanying programs, including this catalogue. This project would simply not have been possible without their support, and we are indebted to both organizations for their continued support of this museum's projects.

In a museum like ours with a small staff, the undertaking of such an exhibition, and the successful realization of the catalogue and the accompanying academic and public programs, requires the participation and collaboration of all staff and many colleagues and friends. To Susan Langdon, the exhibition's guest curator, must go our most profound gratitude for her expertise in selecting the works, editing and contributing to the catalogue, and, more significant, guiding the project throughout its multi-year journey along an exciting and sometimes rocky path. She devoted enormous amounts of time over four years, provided whatever was needed promptly and thoughtfully, put up with the usual unavoidable aggravation involved in a major loan exhibition and catalogue, and, most important, maintained throughout the project the highest academic and professional standards. From the original concept to the last didactic label, this project reflects Langdon's special quality as a scholar and teacher. Our thanks to Langdon should also extend to her husband, Marcus Rautman, associate professor of art history and archaeology at the University of Missouri, who gave many hours of his time to proofreading, working on the bibliographical materials for the catalogue, and assisting with the installation of the exhibition.

An outside advisory group made up of leading American scholars in the field also helped shape the humanities theme of the project and assisted us in developing the present exhibition, its catalogue, and topics for a symposium on the theme of Geometric art and culture held in conjunction with the exhibition in Columbia. They are Jane B. Carter, Department of Classical Languages, Tulane University; Andrew Stewart, Department of the History of Art, University of California, Berkeley; David Gordon Mitten, Department of Classics, Harvard University, who also contributed to the catalogue entries and has been especially helpful securing the loans from the Arthur M. Sackler Museum at Harvard; and Jeffrey Hurwit, Department of Art History, University of Oregon, whose illuminating essay in the catalogue explores the interconnections of Geometric art and literature. Evelyn Lord Smithson offered us valuable insight and enthusiastic support at the beginning of this project; her death is a loss felt by both the exhibition and the greater discipline. Our sincere thanks are also due to Tamsey Andrews, Michael J. Bennett, Marian H. Feldman, J. Michael Padgett, and Aaron J. Paul for their catalogue entries.

We must also mention and thank our University advisory committee of William Biers, Department of Art History and Archaeology; William Bondeson, Department of Philosophy; Alfred S. Bradford, Department of History; John Foley, Department of English and director of the Center for Studies in Oral Tradition; and Theodore Tarkow, Department of Classical Studies and Associate Dean of the College of Arts and Sciences, who have all been regularly available and consulted with by the staff on various aspects of the exhibition and the symposium.

The ever-increasing demands placed on museum directors, curators, and private collectors have made "theme" exhibitions difficult to organize in recent years. The generosity of the lenders has been outstanding, and on behalf of the Museum of Art and Archaeology and the University of Missouri–Columbia, I extend our great appreciation to the many museum directors, curators, boards, conservators, and registrars who put collegiality and public accessibility to their works foremost and agreed to lend to this exhibition. We particularly thank: Ellen Reeder, Walters Art Gallery, Baltimore; Frank A. Norick, Phoebe Appeson Hearst Museum of Anthropology, Berkeley; Jacquelynn Baas, Bonnie Pitman, James Steward, Lisa Calden, University Art Museum, University of California, Berkeley; Adriana Calinescu, Indiana University Art Museum, Bloomington; John Herrmann, Cornelius Vermeule, Emily Vermeule, Mary Comstock, Museum of Fine Arts, Boston; Katharine J. Watson, Bowdoin College Museum of Art, Brunswick; Kevin Smith, Buffalo Museum of Science, Buffalo; James Cuno, Aaron Paul, Amy Brauer, Rachel Vargas, Ada Bortoluzzi, Jane Montgomery, The Harvard University Art Museums, Cambridge; Arielle Kozloff, The Cleveland Museum of Art, Cleveland; William Peck, Suzanne Quigley, Michele Peplin, The Detroit Institute of Arts, Detroit; Bertrand Davezac, Nancy Swallow, Menil Collection, Houston; Anne Schaffer, The Museum of Fine Arts, Houston; Nancy Thomas, Renee Montgomery, Los Angeles County Museum of Art, Los Angeles; Sol Rabin, Los Angeles; Marion True, Karen Manchester, J. Paul Getty Museum, Malibu; Susan Matheson, Yale University Art Gallery, New Haven; Joan Mertens, The Metropolitan Museum of Art, New York; Shelby White, Leon Levy, Shelby White and Leon Levy Collection,

New York; David Romano, University Museum, University of Pennsylvania, Philadelphia; Michael Padgett, Art Museum, Princeton University, Princeton; Florence Friedman, Anne Leinster, Rhode Island School of Design, Providence; Margaret Mayo, Patricia Gilkison, Maureen Morrisette, Virginia Museum of Fine Arts, Richmond; Marie Via, Memorial Art Gallery, Rochester; Wendy Watson, Mount Holyoke College Art Museum, South Hadley; Pamela Russell, Andrew Maass, Tampa Museum of Art, Tampa; Alison Harle Easson, Ronnie Burbank, Royal Ontario Museum, Toronto. We are grateful to Edward H. Merrin for his assistance, which made it possible for us to secure the Buffalo Museum of Science loan.

Needless to say, our museum staff and fine volunteers have shouldered a great deal of the work and deserve a standing ovation. Curator of ancient art Jane Biers lent her experience and knowledge to the exhibition installation in Columbia and other curatorial aspects of the project; the diverse roles and cheerful attitude of Jacque Dunn, assistant director, have been essential to the success of the promotional and public relations campaign for this project and the symposium; Luann Andrews, curator of education, created the superb educational components, including helping with two summer teacher workshops in 1992 and 1993; Jeffrey Wilcox devoted many hours to arrange for all loan and photographic requests; Greg Olson (now of the Nelson-Atkins Museum of Art) and Greig Thompson, preparators, provided preliminary drawings and plans that became the blueprint for the exhibition design with the help of our outside exhibition design consultant Elroy Quenroe, of Quenroe Design

Associates, Inc.; and Diane Buffon (now State Historical Society of Missouri), fiscal officer, made our lives so much easier by her superb financial record-keeping skills. Other important tasks were carried out efficiently by Anne Harwell Brooks, senior secretary, who spent many long hours typing the grant applications and other related materials; Aimée Leonhard, assistant conservator; Tyler Dawson, assistant preparator; and the graduate students in the Museum Studies class of 1992–1993 who helped with various tasks. Leslie Hammond and Lisa Benson, graduate students in the Department of Art History and Archaeology, were especially helpful in undertaking curatorial research, checking references, arranging for interlibrary loans, and handling registrarial matters.

We also owe a debt of gratitude to Chancellor Charles Kiesler, Vice Chancellor for Development Roger Gafke, Provost Gerald Brouder, and especially to Graduate School Dean and Vice Provost for Research Judson D. Sheridon and Associate Vice Provost for Research John McCormick, who have provided vital moral support for this project.

Finally, we must acknowledge all of our friends and colleagues at the University of Missouri Press, without whose hard work and professionalism this publication would not be possible. We are especially indebted to Rhonda Miller for her thoughtful design of the exhibition catalogue, to Jane Lago for her exemplary work as the copy editor, and to Beverly Jarrett, director of the University of Missouri Press, for her grace under pressure and her generosity.

Morteza Sajadian
Director, Museum of Art and Archaeology

FROM PASTURE TO POLIS

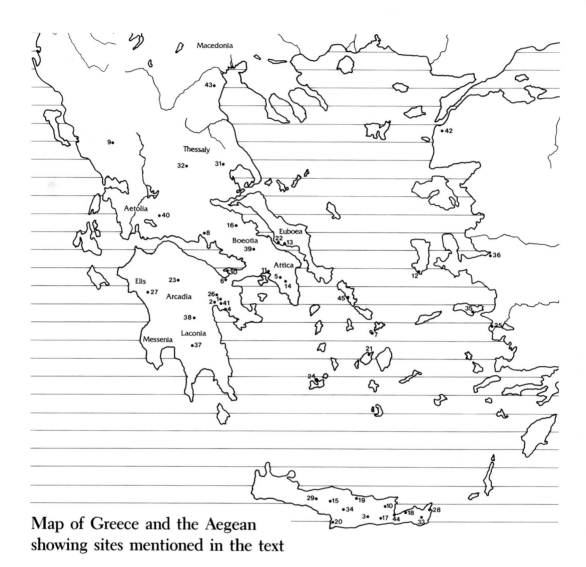

Map of Greece and the Aegean showing sites mentioned in the text

1. Argive Heraion	13. Eretria	25. Miletus	36. Smyrna
2. Argos	14. Hymettus	26. Mycenae	37. Sparta
3. Arkades	15. Idaean Cave	27. Olympia	38. Tegea
4. Asine	16. Kalapodhi	28. Palaikastro	39. Thebes
5. Athens	17. Kato Syme Viannou	29. Patsos Cave	40. Thermon
6. Corinth	18. Kavousi	30. Perachora	41. Tiryns
7. Delos	19. Knossos	31. Pherai	42. Troy
8. Delphi	20. Kommos	32. Philia	43. Vergina
9. Dodona	21. Koukounaries, Paros	33. Praisos	44. Vrokastro
10. Dreros	22. Lefkandi	34. Prinias	45. Zagora, Andros
11. Eleusis	23. Lousoi	35. Samian Heraion, Samos	
12. Emborio, Chios	24. Melos		

1

Plate 1. Neck-handled amphora (9). Buffalo Museum of Science. Height 0.683.

Plate 2. Pair of deities (41). Gift of Leslie Hastings, Esq., courtesy of Museum of Fine Arts, Boston. Height 0.08.

Plate 3. Horse pyxis (29). University of Missouri–Columbia, Museum of Art and Archaeology, Gilbreath-McLorn Museum Fund. Height 0.081.

Plate 4. Small krater (4). University of Missouri–Columbia, Museum of Art and Archaeology, Gift of Museum Associates and Gilbreath-McLorn Museum Fund. Height 0.203.

Plate 5. Triple skyphos (23). Tampa Museum of Art, Joseph Veach Noble Collection. Height 0.128.

Plate 6. Pomegranate vase (22). Bowdoin College Museum of Art, Gift of Edward Perry Warren. Height 0.102.

4

Plate 7. Engraved bow fibula (81). Arthur M. Sackler Museum, Harvard University Art Museums, Ancient Art Acquisition Fund through the generosity of Walter and Ursula Cliff. Photo: Michael A. Nedzweski. Height 0.17.

Plate 8. Stamnoid olla (63). The Art Museum, Princeton University, Museum purchase, John Maclean Magie and Gertrude Magie Fund. Height 0.216.

Plate 9. Oinochoe with figural scene (99). Richard Norton Memorial Fund, courtesy of Museum of Fine Arts, Boston. Height 0.178.

Plate 10. Engraved belt (60). Arthur M. Sackler Museum, Harvard University Art Museums, Gift of Robert A. Kagan. Photo: Michael A. Nedzweski. Height 0.052.

Plate 11. Neck-handled amphora (3). Richmond, Virginia Museum of Fine Arts, The Glasgow Fund, 1960. Photo: Grace Wen Hwa Ts'ao. Height 0.676.

Plate 12. High-rimmed bowl (21). Mount Holyoke College Art Museum, Nancy Everett Dwight Fund, 1935. Height 0.092.

Plate 13. Belly-handled amphora (87). Indiana University Art Museum, Given in Honor of Burton Y. Berry and Herman B. Wells by Thomas T. Solley. Photo: Michael Cavanagh, Kevin Montague. Height 0.71.

Plate 14. Spiral-form earrings (13). Los Angeles County Museum of Art, Gift of Harvey S. Mudd. Diameter of disks 0.028.

Plate 15. Bull figurine (6). University of Missouri–Columbia, Museum of Art and Archaeology, Gift of Marie Farnsworth. Height 0.055.

Plate 16. Pitcher-olpe (79). Arthur M. Sackler Museum, Harvard University Art Museums, Francis H. Burr Memorial Fund. Photo: Michael A. Nedzweski. Height 0.522.

INTRODUCTION

Susan Langdon

The vibrant chapter of early Iron Age Greece from circa 1000 to 700 B.C. was a time of dramatic transformation. During this period the Greek-speaking peoples in the Aegean region gradually emerged from a prolonged Dark Age to establish the basic forms of their classical culture. By 700 this cultural revival had given rise to the polis, or city-state, system in several parts of Greece, to the great Panhellenic sanctuaries dedicated to the Olympian gods, to colonization in east and west, to the alphabet and literacy, to contact with foreign peoples, and to a rebirth of art, especially in sculpture and figural painting.

The cultural revival that characterizes this period must be understood in the context of what preceded it. The dominant Bronze Age culture on the Greek mainland, the Mycenaean palatial civilization, had fallen in successive waves of catastrophe that by 1150 B.C. had dealt a profound blow to its cultural and social systems. Following this widespread collapse ensued a Dark Age lasting nearly four centuries. Archaeological evidence for this period suggests material poverty and social insecurity on a grand scale. Estimates of population decline range from 75 percent to an incredible 90 percent. Material remains point to a transient lifestyle, perhaps uncertain peace and insufficient sustenance, and a nearly complete cessation of foreign contact. During this prolonged period of demographic change the complex inheritance of the prosperous and stable past was preserved through oral poetry and religious myth, eventually to play a remarkable role in the structuring of a newly emerging society. Thus the poetry and art of the Geometric period, so called because of its characteristically abstract and formulaic approach to design, capture the fundamental processes of the birth of the classical world.[1]

This age can truly be called a renaissance—both figuratively, as in a "golden age" of flourishing culture, and literally in its revival of the historical past through literature, as the Homeric epics that date from this period dramatically illustrate. Over the past several decades research in Geometric studies and results of excavations have fueled lively discourse and sometimes ignited controversies that touch on the very foundations of classical Greek civilization. Among the most important questions currently under debate are: to what extent was Greek culture either independently and locally formed, or sparked into life by the sophisticated traditions of its older Near Eastern neighbors? How much of the Mycenaean culture survived the Dark Age to form the basis of the new Iron Age civilization? Is the traditional view of a catastrophically devastated Dark Age the most accurate interpretation of the evidence?

In general surveys of Greek art and culture, the period tends to be briefly reviewed through a familiar approach: the Geometric period is characterized as a prelude to and the foundation of classical civilization. This understanding, however, has become inadequate. Recent archaeological work, new trends in ancient literary analysis, the application of anthropological methods to classical archaeology, and changing theories of economic and political behavior not only enable but require us to consider the Greek Iron Age as a fully developed culture in itself and not just a preliminary phase. Much that characterizes the age in fact does not continue into the Archaic and

Classical periods. For these reasons *From Pasture to Polis* examines this early phase of Greece in terms of the processes of change and a society's mechanisms for adapting to new ideas and shifting structures. The exhibition assembles an often surprising and generally unfamiliar collection of objects whose total impact creates an exciting sense of collective thinking and nascent ideas. Only once before has an exhibition in an American museum featured the art of Geometric and Archaic Greece, in the show *Art in the Age of Homer* organized over twenty years ago (December 1969–March 1970) by the University Museum of the University of Pennsylvania. As part of a broadly based revival of interest in Geometric Greece, the present exhibition synthesizes the advances made by recent scholarly research in the art, literature, and life of this period.

Objects in an exhibition (and in a catalogue) are objects devoid of context. The organization of this exhibition, as reflected in the catalogue, groups objects thematically not only to clarify content but also in order to suggest plausible contexts for the art in terms of its original function and meaning to the people who created it. At the same time, the exhibition draws solely upon objects from North American collections in order to highlight unpublished or little-known works and enlarge the established corpus of early Greek art. The obvious predominance of Attic works, while doing little to mitigate the Athenocentric tendencies of past Geometric studies, reflects the composition of museum collections in Europe and America formed in the early part of the century during the prolonged dispersal of objects from Athenian graves. Some balance

---

1. All Homeric quotations herein are from the following translations, unless otherwise noted: R. Lattimore, *The Iliad of Homer* (Chicago and London 1951, 1961) and *The Odyssey of Homer* (New York 1965, 1967). All pottery dates follow those of Coldstream, *Greek Geometric Pottery* 330 and *Geometric Greece* 385. All measurements are in meters.

is provided by the bronze votive offerings that constitute an almost equally large portion of the exhibition, as they represent for the most part the typical furnishings of Peloponnesian and central and northern Greek sanctuaries.

The objects assembled here offer two paths into the period, first as *realia*, elements of the Geometric world's tangible existence, and second as documentation of how the Greeks represented that reality to themselves. The product of both conscious and unconscious manipulation by its producers and its users, art has a privileged function in the public workings of a society. The use of art to explore cultural transformation can therefore reveal things that other approaches might miss, particularly in the case of a nonliterate and relatively impoverished culture. A general bias toward the individual, usually understood as a characteristic of classical culture, can be detected in the material remains of this period. In Geometric art the steady narrowing of an anthropocentric and narrative focus is aided by the emergence of various recognizable artistic personalities and workshops. In the realm of religious evidence, official cult in the Bronze Age is visibly distinct from popular religious activity; in contrast, numerous changes in the Geometric period laid the foundation for the remarkably religious cultures of Archaic and Classical times, in which popular and public worship have become almost indistinguishable. Bronzeworkers and sculptors in particular aided this process of accessibility to the divine by producing a wide range of representational votive art. Social relationships imply similar trends. Perhaps the most important product of a growing emphasis on the individual was the political basis of the *polis*, in which governing authority resided with the citizens. It is surely no coincidence that the struggle between corporate affiliation and the identity of the individual is a major theme of one of the great artworks of the period, the *Iliad*.

Mycenaean written documents, preoccupied with bookkeeping and inventories, are too prosaic to reveal whether an interest in a shared cultural past was already a Helladic trait before the Iron Age (although a recent discovery of a bit of poetry on a Knossian tablet hints that surprises may yet lie in store). The interest of the Geometric period Greeks in exploring their past through art and poetry seems to have been a matter of both survival and revival. Myths and legends inherited from the Bronze Age not only preserved what was relevant and meaningful to them but became their most effective means of expressing complex moral and social ideas. Recent scholarship has made abundantly clear how the centuries-long interest in the heroic past found expression in the widespread establishment of cults to unknown heroes at Mycenaean tombs, the heroic ambience of figural art, and the general enthusiasm for things heroic in funerals and religious games.

Following the lines of Hesiod, some scholars have interpreted this preoccupation as a deep-seated nostalgia-cum-inferiority complex arising from the unhappy comparison between the ages of Bronze and of Iron. More recent studies have redefined this interest as the "politicization" of the heroic past for the reordering of a scattered society, operating for example in the role of heroic lineage in individual claims to land, or the appropriation of Bronze Age cults for the purpose of extending civic boundaries. Much of the thought that lay behind the later traditions in cult, law, and the obligations of the citizen were encoded in the heroic behavior of epic. The proliferation of this poetry among the social elite was a crucial factor in the developing city-states.

Was the art that accompanied such heroic preoccupations of necessity a geometric style? Its thematic elements might have been successfully conveyed through detailed naturalism, but the evident commitment of the Iron Age Greeks to the orderings of the family, society, the gods, and the cosmos would have lacked a voice. To an eye accustomed to the fluid contours and volumes of classical painting and sculpture, Geometric art might seem "small, bleak, thrifty," as Beazley and Ashmole described it.[2] One of the great benefits of the tabula-rasa beginnings of Protogeometric and Geometric art that distinguishes it from the varied artistic forms of the Bronze Age is its purity of media. The painter of a Geometric pot was uninfluenced by large-scale painting and its expanses of flat surface; the sculptor of bronze figurines had no monumental statues in mind. Taking cues only from the swelling surfaces of the pot's shape, the Geometric artist explored the arresting paradox of the elastic continuum of a pot's contours overlaid by the relentless rigidity of straight lines and right angles. The constant repetition of a limited number of motifs in a series of permutations was controlled by rules of placement and appropriateness. Close study of a Geometric vessel reveals an almost unbelievable precision of measurement and execution. With an impressively minor rate of failure, artists managed the exact spacing of repeated bands, the unvarying regularity of line widths, and the avoidance of crowding or of excess "air"

that the style requires. The painters' apparent contentment with only rectilinear ornaments for nearly 250 years attests to the perfect suitability of form and content and in fact raises the question whether there is more to this abstract decoration than meets the twentieth-century eye. The loss of figural art through most of the Dark Age meant the loss of a major form of communication of symbols and values. It is fair to ask whether the abstract decoration of the tenth through early eighth centuries in some way fulfilled this communicative function, whether there were social messages encoded in the highly repetitive and increasingly complex treatment of pottery surfaces before the advent of the human figure.

The bronze figurines, generously represented in the exhibition, were conceived from the outset as a miniaturist tradition molded by the context of votive offering. While the introduction of the painted animal and human figures into the ceramic decorative system required a conscious rejection of the organic, those figures offered in ritual communication with the divine demanded a certain clarity of identity. Starting from an unpracticed but necessary approximation of naturalism, the bronze sculptor only gradually, through increasing technical confidence and formalization of types, found the geometry that was characteristic of painted figures from the beginning.

The Geometric artistic style, perfected slowly but steadily over several centuries, achieved an expressive force equal to its task of implementing and reflecting the transformation of early Greek society. Created with a spareness that is elegant

---

2. J. D. Beazley and B. Ashmole, *Greek Sculpture and Painting to the End of the Hellenistic Period* (Cambridge 1932) 4.

rather than impoverished, its elements were drawn from a limited palette of warriors, horses, birds, deer, and dancers and repeated in infinite permutations that alert us to the cultural truths they bear. Such richness led Sylvia Benton sixty years ago to observe, "Geometric art is less thrifty than some had supposed."[3]

3. Benton, "Evolution of the Tripod-Lebes" 97.

ART, POETRY,
AND THE POLIS IN THE AGE OF HOMER

Jeffrey M. Hurwit

What may at first glance seem one of the more modest objects in this exhibition of early Greek art is actually one of the most significant items on display: an irregularly shaped potsherd, from the collection of the Yale University Art Gallery, bearing on its battered surface parts of two human silhouettes (98). Above, a warrior has fallen to the ground, his head bent down upon an outstretched and lifeless arm. Below, another soldier marches to the right: he carries two spears and a great, radically incurved shield—a controversial sort known as the "Dipylon shield" (more on that later). Hovering haphazardly about the figures is an assortment of abstract motifs (joined triangles, ovals with rings of dots, a swastika) whose precise symbolism, if symbols they are, eludes us.[1]

The sherd belonged to a huge vase known as a krater, and it almost certainly comes from the same work as do much

---

1. Such motifs are typically called "filling ornaments," as if they are there just to occupy empty space, assuage *horror vacui*, and symbolize nothing. But the joined triangles suggest the shape of a double ax (a ritual instrument with a long history in the Aegean), and the now infamous swastika seems originally to have been an Indic sign symbolizing long life or the sun. That same motif is, however, found at different times in the designs of cultures all over the world (from China to Mesopotamia to Native America), and there is no evidence as to what meaning, if any, it had for early Greeks. Nonetheless, it is likely that at least some of the "fillers" of Geometric art actually meant something in at least some contexts. The few attempts to decode the symbolism of Greek Geometric ornaments include A. Roes, *Greek Geometric Art: Its Symbolism and Its Origins* (Haarlem 1933); Courbin, *La céramique géométrique de l'Argolide* 475–78; N. Himmelmann-Wildschütz, *Über einige gegenständliche Bedeutungsmöglichkeiten des frühgriechischen Ornaments* (Wiesbaden 1968); and Boardman, "Symbol and Story in Geometric Art," who plausibly

Fig. 1. Fragment of krater from the Dipylon ceme-
tery, Louvre A519. (Photo courtesy of the Musée
du Louvre)

larger fragments in the Louvre (Fig. 1).[2]
The vase (originally about a meter high)
was probably painted on commission by an
unknown Athenian artist not long after the
middle of the eighth century B.C. to stand
as a marker over the grave of an important
member of an important early Athenian
family. It was a doubly appropriate monument. First, kraters were typically used for the
serving of wine mixed with water—krater
means "mixing bowl"—at the aristocratic
banquet known as the symposium, and this
was the kind of activity over which the
deceased, a member of the Athenian elite,
no doubt often presided in life. The krater
shape itself, in other words, had inherently
aristocratic associations. Second, whether or
not the images painted upon its surface
bore any relation to the life of the deceased
(for instance, as reflections of his achieve-
ments, aspirations, or fate), the fact that
there were images at all is another indication of his status. In the eighth century
representation was virtually the sole property

of the aristocracy. An image was an aristocratic sign.

Below a tall lip filled with a pattern known
as a double meander, below a narrow strip of
dotted diamonds and two horizontal lines, at
least two zones of the vase's body—the Yale
fragment excerpts bits of both—were filled
with complex scenes of violent combat and
death. Corpses lie piled up at the left of the
upper zone, while warriors duel with swords
and bows beside them. At the right of the
upper zone of the Louvre fragment, amid
more joined triangles and another swastika, a
standing warrior grabs a huge opponent by
the crest of his helmet and drags him from
his chariot (the fallen warrior on the Yale
fragment lay between the two, and the
hooked black splotch just above his head is
the tip of the falling chariot-borne warrior's
Dipylon shield [see Fig. 27]). In the more
damaged zone below, more Dipylon
warriors—the shield-bearer on the Yale fragment is one of them—alternate with birds
pecking at the ground (if they are meant to
be scavengers the mood is not hopeful). The
troops proceed to the right, and since one
soldier raises a foot off the ground, they are
apparently moving on the double. But
behind them, at the very edge of the Louvre
piece, is the incident that truly sets the
scene apart: one shieldless warrior confronts
another who has one body but four legs.

It is possible that on the other, lost side
of the krater there were equally populous
scenes of the ritual mourning of the dead
(the so-called *prothesis*), with the corpse laid
out on its bier amid files of attendant
mourners on foot or in chariots (see **20**).
The question would then be whether the

suggests that the horizontal zigzags often found on pots from Argos signify water.
    2. Louvre A519 (attributed to the Dipylon Workshop). See Davison, *Attic Geometric Workshops* 29; F. Villard, *CVA*
Louvre 11, p. 6, fig. 2. Also Coldstream, *Geometric Greece* 113, 352–53, and "The Geometric Style: Birth of the
Picture," in T. Rasmussen and N. Spivey, eds., *Looking at Greek Vases* (Cambridge 1991) 37–56 at 49–52.

deceased mourned on that side of the vase appeared, alive, in the battle depicted on the other. Whatever the answer, the vase, when whole, would have been covered with perhaps a hundred figures or more. But the ranks of the missing cannot have included any figures more extraordinary than the doomed Dipylon warrior wrenched from his chariot in the upper frieze (he is distinguished from every other preserved figure by his great staring eye), and the Siamese twins in the zone below. Four-legged warriors cannot, of course, have been regular sights on real eighth-century battlefields. But (as we shall see) they do appear in battles and contests preserved in contemporary epic poetry, and so the scenes on this vase, if they were not specifically drawn from legend, may at least have been evocative of mythological, heroic action. As a result, the large funerary vase to which the small Yale fragment originally belonged was one of the most remarkable monuments created near the end of the long "age of Homer."

2

The age of Homer was long because "Homer" is not just what we call the individual composer (or composers) of the *Iliad* and *Odyssey*.[3] The name also commonly serves as shorthand for the venerable oral epic tradition that culminated in the creation of those poems sometime (most think) in the eighth century. It was a centuries-old tradition of preliterate but highly trained bards who, equipped with a lyre (see 17,

101) and a large stock of ready-made phrases that economically fit the dactylic hexameter line (the armature of heroic poetry), created as they sang. Their poems were improvisations assembled from memorized verbal bits and blocks—formulas like "swift-footed Achilles," or "when early-born rosy-fingered dawn appeared," or passages sometimes many lines long—and their art lay in the performance, with each performance serving as a kind of rehearsal for the next.[4] The Greek oral poet must surely have practiced between shows (he was, after all, a professional whose livelihood depended upon pleasing his next audience), and he may even have committed particularly rich and significant passages to memory: the notion that oral composition was completely spontaneous cannot be true. Nonetheless, oral epics were on-the-spot poems. Textless, they existed only so long as they were being performed, and (as studies of roughly analogous oral traditions like the Serbo-Croatian suggest) they would never be sung exactly the same way twice, which is why the *Iliad* and *Odyssey* that we possess—the texts—are recordings not of poems that were orally preserved intact from generation to generation but of poems singularly created at (and perhaps specifically for) the moment of transcription.[5] For the next time Homer or any other oral poet attempted to sing those massive songs, they would have been different, however slightly, from the ones we have—the same songs, made new.[6] The ideas of "fixed text" and "verbatim accuracy" as we understand them did not, before Homer, yet exist,

3. It is not certain, incidentally, that *Homeros* was the poet's real name: the word may mean "he who fits [the song] together." See G. Nagy, *The Best of the Achaeans* (Baltimore 1979) 297–300.

4. Still fundamental to the huge bibliography concerning the theory of oral formulaic composition are the papers of Milman Parry, collected and edited by his son, Adam Parry, in *The Making of Homeric Verse* (Oxford 1971), and A. B. Lord's *The Singer of Tales* (Cambridge MA 1960).

5. See Powell, *Homer and the Origin of the Greek Alphabet,* 189.

6. In the *Odyssey* (1.351–52), Telemachus notes that men praise most the epic that is "most new."

but neither did our conceptions of artistic individuality and originality. Given the oral poet's strong indebtedness to the language and narrative structures of his predecessors, the very idea of creativity needs to be adjusted. Each epic was unique, but each, composed as it was of inherited phrases, set-piece descriptions, and themes, was traditional, too.

The Homeric tradition extended at least as far back as the latter part of the Late Bronze or Mycenaean Age (1550–1100 B.C.)—the age of Mycenae itself and the Trojan War and Agamemnon and Achilles and Hector and Odysseus. But the real kings of Mycenae and the other citadels of thirteenth- and twelfth-century Greece must themselves have been entertained in their palaces by court poets singing tales of still older times, and there is good evidence (both linguistic and archaeological) that the oral epic tradition extended as far back as the Early Mycenaean Age (and almost certainly even earlier).[7] Some of the heroes and weaponry we find in Homer (Ajax, say, and the silver-studded sword) and perhaps even some of the same situations (the long siege of a heavily fortified citadel, for example) would undoubtedly have been found in fourteenth- and fifteenth-century epics as well. Parts of "Homer," then, are of very remote antiquity, and were preserved by the sheer power of the oral tradition itself.

If no oral poem could remain word-for-word the same, if every performance resulted in a new oral poem, the epic tradition itself was remarkably sturdy and stable, and it survived the waves of destruction that swept over the citadels and palaces of Mycenaean Greece around and after 1200 B.C.: the bedrock of the oral formula was unshaken. Deprived of the royal courts in which they had performed, oral poets were probably sustained throughout the succeeding Dark Age (1100–760) by the petty lords, nobles, or "big men" (basileis) who dominated a much diminished Greece (and Greece by now included Aeolis and Ionia in Asia Minor, where Greeks had emigrated in large numbers and where much of the development of the Homeric tradition was played out). Now, precisely what Dark Age basileis heard in their halls—proto-Iliads or proto-Odysseys, or far shorter, more limited poems on Achilles' wrath or Odysseus' return, or poems on other unrelated heroic adventures—we can only surmise. Nonetheless, Homer's raw material negotiated centuries before it took a more or less fixed form in the mid or late eighth century (750–700)—an era whose character was so exceptional that it merits inclusion not at the end of the Dark Age, but at the beginning of the Greek Archaic period.[8]

The Late Bronze Age (which the Iliad and Odyssey are ostensibly about), the Dark Age (through which the oral epic tradition passed and developed), and the eighth

---

7. See M. L. West, "The Rise of the Greek Epic" JHS 108 (1988) 151–72; for criticisms and response, see J. Chadwick, "The Descent of Greek Epic" JHS 110 (1990) 174–77; W. F. Wyatt, Jr., "Homer's Linguistic Forebears" JHS 112 (1992) 167–73; and M. L. West, "The Descent of the Greek Epic: A Reply" JHS 112 (1992) 173–75. It is just possible that we have a Mycenaean representation of a lyre-playing bard, performing before men seated at banquet tables, in a fragmentary fresco from the throne room of the so-called Palace of Nestor; see M. L. Lang, The Palace of Nestor at Pylos in Western Messenia II. The Frescoes (Princeton 1969) 51, 79–80.

8. For a recent review of evidence for the dating of the composition of the Homeric poems, see Powell, Homer and the Origin of the Greek Alphabet 187–220. Powell dates Homer to the first half of the eighth century (800–750), while most others have placed him in the second; see, for example, R. Janko, Homer, Hesiod, and the Hymns: Diachronic Development in Epic Diction (Cambridge 1982) 228–31, where, with staggering precision, the Iliad is dated to 750–725 and the Odyssey to 743–713.

century (in which the *Iliad* and *Odyssey* were composed): these are the three principal "ages of Homer." But the extent to which the *Iliad* and *Odyssey* accurately depict any of them is controversial. The first question is, Was there ever a historical Homeric society? That is, did the Greeks of any one era ever live the way Homer says they did? Is the epic world of Achilles and Odysseus (assuming theirs is the same world) a faithful reproduction of one that once upon a time actually existed? If so, the next question is, Which world would that be—that of the Late Bronze Age, the Dark Age, or the eighth century? The questions may seem simple, but the answers have been almost bewilderingly complex, revolving around such arcane issues as Homer's portrayal of marriage and bride-prices, his description of burial practices, and his knowledge of metallurgy and weaponry. Generally speaking, historians, who (in the absence of chronicles, names, and dates) deal primarily with institutions, practices, and customs, have tended to accept Homer's poetry as reliable sociology and the Homeric world as a consistent picture of a coherent historical society, while archaeologists, who deal primarily with artifacts and are faced with a Homeric material culture that simply does not jibe with the material record recovered from the earth, have tended to reject the notion of "Homer, Social Historian," altogether.[9]

Even among those who accept the essen-tial historicity of Homeric society, there has been no consensus on which of the three "ages of Homer" Homer in fact depicts. From the time of H. Schliemann's late nineteenth-century excavations at Troy and Mycenae until the 1950s, probably the majority view was that the world of the Homeric poems was the world of Mycenaean Greece—a world of walled citadels like Troy; luxurious, treasure-filled palaces like Menelaos' at Sparta (*Odyssey* 4.37–75); and a few genuine Mycenaean "relics" like the silver-studded sword (*Iliad* 2.45), the oxhide-covered "tower shield" (7.219–23; cf. 15.646), and the boar's-tusk helmet (10.261–265) that, though obsolete by the end of the Bronze Age, managed to survive in Homer. It has even been argued that the mind-numbing "Catalogue of Ships" at the end of the *Iliad*'s second book (2.494–759) is a late Mycenaean gazetteer in verse that was preserved virtually verbatim and inserted (rather awkwardly) into the epic.[10] But in 1954 came the first edition of M. I. Finley's influential *The World of Odysseus* and his no-nonsense argument that, despite Homer's obvious attempt to set the actions of the poems in a distant, idealized heroic age, the society Homer actually represents is firmly based upon Dark Age (tenth- and ninth-century) society.[11] In the wake of Finley's book, the number of those who contended that the society Homer describes coherently reproduces the Mycenaean world substantially dwindled.[12] Bronze Age kings, after all,

9. See Whitley, *Style and Society in Dark Age Greece* 34–39. The two camps are not, however, neatly divided: there are archaeologists who accept the authenticity of Homeric society, and historians who do not.

10. See, for example, R. H. Simpson and J. F. Lazenby, *The Catalogue of Ships in Homer's Iliad* (Oxford 1970). But see West, "Rise of the Greek Epic" 168.

11. M. I. Finley, *The World of Odysseus*, 2d ed. rev. (New York 1978). More recently, O. Dickinson has expanded upon Finley's proposed chronological range for Homeric society and added the eleventh century; see "Homer, the Poet of the Dark Age" *Greece and Rome* 33 (1986) 20–37.

12. Defenders of the hypothesis that the most plausible material setting for the society Homer describes is the late Mycenaean age are not unknown, however; see J. Chadwick, *The Mycenaean World* (Cambridge 1976) 180, and M. Wood's popular *In Search of the Trojan War* (London 1985).

did not have dung piled up before their doors the way Odysseus does (*Odyssey* 17.296–99); Homer has no knowledge of the intricate palatial bureaucracies reflected in the Linear B tablets (inventories written on clay in an early form of Greek) from Mycenaean Pylos and Knossos; the Phoenicians, who make their presence felt fairly often in the world of the *Odyssey*, belong to the first millennium, not the second; and the Mycenaeans did not typically cremate their dead—the way Homer, virtually without exception, says they did—but inhumed them.[13] But like the theory he discredited, Finley's own assumes that Homer depicted an actual world that no longer existed when he composed his poems; for him it is a post-Mycenaean but still pre-contemporary world.[14] More recent studies of a variety of oral traditions, however, have emphasized the cultural importance of such poetry, its function as an encyclopedia of information and storehouse of values crucial to the society in which it was created and performed. And so some scholars have concluded that the world of Achilles and Odysseus must accurately reflect Homer's own present, that "the poems essentially report a society which both in its material and political aspects is contemporary with their final date of composition."[15] In other words, the only epic world that would have made any sense to an eighth-century audience was a contemporary world. In this view, obsolete institutions and ways of thinking necessarily disappear from oral traditions. Anachronisms may lend the story an air of authenticity, and the heroes of epic may be dressed in the garb of the Mycenaean past, but it is the eighth-century present that they reenact in their social dealings, and it is an eighth-century mentality that they possess.[16]

But the assumption with which many scholars seem to begin—that Homer was a good social historian, that his poems consistently and accurately depict a single, unitary society (even if there is no agreement on just which one it is)—may not hold. It is not just that many aspects of Greek society probably did not change very much from one age of Homer to the next: especially among the lower classes, life went on pretty much as it always had, and one age was like another. And it is not simply that Homer, even if we assume that he is portraying a specific social and material world, is at best highly selective and thus is, as a cultural historian, necessarily deficient. Rather it is, as A. Snodgrass and others have argued, that Homeric society is an amalgam, a combination of artifacts and practices culled unevenly from the various eras through which the oral tradition passed.[17] Homer's world, like an archaeological site, consists of superimposed layers. It is as artificial as Homer's amalgamated dialect,[18] and just as no Greek ever spoke quite like Homeric

13. One exception to the rule of Homeric cremation may be found at *Iliad* 4.174–77, where Agamemnon refers to the possibility of Menelaos' bones rotting in the plowland of Troy. Similarly, Mycenaeans occasionally used cremation, as at the twelfth-century tumulus recently discovered near Mycenae itself; see H. W. Catling, "Archaeology in Greece, 1984–85" *AR* (1984–1985) 21.

14. Finley, *World of Odysseus* 158.

15. E. A. Havelock, *The Greek Concept of Justice* (Cambridge MA 1978) 56.

16. So, for I. Morris, "The Use and Abuse of Homer" *Classical Antiquity* 5 (1986) 81–138, "the institutions and modes of thought in the poems were ultimately derived from the world in which Homer and his audience lived" (82).

17. A. Snodgrass, "An Historical Homeric Society?" *JHS* 94 (1974) 114–25; J. V. Luce, *Homer and the Heroic Age* (New York 1975), 49–69; Coldstream, *Geometric Greece* 18; E. S. Sherratt, "'Reading the Texts': Archaeology and the Homeric Question" *Antiquity* 64 (1990) 807–24.

18. For the epic dialect see, for example, G. S. Kirk, *The Iliad: A Commentary* I (Cambridge 1985), xxii and 5–7.

heroes speak, so no Greek ever lived quite like Homeric heroes do. In the "cultural stratigraphy" of Homer, one age may have left a thicker deposit than another, and there are certainly Mycenaean and Dark Age relics and purposeful anachronisms, just as there are genuine reflections of Homer's "own day." But his world is nonetheless a composite fashioned, magnified, and idealized by the history and nature of the oral tradition.

One does not necessarily diminish the importance of what Homer has to tell us about specific social institutions and the material culture of particular eras by suggesting that the world of Achilles and Odysseus is, in the end, a selective *literary* construct. But literary imperatives may account for more of the nature of the Homeric world than is usually conceded. I. Winter, for example, has recently pointed out that the way Homer depicts the Phoenicians (who, everyone now agrees, were genuine features of Greek life in the Dark Age and eighth century) seems at variance with what we know about them from other sources. In Homer (especially the *Odyssey*) they are primarily roguish, independent traders of knickknacks, and indeed most Phoenician imports to early Greece are small gold or faience trinkets (see 31, 73). Yet the Phoenicians' mercantile and maritime activities were in reality highly organized and state-controlled and were primarily directed toward the acquisition of metals, and (as we shall see) the Dark Age Aegean knew not only visiting Phoenician peddlers but also permanent Phoenician residents (about whom Homer knows, or says, nothing). Now, Homer did not necessarily get his facts wrong so much as he invented his own

Phoenicians to act as foils for his own epic characters—as deceitful, dishonorable contrasts for the resourceful Odysseus and the honorable Phaiakians. For Homer (the first "Western" poet), the Phoenicians were the stereotypical "other" (the first "Orientals"), and his representation of them has more to do with his literary, fictional goals—and with the representation of his heroic Greeks—than with any truly historical impulse: ethnographic accuracy was beside the point.[19]

Homer's (or his tradition's) principal goal cannot have been to document an *actual* society: his (or its) real task was to re-create a narrative set in a *plausible* society, replete with enough archaisms and enough familiarities to make the story and the world he describes both heroically distant and convincing to his own audience. The real question, that is, is not the documentary truth or accuracy of the world Homer depicts, but its verisimilitude, its *appearance* of truth. It needed only to *seem* accurate. Those who wish to locate "Homeric society" firmly in this period or that will continue to have no trouble finding passages in the poems to support their cases. Nonetheless, attempts to use the *Iliad* and *Odyssey* as social history are in the end misguided. For "the Homeric world" is rooted not so much in any one period or even any combination of periods as it is in a monumental and selective literary imagination.

3

It is a truism by now that the Greek Dark Age is no longer as dark as it used to be, and it is possible to underestimate the degree of continuity in some spheres between the Mycenaean and the Dark Age,

---

19. I thank Professor Winter for her kind permission to refer to her as yet unpublished "Homer's Phoenicians: History, Ethnography, or Literary Trope?"

on the one hand, and between the Dark Age and the Archaic period on the other. But certainly compared to the preceding Late Bronze Age, with its citadels and frescoed halls and gold- and ivory-filled graves, Dark Age Greece was a less populated and poorer place, its context no longer fully international, as the Mycenaean had been, but provincial, cut off (at least for a time) from the stimulus of contact with the Near East. Dark Age economics was simpler stuff, dependent upon the welfare of the individual *oikos* (household or family estate) and *genos* (clan) rather than of the palatial state, and life (or at least many lives) was largely pastoral, dependent on shepherding and seasonal movement more than upon agriculture and its associated sedentary ways. One of the clearest archaeological features of the Early Dark Age—the relative dearth of sites—may best be explained by a surge in pastoralism.[20] Interestingly, though, the pastoralist phase seems to have been already on the decline by the ninth century (if the dedication of bronze figurines of cattle and flocks of sheep [6, 49–51] suggests the continued importance of stock-rearing, Geometric funerary offerings such as terracotta model granaries [14]—symbols of agrarian wealth—also testify to the rise of arable farming once more). Similarly, Greece's isolation from the Near East, the source of so much inspiration and matériel, now seems to have been considerably briefer than was once thought: some contacts may even have been renewed by the late eleventh century. It is, moreover, increasingly clear that the so-called Orientalizing period of Greek art, usually confined in our textbooks to the late eighth and seventh centuries (when Eastern influences upon Greek art were indeed particularly intense; see **65**), actually got its start much earlier, and that, in fact, our picture of the development of early Greece is not enhanced by the old, rigid polarity (established by the Greeks themselves) between Greek and Eastern, between occidental and oriental. This is true for the literary record as well as the archaeological: there are passages in Homer that come close to being translations of Eastern epic, and when in the *Iliad* Achilles anguishes over Patroklos' body "like a lion whose cubs have been stolen" (18.318–19) and later tries to embrace his ghost (23.99–101), he acts like Gilgamesh already had.[21] In short, the cultural spheres of Greece and the Near East had begun to interpenetrate again as early as the early Dark Age: to some extent, Greek culture had been "orientalizing" all the time.[22]

Although there is nothing in the Dark Age to compare to the palaces and tombs of Mycenaean royalty, over the last twenty years or so a nearly constant stream of archaeological surprises has forced us to revise our view of the cultural capacities of the era. From one site alone—Lefkandi on the island of Euboea—have come: a nearly fifty-meter-long hall (dated ca. 1000) whose cremated "hero" and inhumed, gold-bedecked "heroine," buried beneath the floor, may anticipate the proliferation of Greek hero-shrines three centuries later, and whose surrounding colonnade may also

20. See Snodgrass, *An Archaeology of Greece* 190–209. No Greek society, of course, was purely pastoral or purely agricultural: both Mycenaean and Dark Age economies were mixed. It was the proportions of the mixture that differed.

21. West, "Rise of the Greek Epic" 171.

22. See now S. Morris, *Daidalos and the Origins of Greek Art*, and W. Burkert, *The Orientalizing Revolution: Near Eastern Influence on Greek Culture in the Early Archaic Age* (Cambridge MA 1992).

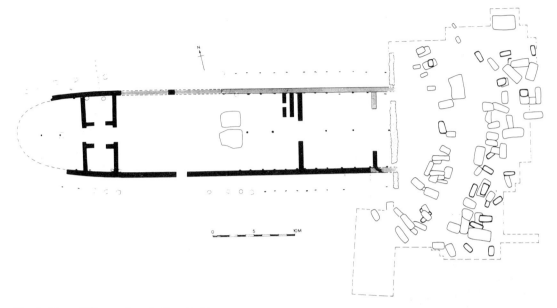

Fig. 2. Plan of "heroon" at Lefkandi. (From AR *[1988–1989] 129, fig 28; reproduced by permission)*

prefigure a canonical peripteral architecture that is later still (Fig. 2);[23] a painted terracotta centaur (dated ca. 900) that is the earliest true mythological figure in Greek art (Fig. 3);[24] and a Phoenician bronze bowl, found in a grave of around 900 and decorated with sphinxes and palms, that is one of the earliest securely datable works of its kind found outside the Levant and that is precisely the kind of Sidonian-made metal bowl that so impressed the Homeric tradition.[25] The level of Dark Age architectural, artistic, and commercial achievement, unsuspected not so very long ago, seems to rise with each year's excavations. And so the eighth century, the last of the ages of Homer, should now be considered less a completely new start in the course of Greek cultural history

than a rapid intensification of cultural, social, and economic patterns that had already been established in the Dark Age.

It is nonetheless still appropriate to consider the eighth century, Homer's own age, an era of "renaissance"[26] and of intense Greek self-definition. This view is justified because the century witnessed the appearance or emergence of four cultural phenomena in particular that would lay the foundations of Greek civilization as we usually conceive it, shaping it for the rest of its history: (1) the Greek alphabet, whose invention can be seen not only as one symptom of a larger pattern of interchange between Greece and the Near East but also as a creative reworking of the borrowed Eastern prototype; (2) the "textualization" of

23. Whitley, *Style and Society in Dark Age Greece* 185–86, has questioned the interpretation of the Lefkandi structure as a "heroon," suggesting instead that the building was originally the house of a *basileus*, or "big man," of Lefkandi, where he entertained his followers and entourage and cemented patterns of personal loyalty, and that it went out of use after his death and burial beneath the floor and the construction of a tumulus over the house.

24. It is probably a representation of the good centaur Cheiron; see Hurwit, *The Art and Culture of Early Greece* 60–61.

25. M. R. Popham et al., "Further Excavation of the Toumba Sanctuary at Lefkandi, 1984 and 1986" AR (1988–1989) 118 and Fig. 5; also Winter, "Homer's Phoenicians." Cf. *Iliad* 23.741–45; *Odyssey* 4.615–19.

26. See *The Greek Renaissance of the Eighth Century* B.C., ed. Hägg.

Fig. 3. Terracotta centaur from Lefkandi. (Courtesy of the British School at Athens)

The paradox bears emphasis: the *Iliad* and the *Odyssey*, masterpieces of a long oral tradition, exist only because someone, somewhere, sometime, wrote them down. The poems that we have, the ones we hold in our hands, are not oral poems, no matter how much they may be like oral poems or faithfully preserve the record of two oral performances. They are texts. Whether the use of writing to transcribe (and so "fossilize") the poems affected the nature of the poems themselves (for instance, by allowing for greater planning or organization), whether the existence of literacy itself "kills" orality, whether Homer wrote the poems down himself or dictated them to a scribe, whether there were actually complete eighth-century manuscripts of the *Iliad* and *Odyssey* (on papyrus or leather scrolls)—these are all arguable points, and reasonable people disagree.[27] What is beyond dispute is that the Greeks (who had lost the art of writing after the fall of the Mycenaean palaces and the collapse of their Linear B bureaucracies) had learned how to write again by the time Homer is generally believed to have composed his epics, and that they learned how from the very same Phoenicians who, though sometimes praised as fine craftsmen, are more often maligned as greedy tricksters and treacherous kidnappers (*Odyssey* 15.415–84). The Greeks admitted as much: according to Herodotus, the inventor of the Greek alphabet was Kadmos, an immigrant from Phoenician Tyre who founded Mycenaean Thebes.[28]

By the eighth century, the Greeks (or some Greeks) had already become very familiar with this essentially seagoing people from the East. In the late tenth and ninth

the Homeric poems themselves and thus the fixing of a Greek "national literature" and identity; (3) the establishment of the representation of the human form and mythological action as principal subjects of Greek art; and (4) the rise of the multivalent institution known as the *polis*, or city-state. It is just beginning to be realized how interrelated or interdependent these various phenomena may have been.

27. For a recent review of the controversies, see R. Thomas, *Literacy and Orality in Ancient Greece* (Cambridge 1992) 29–51.

28. Herodotus, 5.58. The Greeks adopted the Phoenician names of the signs (for example, *aleph*, derived from a pictograph of a bull's head and meaning "bull," became *alpha*, which is meaningless in Greek); they called their letters *phoinikeia*, "phoenicians"; and on late Archaic Crete a scribe was called a *p[h]oinikastas*, "a phoenicianizer."

centuries, for example, Eastern luxury goods in bronze and gold and faience began appearing in some quantity in Greek tombs not only at Lefkandi but also at Tekke and Fortetsa (the cemeteries of Knossos) on Crete.[29] And while it is usually impossible to tell whether a given import arrived on a Greek ship or an Eastern one, the goods at Lefkandi and Knossos were almost certainly brought to the Aegean by Phoenicians, since their burial predates the earliest likely Dark Age visits of Greeks to the Levant.[30] The Phoenicians may have been interested in Euboea because of its plentiful copper and iron ores.[31] But they were interested in Crete for other reasons: they used the south Cretan harbor of Kommos as a port of call by the end of the tenth century, and the site's Temple A (ca. 925–800) was for all intents and purposes a Phoenician shrine, a facility for Eastern seamen on their way farther west.[32] It is even likely that whole families or guilds of migrant Phoenician craftsmen (master goldsmiths, in particular) settled in such places as Knossos and Athens by the end of the ninth century, increasing or earning their reputation for fine workmanship preserved in Homer. In the Dark Age, then, Greeks and Phoenicians did not merely meet, barter, and go their separate ways; in several corners of the Aegean—Euboea, Crete, Athens, and Kos in the Dodecanese—they lived side by side.[33]

And that is all it took for the invention of the Greek alphabet: one literate Phoenician, living among illiterate Greeks, able to speak their language in a rudimentary way, who possessed the necessary tools (styluses, leather scrolls or wooden writing tablets)[34] and the willingness to teach someone how to read and write, and one teachable Greek, who was able to convert the West Semitic script of his tutor to an alphabet better suited to his own language, and ingenious enough to invent something the Phoenician script did not have: vowels. Until recently it was commonly believed that the lesson was learned in the East, at the supposedly Greek-founded emporium of Al Mina on the North Syrian coast, when Euboeans, having (it was thought) settled there in the late ninth century, finally realized that they needed writing for commercial purposes. But Al Mina may not have been founded as early as the ninth century after all, it is not likely to have been a Greek settlement originally in any case, the presence of Euboean pottery at the site does not necessarily mean Euboeans actually dwelt there at the start,[35] and there is only one Greek inscrip-

---

29. Conversely, Greek Protogeometric pottery made its way to Tyre in the tenth century; see P. Bikai, *The Pottery of Tyre* (Warminster 1979) pls. XXIIA.1 and XXX.3

30. See J. N. Coldstream, "Greeks and Phoenicians in the Aegean," in Niemeyer, *Phönizier im Westen* 261–72. Coldstream notes (266) that a pair of gold earrings of Eastern design from Lefkandi seem to be excellent prototypes for earrings worn in Homer by Hera and Penelope (*Iliad* 14.183, *Odyssey* 18.298). See also P. J. Riis, "Griechen in Phönizien" in Niemeyer, *Phönizier im Westen* 237–55.

31. S. Morris, *Daidalos and the Origins of Greek Art* 139–40.

32. See J. W. Shaw, "Phoenicians in Southern Crete" *AJA* 93 (1989) 165–83. In one of his tall tales, Odysseus claims he sought the aid of Phoenicians anchored off the coast of Crete (*Odyssey* 13.255–86), a detail made entirely plausible by the discoveries at Kommos.

33. Coldstream, "Greeks and Phoenicians" 269–70. See also O. Negbi, "Early Phoenician Presence in the Mediterranean Islands: A Reappraisal" *AJA* 96 (1992) 599–615, and M. E. Aubet, *The Phoenicians and the West: Politics, Colonies, and Trade* (Cambridge 1993). Burkert, *The Orientalizing Revolution*, has forcefully argued for the presence of migrant Eastern seers and healers in the Aegean as well as traders and artisans.

34. Homer knows of papyrus, but not as a medium for writing (*Odyssey* 21.390–91).

35. See A. J. Graham, "The Historical Importance of Al Mina" *Dialogues d'histoire ancienne* 12 (1986) 51–65, who

tion from Al Mina possibly as early as the eighth century.[36] Moreover, no early Greek inscription, from anywhere, is commercial in content. As a result, focus has shifted from the Levant as the probable birthplace of the Greek alphabet to the Aegean, where there were also Phoenicians and where eighth-century inscriptions are far more common, and from commerce as the probable motivation for the invention to the need to establish ownership of an object, the need to dedicate an object, and even the desire to transcribe poetry.

While several plausible candidates for the birthplace of the Greek alphabet have been proposed—Crete, Rhodes, Athens, Cyprus (whence comes 72, a local product with Phoenician characters painted on the lower body), to name a few—a very strong case can be made for Euboea, or, at least, for some place in the Euboean sphere.[37] It was, again, Euboeans who were among the first Greeks to benefit from renewed contacts with the Levant. Probably our earliest examples of written Greek (brief though they are), datable to a little before 750, appear on potsherds from Lefkandi,[38] and other

inscribed sherds nearly that early have been found on the island of Pithekoussai (Ischia), off the bay of Naples, which Euboeans settled around 770 (Phoenician or Aramaic inscriptions have been found there, too).[39] The evidence is circumstantial, but a reasonable verdict is that the inventor of the Greek alphabet was a Euboean—either a trader who had been East, or a student of a Phoenician resident of or visitor to an Euboean town such as Lefkandi, Chalkis, or Eretria. And it is worth noting that according to one Greek tradition (clearly a jingoist response to the tradition that Kadmos the Phoenician first brought letters to Greece) the inventor of the alphabet was Palamedes, a native of Euboea.[40]

The date of the invention remains a problem. Since no extant Greek inscription is much earlier than 750 or so, most Hellenists (conventionally assuming a generation between the invention of the alphabet and the first extant specimens) accept the early eighth century as the most likely date for the adaptation. Semiticists and Orientalists, however, are another matter. Comparing the forms of the earliest Greek letters to

---

points out that there is plenty of Greek pottery at Tyre, too, and a Greek enclave there is most unlikely; see also Bikai, *The Pottery of Tyre.* Cf. J. Boardman, "Al Mina and History" *OJA* 9 (1990) 169–90.

36. It appears on an otherwise nondescript potsherd; see J. Boardman, "An Inscribed Sherd from Al Mina" *OJA* 1 (1982) 365–67, where it is described as Attic Late Geometric, and L. H. Jeffery, *The Local Scripts of Archaic Greece,* rev. ed. with supp. by A. W. Johnston (Oxford 1990), 426 and 476 (D). But see Graham, "Historical Importance of Al Mina" 55 and 63 n. 64, who suggests the sherd may in fact belong to the seventh century.

37. A strong case for Cyprus has been made by A. Johnston, "The Extent and Use of Literacy" in *The Greek Renaissance of the Eighth Century* B.C.; the case for Crete (also strong) has been made, most recently, by S. Morris, *Daidalos and the Origins of Greek Art* 159–60. See also Burkert, *The Orientalizing Revolution* 26–27, and Thomas, *Literacy and Orality* 53–56.

38. An inscription from Grotta on Naxos is not necessarily as early (ca. 770) as its excavator claims; see V. Lambrinoudakis, "Anaskaphai Naxou" *Praktika* (1981) 294, and Jeffery, *Local Scripts of Archaic Greece* 466 (where it is simply dated "eighth century") and pl. 78 (5–6).

39. One brief inscription on a sherd from Ischia has been read by some as Aramaic, by others as Greek, and in another case Aramaic and Greek graffiti appear on the same vase; see Johnston, "The Extent and Use of Literacy" 64, fig. 2. For the Euboean settlement and archaeological history of Pithekoussai, see D. Ridgway, *The First Western Greeks* (Cambridge 1992).

40. See Powell, *Homer and the Origin of the Greek Alphabet* 12–18, 233–36. Yet another tradition, preserved in Aeschylus, is that it was the Titan Prometheus who taught men "the compositions of letters"; see *Prometheus Bound,* 460.

Phoenician ones and arguing that the formal variety of even the earliest Greek inscriptions implies a long history of divergence from a single common source, some have argued that the borrowing of the script must have occurred in the eleventh century (that is, at the very beginning of the Dark Age), while another has even argued that the Greek alphabet must have been invented before ca. 1400.[41] The dispute is complex, largely epigraphic or stylistic (is the *alpha* of this Greek graffito more like the *aleph* on this Phoenician inscription, or that one?), and thus, given the fact that there are fewer than a dozen early Phoenician inscriptions to compare the Greek ones to,[42] very subjective.

Into the argument a tantalizing piece of evidence has recently come: a bronze bowl, found in Tomb J at Tekke near Knossos, with a Phoenician inscription, twelve letters long, cut into its rim saying "Cup of Shema, son of L . . ." (Fig. 4).[43] To judge from its context in the tomb, the bowl was deposited around or just after 900, though it could have been made and inscribed much earlier than that (a century or two earlier, according to some). What the discovery of Shema's cup does *not* prove is that the Greeks learned the alphabet as early as

900.[44] It does prove that they had the *opportunity* to do so, and that they had the opportunity to do so somewhere other than the Levant. In other words, it is now likely that at least some Greeks—on Crete and wherever else they came into contact with Phoenicians—knew there was such a thing as writing (and reading, too) at least a century and a half before the oldest preserved specimens of written Greek. But that knowledge may not in itself have been sufficient stimulus for the invention of the Greek alphabet, and although arguments from silence are notoriously perilous, the silence remains, after decades of excavation, total and deafening. The simple facts are these: the earliest extant Greek inscriptions are incised or painted on mid-eighth-century pots and sherds; there are plenty of ninth- and tenth- and eleventh-century pots and sherds; but there is no writing on any of them. Now, facts change, and a Dark Age Greek inscription may one day turn up: as we keep finding out, the Dark Age is full of surprises. But until one does, the invention of the Greek alphabet is best placed at the turn from the ninth to the eighth century.[45]

If the alphabet was in use by 800 or so, and if the composition of the *Iliad* and

41. Eleventh century: J. Naveh, "Some Semitic Epigraphical Considerations on the Antiquity of the Greek Alphabet" *AJA* 77 (1977) 1–8, and *The Early History of the Alphabet* (Jerusalem and Leiden 1982); J. F. Healey, *Reading the Past* (Berkeley 1990) 230–32. The argument in favor of gradual development and branching from a common source is forcefully countered by Jeffery, *Local Scripts of Archaic Greece* 14–16. Around 1400: M. Bernal, *Cadmean Letters: The Transmission of the Alphabet to the Aegean and Further West before 1400 B.C.* (Winona Lake IN 1990). Bernal's eccentric theory would mean the Mycenaeans had the alphabet as well as the Linear B syllabary, though no alphabetic text from the Mycenaean world has ever been found.

42. Powell, *Homer and the Origin of the Greek Alphabet* 20.

43. M. Sznycer, "L'inscription phénicienne de Tekke, près de Cnossos" *Kadmos* 18 (1979) 89–93; F. Cross, "Newly Found Inscriptions in Old Canaanite and Early Phoenician Scripts" *BASOR* 238 (1980) 1–20; O. Negbi, "Evidence for Early Phoenician Communities on the Eastern Mediterranean Islands" *Levant* 14 (1982) 179–82.

44. Coldstream, "Greeks and Phoenicians" 271–72, points out that the Cretans could not have taken the Tekke bowl as the model for their alphabet since "if they had done so, there would surely be some trace in their script of the archaic [letter forms] seen in this graffito. In fact, these forms are considerably older than the versions of these letters which were imitated in the earliest Greek inscriptions."

45. See Burkert, *The Orientalizing Revolution* 27–28; S. Morris, *Daidalos and the Origins of Greek Art* 160, suggests that for a considerable time before the Greeks decided to learn how to write for themselves, they left the skill in the hands of Phoenician scribes.

Fig. 4. Phoenician inscription on bronze bowl from Tekke, Tomb J, Knossos. (Courtesy of the British school at Athens)

Odyssey occurred in the second half of the eighth century, then, obviously, Greek writing predates Homer, and the supposedly quintessential oral poet would have lived in a world that was, or was fast becoming, literate. The crucial question then becomes, Did Homer know of the alphabet? And if he knew of it, did he use it? If the *Odyssey* is, as some think, a Euboean poem (its principal dialect is the sort of Greek spoken in the vicinity of the island),[46] it is especially hard to believe that its poet could have been unaware of alphabetic writing: average Euboeans were writing a lot. Yet there is only one passage anywhere in Homer that might refer to the new technology, and it is found in the *Iliad*, where it is said that Bellerophon was once sent to Lykia with a folded tablet engraved with "baneful signs," "life-destroying things" (6.168–70). The passage is open to different interpretations: for some, the reference is to Mycenaean Linear B; for others, it is to the recently learned but still mysterious alphabet; for still others, it is to mere pictographs.[47] Homer clearly refers to markings of some kind, but the passage is simply too vague for us to be sure what sort of marks he (or his tra-

dition) had in mind. The absence of unambiguous references to the alphabet in Homer suggests to some that the technology was too recent an innovation to have penetrated the epic tradition. To others, it is an intentional anachronism: a known feature of contemporary life is banished from Homeric society to make it seem more heroically distant.

The earlier one places the invention of the alphabet, of course, the harder it is to imagine an eighth-century Homer who did not at least know of the new technology, or even how to use it. It is even harder to imagine a Homer who had no idea what the alphabet was or what value it had deliberately and painstakingly dictating his poems, over many hours spread over several days, to a person who knew how to write (what on earth did he think the scribe was doing?).[48] It is, however, possible to imagine oral composition proceeding in a newly but still crudely "literate culture" very much as it always had, which is to say, by calculated improvisation. It is, at all events, misguided to search the epics themselves for telltale signs of literate composition: their monumental designs, their complexities and cross-references, their sophistication and "quality," are not in themselves proof of the literacy of their creators (as some would have them). On the other hand, the clearly oral diction and traditional language of the poems are not in themselves proof that they were composed without the aid of writing:

46. West, "Rise of the Greek Epic" 166, 172. The *Iliad*, however, seems firmly rooted in Ionia, which raises the age-old question of whether the Homer of the *Iliad* could have been the same poet as the Homer of the *Odyssey*.

47. See Powell, *Homer and the Origin of the Greek Alphabet* 198–200, who suggests the reference is part of a "fatal letter" motif borrowed from Eastern folklore and literature and that Homer could not have meant any specific writing system. A problematic passage in the *Iliad* (2.339–41) that mentions "submitting the counsels and *spondai* (agreements) of men to the flames" may, however, also refer to written (and flammable) documents.

48. Powell, *Homer and the Origin of the Greek Alphabet* 162, notes that research suggests that "oral poets are not interested in the power of writing to preserve their words." But, if Homer did not write down the poems himself, the transcription of his epics in the late eighth century must still have been a monumental collaboration, with the singer often waiting patiently for the scribe to catch up, and probably often repeating what the scribe could not get down the first time. The poet, in this scenario, must have been very interested in the preservation of his words. On the interaction of the arts of oral poetry and writing, see A. Ford, *Homer: The Poetry of the Past* (Ithaca NY 1992) 131–71.

"traditional" hexameter poetry was composed in the seventh and sixth centuries, too, when the use of writing was widespread. Everyone can agree that Homer's tradition was oral, and that his poems (like Greek poetry in general) were aural—intended to be sung aloud and be heard by an audience, not read alone in silence. But as for Homer's own literacy or illiteracy, opinion is divided, and only the agnostic is safe.

Whether Homer wrote poetry or not, some late eighth-century Greeks certainly did. Many of the earliest extant Greek inscriptions simply name names, presumably the owners of the vases on which they were written ("Aischrion," for example). Others (like the much earlier Phoenician "cup of Shema" [Fig. 4]) declare ownership more directly ("I am the kylix of Korax," says a fragmentary late eighth-century cup from Rhodes) or name the maker of the pot (". . . inos made me," on a fragment of a bowl from Pithekoussai). A few may have recorded dedications to the gods (in the form "So-and-so dedicated me"). But unquestionably the most intriguing eighth-century Greek inscriptions are longer ones written in dactylic hexameters, the meter of Homeric epic. The earliest Greek inscription

of any real length, incised on the shoulder of a prize-jug from Athens dated to ca. 740–730, begins with the perfect hexameter line "He who now of all the dancers most playfully dances . . ." before becoming incoherent. And there is the only slightly later but even longer inscription, mostly in hexameters, on a cup from Pithekoussai (Fig. 5):

> I am Nestor's cup, good to drink from.
> Whoever drinks from me will at once be
>   seized
> By desire for fair-crowned Aphrodite.[49]

It is, in fact, surprising to find so many of the earliest Greek inscriptions in meter, and the percentage is high enough that some scholars (discounting the even higher percentage of proper names) have argued that the Greek alphabet and its vowels were invented for that very purpose—to write down poetry, not commercial accounts, signatures, or notes of ownership.[50] Recently, B. Powell has gone even further than that. The alphabet, he argues, was invented not to write down just any poetry, but the poetry of Homer: that is, the inventor of the Greek alphabet and the person who

---

49. For the Nestor cup, see Ridgway, *The First Western Greeks* 55–57. H. R. Immerwahr, *Attic Script: A Survey* (Oxford 1990) 18–19, suggests the inscription on the cup (which is surely a humorous allusion to the great gold cup of King Nestor described at *Iliad* 11.632–35, demonstrating that at least this part of the Homeric epic was familiar by the last third of the eighth century) was written by someone who knew what a "book" was. For another review of early inscriptions, see M. L. Lang, "The Alphabetic Impact on Archaic Greece" in D. Buitron-Oliver, ed., *New Perspectives in Early Greek Art* (Hanover and London 1991) 65–79.

50. H. T. Wade-Gery, *The Poet of the Iliad* (Cambridge 1952); K. Robb, "Poetic Sources of the Greek Alphabet," in E. A. Havelock and J. P. Hershbell, eds., *Communication Arts in the Ancient World* (New York 1978) 23–36; Hurwit, *The Art and Culture of Early Greece* 88–91. The vowels are generally supposed to have marked the critical Greek departure from the West Semitic prototype, and their invention is often explained by the demands of Greek poetry. Greek meter depended not upon "stress" but upon the "quantity" of syllables: that is, the rhythm depended upon whether a syllable was "short" or "long," and length depended in turn on the sort of vowel(s) the syllable contained. Greek business accounts could be written without vowels; Greek poetry could not. But as Thomas, *Literacy and Orality* 55, points out, vowels were needed for other reasons: for example, to spell out the case-endings of inflected Greek nouns, which often end in vowels. Vowels were necessary not only to write down Greek poetry, but also to give grammatical sense to any specimen of written Greek.

*Fig. 5. Inscription on "Nestor's Cup" from Pithek-
oussai. (Drawing after Powell,* Homer and the
Origin of the Greek Alphabet *164 no. 59)*

first committed the *Iliad* and *Odyssey* to
writing were one and the same.[51] If he is
right, one of the great accomplishments of
the Greek Renaissance was created specifically so that another could be preserved for-
ever. But even if he is wrong, the eighth-
century appearance of the alphabet and the
eighth-century composition of the Homeric
epics are unlikely to have been coincidental:
we have the poems in the first place
because of the technology.

One of the ways in which "Homeric
society" does not correspond with any of
the several ages through which the oral epic
tradition passed is the absence of pottery,
especially painted pottery, from its material
culture. The most plentiful category of
manufactured object actually left to us from
the Mycenaean period, the Dark Age, and
the eighth century virtually does not exist
in the *Iliad* and *Odyssey*.[52] Homer's neglect
of the crafts of the potter and pot painter
suggests, perhaps, that they were held in no
great esteem. Yet it is the development of
painted pottery that has allowed archaeologists to establish the sequence of periods in
early Greece and its regions, and it is on

the surface of eighth-century pots that we
witness a monumental achievement comparable to the introduction of the alphabet
and the composition of the Homeric epics:
the establishment of the image—particularly
the human figure and the figured scene—as
the principal matter of Greek art.

Until the eighth century, in fact, it was
not clear that Greek vase painting would be
an art of images rather than of geometric
ornaments, of abstract motifs. After the collapse of the Mycenaean citadels and the
withering of their palatial economies, the
vase painter (a relatively minor artist in the
Late Bronze Age who depended heavily on
the inspiration provided by other "finer"
media, such as ivories, frescoes, and works
in gold and silver) was left to his own
devices, and in those Dark Age circumstances representation almost died out.[53]
But although the styles of vase painting
produced during the Dark Age were essentially styles of abstraction, they are not
necessarily inferior for that: abstraction (as
twentieth-century art demonstrates to any-
one who needs convincing) is a perfectly
valid and powerful means of expression.
And the values expressed on the formu-
laically patterned pots of the Dark Age are
the values of definition, clarity, rhythm, balance, order, and harmony. There is a word
in Greek for the kind of studied relation of
part to part and interaction of part and
whole that we see in the finest examples of
Dark Age vase painting: *symmetria* (not
"symmetry" but "commensurability").[54] In
various forms, *symmetria* would become a

51. Powell, *Homer and the Origin of the Greek Alphabet* 232.

52. A pot is referred to at *Iliad* 9.469; the action of a potter at the wheel is referred to once, in a simile, at *Iliad*
18.601. It is not clear what material the *pithoi* (storage jars) full of good and evil gifts set at the door of Zeus (*Iliad*
24.527–33) are made of.

53. See Hurwit, *The Art and Culture of Early Greece* 53–54.

54. For the term, see J. J. Pollitt, *The Ancient View of Greek Art* (New Haven 1974) 14–22, 256–58.

Fig. 6. Attic Protogeometric belly-handled amphora
(Kerameikos 1073). (Photo courtesy of Deutsches
Archäologisches Institut, Athens, neg. Ker. 4245)

principle of Greek art throughout its history.
But it was a Dark Age principle first.

It was not, admittedly, the concern of
some of the very earliest Dark Age potters
and painters, purveyors of the depressing
style of pottery called "Submycenaean" (see
1). This style has frequently been equated
with an entire period (specifically the years
between 1100 and 1050 or so), but in fact it
was a regional phenomenon essentially limited to Athens and its vicinity: Submycenaean pottery such as we have from Attica
was not produced all over Greece.[55] And a
good thing, too: workmanship is generally
sloppy, pots sag or are lopsided, and shapes
and decorative motifs are derivative and uni-
maginative. The Submycenaean style's principal virtue was, in fact, its brevity, and
around the middle of the eleventh century

it was supplanted in Athens by the style
known as Protogeometric.

Here, too, an Attic style has often been
confused with an entire period of Greek
history, and the years between 1050 and
900 are often called the "Protogeometric
period," a title that wrongly makes Athens
the center of the Greek cosmos and ignores
the great variation in styles (and the varying
chronologies of those styles) in other parts
of Greece. Still, there can be no question
that the Attic Protogeometric vase (Fig. 6)
was the finest ceramic product of the day:
the contour (or profile) of the typical
amphora, for example, is crisp and taut, the
curve of the body is answered by the countercurve of the neck, and concentric motifs
drawn not freehand, roughly, but with
brushes affixed to compasses, carefully, are
deployed to intimate the nature of the vase
that bears them. The concentric semicircle,
uniformly placed on the shoulder of the
vase, suggests the hemisphere of the upper
half of the vase (when placed below the lip
of a skyphos or krater [see 4] it intimates a
lower hemisphere). The concentric circle,
typically placed at the widest diameter of an
amphora, evokes the full globe that is the
body of the vase. Two-dimensional motifs
are employed to suggest underlying volumes: this precise relation of ornament to
structure, of motif to whole, in Protogeometric vase painting is the first great
expression of *symmetria* in Greek art.

The second is found in the next style of
Athenian vase painting: the Geometric
(900–700).[56] Surface ornament is once again
used to analyze the nature of the vase
beneath, but it is not the seamless volumes
of the interior that the new decorative reper-

55. For warnings against confusing ceramic styles with historical periods, see W. D. E. Coulson, *The Greek Dark Ages* (Athens 1990) 8–14.

56. The dates for both the Protogeometric and Geometric styles are conventional, and the chronology of the per-

toire is meant to suggest, but the construction of the vase, its assembly from separate clay parts stacked atop one another. In Early and Middle Geometric vase painting (900–760), rectilinear designs such as the battlement and meander (designs that consist entirely of right angles and that thus emphasize the vertical and horizontal dimensions of the vase) and vertical strokes, hourglass motifs (or double axes), and dog-teeth at first fill narrow continuous bands at the middle of the body of the vase and precisely limited panels at the center of the neck, thus emphasizing the two basic building blocks of the vase (see **2**). As the style develops, geometric designs appropriate more and more of what had been black-glazed surface: the shoulder of the vase is decorated next, then more and more of the space in between. But the expansion is constrained by fairly strict syntactical rules: the principal patterns, for example, will generally be found at the level of the handle zones, at the widest diameter of the vase, or at the center of the neck, and the major motifs are set off or prepared for by subsidiary patterns above and below. There is something formulaic about the tapestry-like designs of Attic Geometric pots: one senses that the vase painter's originality (like the oral poet's) consisted of his ability to marshal and vary standard combinations of traditional themes and motifs. And the process of formulaic composition culminates at the beginning of the Late Geometric period (ca. 760–700), when the artist known as the Dipylon Master potted and painted the huge, superb vase mundanely called Athens

804 (Fig. 7) a masterpiece of design and *symmetria* (the neck of the vase is half the height of the body, the width of the body half the height of the vase) that is the ultimate precursor of many of the smaller vases in the present exhibition [cf. **3, 9, 20, 25**].

In the handle zone of Athens 804, the Dipylon Master placed his principal design: a figured scene representing the formal, ritualized burial of the dead, the *prothesis*. It is with this scene, in my view, that the representational focus of Greek vase painting is assured: the human figure, geometricized into a motif that has a triangle for a chest and a circular blob for a head, has been set at the center of the Geometric fabric. Yet, paradoxically, the achievement of the Dipylon Master—his successful reconciliation of the abstract with the figural—carried within it the seeds of the destruction of the very aesthetic he had perfected. Geometricized or no, the human figure proved too attractive an inhabitant, too strong a force, for its abstract context. The balance could not hold, and in the last decades of the eighth century, geometric friezes and panels rapidly shrank and withdrew before the advance of more and proportionately larger scenes of human action (see **25**).

The Dipylon Master was hardly the first Greek (or even the first Athenian) artist to paint a figure on a vase, and Athens was not the only home of early Greek image-making. In fact, Dark Age Athenian vase painters, tenaciously committed to abstract design, almost seem to have resisted or repressed pictorial impulses to which vase painters elsewhere gave in more readily.

---

iods that produced them have lately been challenged: see, for example, E. D. Francis and M. Vickers, "Greek Geometric Pottery at Hama and Its Implications for Near Eastern Chronology" *Levant* 17 (1985) 131–38, and P. James et al., *Centuries of Darkness* (London 1991), who want to lower the end of the Bronze Age to ca. 950 and thus see a much more rapid stylistic development of Dark Age pottery than orthodoxy allows. No chronology for this period is unassailable; too few of the fixed points we require exist, and the correlations with other chronologies (say, Egypt's) are too tenuous and problematic, to inspire complete confidence in the conventional scheme.

Fig. 7. Attic Late Geometric belly-handled amphora by the Dipylon Master (Athens NM804). (Photo courtesy of Deutsches Archäologisches Institut, Athens, neg. NM5944)

Dark Age Lefkandi, for example, has now produced a scene of rubbery archers taking aim at each other across the panel of an apparently imported hydria (ca. 1000), a monumental krater decorated with four pairs of tall trees (ca. 1000), and a pyxis with a panel filled with a ship, birds, and fish (ca. 850).[57] On Crete, wild goats decorate a ninth-century krater from the cemetery of Fortetsa at Knossos; two "snake-goddesses" appear beneath the handles of a pithos from the same place; two sphinxes or griffins confront each other on one side of a krater from Tomb E at Tekke, while on the other side an armed man is savaged by two lions (ca. 850); and on the sides of another, early ninth-century krater from Tekke (Tomb F) two men hunt down a stag with spears (or is it the same man in two stages of the chase?).[58] On Cyprus (beyond the boundaries of the Aegean but part of the Greek world nonetheless) a Dark Age pictorial tradition was also strong: the complex but enigmatic scene on the neck of the fragmentary amphora in the exhibition (70), for example, might be as early as the mid-ninth century. Whether the representational efforts of non-Athenian artists of the Dark Age sprung untutored from their own desires, or whether they were instead triggered by figured Eastern imports (such as the bronze bowl embossed with sphinxes, "trees of life," and lions recently found at Lefkandi, by rediscovered Minoan or Mycenaean artifacts, or even by traditions that

survived the end of the Bronze Age, their capacities for imagemaking have been regularly underestimated.[59]

There was, however, no representational vacuum even in Dark Age Athens: small, cursory horses had wandered onto the surfaces of a few Protogeometric cremation amphorae (the animals were surely symbolic of the status of the horse-rearing—and thus aristocratic—dead, a symbolism that the horses, both painted and modeled, on later Geometric vases [16, 27–29] also shared). And horses, pigs, birds, deer, and human figures (mourners and warriors, primarily) appeared with increasing frequency, and in increasingly complex scenes, on Early and Middle Geometric works. The Dipylon Master was not even the first Athenian artist to paint a full *prothesis*.[60] But after the creation of Athens 804 and other, far more densely populated vases from his workshop (such as Louvre A519, Fig. 1), there was no longer any doubt that the human figure would be the proper study of Greek art. The late eighth century was really the first great age of Greek representation since the end of the Bronze Age, and the first great tradition of figured vase painting was driven primarily by the artisans of Athens. With the representational explosion on Attic Late Geometric vases, the course of Greek imagemaking is securely set.

Funerals, parades, and battles are the most popular subjects of Attic Late Geometric vase painting, and they are usually

---

57. For the "archer hydria," see Popham and Sackett, *Lefkandi* I. *The Iron Age* 127–28, pls. 254b, 270d-e; for the krater with trees, which was found on the floor of the "heroon," where it may have served to mark the graves of the hero and heroine, see Catling and Lemos, *Lefkandi* II, pt. 1. *The Pottery* 25–26 and pls. 17–18, 54–56 (two later Protogeometric trees appear on a lekythos from Lefkandi and a flask from Skyros; ibid., 25 and n. 68); for the ship pyxis, see M. Popham et al., *AR* (1988–1989) 120 and fig. 21, and "An Early Euboean Ship" *OJA* 6 (1987) 353–59.

58. For the "agrimi krater," see Brock, *Fortetsa* 11–15; for the "goddess pithos," see Coldstream, "The Geometric Style" 43–45; for the Tekke vases, see H. W. Catling, *AR* (1976–1977) 15–16.

59. See Hurwit, *The Art and Culture of Early Greece* 64–70; Whitley, *Style and Society in Dark Age Greece* 47–48.

60. See Hurwit, *The Art and Culture of Early Greece* 62–64, 94–96.

interpreted as abstracted or generalized "scenes from everyday life." And most eighth-century images, Attic and non-Attic alike, whether painted on vases or cast in bronze, are surely rooted in contemporary reality. The dancers on a fragment of an Argive vase (52) or the charioteers on a neck-handled amphora (3) or the warriors fighting hand to hand on an Attic figural stand (37) or the bronze group of a man leading his ram to the sacrifice (51) or the many single bronze horses in the exhibit (for example, 97) do not represent particular people or particular animals or particular events but stand for people or horses in general, and for any and all such activities. The world of Geometric art is, for the most part, a world that is nonspecific, its inhabitants all-purpose.

Interspersed among these generic images, however, are a few idiosyncratic ones that depict not "real life" but legend or myth. On one side of the catchplate of a badly damaged bronze fibula (or safety pin) in Philadelphia (Fig. 8), for example, is an engraved scene of two men struggling with a multiheaded snaky beast: the men can only be Herakles and his companion Iolaos, and the monster can only be the Hydra of Lerna (the crab between the feet of one of the heroes, sent by Hera to bother Herakles, clinches it).[61] Most often, however, the mythological content of Late Geometric images is not so clear: on the other side of the fibula, another man grabs a deer by the horns: Herakles' struggle with the Keryneian hind is the likely, but not quite cer-

tain, subject. Frequently, Late Geometric images are open to mythological interpretation, while remaining ambiguous. On one Attic oinochoe (99), for example, two figures, holding hands, flank another who is set upside down, surely an indication that he is dead. The deceased has an empty scabbard at his waist; the standing figure at left holds a sword in his hand; the two live, linked figures have apparently conspired to kill the third with his own weapon. It is an extraordinary scene, a strong departure from the standard burials and parades and duels of Late Geometric iconography, but is it myth? One thinks of Klytemnaestra and her lover Aigisthus murdering her husband Agamemnon upon his return from Troy (cf. *Odyssey* 11.405–11), but neither conspirator is identifiably female, and one has no proof.

So, too, with Louvre A519 (Figs. 1, 27), the great krater from the Dipylon Workshop to which the little Yale sherd (98) belongs. The Siamese twins fighting at the edge of the Louvre fragment are probably the mythological Aktorione (or Molione) mentioned by Homer and the slightly later epic poet Hesiod, and their opponent might then be Nestor, legendary king of Mycenaean Pylos, who recalls his youthful victory over the pair in the *Iliad* (they escaped).[62] J. N. Coldstream has suggested that since one of the most important families of Athens—the Neleids—traced their descent from Nestor, the image on the krater may have served as an emblem of this clan, a "family crest" identifying as a Neleid the man

61. See Schweitzer, *Greek Geometric Art* 207.

62. *Iliad* 11.709–10, 750–52; Hesiod, Fr. 17b (Merkelbach-West). Not all scholars agree that the double figure represents the mythological Siamese twins; Boardman, "Symbol and Story in Geometric Art" 25–26, for example, argues that the double figure was a conventional way of indicating two warriors fighting side by side, so much in tandem that they could be represented with a single body. But the Siamese twins appear less than a dozen times in all of Late Geometric art—not often enough, in my view, to be "a convention."

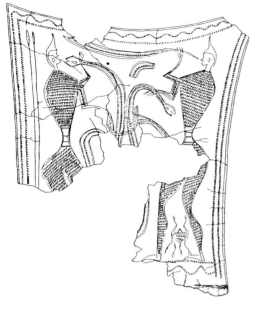

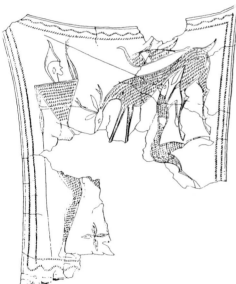

Fig. 8. Fragmentary Late Geometric bronze fibula, two sides. (Philadelphia, University Museum 75–35–1, reproduced by permission)

whose tomb the krater itself marked.[63] But

what, then, of the rest of the figures on the vase: are they heroes, too, or just everyday eighth-century soldiers? Is the complex scene as a whole a depiction of a specific mythological battle, or a generic representation of the kind of battles fought in the late eighth century?

The answer may be: neither one. The usual practice of trying to distinguish rigidly between "everyday life" and "myth" in Late Geometric imagery is simplistic. For there is, as A. Snodgrass has argued, a third possibility: the "generalized heroic" scene.[64] That is, while not specifically or identifiably mythological, many scenes are nonetheless given a legendary ambience or character through the presence of heroic features such as the war chariot (the vehicle was not used the way Homer's heroes—or the fallen figure at the top of Louvre A519—use it) and the scalloped Dipylon shield. This curious piece of work, found over and over again in Late Geometric vase painting, has been variously interpreted as (1) an "art-shield," an object that never actually existed in the eighth century but that consciously quoted rediscovered Mycenaean types (it would thus stamp its bearer Bronze Age Hero and transport any scene in which such Dipylon warriors appeared vaguely back to the heroic age); (2) a stylized representation of a real but ordinary sort of eighth-century shield with no heroic implications whatsoever; and, in a compromise, (3) a representation of a shield that was actually manufactured in the eighth century but that was intended to allude to the heroic world, a shield that was both real

63. Most recently, "The Geometric Style" 51. On the other hand, the twins appear on many non-Attic Geometric pots and pins, where they obviously could not have been intended as Athenian heraldic devices. But Nestor was not their only opponent: Herakles, a panhellenic champion, slew them (cf. Apollodoros 2.7.2), and that battle may be represented, too.

64. "Towards the Interpretation of the Geometric Figure Scenes" AM 95 (1980) 51–58.

and ennobling.[65] That the Dipylon shield was indeed no ordinary armament, that it was in fact emblematic of heroism, is suggested by a Boeotian kantharos (12) on which it is the principal subject.

At all events, the presence of warriors bearing Dipylon shields or driving chariots into battle does not by itself make any scene an illustration of a particular myth, but such illustration was probably not the point: it may have been the function of such shields and chariots merely to blur the distinction between eighth-century reality and the age of heroes, to make the two worlds interpenetrate. The elevation of the everyday to the level of the heroic would have served the purposes of the aristocracy for whom such images were painted, an exclusive elite that in the late eighth century virtually controlled representational activity—especially the painting of mass figured scenes like those on Louvre A519 (Figs. 1, 27)—for the sake of its own self-promotion. When representation is almost solely the preserve and property of an elite, as it was throughout the ages of Homer, it is, at some level, self-representation. It is an instrument of social power, a token of honor, a means of arguing for continued elite status. It is thus rhetoric, and the need for it in the late eighth century must have been made more acute by the rise of the last major phenomenon of Greek Renaissance, one that threatened the independent authority of the *oikoi* and the dominant position of the lords and nobles (*basileis*) who had exerted control over all aspects of culture: this was the *polis*, or city-state.

There is now a fair amount of excavated Dark Age and eighth-century architecture, and it has even been possible to draw up the plans of a number of towns from across these ages of Homer: Kavousi on Crete, Old Smyrna in Ionia, Emborio on Chios, Zagora on the island of Andros (Fig. 9), Koukounaries on Paros, the settlement on Donousa (a small island just off Naxos), Assiros in Macedonia, to name a few.[66] But a town alone—a physical, urban setting— does not a *polis* make. The Greeks themselves realized that a city-state was more than an aggregate of buildings or cluster of houses: it was a collection of like-minded men; it was a state of mind, a communal attitude. "*Poleis*," said the lyric poet Alkaios around 600, "are not stones or timbers or the artfulness of builders, but wherever there are men who know how to defend themselves, there are walls and *poleis*."[67] Still, *polis* is a hard word. At first meaning simply "citadel," it later came to be used for "city" proper, for both the citadel and the town that spread out at its slopes—a residential and urban concentration (the citadel proper then came to be called the *akropolis*, or "high city"). But it is not always easy to tell when *polis* is used more abstractly for "city-state" in the classical sense of "an autonomous political unit, incorporating a town and its territory as the inseparable parts of that unit,"[68] in which civic life is organized by customs, laws, or institutions that cut across ties of kinship or private privilege (that is, by settled procedures that form what might as well be called a "constitution") and in which there is both some

65. See J. M. Hurwit, "The Dipylon Shield Once More" *Classical Antiquity* 4 (1985) 121–26, and Whitley, *Style and Society in Dark Age Greece* 51.

66. See Coulson, *The Greek Dark Ages* 19–22; Coldstream, *Geometric Greece* 303–16; for Assiros, see AR (1988–1989) 62–66.

67. Alkaios, Frag. 426 (Loeb). Cf. Thucydides, *Peloponnesian War,* 7.77.7.

68. A. Snodgrass, *Archaeology and the Rise of the Greek State* (Cambridge 1977) 7.

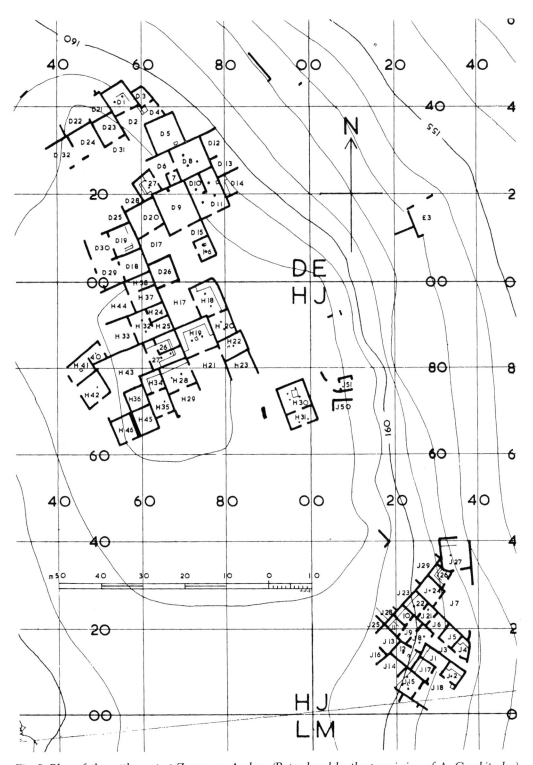

Fig. 9. *Plan of the settlement at Zagora on Andros. (Reproduced by the permission of A. Cambitoglou)*

specialization of government roles and some centralization of authority. Though Homer uses the word *polis* often enough, and though the idea of the city is clearly fundamental to our understanding of his epics (especially the *Iliad*, where the action is played out before and within city walls, where the fated destruction of Troy looms so large),[69] yet another vigorous debate has raged over whether he ever uses the word to mean "city-state," and thus whether Homeric society can be used to document the rise of the *polis* in the eighth century. For some, the existence of the full-blown, sovereign city-state is implicit in the description of the cities on Achilles' marvelously figured shield (*Iliad* 18.490–540) or in the description of Scheria (*Odyssey* 6.9–10, 262–67), or, by way of contrast, in the depiction of the stateless way of life of the Cyclops (*Odyssey* 9.112–15). For others, the city-state is nowhere to be found, and Homeric society is not even on the brink of *polis*hood (Odysseus' Ithaca, for example, is a mere semistate).[70]

But whether Homer acknowledges the *polis* or ignores it, it is almost universally agreed that the institution had in fact emerged by the end of the eighth century.[71] Though there would in time be hundreds of them, *poleis* certainly did not emerge everywhere in Greece,[72] and they did not appear all at once: some city-states took

longer to develop than others. Nor can we say exactly what an eighth-century *polis* looked like; indeed, there must have been considerable physical variation among early examples—some, for instance, consisted of clusters of villages rather than of a single great urban center—so we cannot always be sure we know a *polis* when we see one. Similarly, the social and political structures of early examples—even the ways in which their territories were spatially defined—were extremely diverse: the Athenian *polis* would have been a very different place from the Argive.[73] Still, we intuit or deduct the existence of the eighth-century *polis* from a number of architectural and cultural phenomena that, taken together, strongly suggest the kind of corporate effort, communal identity, and common will that only a city-state could inspire or entail. Inevitably, different scholars have drawn up different lists of symptoms that indicate the existence of true *poleis* in the eighth century, but the following would appear on most:

1. The construction of large temples and sanctuaries sacred to the city's patron god or goddess either at the center (for example, on the acropolis) or at the margins of the territory of the *polis*. The emergence of such sanctuaries—and the dedication within them of the sort of objects that had once been found only in graves, as offerings to

69. S. Scully, *Homer and the Sacred City* (Ithaca NY 1990), suggests that the composition of monumental epic in the eighth century was largely inspired by the contemporary rise of walled cities (96).

70. For a range of opinions, see J. V. Luce, "The *Polis* in Homer and Hesiod" *Proceedings of the Royal Irish Academy* 78 (1978) 1–15; W. G. Runciman, "The Origins of States: The Case of Archaic Greece" *Comparative Studies in Society and History* 24 (1982) 351–77; I. Morris, "Use and Abuse of Homer"; Scully, *Homer and the Sacred City* 90–91.

71. It has been suggested that the model of the Phoenician urban state had a major impact upon the development of the Greek; see A. Snodgrass, *Archaic Greece* (London 1980) 31–32; S. Morris, *Daidalos and the Origins of Greek Art* 123–24, 168–69.

72. The *ethnos*, a tribal system typically lacking towns but unified by a common religious center, dominated large areas such as Thessaly, Aitolia, Boiotia, and Achaia; see Snodgrass, *Archaic Greece* 42–44. E. Ruschenbusch, *Untersuchungen zu Staat und Politik in Griechenland vom 7.–4. Jh. v. Chr.* (1978), points out that there were eventually six to seven hundred individual *poleis* in Greece.

73. F. de Polignac, *La naissance de la cité grecque* (Paris 1984).

individuals—signals the eclipse of familial cults and personal status by the rise of state religion, and, with it, state identity. The *polis*, not the *oikos* or *genos*, was now the anchor of religious practice, and its sanctuaries became the centers of the greatest votive and material investment (in the form, for example, of splendid bronze figurines like **80** or monumental tripod cauldrons like **62** and Fig. 20). It is, in fact, not going too far to say that the consolidation of Greek religion and the rise of the *polis* went hand in hand: religion was "the *polis*' central ideology," and the *polis* provided Greek religion its structure.[74]

2. The widespread establishment, soon after 750 or so, of communal hero cults—rituals of worship at rediscovered Mycenaean tombs identified as those of legendary heroes (some but not all of them known from Homeric epic)—that seem to indicate an expropriation and canonizing of mythological figures as central to the ideology, legitimization, and self-definition of the individual *polis*. Each city-state needed its own local hero, and when one was not readily available, one was often invented. Broadly speaking, the identity of each *polis* was in large measure a function of its myths, especially those of its hero.[75]

3. The foundation, beginning before the middle of the eighth century, of the first Greek outposts and colonies in south Italy and Sicily (Pithekoussai, for example, founded by Eretria and Chalkis ca. 770).

Colonization indicates that some *poleis* were organized and centralized enough to reproduce for the sake of trade or (given population increases or other social pressures) out of the need for land.

4. The rise of new bronze armor and battle tactics in the late eighth century centering on the role not of elite warriors who fought each other one-on-one (as Homeric heroes and Geometric warriors usually do), but of heavily armed hoplites who fought closely side by side, shield overlapping shield, in massed lines or phalanxes that militarily expressed the collective identity of the state.[76] Hoplite tactics required lots of men, and so battle was no longer the business of the few. The rise of the hoplite, drawn mostly from the ranks of nonaristocratic but still prosperous landowners, suggests that the exclusivity of warfare had been broken: it had become the business of the *polis*.

5. The sharper definition of separate, local styles of vase painting and sculpture that reflect the differing aesthetics of different *poleis*. It is, for example, a relatively easy matter to tell an Arcadian Geometric bronze horse (**55, 95**) from a Laconian one (**92**), or a Laconian one from an Argive (**94**).[77] Similarly, there is no mistaking the Corinthian (**89**) or Argive Late Geometric style (**52, 90**) for the Athenian. To be sure, not every *polis* had its own distinct style, and at the end of the eighth century Eretria and Chalkis, now bitter enemies,

---

74. See C. Sourvinou-Inwood, "What Is *Polis* Religion?" in O. Murray and S. Price, eds., *The Greek City: From Homer to Alexander* (Oxford 1990) 295–322.

75. Snodgrass, *Archaic Greece* 38–40; Coldstream, *Geometric Greece* 346–48. Also D. C. Pozzi and J. M. Wickersham, eds., *Myth and the Polis* (Ithaca NY 1991) 2–3, 9; C. Bérard, "Récuperer la mort du prince: héroisation et formation de la cité" in G. Gnoli and J.-P. Vernant, eds., *La mort, les morts, dans les sociétés anciennes* (Cambridge 1982) 89–105; and A. J. M. Whitley, "Early States and Hero Cults: A Re-appraisal" *JHS* 108 (1988) 173–82.

76. Massed infantry tactics of some sort are referred to in the *Iliad* at 12.105–7, 13.125–34, and 16.210–17. For hoplite tactics in general, see V. D. Hanson, ed., *Hoplites: The Classical Greek Battle Experience* (London 1991).

77. See Zimmermann, *Les chevaux*.

used the same style of pottery. But as a whole political autonomy encouraged artistic independence and diversity.[78]

6. The rise of Panhellenic sanctuaries and contests such as those at Olympia and Delphi. Though the traditional, ancient date for the first Olympic Games (776 B.C.) is suspect,[79] the Panhellenic movement itself implies the existence of discrete political units that, despite their independence, promoted the periodic expression of "Greekness." The existence of the *polis*, in other words, was a prerequisite for the development of such "interstate" sanctuaries.[80]

Not all of these phenomena appear on everyone's list of *polis* symptoms (many would remove the so-called hoplite reform, for example),[81] and some would add others (the presence of fortification walls protecting the community as a whole, for example). Individually, none is by itself sufficient to prove the existence of a fully formed city-state. But, taken together, they are formidable indications indeed, and the diagnosis of the existence of the *polis* in the eighth century is virtually assured.

4

Art and poetry are interlocking strands in the web of culture. They are among a society's strongest expressions and communications, and changes in the fundamental structure of a society will likely stimulate equally great changes in its poetry and art.

It is thus fair to ask whether the changes brought about by the rise of the *polis* in the eighth century had anything to do with the apparently contemporary textualization of Homer and the rise of representation and mythological content in art. To put the question another way: Who would have benefited from the transcription of the *Iliad* and *Odyssey*, and who from the explosion of images?

For some, the answer is aristocrats, and aristocrats alone. I. Morris, for example, has argued that the *Iliad* and the *Odyssey* are above all polemical texts and were first written down in the late eighth century specifically to serve the purposes of highborn nobles (the *basileis*) whose traditional stature was at risk in the social ferment accompanying the development of the *polis*. The transcription of Homer was a response to a threat, a defense of the status quo, an attempt on the part of the nobility to promote its elite ideology and legitimize its traditional powers and prerogatives in the face of the coalescing *demos* (the people). Homer was, in this view, a tool of the aristocracy, and the act of writing down his poems was a political act—a glorification of individual, "heroic" rulers, a promotion of "the good *basileus*" (like the one described at *Odyssey* 19.109–14), an argument for the continued concentration of power in the hands of a few, to the detriment of the people.[82] Now, it is true that epic poets must have been regular fixtures in the halls of *basileis* and

78. See J. N. Coldstream, "The Meaning of the Regional Styles in the Eighth Century B.C.," in *The Greek Renaissance of the Eighth Century B.C.*, 17–25. Similarly, the various local or epichoric alphabetic scripts of early Greece are clear indications of political heterogeneity.

79. C. Morgan, *Athletes and Oracles* (Cambridge 1990) 47–49.

80. See Pozzi and Wickersham, *Myth and the Polis* 5, 9. Morgan, *Athletes and Oracles*, 16–20, argues, however, that in the eighth century prominent individuals or families were far more active than *poleis* at interstate sanctuaries.

81. For a recent discussion, see I. Morris, *Burial and Ancient Society: The Rise of the Greek City-State* (Cambridge 1987) 195–201.

82. I. Morris, "Use and Abuse of Homer."

often performed at contests held at the funerals of the great.[83] And it is important to stress that the eighth-century *polis* was still a highly stratified place: it was no democracy. But it is hard to reconcile the notion of exclusive aristocratic control over epic with the very name of the blind bard tenderly portrayed in Homer's own *Odyssey*: Demodokos ("Welcomed by the People").[84] And if the *Iliad* and *Odyssey* had been solely "court poems," if their ideology had been identified solely with the interests of the elite, it would be difficult to explain their enduring and universal popularity in the *poleis* of Archaic and Classical Greece and their rapidly acquired status as the texts of Panhellenism, poems that helped define what it was to be Greek (not just a Greek aristocrat).[85]

Bards performed not only in aristocratic halls, for the amusement of the few, but in marketplaces and in public contexts such as religious festivals, for the pleasure of the many.[86] The audience of epic was also a popular audience, a *polis*-audience. And recently I. Winter, citing parallels with the lays of Chrétien de Troyes and the urbanization of twelfth-century A.D. France, has proposed that the *Iliad* and *Odyssey*, far from being exclusive aristocratic instruments, "displaced" into the realm of saga the sort of individualistic and often destructive behavior that heroes like Achilles might exhibit but that the *polis* could no longer endure or tol-

erate.[87] By channeling and confining heroic ideals to a "golden age," where they could be admired safely from an imaginative distance, the textualization of Homer allowed and nurtured the development of new ideals and newly political (*polis*tical?) behaviors. In this view, the motivation behind the transcription and thus fossilization of Homer was a civic rather than an aristocratic one. In either case, the eighth-century creation of the texts is considered another symptom of the rise of the city-state.

But what of representation and, especially, heroic imagery? Here, the notion of continued aristocratic control makes some sense, for there is virtually no such thing in the eighth century as "state art," art overtly placed in the service of the *polis* itself. With the exception of early cult statues like those that stood in the eighth-century temples of Hera on Samos and of Apollo at Dreros on Crete (Fig. 19),[88] Late Geometric art was still mostly the property of the elite: grand, publicly financed artistic programs—programs that visually expressed the ideology and mythology of the *polis*—are not yet known. The large figured vases that stood over or were placed in tombs, the bronzes that were now thickly dedicated in public sanctuaries, the engraved fibulae that fastened the clothing of the well-to-do: these were the status-charged memorials, offerings, or equipment of individuals, not of the *polis*. They were, and bore representations

83. Hesiod tells us as much in *Works and Days*, 653–59.

84. See W. G. Thalmann, *Conventions of Form and Thought in Early Greek Epic Poetry* (Baltimore 1984) 131, who notes the importance of the oral poet to the entire community, claiming he was "not just a court poet who provides amusement to aristocrats in their idle hours." Also note that the bard is ranked among the *demioergoi* ("workers for the people") listed at *Odyssey* 17.383–85 (along with prophets, healers, and skilled workmen). Cf. C. Segal, "Bard and Audience in Homer," in R. Lamberton and J. J. Keaney, eds., *Homer's Ancient Readers: The Hermeneutics of Greek Epic's Earliest Exegetes* (Princeton 1992) 3–29 at 5.

85. See Scully, *Homer and the Sacred City* 98.

86. See Thalmann, *Conventions of Form and Thought* 118–19.

87. Winter, "Homer's Phoenicians."

88. See A. F. Stewart, *Greek Sculpture: An Exploration* (New Haven 1990) 104–5.

of, elite displays. But rather than see the generation of specifically mythological images on such artifacts as antagonistic rhetoric, as evidence of blatant aristocratic opposition to the emerging *polis*, one should perhaps regard the birth of mythological art as an attempt to co-opt the *polis's* emerging mythology. With such images aristocrats could publish their supposedly heroic pedigrees and fuse them with the identity of the city-state (just as noble and commoner alike joined in the communal hero-cult), and so stake out certain boundaries within a state that was itself acquiring definition partly through the consolidation of myth and legend. Mythological representation was a discreet means of arguing for continued power and influence in a different political climate.

There were, again, images in Greek art long before the end of the eighth century, just as there had long been epic poetry. But unless we assume that art is driven entirely by impersonal evolutionary forces and that complex paintings like those on Louvre A519 (Figs. 1, 27) were just "bound to happen," the burst of images and the appearance of mythological subject matter in the decades before 700, like the phenomenon we call Homer, are best explained in the context of the *polis*. The rise of representation and the culmination of the epic tradi-

tion were part of the same complex process of Greek self-definition that fueled the rise of the *polis* itself and cannot be viewed in isolation: the art and poetry of the Late Geometric period both made the world of heroes more accessible. And this is the principal relationship between Homer and Late Geometric imagery: they were tools in the recovery of the heroic past, a past that was employed to define and elevate the Greek present. One cannot argue any longer that the dissemination of the *Iliad* and *Odyssey* specifically inspired Late Geometric artists to deviate from their generic ways of rendering and to experiment with mythological narrative: most early Greek narrative scenes are not specifically "Homeric" in content anyway. And the days are now fortunately gone when the Greek artist, early or late, was considered a slavish illustrator of Homer's epics and other poetic texts.[89] Instead, Homer and the rise of mythological narrative in art were cognate responses to the rise of the *polis* and its need to define itself both as an autonomous entity, with its own favored cults and heroes, and as a Greek state among other Greek states, sharing the common heritage stored in epic. It is the construction of this dynamic relationship between the *polis* and its art and poetry that signaled both the climax of the age of Homer and its end.

---

89. The literature on this problem is now extensive; see, for example, Hurwit, *The Art and Culture of Early Greece* 122–24.

*For it is not a bad place at all, it could bear all crops
in season, and there are meadow lands near the shores of the gray sea,
well watered and soft; there could be grapes grown there endlessly,
and there is smooth land for plowing, men could reap a full harvest
always in season, since there is very rich subsoil.*

(Odyssey 9.131–35)

LIFE AND
SOCIETY IN GEOMETRIC GREECE

Greece in the eleventh to eighth centuries was a different world from that of the classical period. In decided contrast to the democratic ideals and civic orientation of the Classical polis, the world of Geometric Greece continued the more pastoral existence of the Dark Age. Its major religious sites were not city shrines but altars in the countryside; its art focused on the natural world. Within this setting, the social structure of Geometric Greece was in flux. An aristocratic class arose from the remains of the fallen Bronze Age kingdoms during a time when material means of expression were limited. Available evidence suggests that this elite class defined itself in part through an awareness of the past and the kindling of heroic ideals together with a new sense of panhellenism. The setting and motivating forces of this changing social structure appear in objects that transmitted the symbols and messages of the aristocracy in both daily life and the funeral, realms

that reaffirmed group identities. Viewed through the filters of epic poetry, artistic representation, and modern excavations, the realities of life and death in early Greece appear unusually accessible yet remain incompletely understood. Recent scholarship has been reconsidering precisely how "dark" the Dark Age was. Excavations at Lefkandi, Knossos, Eleutherna, and Zagora are dispelling the received tradition of a bleak, impoverished land cut off from the outside world and bereft of the amenities of civilization.

The twin-handled wine container (amphora) is perhaps the most familiar of all Greek vessel shapes. Although it developed within the Mycenaean culture, it never attained there the status it was to achieve in the Iron Age as cultural symbol and objet d'art. Technically a storage vessel for wine and oil, this vase type for a brief phase served as a cinerary urn, a use that was gradually phased out from the earlier eleventh century on in the face of inhumation's rising popularity. About the time it ceased to contain cremations, its surface became the field for figural representations, a tradition that continued down to the Red Figure style of the Classical period. The amphorae that open the exhibition (1–3) reflect successive stages of the remarkable changes that transformed Greece between 1100 and 700 B.C. The Submycenaean example of about 1075 (1) belongs to the waning of the Greek Bronze Age. As the witness to a dissolving artistic tradition, its loose, plump profile and simple freehand decorative curves are a stark reminder of the once-elegant pottery of the Mycenaean palaces in the years before their collapse. Half a century later, the development of a new technology based on a compass and multiple brush has given the artist of the Protogeometric period complete control over the decoration, resulting in a new spirit of order and formality (Fig. 6). This new aesthetic increasingly uses decoration to complement the form of the vessel. Now made up of rectilinear geometric designs, the decoration of the Middle Geometric amphora of about 850 B.C. (2) is characterized by a mathematically precise organization that highlights the vase's structure against a black background. Finally, the Late Geometric amphora, 725–700 B.C. (3), illustrates the profoundly significant shift of focus from abstract design to the human figure. Its bands of ornamentation vibrate with animal and human life and anticipate the leading role that the human figure will henceforth play in Greek art.

Among the earliest objects in the exhibition are a Protogeometric skyphoid krater (4) and straight pin (5). Although both ultimately derive from Mycenaean ancestors, their functional simplicity and aesthetic understatement belong quintessentially to the sober new post–Bronze Age world, displaying the subtle but profound differences that have fueled the long-standing controversy over how much cultural continuity linked the Bronze and Iron ages.

Perhaps surprisingly, few objects from the Geometric period refer overtly to agriculture and animal husbandry. Only in votives offered with a prayer for divine protection can we sense the concerns of the average Greek citizen. A small bronze wolf grasping a lamb in its mouth embodies the farmer's fears (7). A bronze bull figurine (6) and pottery painted with horses and their foals (8) symbolize his source of security: ownership of bulls or horses implies ownership of land, the basis of all real wealth in this period. A small model granary (14 and Fig. 15), one of only a few such objects known, would have been buried with a deceased landowner upon his or her death to proclaim the status of the departed soul and, perhaps more to the point, the status of that soul's surviving family. Round structures recently excavated at Lefkandi in Euboea may offer concrete parallels for the models.

Direct evidence for an elite group grows as the period progresses, with material wealth evident in metal objects, made innately precious by the scarcity of copper, tin, and gold deposits in Greece. The spectacular Late Geometric gold earrings with elaborate decorative granulation (13) attest not only to the reestablishment of contact with metal sources but also to the learning anew of lost metalworking techniques. An iron knife (15) is a rare example of the metal that characterizes the new age. Nevertheless, at a time when the material means of expression are still limited, it is easier to trace the development of an aristocratic class through artistic images and the use of symbolism. The newly invented or recaptured figural style focuses not on the mundane world of the farmer and the fisherman, but rather on a heroic world of aristocratic warriors and their equipment. Expensive to maintain above all other animals, the horse became a natural emblem of the aristocracy. Horse symbolism crops up everywhere in Geometric art, as on the sides of a drinking cup (16). Inside another skyphos (10), upon finishing his wine the drinker found scenes of horses being trained by riders standing on the animals' backs.

The armed warrior, the chariot, and the horse are the most familiar symbols of the age, all assembled here on an amphora (9) and variously encountered throughout the exhibition. Certainly the most long-standing issue in Geometric art studies is the extent to which these images of military preoccupation reflect a real world of military threats and conflicts among the developing poleis and to what extent the images were understood by contemporary viewers to refer to the heroic deeds of their ancestors. Odysseus' invented identity as a professional freelance warrior may equally characterize the armed figures of Geometric pottery and reflect a pattern of life at the beginning of the Dark Age:

> but labor was never dear to me,
> nor care for my house, though that is what
> raises glorious children;
> but ships that are driven on by oars were
> dear to me always,
> and the wars, and throwing spears with
> polished hafts, and the arrows,
> gloomy things, which to other men are
> terrible

(*Odyssey* 14.222–26)

Reference to courage and physical prowess could be overt, as in scenes of war on land (**24, 37, 98, 99**, Figs. 1, 27) and sea (Figs. 10, 18), but could also reside implicitly in animal imagery (**11**). Motifs like the so-called Dipylon shield, a round body shield with

Fig. 10. *Attic krater with ship scene, Metropolitan Museum of Art 34.11.2 (Photo courtesy of Metropolitan Museum of Art, Fletcher Fund, 1943)*

cutout sides, here pictured on a skyphos (**10**) and a Boeotian kantharos (**12**), are widely interpreted as an (incorrect) attempt to portray actual Bronze Age armor revived for the sake of heroic atmosphere in Geometric art.

Evidence suggests that the aristocracy of the Iron Age defined itself not only in material wealth but also through references to the past transmitted through Homeric poetry. The origin of the symposium, the Greek institution providing a crucial forum for exchange of ideas and aristocratic intragroup bonding, may be archaeologically detected in the focus of the Greek master potter and painter on vessels produced for elaborate drinking ceremonies: large jugs (oinochoai), tankards, mixing bowls (kraters), and cups (skyphoi and kantharoi). In the symposium setting the Homeric epics may have spread across Greece, linking cities and regions through the awareness of a common past. The small bronze figure of a man playing a lyre captures the nature of Homer himself, in the essential role of the blind bards of the *Odyssey* as preservers of ancestral Greek history and legends (17).

The early Greek hero, of course, was not actualized only on the battlefield, but embodied excellence in all its forms. Legendary heroes were therefore associated with important social functions: they founded cities and sanctuaries; they organized civic institutions; they made laws and settled disputes. It is no mystery that at a time of accelerated civic and social development the boundaries between heroes and aristocrats are permeable and that both inhabit public art as interchangeable images. The ascendancy of the human subject out of a non-figural artistic tradition accompanies the social developments in Greece from 1000 to 700 B.C. From the tenth century on, the unsettled pastoral Dark Age existence supported an increasing importance of the town, or polis, as the organizational focus of life, laying the foundations for the uniquely Greek role of the individual citizen as the basis of the state for the first time in history. Archaeological evidence from the late eighth century begins to reveal that component parts of a functioning, citizen-driven polis were in place: a separately defined agora, or public meeting place, an acropolis with both religious and defensive functions, and a necropolis, the resting place of the community's dead. The democratic nature of these developments should not be exaggerated; the period's art speaks in an aristocratic voice, reminding us by whose hands the period's major transformations were effected.

S. L.

1 NECK-HANDLED AMPHORA

Submycenaean, ca. 1075–1050 B.C.
Height 0.413.

Ceramic; handles and base of neck broken and repaired.
Yale University Art Gallery, Gift of Rebecca Darlington Stoddard, 1913 (1913.49).

The amphora features a globular body with sloping shoulder onto which is set a tall, narrow neck. Vertical handles rising from the shoulder attach below the hollow lip. The vessel's minimal decoration is rendered in dark-brown glaze on an almost completely reserved body. Typical of Submycenaean and Protogeometric amphorae, the shoulder bears the main decorative zone, containing pairs of freehand antithetic loops. Simple horizontal bands articulate the structure of the vase, appearing just above and below the point where the vessel reaches its widest girth, marking the lower body where it begins a swift tapering to the foot, framing the neck at base and lip, and reiterating the vertical lines of the handles.

The Yale amphora is similar in shape and decoration to examples from the Kerameikos cemetery. Corresponding in shape more to the transitional Submycenaean/Protogeometric amphorae (Kerameikos inv. 556 and 915) than to the more globular Submycenaean versions (Kerameikos inv. 422 and 519), the Yale amphora shows in its emphasis on the lip and the lengthening of the neck the developing articulation of vessel parts in greater distinction from one another that characterizes late Submycenaean ceramics. Its large size also indicates its relatively later date in Submycenaean, when the gradual abandonment of small cist-grave inhumations for cremations in Attica allowed for larger funerary vessels. The purely Submycenaean decoration finds correspondence in the loose antithetical spirals on a belly-handled amphora from Salamis and the spirals on another neck-handled version from Deiras. Its shape inherited from the Late Mycenaean repertoire, the Submycenaean amphora launched a centuries-long tradition of using such vessels as containers for ashes of the dead. Apparently from the start these ash-urns were sex-linked by handle placement, with the present neck-handled

1

form employed for male burials and the belly-handled and shoulder-handled for female.

Controversy surrounds the use of the term *Submycenaean* to describe the material remains in Greece following the final catastrophes the Mycenaean palaces suffered around 1125 B.C. Some use the term to denote a chronological phase distinct from the latest Mycenaean material (LHIIIC2), while others argue for Submycenaean pottery as a specifically funerary ware produced contemporary with LHIIIC2. In comparison with earlier Mycenaean culture, however, the term is consonant with aesthetic and technical degeneration, as Submycenaean pottery seems to show signs of a profoundly affected cultural spirit. At its most extreme, this is detected in listless ornamentation and clumsy, baggy shapes, as if the task of pottery making were suddenly in the hands of amateurs, as might actually have been the case. At the form's finest, as in the example here, the potter maintains high technical standards and treats the vessel with an eloquent simplicity and a lightness of touch that join the artistry of the past with the reviving spirit of the early Iron Age.

PUBLISHED

Baur, *Catalogue of the R. D. Stoddard Collection* 44–45 no. 49, fig. 8.

Desborough, *Protogeometric Pottery* 8.

Matheson Burke and Pollitt, *Greek Vases at Yale* 3, 4, no. 7.

NOTES

On Submycenaean pottery: C. G. Styrenius, *Submycenaean Studies* (Lund 1967); Desborough, *The Last Mycenaeans and Their Successors*; Desborough, *The Greek Dark Ages*; P. M. Mountjoy, *Mycenaean Decorated Pottery: A Guide to Identification* (SIMA LXXIII, Göteborg 1986) 194–200.

Parallels: from Athens, Kriezi Street grave 70, *AD* 22 (1967) B pl. 85a; W. Kraiker and K. Kübler, *Kerameikos* 1 (Berlin 1939) pl. 26, inv. 422 and inv. 519, pl. 56, inv. 556; K. Kübler, *Neufunde aus der Nekropole des 11. und 10. Jahrhunderts* (Kerameikos IV, Berlin

1943) pl. 5, inv. 915; Styrenius, *Submycenaean Studies*, transitional Submycenaean/Protogeometric Kerameikos amphorae figs. 35–36, amphora from Deiras chamber tomb XXIV fig. 50; Mountjoy, *Mycenaean Decorated Pottery* 197 fig. 261 FS70; amphora from Salamis, *AM* 35 (1910) pl. VI, 6.

S. L.

2 NECK-HANDLED AMPHORA

Attic, Middle Geometric I, 850–800 B.C.
Height 0.530.
Pottery; neck and rim broken and mended on one side; two large chips on foot restored.
University of Missouri–Columbia, Museum of Art and Archaeology, Gilbreath-McLorn Museum Fund (91.255). From a German private collection, acquired in the 1960s.

The amphora comprises an ovoid body set on a low ring foot, the shoulder sloping to a tall, slightly concave neck with flaring rim; strap handles attach at neck and shoulder. The decoration features two sets of triple reserved bands on the lower body; on the upper body, a band of dotted double axes alternates with groups of vertical lines, with two sets of triple reserved bands above and below. The neck bears a panel framed by triple reserved bands enclosing a hatched meander above a row of dogtooth. Simple double axes alternating with vertical strokes encircle the lip. Two diagonally hatched columns decorate the handles.

The relatively slender profile with high center of gravity supports a dating of this vessel in the second half of the ninth century. The hatched meander of the neck panel, a motif invented at the outset of the Geometric period, shows the new precision of execution that followed the unsure efforts of Early Geometric artists. The use of this quintessentially continuous motif in an abbreviated window panel succeeds by using the vertical arms of the meander to frame the panel. (Compare the Early Geometric amphora in Coldstream, *Greek Geometric Pottery* pl. 2f, for a less satis-

application of horizontal lines. The refinement of high-quality black slip inspired a preference for dark ground effects that encouraged decoration in bands and windows rather than the freer approaches of previous light-ground ceramic styles. Perhaps most significant, the new decorative systems and motifs attest to the development of precise measuring techniques for three-dimensional surfaces. The fundamental control over decoration that these improved techniques offered the painter resulted in a new aesthetic of rationality, dominated by rectilinear motifs applied so as to complement the form of the vessel. The Missouri amphora, with its areas of well-preserved black slip, exemplifies the balance of restrained ornamentation and predominately dark ground that makes the Middle Geometric pottery perhaps the most visually powerful of the Geometric period.

PUBLISHED

Galerie Günter Puhze, *Kunst der Antike* cat. 9 (Freiburg 1991) 18, no. 184.
GBA no. 1478 (March 1992) 54 no. 178 (ill.).
"Acquisitions 1991" *Muse* 25 (1991) 55 (ill.).

NOTES

For Eleusis amphora 816 with dots and double axes: P. Kahane, "Die Entwicklungsphasen der attisch-geometrischen Keramik" *AJA* 44 (1940) 464–82 at 470, pl. 19, 2.

Neck-handled amphora from Kerameikos grave 36, inv. 2155: Kübler, *Die Nekropole des 10. bis 8. Jahrhunderts* pl. 29 dated 875–850 B.C.; Coldstream, *Greek Geometric Pottery* 17 and pl. 3a, sets its date nearer 850.

Neck-handled amphorae from Kerameikos grave 37, inv. 866: Kübler, *Die Nekropole* pl. 29; Coldstream, *Greek Geometric Pottery* pl. 3d; from grave 23, inv. 236, Kübler pl. 30, dated near 800 B.C.

Similar amphora with "killed" sword from Athens, Mitsaion Street: *AD* 22 (1967) B pl. 94b.

For the handle pattern: Kübler, *Die Nekropole* pl. 151 inv. 866.

2

factory solution.) The motif of double axes between vertical strokes originates in the Middle Geometric period, although the use of dots above and below the double axes on the body is unusual. A similar combination appears on a neck amphora from Eleusis, where the ornamentation of both neck and body is increased through additional bands of decoration. Closer in overall appearance are three amphorae from the Kerameikos cemetery, particularly inv. 2155 with plumper body and identical neck design.

During the two centuries between the Yale Submycenaean amphora (1) and the ninth-century Missouri amphora, new ceramic technologies changed the direction of Greek pottery. An improved potter's wheel facilitated a tautening of vessel profiles and the precise

S. L.

3

3

3 NECK-HANDLED AMPHORA

Attic, Late Geometric, ca. 725–700 B.C.
Height 0.676, maximum diameter 0.342.
Ceramic; restored from large fragments,
 missing two small sections of plastic
 snake.
Virginia Museum of Fine Arts, The
 Glasgow Fund, 1960 (60.50).
See Plate 11.

Resting on the standard low foot, the body
follows a relatively taut contour to a rounded
shoulder; the neck is cylindrical, flaring slightly at the top, and is proportionally shorter

than on many contemporary examples. Lip
and handles each carry a wavy plastic snake.
Above the solid foot, thin banding alternates
with subsidiary motifs on the body: sigmas,
tight horizontal zigzag, blind lozenge chain,
simple hatched meander, tightly overlapping
lozenges, and double horizontal zigzag. The
two figural zones are at belly and shoulder.
The neck features a complicated hatched
meander with a simple meander below, zigzags and single hatched zigzag above. The
snakes are solid.

Seven men parade around the belly in
single-horse chariots amid filling ornaments of
zigzags, double axes, and birds. Each unarmed
driver holds a crop and three reins in his
hands, the latter thought to signify that not
one horse, but two or three pull the chariot.
Interestingly, one driver is clad in a long robe.
The chariot boxes are small with loops representing front and side rails. On the amphora's
main side the drivers' legs disappear into the
box floor shown as a broad horizontal line
angled down at the back, except for one in
which three horizontal strokes seem to indicate the side construction. On the back,
chariot boxes are reduced to a negligible
thickening of the top of the wheel. In the
smaller figural zone on the shoulder, five deer
on either side graze on crosshatched triangles;
zigzags and quatrefoil lozenges fill space
above and below the animals.

All elements of this handsome amphora
indicate that it was painted by an artist following closely in the footsteps of the great
Dipylon painters. The later eighth-century
followers retained some of the monumentality
achieved by the earlier workshops in both pot-
ting and painting. Unlike those who experimented outside the Classical traditions
established by the Dipylon and Hirschfeld
Masters, the Dipylon followers added relatively
few new motifs to their repertoire and
focused instead on the staid chariot processions. The overall decorative scheme of the
Richmond amphora is typical of this group.
The neck carries the customary complicated
meander and a strong hatched zigzag that, as

on other vessels of this group, overwhelm the perfunctory bands of sigmas and lozenges that cover the rest of the vase. The figural friezes stand out much more assertively in this quiet setting than the earlier artists would have allowed.

Although the particular one-horse-chariot form seen here appears more commonly on vessels of the Late Geometric Ia Sub-Dipylon Workshop that immediately succeeded the Dipylon productions, other elements indicate the origin of the Richmond amphora in the prolific Workshop of Athens 894. As in that group, the grazing deer of the Richmond vase derive directly from the animal files introduced by the Dipylon Master, an old motif derived from Near Eastern art. These files are absent in Sub-Dipylon work and seem to have been revived by the slightly later Philadelphia Painter and the Athens 894 Workshop. Also introduced in these two groups, this time under Corinthian influence, are the one-legged "soldier-birds" that fill space between the chariots.

The robed charioteer on the Richmond vase is preceded by only two earlier examples, but the motif occurs on several amphorae by the Workshop of Athens 894. Generally the horses of that workshop are cursive in style, although none so much as the Richmond horses with their full, rounded chests and equally contoured backs rising to a high rump. Amphorae with a similar decorative scheme of chariot procession around belly and complicated meander on neck as the two main zones reside in Hanover, Paris, Berlin, and Athens collections; all these have proportionally higher necks than the Richmond vase.

Although not a first-generation figural vase, the Richmond amphora captures the fundamental developments in Late Geometric pottery. Its monumental size is a response to changing social usage that by the eighth century ranks certain individuals by visible marks of distinction accompanying burial. Vases have long abandoned large areas of solid black in order to open up the surface to increasingly explicit discourse through images. The belly, shoulder, and neck zones that formerly received the amphora's sole decoration retain their primary roles, but the once-featured geometric ornamentation now provides a muted backdrop to the drama of human action.

The chariot procession was the most important inheritance of the great pioneering workshops that standardized the human figure and established iconographic motifs. The significance of this motif—specifically, the question of whether it represents the military concerns of eighth-century life, funeral games in honor of the deceased, a funeral cortege to the grave site, or a more rarified evocation of a heroic age—is much debated. That the horse-and-chariot was a highly charged image in Greece, probably encompassing multiple meanings, is clear. It pervades Late Geometric art, appearing on painted pottery, gold bands, bronze and terracotta figurines, and engraved bronze fibulae. Yet no clear chariot remains have been found in Greece, a lack that has kept alive controversy surrounding the actual use of chariots in this period. The chariot was not a new Iron Age artistic device but rather an important Helladic emblem of aristocracy prevalent in Mycenaean palace frescoes, painted kraters, and engraved gems. The resemblance of painted Geometric chariots to Mycenaean examples suggests to some that the sources upon which the later artists drew included accidental encounters with Mycenaean pictorial art.

The significance of chariot-frieze amphorae is explored further in 9 and 25.

PUBLISHED

Ancient Art in the Virginia Museum Richmond 1973) 69, no. 81.

M. Mayo, "Tradition and Imagination: Five Centuries of Greek Ceramic Art" *Apollo* 286 (1985) 428–35 at 428 fig. 1.

EXHIBITED

The Greek Line, Norfolk Museum of Arts and Sciences, October 1962.

NOTES

On the Sub-Dipylon Group and Workshop of Athens 894: Cook, "Athenian Workshops around 700" 146–49; Davison, *Attic Geo-*

4

metric Workshops 41–45, 65–73; Coldstream, *Greek Geometric Pottery* 55–64.
Similar amphorae: Hannover 1953.148, CVA Hannover 1, 11–12, pl. 1.1–4; Louvre CA 2503, Villard, *MonPiot* 1957 figs. 18, 19; CVA Louvre 16, 24–25, pl. 34.1–2; Berlin atliche Museen, *AK* 15 (1972) 3–6; Athens (184) 1044, *JdI* (1899) 193, fig. 56; Davison, *Attic Geometric Workshops* fig. 96; U. Gehrig, *Antiken aus Berliner Privatbesitz* (Berlin 1975) no. 30.
For the funerary significance of the snakes, see **20**.

S. L.

4 SMALL KRATER

Euboean, Protogeometric, 950–900 B.C.
Height 0.203, rim diameter 0.215, foot diameter 0.090, foot height 0.035.

Ceramic; mended; small section of foot, root of one handle, and several areas of rim restored.
University of Missouri–Columbia, Museum of Art and Archaeology, gift of Museum Associates and Gilbreath-McLorn Museum Fund (90.109). Previously Erlenmeyer Collection.
See Plate 4.

The small deep-bodied krater with high flaring lip and tall foot features four sets of ten pendent concentric semicircles made by compass and multiple brush. Compass holes are visible.

This handsome drinking vessel embodies the new aesthetic spirit of the Protogeometric period. The artist employed painted decoration to interpret the bowl as a constructed object. Solid areas of paint balance lip and foot and frame the decorative zone between dark bands and painted handles. The pendent concentric semicircles display the new compass technology that offered the artist a strict mechanical control over the decoration and rid the old Mycenaean motif of all its previous irregularities. Just as the bands divide the pot into its component parts, the semicircles express its volume as the two-dimensional equivalent of the vessel's deep hemisphere. As simple as the decoration is, it forms the foundation of all later Greek pottery in its sympathetic relationship between ornament and structure.

The krater is datable by similar pots in the assemblage from the Protogeometric building at Toumba, Lefkandi, which belongs to the first half of the tenth century. Several of the vessel's early features betray connections with local Mycenaean pottery: the pedestal foot, size and proportion of the deep bowl, high flaring lip, reserved lower body, and nonintersecting semicircles. These pedestaled bowls with pendent semicircles are prototypes of the later smaller skyphos version that constitutes the most widespread of all Greek Geometric pottery types, found not only throughout Greece and the Cyclades but exported as far as Cyprus, Syria, Italy, and Sicily (compare **71**).

The Columbia bowl is important as one of the best-preserved links between the local Mycenaean tradition and the origin of the Thessalo-Cycladic pendent semicircles skyphoi. Moreover, its closest parallels, which come from Koundouriotissa Pieria in Macedonia, the island of Andros, and Lefkandi, support the contention of an independent northern development of Protogeometric style, uninfluenced by Attica. The lack of mica in the ceramic fabric locates its provenance in Euboea rather than Thessaly or Macedonia, and the slip preserved in several places suggests that it may have come from Lefkandi, since other Euboean sites have tended to produce only unslipped vessels.

This small, elegant krater was probably used for food as well as for drink. The monochrome interior is completely worn away. We may imagine it as a favorite vessel, used for the last time at the graveside funerary meal and then deposited with the burial.

PUBLISHED

H. Erlenmeyer, "Über Philister und Kreter. II" *Orientalia* 29, 4 (1960) 241–72 at 249, pl. LXXII, fig. 65.

Schefold, *Meisterwerke griechischer Kunst* 121–22, 136.

Coldstream, *Greek Geometric Pottery* 153.

Catling and Lemos, *Lefkandi* II, pt. 1 *The Pottery* 22–23.

Sotheby's, *Antiquities from the Erlenmeyer Collection*, London, July 9, 1990, no. 146.

"Acquisitions 1988–1990" *Muse* 23–24 (1989–1990) 114.

NOTES

On Protogeometric pottery from Toumba: Catling and Lemos, *Lefkandi* II, pt. 1 *The Pottery*; on similar skyphoi and krater-bowls, 22–23, pls. 5i, 14, 15, 48 no. 156, 49 no. 157, 52 nos. 293, 294.

For the origin of the type: Kearsley, *The Pendent Semi-circle Skyphos* 109–14; for the Koudouriotissa Pieria skyphos, 110, pl. 7c.

For the skyphos from Andros: Desborough, *Protogeometric Pottery* pl. 16, no. 146.

For similar shape, krateroid skyphos, inv. C2: A. Cambitoglou, *Archaeological Museum of Andros, Guide* (Athens 1981) 101 no. 339, 102 fig. 59.

On local development of Protogeometric style: D. Theocharis, "Iolkos" *Ergon* (1960) 55–61 and *Ergon* (1961) 51–60.

For comparative fabric studies: Kearsley, *The Pendent Semi-circle Skyphos* 75–83; M. Popham and I. Lemos, review of Kearsley, *Gnomon* 64, 2 (1992) 152–55, esp. 154.

S. L.

5 DRESS PIN

Submycenaean to Protogeometric, 1075–900 B.C.

Length 0.225, diameter of head 0.008.

Bronze, gray-green patina; complete, shaft mended in one place.

5

University of Missouri–Columbia, Museum of Art and Archaeology (59.44).

The pin's long shaft is round in section and features a flat disk head and a spherical globe, made separately, on the shaft.

This type of bronze straight pin was commonly used during the Submycenaean period in Greece and continued fundamentally unchanged in form through the Protogeometric period. The main development in this later period was in material, and straight pins made of iron seem to have predominated over the bronze versions. Whether this pin dates to Submycenaean or Protogeometric is uncertain. It has no projection of shaft above the disk, which Jacobsthal designated as a late feature, yet many of the less progressive areas of Greece long continued to make near-replicas of very late Bronze Age objects. In grave contexts pins usually occur in pairs in women's burials, one on each shoulder of the skeleton, and less frequently in men's burials, as a single cloak fastener on one shoulder.

The ultimate origin of these long dress pins was once generally accepted as Central Europe where they appeared around 1500 B.C. in the Tumulus Culture. They have been cited, along with other types of bronze objects that first appear in the LHIIIC period, as evidence of a wave of intruders into Greece, explaining the widespread disturbances observable in the archaeological record. Specifically, these pins were seen as evidence of a heavier woolen wardrobe than that worn by the Mycenaeans, presumably coming from the north. This view has more recently been challenged in light of Mycenaean antecedents, the lack of demonstrably earlier Central European examples, and the distribution pattern of straight pins, which excludes northern Greece. Moreover, a reexamination of late Mycenaean pin finds in graves reveals that

the use of long pins in pairs was not an innovation of the Submycenaean period but occurs earlier.

UNPUBLISHED

EXHIBITED
Jewelry of the Ancient Mediterranean, The California Palace of the Legion of Honor, San Francisco, December 1969–February 1970.

NOTES
General discussions of the type: Jacobsthal, *Greek Pins* 2–3, nos. 4–8; I. Kilian-Dirlmeier, *Nadeln der frühhelladischen bis archaischen Zeit von der Peloponnes* (Prähistorische Bronzefunde XIII, 8, Munich 1984) pls. 7–8 nos. 199–215, type B1 (Submycenaean and Protogeometric); Philipp, *Bronzeschmuck aus Olympia* 35–36, pl. 26, 3 and 5, Submycenaean to Protogeometric; Desborough, *The Last Mycenaeans and Their Successors* 53–54; Desborough, *The Greek Dark Ages* 296 fig. 33 F; Snodgrass, *The Dark Age of Greece* 226–28, fig. 81, 1.

Examples from Argos: J. Deshayes, *Fouilles de Deiras* 205, pl. 24 DB 17, 18; DB 23, dated to end of LHIIIC; examples from Corinth, *Hesperia* 39 (1970) 20 no. 33, 34, pl. 9.

On the function and origin of long pins: S. Hood, "A Note on Long Bronze Pins" *BSA* 63 (1968) 214–18.

Against the specific connection with a Dorian invasion: I. Kilian-Dirlmeier, "Der dorische Peplos: Ein archaeologisches Zeugnis der dorischen Wanderung?" *ArchKorrBl* 14 (1984) 181–91.

S. L.

6 BULL FIGURINE

**Allegedly from a hoard found at Olympia, Late Geometric, 750–700 B.C.
Length 0.055, height 0.055.**

6

Bronze; intact, deep scratch on left side of neck; smooth dark greenish brown patina. University of Missouri–Columbia, Museum of Art and Archaeology, Gift of Marie Farnsworth (86.60). Purchased by the donor in Athens before World War II. See Plate 15.

The small bronze bull represents an unusually graceful rendering of this animal in a time when bull figurines are typically short-legged, thickset, and somewhat angular. The alert-looking animal stands on long slender legs that taper at the hoof, giving the animal's stance a springy effect. The head features a flattened muzzle, slender pointed horns, and small ears. The gently rounded modeling and fluid contours of the narrow torso and flanks create the impression of a spirited young animal, an effect enhanced by the surprising corkscrew tail.

Said to come from Olympia, this bull was likely made at the site. In proportions, body shape, and the incurving arch of the legs, it shares affinities with certain animal votives at Olympia believed to represent production done on the site by bronzeworkers from the Argive plain in southern Greece. These works are characterized by a broad, usually unbroken, arching curve of legs and belly in response to the swinging contour rising to

mane and hindquarters. The legs have a slight bend that grants the figures an agile grace and gives this group a liveliness not associated with the static tectonic construction of other major workshops. Such features also tend to be characteristic of figurines made by local Olympian artisans under the influence and perhaps even training of Argive masters.

This bronze bull was, like all other Geometric bronze figurines, a votive offering. Its significance was likely tied to the economic realities of Geometric period Greece. In epic poetry cattle served as a standard of value and a major food source. This pattern may reflect the high proportion of cattle to other animals in the Dark Age diet, archaeologically detectable at certain sites. The number of such bull statuettes dedicated at Olympia declined steadily from the tenth through the eighth centuries, during which time they were overtaken by horses and other animal types. Recent studies suggest that this decline in the popularity of bull votives reflects the economic environment of early Iron Age Greece, which was evolving from a pastoral lifestyle based on stock-rearing to one centered on settled farming and close ties to the land. Consequently, as the later Geometric period saw the shifting patterns of land use first crystallize with the emergence of towns and land ownership, the number of votive offerings intended to protect and increase roving herds of cattle diminished.

PUBLISHED
S. Langdon, "In the Pasture of the Gods" *Muse* 21 (1987) 55–64.
"Acquisitions 1986" *Muse* 21 (1987) 30, ill.

NOTES
Bronze bull figurines from Olympia: Heilmeyer, *Frühe Olympische Bronzefiguren.*
Other bull figures with corkscrew tails: Neugebauer, *Staatliche Museen zu Berlin: Katalog der statuarischen Bronzen im Antiquarium* no. 143; Heilmeyer, *Frühe Olympische Bronzefiguren* pl. 70, 527, pl. 76, 591; Pilali-Papasteriou, *Die bronzenen Tierfiguren aus*

Kreta fig. 40, from Olympia, no. 143, Gia-
malakis Collection.

For Argive production at Olympia: Heilmeyer,
Frühe Olympische Bronzefiguren pl. 19, 135,
pl. 20, 136, pl. 22, 152, pl. 24, 168; for
Argive-Olympian work, pl. 46, esp. 387–90.

On early Iron Age economy: Snodgrass, *An
Archaeology of Greece* 205–7; M. H.
Jameson, "Sacrifice and Animal Husbandry
in Classical Greece" in C. R. Whittaker,
ed., *Pastoral Economies in Classical Antiquity* (Cambridge 1988) 6–34.

Arguments against a pastoral Greek Dark
Age: J. F. Cherry, "Pastoralism and the Role
of Animals in the Pre- and Protohistoric
Economies of the Aegean" in Whittaker,
ed., *Pastoral Economies* 6–34.

S. L.

7 WOLF WITH PREY

Late Geometric, 750–700 B.C.
Height 0.045.
Bronze; intact, smooth blue-green patina.
Walters Art Gallery, Baltimore (54.2413).

With head held high and ears at attention,
a canine animal grasps a small quadruped in
its mouth. The narrow figure is triangular in
section from its splayed front legs to its high,
flat haunches. A long tail curves out behind.
Front legs curve forward from broad shoulders
down to long front feet. With almost no neck,
the low flat head is nearly overwhelmed by its
tall vertical ears with diagonal incisions on the
edges. Projecting from its mouth is the flattened profile of a tiny quadruped, hardly
more than two-dimensional. Fine incised lines
decorate the larger animal's front shoulders
and waist. It stands on a rectangular base
with rounded corners, perforated with two
rows of four triangles and one centered
triangle.

With its massive haunches and exaggerated
ears, this unique animal has no close stylistic
parallel. The curving contours of the flat shoulders and flanks are related to Corinthian
bronzework and its derivative Thessalian style.

7

This figurine is one of over a dozen examples
in bronze that represent a canine holding a
small quadruped in its mouth. These animals
have been interpreted as either a domestic dog
or a wolf gnawing its prey or carrying its young.
The suggestion of a mother animal carrying its
pup finds no parallel in Geometric art; the fertility of the animal world was an important
theme among votive bronzes, including figures
of deer, horses, and cows with their young, but
in these the maternal relationship is expressed
through suckling. More often the group is identified as a formulaic hunting scene of a dog
with hare or a wolf with lamb. Both subjects
have a well-documented place in Geometric art
and probably signified quite different things to
the votary selecting a bronze offering for a god
or goddess.

Like the stock dog-chasing-hare motif of
Attic and Protocorinthian vase painting, the
dog with prey in its mouth is the subject of a
series of Archaic bronze and terracotta figurines in which the dog usually seizes the back
legs of the hare, whose front half protrudes
forward from its mouth. Their simple terra-
cotta-like style of rolled limbs and pinched
features is characteristic of the seventh and
sixth centuries rather than the more carefully
abstracted styles of Geometric art, and most
likely this type developed from the Geometric
animals that grasp their prey sideways. In

none of the eighth-century examples does the victim have the long ears of a rabbit.

There are, however, no positively identified wolves among Geometric bronzes, where the lion is the predator par excellence and is distinguished by its long tail curled over its back. The nearest parallel to our group is a pair of beasts with small prey in their mouths who stand side by side on a shared base, in a private Geneva collection. Like the present group, the Geneva animals have fine striations on their necks, bases pierced with triangles, and flattened heads with prominent ears. The lion of the long-lost and recently recovered Samian lion group holds in its enormous jaws a small flat lamb much like that of the Baltimore figure.

The figurine's precise meaning is better understood within the context of votive dedications. Although in later times the dedication by a hunter of a terracotta representation of his dog or his day's catch became customary, for the Geometric period the same subject seems slightly trivial when translated into the more precious medium of bronze. The importance of a square meal notwithstanding, of greater significance would seem to be the shepherd's seasonal request for a deity's protection of his flock against marauding beasts. In this interpretation, the fantastic duplication of such a scene in the Geneva group takes on a nightmarish quality. These Geometric bronze wolves-with-prey can be seen as simplified versions of the famous scenes in bronze and painting in which a man and his hound defend his flock against a lion. The heroism of the shepherd who faces the predator is fully equal to that of the hero of the battlefield who may, like Odysseus, be a shepherd as well. The donor of the small bronze wolf could be especially proud of the imagery by which the divine recipient would remember him. The figurine may have been offered to Apollo Lykeios, who was particularly concerned with the protection of flocks against wolves.

PUBLISHED
D. K. Hill, "Other Geometric Objects in Baltimore" *AJA* 60 (1956) 35–36, pl. 28, 1.

Expedition 12, 1 (1969) 7, no. 9.
Dörig, *Art antique* no. 109.
Buchholz, Jöhrens, and Maull, *Jagd und Fischfang* pl. I.
Heilmeyer, *Frühe Olympische Bronzefiguren* 181 n. 221.

EXHIBITED
The Age of Homer, University Museum, University of Pennsylvania, December 1969–March 1970.

NOTES
For Geometric and Archaic bronze dog-and-prey figurines: list of examples in Heilmeyer, *Frühe Olympische Bronzefiguren* 181 n. 221; Buchholz, Jöhrens, and Maull, *Jagd und Fischfang* 42–43, pl. I.
For dogs alone: Dawkins, *The Sanctuary of Artemis Orthia at Sparta* pl. 76 f; Waldstein, *The Argive Heraeum* II, pl. LXXIII 16; from Tegea, *BCH* 45 (1921) 345 fig. 6, 20.
Pair of canines with prey, in Ortiz Collection: Dörig, *Art antique* no. 109.
Lion-fighting scenes: Samos B190, Schweitzer, *Greek Geometric Art* pls. 186–87; Ortiz collection, Rolley, *Greek Bronzes* 66–67, fig. 35; on an Attic tripod, Kübler, *Die Nekropole des 10. bis 8. Jahrhunderts* pl. 69, lower left.
On the peasant-hero in Homer: J. Griffin, "Heroic and Unheroic Ideas in Homer" in J. Boardman and C. E. Vaphopoulou-Richardson, eds., *Chios. A Conference at the Homereion in Chios 1984* (Oxford 1986) 3–13.

S. L.

8 FRAGMENT OF A LARGE VESSEL

Argive, from the Heraion, Late Geometric I, ca. 750–725 B.C.
Height 0.082, width 0.073.
Ceramic; fragment, exterior painted with red-brown slip, interior unslipped, fine buff-colored clay with no inclusions.
Arthur M. Sackler Museum, Harvard University Art Museums, Transfer from the Department of Classics, Harvard

University, Gift of George H. Chase
(1977.216.1834.2).

This fragment originally formed part of a large vessel whose interior was unslipped and therefore may have been of a closed-shape form, like an amphora or a pithos. The animal figures in the scene probably formed the central focus for one of several metope compositions that were painted on the vase between other metope panels containing geometric designs. Bands of zigzags, spirals, and meander ornament would have filled the remaining vase surface.

Depicted on the fragment is a mare with a foal beneath her. Together they continue the basic Argive theme of horse compositions found in four primary arrangements: a horse alone, a man with a horse ("horse-leader"), a man between two horses ("master of horses"), and this fourth type composed of mare and foal. Both horses stand on a ground line, or band, of which two painted horizontal lines are preserved. Their bodies are elongated in the style of Argive representation for these animals, and their hocks are indicated by the sharply curved thighs, which are set off from straight lower legs. A bird, probably a water bird, stands on the mare's back and is completely preserved except for the head, its body and wing decorated with diagonal parallel lines. The filling ornament consists of eight-pointed stars, stacked chevrons, and a multiple zigzag, all of which soften the relatively stark silhouettes created by the horses. (See reconstruction, Fig. 11.)

The decoration of the vase shares certain affinities with one of the more important pieces of Argive Late Geometric I pottery, Argos C209, a large vessel, called a globular pyxis, which measures just over a meter in height. Filling ornament like the star, which is a continuation of the usual filling ornament from the Argive Middle Geometric period, is painted on our fragment as well as on Argos C209. Floating stacks of chevrons and multiple zigzags are also common filling ornament for both pieces. Horses depicted with elongated bodies, and boldly curving, almost semicircular, necks and thighs are found on both, as are water birds decorated with diagonal lines and a body center line as a demarcation between the backs and lower bodies of the birds. The similarities between this fragment and the globular pyxis provide us with a date for the fragment to the Late Geometric I period.

8

Fig. 11. Reconstruction of vessel fragment 8. (Drawing by Susan Langdon)

This "pastoral" scene is significant in that it may both symbolize the wealth of the Argolid as well as embody the daily Argive concerns with animal husbandry and the agricultural resources necessary to retain these animals. The position of the foal's head beneath its mother's hindquarters suggests that it is about to nurse, and this may be an allusion to the fecund and fertile lands of the Argolid. The reputation of Argos for horse breeding is known from the Homeric descriptive term *ippoboton*. Together with the Homeric epithet for Argos, *polydipsion*, meaning "thirsty," these two terms may aptly reflect the visual image conveyed on this vase fragment, that is, the rural economy of Argos dependent for comfort and survival upon its lands, thirsty but well watered and prosperous.

UNPUBLISHED

NOTES

For the early excavations of the Argive Heraion: Waldstein, *The Argive Heraeum* II.

For Argos C209, the Asine amphora: Courbin, *La céramique géométrique de l'Argolide* pls. 12, 100–104; Coldstream, *Greek Geometric Pottery* 125–31, pl. 26; Schweitzer, *Greek Geometric Art* pls. 77, 78.

For horses in Argive figure repertoire: Schweitzer, *Greek Geometric Art* 62–63.

For a comparable bronze group with mare, fawn, and bird: Comstock and Vermeule, *Greek, Etruscan and Roman Bronzes in the Museum of Fine Arts, Boston* 5, no. 3.

For Argive iconography: Boardman, "Symbol and Story in Geometric Art" 20–23.

A. J. P.

9 NECK-HANDLED AMPHORA

Attic, Late Geometric IIb, 720–700 B.C.
Height 0.683, width at mouth 0.25, maximum diameter 0.32, width at handles 0.305.
Ceramic; restored from numerous fragments, small areas of reconstruction on body.

Buffalo Museum of Science, acquired 1938 (C 12847).
See Plate 1.

The amphora's egg-shaped body rests on a small foot. From the sloping shoulder the tall neck rises abruptly and flares at the top. Plastic serpents adorn the rim and the handles, which are attached at shoulder and upper neck. Decoration in dark slip includes three figural zones at lower body, midbelly, and shoulder, separated by simpler ornamentation. Bands of sigmas cover the foot below a solid dark zone and frame the bottom figure frieze; the upper body has a band of checkerboard and a hatched meander. Around the shoulder extends a file of grazing deer, each of which has a bird between its front feet and a quatrefoil under its belly. The neck features a central complicated hatched meander with a simple meander at bottom and top; between are multiple zigzags, a bird file, and a checkerboard zone. The snakes are solid black; on the handles are hatched triangles among the snakes' curves. Directly above the handles on either side is a small panel containing two horses.

In the lowest figural frieze twenty-one warriors on foot stride to the right, their bodies covered by great round shields to just above their knees. Each figure is armed with a crested helmet and two spears and is accompanied by a small bird between his feet. Chevrons, zigzags, and two-headed snakes compose the filling ornaments around the warriors.

At the amphora's greatest diameter on the belly five two-man chariots populate the figural zone, which is organized so that one chariot, the largest and now the best preserved, is centered on the front. These vehicles are drawn by teams of three horses; both wheels are depicted side by side beneath the chariot boxes. In addition to a front frame, the "main" chariot box has a long side railing; the other four chariots have instead a vertical back railing identical to the front. The occupants of all the vehicles are similar: an unarmed driver leans forward with the reins

9

9, *detail*

9, *detail*

in his hands, while the passenger faces rear and holds a spear upright in each hand. A bird perches on the back rail, facing rear. Each horse team shares a single body with three heads and tails and twelve legs. Directly behind the central chariot a lone horseman rides one horse while a spare trots alongside; his animals are rendered with a single body, two necks, and eight legs. The rider grasps the horses' reins in his left hand while brandishing a spear in his right. A thick horizontal line painted at his waist depicts the bottom edge of what is thought to be the earliest representation of a bell corselet in Greek art. Like the marching warriors and the charioteers, he also has a bird companion among his filling motifs.

This important vase documents a turning point in Greek social history in its depiction of both the old and the new in military equipment and fuels the discussion of the meaning of these chariot amphorae. Belonging, as do several of the amphorae in the exhibition, to the prolific Workshop of Athens 894 group, this vessel's closest parallel is in fact the name vase in Athens. Although by a different artist, the Athens amphora also features a frieze of double-occupant chariots and a lower band of processing infantry with round shields; the organization of the neck is nearly identical to the Buffalo vase, although the small horse panels above the handles on the latter find no close parallels.

While many of the elements on the Buffalo amphora are standard for this group—the complicated neck meander, grazing deer, plastic snakes, and the pairing of chariot and warrior friezes—other features are unusual, most notably the chariot groups and the rider. The combination of a three-horse chariot with a shieldless driver and warrior occurred in the Late Geometric I Dipylon Workshop but is otherwise unknown in Late Geometric II; it may reflect a conscious imitation of the earlier works, particularly in showing both chariot wheels. The presence of an armed passenger raises the ongoing controversy over the use of chariots in eighth-century Greece: were chariots ever used for anything but processions and taxi service to the battleground? Combat in the *Iliad* takes place primarily from chariots, some of which are drawn by three horses, presumably to aid in quick turns. Many scholars doubt the reality of chariot fighting in Greece, where, unlike the flat, open plains of Egypt and the Near East that fostered highly developed chariot warfare, the terrain is unfavorable for the maneuverability required in battle. Evidence for Geometric battle chariots consists largely of Homeric poetry and artistic representations, both of which were subject to Near Eastern influences. Preserved Geometric chariot remains are lacking, and archaeological evidence for horse armor is limited to a few cheekpieces dedicated in sanctuaries. It has also been observed that due to limited means ninth- and eighth-century society was unlikely to have maintained large numbers of these expensive vehicles. The less risky use of chariots for processions and races is more plausible and probably forms the basis of the amphora friezes.

Although the chariots of the Buffalo vase may betray the artist's archaizing tendency, one figure is quite "modern" in his military dress. The rider's bell corselet precisely parallels a bronze corselet found in a grave of ca. 725 B.C. in Argos. Its waist-length form with flaring bottom edge seems appropriate for a mounted warrior as shown here but is depicted in later art as worn by fighters on foot. As with the chariots, there is disagreement as to whether cavalry fighting was practiced before the sixth century; in Geometric art an armed rider may refer simply to infantry who used their mounts as transportation to the battlefield, an image familiar from Archaic art as well. Despite the novelty of the corselet, the round shields carried in the bottom register probably represent the Late Geometric round shield with a single handgrip rather than the hoplite shield with armband and handgrip. When the outer surface is shown in art, the hoplite shield is distinguished by a blazon, which requires the "fixed" position given by the handgrip. Similarly, the twin spears carried by the warriors were standard Geometric period fighting equipment, difficult to handle with a hoplite shield. Even if the shields are of the traditional Geometric type, the appearance on this late eighth-century vessel of the rider's short body armor signals the profound change in military organization that had begun by the end of the eighth century. The establishment of hoplite armies, citizens who could afford the round shield and armor and took military power out of the hands of an aristocratic minority, paralleled the development of the citizen-based polis.

The artist's apparent singling out for emphasis of certain elements may have involved reference to the deceased owner's social status and life. Is he depicted in the lone mounted figure, or perhaps symbolized in the riderless horse? Does he have pride of place as the chauffeured warrior in the large centered chariot? Any of these interpretations is likely, although a brief comparison with other Workshop 894 amphorae (for example **3**, **20**) suggests that such standardized imagery was purchased off the shelf and not painted to order. Even the insertion of a single mounted or standing warrior into a chariot frieze may be a simple solution to planning problems rather than a significant reference. (Compare amphora **25** with its single, less prominent Dipylon warrior among chariots; **3** with its lone robed charioteer similarly selects one figure for attention.) Is it also merely ill-planning that inspired the artist to insert two birds in the bottom frieze in direct alignment with the main chariot above? The studied pairing of birds with figures throughout the Buffalo vessel gives them the force of "soul" symbols, much like the "soul birds" of later Greek art, and alerts us to the potential of these seemingly formulaic chariot amphorae to encode information.

PUBLISHED

H. Phelps Clawson, *By Their Works* (Buffalo 1941) frontispiece.

A. Alföldi, "Die Herrschaft der Reiterei im Griechenland und Rom nach dem Sturz der Könige" in M. Rhode-Liegle, H. A. Cahn, and H. Chr. Ackermann, *Gestalt und Geschichte: Festschrift K. Schefold* (Berne 1967) 13–47 at 20, 24, n. 94, pl. 7, 1.

Coldstream, *Greek Geometric Pottery* 59 no. 21a.

J. Wiesner, *Fahren und Reiten* (ArchHom I, F, Göttingen 1968) 119 n. 397, pl. IV a.

A. Snodgrass, "The First European Body-armour" in J. Boardman, M. A. Brown, and T. G. E. Powell, *The European Community in Later Prehistory* (Totowa NJ 1971) 31–50 at 45–46 and pl. 5.

Ahlberg, *Prothesis and Ekphora* 200 n. 2.

Greenhalgh, *Early Greek Warfare* 47, 88 no. 38.

Coldstream, *Geometric Greece* 149.

J. H. Crouwel, *Chariots and Other Means of Land Transport in Bronze Age Greece* (Amsterdam 1981) 48–49, pl. 112.

Rombos, *The Iconography of Attic Late Geometric II Pottery* 146, 171, 382, 439 cat. 154.

NOTES

Amphora Athens 894: *JdI* 14 (1899) 197, fig. 61; Cook, "Athenian Workshops around 700" 146–49, pl. 22b; Davison, *Attic Geometric Workshops* 41–45, fig. 33; Coldstream, *Greek Geometric Pottery* 58 no. 4.

For grazing deer on an amphora shoulder, see 3.

On chariot and cavalry fighting in Greece: Lorimer, *Homer and the Monuments*; A. M. Snodgrass, *Early Greek Armour and Weapons* (Edinburgh 1964) 163–64; Greenhalgh, *Early Greek Warfare* 19–39; J. K. Anderson, "Greek Chariot-Borne and Mounted Infantry" *AJA* 79 (1975) 175–87; Crouwel, *Chariots and Other Means of Land Transport* 48–50; Wiesner, *Fahren und Reiten* 63–69.

Argos corselet: P. Courbin, "Une tombe géométrique d'Argos" *BCH* 81 (1957) 322–86; Snodgrass, "First European Body-armour" pl. 4.

Generally on early Greek shields and corselets: Snodgrass, *Early Greek Armour and Weapons* 61–67, 71–84.

S. L.

10 CUP WITH RIDERS

Attic, Late Geometric IIa, 740–720 B.C.
Height 0.057, width at handles 0.172, rim diameter 0.139.
Ceramic; mended, complete.
Los Angeles County Museum of Art, the Hans Cohn Collection (1992.152.2).

The flat-bottomed cup has a broad, low body with an offset flaring lip; handles rise at a slight angle from the midpoint of the body. Within a dotted lozenge chain frame on the rim, a frieze contains men and horses parading around the interior of the cup. On each of the four horses stands a bareback rider, perched above the horse's rump and grasping the reins in one hand. Between each pair of horses a warrior wearing a Dipylon shield and plumed helmet carries two spears that project from the top and bottom of the shield. The tondo around which this scene unfolds is a false-spiral ring with rayed border surrounded by a checkerboard band. Outside, a panel of stacked zigzags fills the handle zone above rows of summarily drawn checkerboard and crosshatched triangles near the base.

This special type of fine drinking cup was ultimately inspired by Syro-Phoenician bronze bowls with concentric figural scenes on the interiors that were exported to Greece, Crete, Italy, and Cyprus in the later ninth and eighth centuries. This particular cup belongs to an earlier stage of the series when the lower body is nearly conical, rising to a rounded shoulder from which the lip turns abruptly out. The sharply offset lip and low open bowl form are particularly well suited to metalworking, although this skyphos shape has greatly evolved from its metal prototypes. The shape of the Los Angeles cup is close to examples in Munich and Athens. Although no precise parallel for the interior scene is known, it is one of a small number that features human figures; thematically closest is Athens National Museum 13038 with riders and a Dipylon warrior.

This interior scene has been interpreted as relating to a cult of the dead, with a hero or deity, perhaps Poseidon, on horseback. A more literal reading sees it as a "circus" scene, a group performance by Dipylon warriors and acrobatic equestrians. The riders standing on horses are unique in Attic vase painting, although the motif occurs at least twice again in Geometric art. A well-known bronze tripod leg at Olympia bears a decorative panel enclosing a figure with raised arms standing on a horse. This is arguably a divine epiphany, as the pose suggests, influenced by Syro-Hittite iconography that places deities on their symbolic animals. A goddess on horseback is similarly depicted by a bronze disc from Tegea, which shows an apparently female figure holding a pomegranate in one

10

10

hand and standing on a horse's back. Usually a funerary or fertility symbol, the pomegranate suggests that the rider is not an ordinary mortal.

The Los Angeles cup, however, includes no symbolism that compels us to look beyond the everyday world for explanation. The standing position of the riders, although awkward, need not signify acrobatic stunts; on a bow fibula from Thisbe, a Dipylon warrior fights while standing on his horse. The combination here of standing warriors and unarmed riders recalls Attic scenes of horse training such as on a mug from the Kerameikos and a related skyphos in Athens with a similar interior frieze: a Dipylon warrior holding two horses beside unarmed riders, one of whom wields a crop as well as reins. As a breeder and trainer of horses, the Geometric period aristocrat embodies a new kind of "Master of Animals." The message of the Los Angeles cup could not be clearer.

PUBLISHED

R. G. Hood, "Daredevil Divinities?" *Getty-MusJ* 1 (1974) 95–100.

Borrell, *Attisch geometrische Schalen* 22, 64, 96, no. 82.

Ahlberg-Cornell, "Games, Play and Performance" 78, fig. 28.

Rombos, *The Iconography of Attic Late Geometric II Pottery* 161, 168–70, 175, 380, 383, 470, no. 228.

N. Thomas and C. Oldknow, eds., *Judgment of the Eye, The Varya and Hans Cohn Collection* (Los Angeles 1991).

NOTES

On Syro-Phoenician bronze bowls in Greece: G. Markoe, *Phoenician Bronze and Silver Bowls from Cyprus and the Mediterranean* (Berkeley 1984) esp. 110–27; Borrell, *Attisch geometrische Schalen* 74–94.

For the shape: Munich, Museum antiker Kleinkunst 6029 and 6220, CVA Munich 3, 23–24, pl. 124.1–4, Borrell, *Attisch geometrische Schalen* pls. 2, 17; Athens National Museum 874, CVA Athens 2, pls. 10.1–2, 11.1–3, Borrell, *Attisch geometrische Schalen* pl. 14.

Funerary interpretation of the Los Angeles cup: Hood, "Daredevil Divinities?" 100.

Acrobatic interpretation: Ahlberg-Cornell, "Games, Play and Performance" 78; Rombos, *The Iconography of Attic Late Geometric II Pottery* 169–70.

Tripod leg, Olympia B1665: Schweitzer, *Greek Geometric Art* pl. 215.

Tegea disc: *BCH* 45 (1921) 384 fig. 45; Schweitzer, *Greek Geometric Art* 178 fig. 105.

Kerameikos mug inv. 2159: Kübler, *Die Nekropole des 10. bis 8. Jahrhunderts* pl. 141.

Skyphos with horse training, Athens NM 13038: Borrell, *Attisch geometrische Schalen* 63 fig. 10; Schweitzer, *Greek Geometric Art* 49 fig. 16.

Bow fibula from Thisbe, Berlin Staatliche Museen 8396: Schweitzer, *Greek Geometric Art* 212 fig. 124.

For discussion of the Dipylon shield, see **12.**

S. L.

11 FEEDING CUP

Attic, Late Geometric, ca. 725 B.C.
Height 0.044, diameter 0.062.
Ceramic; complete except for rim of spout; slip decoration missing in places.
University of Missouri–Columbia, Museum of Art and Archaeology (64.10).

The feeder is a one-handled spouted cup with flat bottom, broad body, flaring rim, and a spout on the shoulder. A horizontal strap

11

11

handle attaches to rim and lower body. The rim is banded inside and out, with a row of dots on the exterior. Both spout and handle are banded. The body of the cup is solid black with figural decoration added in a light pinkish slip. Level with the spout are four slender dogs, only one of which is well preserved, who chase a bushy-tailed fox. A second row of figures around the lower body is meant to be viewed by turning the cup over. Directly below the spout crouches a lion with large chest and head, gaping tooth-filled jaws with long tongue, and tail curled over its back; a reserve circle forms its eye. A large dog faces the lion, their jaws and front paws overlapping in fight. Two more dogs run behind the lion.

Its shape dates the Missouri feeder to the

later eighth century. One-handled cups from graves and wells in the Athenian Agora offer a clear development from a low, broad profile to a deeper shape with taller rim. The Missouri cup falls into the middle of this sequence.

The combination of several unusual features makes this cup unique. Although uncommon, other spouted cups are known. A cup from a Kerameikos grave, of a somewhat later form, has a similarly banded handle and a spout on the shoulder but lacks any figural decoration. A child's grave at Tiryns yielded a two-handled spouted cup. The most striking feature of the Missouri cup is certainly its technique, with the decoration in added slip over the fired slipped black surface. The use of added white paint is not unknown in Geometric pottery. It appears first on Middle Geometric Corinthian vessels for small decorative motifs like circles and continues, although rarely, in Late Geometric. On Late Geometric II Attic vases details are added in white to dot plastic snakes and individualize warriors' shields. By the end of the period Argive and Euboean painters occasionally adopted the technique, probably through Corinthian influence.

The hunt motif is also unusual. Dogs hunting a hare is a popular Late Geometric motif and occurs below the rim of a one-handled cup also from the Kerameikos. Fox-hunting scenes, as on this feeder, are much less common, and the attack of a lion by dogs is unparalleled. This can hardly be a reduced version of a man with his dog fighting a lion, since the scheme is unknown in Late Geometric two-dimensional media, and the dog appears in a lion hunt only in a pair of bronze figurine groups. The significance of this artistic motif may lie in its use as a visual metaphor akin to one of Homer's similes for heroism:

> As when some hunting hound in the speed of his feet pursuing
> a wild boar or a lion snaps from behind at his quarters

or flanks, but watches for the beast to turn
   on him, so Hektor
followed close upon the heels of the flowing-
   haired Achaians,
killing ever the last of the men; and they fled
   in terror.

                                (*Iliad* 8.338–42).

One can imagine in the choice of such a
heroic image for a baby's feeding cup both
the hopes of the parents for their child's well-
being and the game of turning over the
emptied cup to recite the tale.

UNPUBLISHED

NOTES

Similar cup shapes from the Agora: Brann,
   Late Geometric and Protoattic Pottery 52–53,
   nos. 177–79, pl. 10.
One-handled feeding cup: Kübler, *Die
   Nekropole des 10. bis 8. Jahrhunderts* pl. 106
   inv. 321, Gr. 56 (740–730 B.C.); dated by
   Coldstream, *Greek Geometric Pottery* 83–84,
   to 720–700 B.C.
Two-handled spouted cup from Tiryns: A.
   Frickenhaus, W. Müller, and F. Oelmann,
   Tiryns I (Athens 1912) pl. XVIII, 9.
On the use of added white in Geometric
   pottery: Coldstream, *Greek Geometric
   Pottery* 57–58, 97, 100.
For hunting dogs on a one-handled cup:
   Kübler, *Die Nekropole des 10. bis 8.
   Jahrhunderts* pl. 138 inv. 1240, Opferrinne 2,
   dated 720–700 by Coldstream, *Greek
   Geometric Pottery* 83–84.
For fox-hunting scenes on Attic LG pottery:
   Rombos, *The Iconography of Attic Late
   Geometric II Pottery* 317, 320–22; on Late
   Geometric lions, 185–208.

                                          S. L.

12 KANTHAROS

Boeotian, Late Geometric, 720–700 B.C.
Maximum height 0.152, width at handles
   0.216, diameter 0.162.
Ceramic; repaired from few large fragments,
   some reconstruction under one handle.

**Virginia Museum of Fine Arts, the Glasgow
Fund (87.392).**

The flat-bottomed drinking cup has a deep
rounded body with plain rim and two high
strap handles. Above a solid lower body identical decoration on both sides features a Dipylon shield flanked by a pair of marsh birds
and crosshatched triangles. Dot rosettes fill
the concavities of the shield and the space
above the birds' backs. The two-toed birds
have hatched bodies, tall curving necks, and
reserved eyes. The shield has a reserved rim
from which crosshatched triangles project to
the center.

This characteristic Boeotian shape, ultimately based on an Attic Late Geometric IIa kantharos type, is datable to the second half of
Boeotian Late Geometric on the basis of its
negligible lip, flat bottom, and somewhat baggy profile. The free-field setting of large, bold
ornaments is typical of the decorative
schemes of Boeotian kantharoi and appears
also in the concentric circle friezes of Boeotian oinochoe 91. Antithetical birds frequently
flank a single motif, as in a serpent on a kantharos in Boston, the wheel design on a similar vessel in Athens, or the crosshatched loop
on a kantharos in Heidelberg. The crosshatched triangle is a favorite Boeotian filling
motif.

Coldstream has noted that the conservative
Boeotian style owed much more to the Dipylon generation of Late Geometric I Athens
than to later Attic work. The Richmond kantharos illustrates this point, for the Dipylon
shield that played such a large role in Late
Geometric I figural scenes tended to be
reduced to a simple silhouette in Late Geometric II. The shield on the Richmond example reflects the same interest in its inner
design seen in the earlier Attic shields. A kantharos in Bonn has a nearly identical Dipylon
shield as the central ornament between two
sets of concentric circles. A single shield,
although not precisely of Dipylon form,
appears on a kantharos in Chicago and on a
small oinochoe in Munich. The freestanding

12

Dipylon shield seldom appears on Geometric pottery outside Boeotia and Attica. In Attic pottery isolated Dipylon shields occasionally play a featured role. Two identical kantharoi from Kerameikos grave 57 preserve very debased versions of the scheme found on the Richmond cup: in an empty field two simple birds flank a crudely drawn shield. The Dipylon shields appearing between figures seated at a table on scenes of the Rattle Group are believed to indicate the graves of warriors. The importance of kantharoi in Attic and Boeotian funerary deposits suggests that the Dipylon shield kantharoi might have been especially intended for a man's grave.

The Dipylon shield is one of the great icons of Geometric art and, fittingly, its interpretation has been among the longest-running debates in Geometric scholarship. Many have concluded that it was an artistic invention, probably based on misunderstood Mycenaean depictions of figure-eight shields. Indeed, the Dipylon shield does not correspond to documented Greek shield types and is apparently ancestral to the "Boeotian" shield, which is generally accepted as an artistic fiction. In this view, its function in Geometric art was to endow battle and chariot scenes with heroic atmosphere. The alternative view, that the Dipylon shield was not only real but a common type in eighth-century Attica, is supported by its appearance in art alongside round and rectangular shields; its disappearance from art at the end of Geometric may reflect the change to hoplite equipment. The absence of material evidence for a Dipylon shield is no more significant than the similar lack of Mycenaean figure-eight shields, since both were presumably made of perishable materials. In Geometric painting Dipylon shields were apparently used by artists to distinguish their wearers in some way from other warriors. Similarly, the Boeotian shield, a tall oval with side cutouts related to the Dipylon shield, is carried by heroes in Archaic art.

UNPUBLISHED

NOTES

On Boeotian kantharoi: Ruckert, *Frühe Keramik Böotiens* 35–37, 103–8; P. Courbin, "Les origines du canthare attique archaique" *BCH* 77 (1953) 322–45 at 343 n. 7; F. Canciani, "Böotische Vasen aus dem 8. und 7. Jahrhundert" *JdI* 80 (1965) 18–75, esp. 41–46, 73.

Parallels: Kantharoi in Boston, Ruckert, *Frühe Keramik Böotiens* cat. Ka 5, pl. 27; in Heidelberg, cat. Ka 14, pl. 27; in Athens, Coldstream, *Greek Geometric Pottery* pl. 44a; *AD* 26 (1971) pl. 188 top center; with Dipylon shields: Bonn, Akademisches Kunstmuseum Inv. 1000, Canciani, "Böotische Vasen" 42, 72–73, fig. 20; University of Chicago, Classical Collection, *AJA* 53 (1949) 243–44, pl. 33B; oinochoe in Munich, Antikensammlungen, *AA* (1957) 373–74, figs. 1–2.

Kerameikos kantharoi: Kübler, *Die Nekropole des 10. bis 8. Jahrhunderts* pl. 88, grave 57 inv. 323, 324, dated LGIIb by Coldstream; sherd from Mt. Hymettus, M. K. Langdon, *A Sanctuary of Zeus on Mount Hymettos* pl. 24 no. 291.

For the reality of the Dipylon shield: Carter, "The Beginning of Narrative Art in the Greek Geometric Period" 55–58; Boardman, "Symbol and Story in Geometric Art" 27–33.

For the unreality of the shield: Lorimer, *Homer and the Monuments* 152; T. B. L. Webster, "Homer and Attic Geometric Vases" *BSA* 50 (1955) 38–50; A. M. Snodgrass, "Towards the Interpretation of the Geometric Figure Scenes" *AM* 95 (1980) 51–58; J. Hurwit, "The Dipylon Shield Once More" *Classical Antiquity* 4 (1985) 121–26.

S. L.

13 SPIRAL-FORM EARRINGS

Attic, Late Geometric, ca. 750 B.C.
Diameter of cones 0.027, of disks 0.028.
Gold; one earring complete except for missing inlay; second earring lacking its disk; the other disk is from a similar earring, also missing inlay.
Los Angeles County Museum of Art, Gift of Harvey S. Mudd (M.47.6.8 a, b; M.47.6.1; M.47.6.2).
See Plate 14.

The pair of gold ornaments represents one of the most splendid of early Greek earring types. A thick curved wire holds at one end a conical element, at the other a detachable disk. Minute granulation covers the surfaces in a lavish web of geometric design. The outer face of the cone has a rim of simple meander around a decorative scheme found on Attic Middle Geometric I grave vessels: a circle containing a St. George's cross, the arms filled with columns of *M*s and the quarters filled with a chevron. On the underside six drop-shaped cloisons, outlined with granulation, form a rosette with zigzag columns between the petals. By comparison with earrings from Eleusis the drop-shaped inlay might have been of amber; other possibilities are rock crystal or glass. The flat disc at the other end of the earring similarly bears a simple meander around the rim of a once-inlaid center. The disk on the other ornament, similarly granulated, has an arcaded edge around a central round inlay.

The thickness of the spiral rod reveals a fashion for piercing quite a large hole in the ear. How these were worn is shown by the sockets under the disks into which the rectangular rod-ends of the cones fit precisely. A cord or wire passed through the small holes in both parts would have secured them to the ears.

As a type, these pieces are related to earrings with conical elements, one detachable, at both ends of the spiral wire. Examples are known from Perachora, the Argive Heraion,

13

Olympia, and Thebes. A related type is represented by three pairs of gold earrings with disks and double-pyramid "tails," which must have been suspended from the ear by a hook through the lobe. One fragment comes from near the Artemision on Delos; two pairs are in the British Museum and a Swiss private collection. These are so close in style to the Los Angeles earrings that they have been attributed to the same artist. Also closely related is an important set of gold plaques found at Eleusis, giving the nickname the "Eleusis School" to the workshop that produced all these pieces of gold jewelry.

These ear ornaments clearly connote great wealth, at a time when Athens enjoyed a renewed prosperity. It is believed that these were made by Attic goldsmiths trained by immigrant Phoenician craftsmen ("a semi-hellenized guild") who set up shop in Athens and worked by commission. The cloisons and granulation are oriental, while the meander, cross, and zigzags belong to a purely Geometric decorative tradition. The St. George's cross with chevrons in the corners is a favorite scheme on Middle Geometric belly-handled amphorae.

The find-context of these earrings is unknown, but we may surmise that they were some woman's loved and often-worn possession. When the back of one was lost, she replaced it with the disk of a similar earring. We might also imagine that she wore her hair pinned up, the better to show off the extravagant ornamentation on both front and back of the earrings. Upon her death the earrings may have gone into the ground with their owner; on the other hand, it is equally likely that they were handed down in the family and eventually dedicated to Athena or Hera as an offering. Unlike the earlier gold earrings in the so-called Rich Athenian Woman's grave, and in the Isis grave and Tomb A at Eleusis, related contemporary earrings of known provenance have come from sanctuary deposits.

PUBLISHED

R. Higgins, "Early Greek Jewellery" BSA 64 (1969) 143–53 at 148–49, pls. 39b, 40 a and b.

D. L. Carroll, "A Group of Asymmetrical Spiral-form Earrings" AJA 74 (1970) 37–42.

R. Higgins, Greek and Roman Jewellery, 2d ed. (Berkeley and Los Angeles 1980) 98, pl. 14C.

B. Deppert-Lippitz, Griechischer Goldschmuck (Mainz 1985) 73, fig. 33.

NOTES

For conical earring type: H. Payne, *Perachora I Architecture, Bronzes, Terracottas* (Oxford 1940) pls. 18:16–18, 83:1, and 84:13; *MonPiot* IX (1902–1903) 148; Higgins, "Early Greek Jewellery" pl. 39a.

For earrings of related style and artist: Elgin Jewelry, *BMQ* 23 (1961) 101; Higgins, "Early Greek Jewellery" pl. 41 a–d; Higgins, *Greek and Roman Jewellery* 98, pl. 14 D, E; Coldstream, *Geometric Greece* 126.

For dating of Los Angeles earrings: Carroll, "A Group of Asymmetrical Spiral-form Earrings" 42, alone dates them to Protoattic; Higgins, "Early Greek Jewellery" 148 (750–725 B.C.), but cf. *Greek and Roman Jewellery* 98 (800–750 B.C.); Coldstream, *Geometric Greece* 126 (LGI, ca. 750).

On Phoenician jewelers in Athens: Smithson, "The Tomb of a Rich Athenian Lady" 77; Coldstream, *Geometric Greece* 126, on the "Eleusis School."

S. L.

14 GRANARY MODELS

Attic, Early Geometric II–Middle Geometric I, ca. 850 B.C.

Preserved height 0.055, length 0.08, greatest diameter 0.04.

Ceramic; broken and repaired, with small lacunae. The base is missing.

The Art Museum, Princeton University, Gift of Hetty Goldman (y1951–13).

The curious object, said to have been found at Phaleron, near Athens, is more important than its size and humble fabric first suggest. Consisting of two mammiform or dome-shaped vessels joined at the waist, it is a granary model, a variant of the famous models discovered in Athens 1967 in the so-called Tomb of a Rich Athenian Lady. Like their painted, wheelmade counterparts, these models have a small opening at the top with a flap above, imitating the entrance of an actual granary, set high on the sloping walls to keep out rodents. The Rich Lady's tomb con-

14

tained an individual granary model as well as a much more elaborate one, with five granaries set in a row on the lid of a model chest, their sides not touching (Fig. 15). The Princeton example is apparently unique in consisting of two granaries joined at the sides. The pair probably did not sit on a chest lid, for there are not only no other granary models known in Attic Handmade Incised Ware, but no fragments of chests either.

Handmade Incised Ware is a fabric peculiar to Attica, where it was produced in limited quantities throughout most of the ninth century. The most common shapes are hemispherical bowls and pointed pyxides, but there are also balls, beads, spindle whorls, loom weights, tripod jars, and dolls with movable legs. The micaceous, pinkish gray clay of these granary models is typical, as is the dark gray slip coating them. The white substance filling the incised designs is encrusted earth, not intentional coloring. The matt surface was originally polished, and Smithson has suggested that the dark exterior and pinkish interior show it was burned on a pyre. As most examples of Attic Handmade Incised Ware are found in graves of inhumed children and cremated women, this one, as well as two bowl fragments probably found with it, is probably from a woman's grave, like that of the cremated Rich Lady. Another wheelmade granary model was found in the so-called Isis Grave at Eleusis, a cremation burial of a woman dating about 800 B.C.

The domes of the models are hollow and taper to a point. They were made separately in a simple mold and then joined with added clay smoothed between them. The incised decoration, the same on each granary, is found on other shapes in this fabric, particularly spindle whorls. The tip is ringed, and below this is a band of herringbone. On the back of the shoulder is a broad band containing a stroke-filled zigzag. On either side of the hole in front are circles surrounded by stroke marks. Below these is a band of herringbone, which extends across the join between the two granaries. The broad belly zone is divided into panels by vertical bands of herringbone. The panels beneath the holes contain stroke-ringed circles enclosed within lozenges; between them, in the center, are three "three-barred sigmas" with strokes between them. Of the panels on the backs and sides, two contain stroke-ringed circles and three have pairs of horizontal chevrons with strokes between them. Herringbone decorates the added clay at the bottom, where the models were joined to the lost base.

The interpretation of models such as this as granaries seems beyond reasonable doubt; certainly they do not represent beehives. Examples of clay granary models from Egypt, although differing in shape, were also set side by side on narrow bases, and may have provided the inspiration for similar provisioning of graves in ninth-century Athens.

Both these models and the ones from the Tomb of a Rich Athenian Lady are in the shape of pointed pyxides, several examples of which, both wheelmade and handmade, were also found in the tomb. The pyxides are larger, fully functional vessels, but it is obvious that their form was the basis for the models, which needed only to be turned over, reduced in size, and provided with an entry hole to suggest the granaries that were among the most visible and tangible marks of an Athenian aristocrat's wealth. Smithson has suggested that the five granaries on the model from the Tomb of the Rich Athenian Lady might sig-

nify her membership in the *pentakosiomedimnoi*, the highest social class in early Athens.

PUBLISHED

E. L. Smithson, "Twin Granaries from Phaleron" *Record of the Art Museum, Princeton University* 28, 2 (1969) 3–14.

NOTES

On the Princeton granary model, with parallels for shape, fabric, and decoration: Smithson, "Twin Granaries."

On the Tomb of a Rich Athenian Lady: Smithson, "The Tomb of a Rich Athenian Lady."

For earlier examples of Attic Handmade Incised Ware, including a doll: E. L. Smithson, "The Protogeometric Cemetery at Nea Ionia, 1949" *Hesperia* 30 (1961) 145–78 at 170–72, nos. 54–56, pl. 30; see also Kübler, *Die Nekropole des 10. bis 8. Jahrhunderts* pl. 157; *CVA* Adolphseck 2, pl. 56, no. 90; D. Burr, "A Geometric House and a Protoattic Votive Deposit" *Hesperia* 2 (1933) 542–640 at 564–65.

For a list of other wheelmade granaries: Smithson, "The Tomb of a Rich Athenian Lady" 92, n. 41.

For the granary from the Isis Grave at Eleusis: A. N. Skias, "Panachaia eleusiniake nekropolis" *ArchEph* (1898) 29–122 at 113, fig. 32; Coldstream, *Geometric Greece*, 78–79.

For an Egyptian granary model: Smithson "Twin Granaries" 11, figs. 10–11.

For the *pentakosiomedimnoi*: Smithson "The Tomb of a Rich Athenian Lady" 96; Coldstream, *Geometric Greece* 55.

J. M. P.

15 KNIFE

From Vrokastro Bone Enclosure VII, Crete, eighth century B.C.
Length 0.127.
Iron; corroded, handle missing.
The University Museum, University of Pennsylvania (Neg. #S4-140824) MS 4764.

Serving as both weapons and cutting tools, knives were important personal belongings in

15

ancient times and were frequently buried in graves. The single-edged iron knife blade has a straight back, curved cutting edge, and rectangular end. It was found in Bone-Enclosure VII, one of twelve examples of this peculiar grave form unique to Vrokastro. Irregular multi-compartmented structures, the bone-enclosures contained adult cremations and child inhumations deposited with varied grave goods. Along with the knife in one of the five compartments of VII were found a bronze fibula, a bronze saw, and a Cypriot-type flask.

Iron tools and weapons are unusually abundant at Vrokastro, a site important for its continuous occupation from Subminoan through Geometric times. Iron appeared first in areas like eastern Crete where contact was maintained with the eastern Mediterranean throughout the Dark Age. The number of Cypriot-related objects from the Vrokastro tombs, such as a bronze rod tripod, suggests the means by which knowledge of ironworking entered the island, and indeed the entire Aegean area. Whether the iron objects in eastern Crete were of local or imported metal is uncertain. Nearly thirty deposits of iron ores are known on Crete, three of them reasonably near Vrokastro. Although there is no direct evidence that these were worked in the early Iron Age, they tend to occur in association with copper ores and thus are likely to have been discovered by accident.

The first use of iron in Greece and Crete predates the Iron Age. Iron finger rings were among the grave gifts deposited in Mycenaean tholos and chamber tombs at Vapheio, Kakovatos, Dendra, Asine, Thebes, and Mycenae. During the Late Bronze Age iron was treated as a precious metal, used primarily for objects of personal adornment. A rare exception is an iron drill point found in a jeweler's workshop in the Theban Kadmeia. Until quite late the Bronze Age technology employed for ironworking did not yield a product superior to or even as satisfactory as bronze for weapons and tools. This early status of iron is recalled in the *Iliad* (23.826–835), where a lump of pig iron is offered as a prize in Patroklos' funeral games. However, the new Iron Age attitude is apparent some lines later when Achilles remarks that the winner's shepherd and plowman will be able to put the iron to good use, suggesting that it was considered a desirable material for tools.

Cypriot smiths experimented with the possibilities of this unattractive but promising material first on knives. By 1000 B.C. in Cyprus and almost simultaneously in the Aegean an iron knife could be quench-hardened to produce as fine a blade as one could wish. This technique must have become commonplace by the time Homer in an unforgettable passage described the piercing of the Cyclops Polyphemus' eye with a red-hot stake: "As when a man who works as a blacksmith plunges a screaming great ax blade or plane into cold water, treating it for temper, since this is the way steel is made strong, even so Cyclops' eye sizzled about the beam of the olive" (*Odyssey* 9.391–94). The flip side of this practical resource was expressed by Hesiod, who applied it to characterize the morally and ethically regressive nature of his time, as compared with the bygone ages of Gold and Silver (*Works and Days* 110).

PUBLISHED
Hall, *Vrokastro* 165–66, no. 4.

16

NOTES
Other Cretan iron knives: Brock, *Fortetsa* 202
    and pl. 172.
On the introduction of iron to Crete and
    Greece: Snodgrass, *The Dark Age of Greece*
    251; J. Muhly, "The Bronze Age Setting"
    in *The Coming of the Age of Iron* ed. T. A.
    Wertime and J. D. Muhly (New Haven and
    London 1980) 25–67, esp. 51; opposing
    view, J. C. Waldbaum, *From Bronze to Iron*
    (SIMA LIV, Göteborg 1978) esp. 67–73.
On iron ores in Crete: P. Faure, "Les miner-
    ais de la Crète antique" *RA* (1966) 61–66;
    Waldbaum, *From Bronze to Iron* 63, 65.
Iron objects in Bronze Age Greece: Wald-
    baum, *From Bronze to Iron* 18–19; J. C.
    Waldbaum, "The First Archaeological
    Appearance of Iron" in *The Coming of the
    Age of Iron* 77–78.
Iron objects in Homer: D. H. F. Gray, "Metal
    Working in Homer" *JHS* 74 (1954) 1–15;
    Muhly, "The Bronze Age Setting" 49–52.
On early Aegean iron knives: Gray, "Metal
    Working in Homer" 11; A. M. Snodgrass,
    "Iron and Early Metallurgy in the Mediter-
ranean" in *The Coming of the Age of Iron*
341–45.

S. L.

16 SKYPHOS WITH HORSES

**Attic, Late Geometric, probably ca.
725–700 B.C.**

**Height 0.067, rim diameter 0.107, width at
handles 0.149.**

**Ceramic; broken and mended, some chips at
lip and foot.**

**Museum of Art, Rhode Island School of
Design, Providence (26.398).**

Resting on a disc foot, the deep-bodied profile rises to a rounded shoulder and short
everted lip. At the widest diameter paired
handles attach at a slight angle. The exterior
is covered in streaky red glaze and only the
handle zone is decorated. This is divided on
either side into three metopes and set off
from the handles by vertical lines and a zigzag. The central panel carries a quatrefoil of
hatched leaves with dot rosettes between
them. In the flanking panels a horse faces

center, surrounded by zigzags; under its belly is a lozenge.

There is no exact parallel for this vessel. Its decorative scheme is based upon the popular series of Attic "bird bowls" in which birds in metopes flank a central quatrefoil (compare 74). Unique, however, is the appearance of horses instead of birds in these metopes. Other unusual features include the heavy foot, the strongly flaring lip, and the absence of thin horizontal lines framing the picture zone above and below. These irregularities have prompted the suggestion that the cup is the work of a provincial Attic artist who was familiar with fine Athenian work.

Other types of Attic drinking cups occasionally carried horses in panels on their exteriors. An unpublished kantharos from Merenda features two horses facing a central ornament, a kantharos from an Agora grave has two horses in a single panel facing right, and two metopes on a cup in Brussels frame horses facing left and right. On a local miniature Late Geometric krater from Xeropolis in Euboea two horses face a hatched quatrefoil without metope divisions. In view of the aristocratic connotations of horse imagery and the settings in which drinking cups were deployed, it is surprising to note that the treatment of the Providence skyphos represents a departure from the standard range of decorative schemes for skyphoi.

PUBLISHED
CVA Providence 1, 18, pl. 8.5.
CVA Fogg Museum and Gallatin Collections, 18, pl. 3.6.
Ashmead and Phillips, *Classical Vases*, no. 26, pl. 88.
Rombos, *The Iconography of Attic Late Geometric II Pottery* 541 cat. 426.

NOTES
For shape: Brann, *Late Geometric and Protoattic Pottery* pl. 8, nos. 135–37, 139, variously dated third quarter eighth century to early seventh century; Kübler, *Die Nekropole des 10. bis 8. Jahrhunderts* pl. 100 inv. 366.

Horses on drinking cups: *AD* 23 (1968) B, pl. 46c; Young, *Late Geometric Graves and a Seventh Century Well in the Agora*, fig. 112 C63; Rombos, *The Iconography of Attic Late Geometric II Pottery* 544 cat. 446; *CVA* Brussels 3, 3, pl. 3.5; Popham and Sackett, *Lefkandi* I 60 no. 30, pls. 39 and 61.

S. L.

17 SEATED LYRE-PLAYER

Cretan, Late Geometric, 750–700 B.C.
Height 0.045.
Bronze, dark green patina with some brown incrustation; intact.
Leon Levy and Shelby White Collection.
Previously, James Coats Collection.

Sitting on a simple low stool, the small man hunches pigeon-toed over his instrument, a large four-stringed lyre. In a lapse of artistic observation, both three-fingered hands seem to pluck the same string. The musician's pierced ears are large enough to catch every note of the song that passes between his modeled and slightly parted lips. His nose and eyes are similarly rendered in high relief, as is his browline, creating a fervent expression that augments his intent posture.

It is nearly impossible to look at this seated figure absorbed in his composing and not think of Homer and the great Aegean bardic tradition. Yet all the evidence offered by the small bronze demands a different interpretation. Its closest parallel, down to the three-fingered hands, ungainly head, and pierced ears, is a famous bronze lyre-player in Heraklion, found in Crete. The two works are close enough in all details to have been made at the same time and in the same place. Among the range of Geometric Greek figurines, the Heraklion harpist looks odd enough in style to have been called Syrian by more than one Near Eastern scholar; Greek specialists, however, have readily accommodated it, perhaps seduced by its "Homeric" iconography.

The importance of the lyre and the bards who played it makes our interpretation of a

17

specific votive offering difficult, for music pervaded the most critical events of life in early Greece. Lyre-players are present at funeral feasts on Attic vessels; even more often they lead lines of dancers in scenes that surely capture in paint the heart of every religious festival. If considered in its purely Geometric Greek context, the bronze figure might be a generic musician engaged in the quite ordinary but highly regarded pastime of music-making and especially poetry recital. As a votive offering it could have commemorated a victory in a poetry competition, the very circumstances under which Homeric epic likely traveled through Greece and Crete. In a similar vein, it might symbolize the festival occasion on which dances honored the god or goddess of a sanctuary, much as the upper

half of a Geometric terracotta lyre-player from Arkades Tomb R recalls the tradition of this motif on Crete.

On the other hand, the foreign affinities of these two bronzes cannot be ignored. Details like the pierced earlobes and the over-large head with emphatic features are regular attributes of Bronze Age to Iron Age bronze figurines from the Syro-Palestinian coast, where the lyre-playing motif is even more common than in Greek art. Particularly in North Syria the ubiquitous banqueting scenes include both seated and standing musicians and apparently inspired the seals of the so-called Lyre-Player Group, probably of Cilician manufacture; the musicians for which the group is named represent an excerpt from such scenes (see also 75). Alternatively, a group of bronze Phoenician lyre-players that circulated in the eastern Mediterranean might have inspired the Cretan versions, if these are not actual imports. Despite the family resemblances, the exotic details are more pronounced in the slightly larger figure in Heraklion than in the Levy Collection bronze; it may have served as the model for the smaller one, or at least remained closer to the original Levantine prototype.

Among this bounty of lyre-playing representations in Greece and the Near East, the majority seem to represent a generic situation. In Cyprus, however, and perhaps in the Aegean, a few representations seem to single out a musician and raise him to supernatural status. Scenes depicting homage to a seated lyre-player decorate two four-sided bronze stands in the British Museum. A Proto-White-Painted kalathos from Kouklia-*Xerolimni* bears an impressive lyre-player whose sword distinguishes him from garden-variety musicians; a tree in a neighboring panel may signify the sacred tree that accompanies the musicians of the stands. These figures have been linked to Kinyras, the semidivine musician-king of Cyprus who received worship at Paphos. His name since ancient times has been linked with the Semitic word for harp, *kinnor*; he may in fact have been a Levantine ruler. A similar scene on a twelfth-century strainer-jug from Megiddo, depicting a lyre-player walking among animals and birds, provides a Philistine parallel, although Near Eastern specialists note its Aegean flavor. These twelfth- and eleventh-century representations echo the somewhat earlier Mycenaean fresco from the Pylos throne room and the Late Minoan IIIB pyxis from Chania in giving a lyre-player an iconographical context that makes him seem larger than life and suggests perhaps a semidivine status.

As for the small Cretan bronzes, their Near Eastern connections evoke a wealth of iconographical associations that enlarge their possible interpretations and give broader scope to the motif in Greek art.

PUBLISHED

J. M. Hurwit, "*Thespis Aoidos*: A Bronze Harper from the James Coats Collection" *Yale University Art Gallery Bulletin* 38 (1982) 18–23.

NOTES

Related bronze lyre-player: Heraklion Museum Inv. 2064, Schweitzer, *Greek Geometric Art* pl. 203; Verlinden, *Les statuettes anthropomorphes crétoises* cat. 230, pl. 90.

Terracotta musician from Arkades: *ASAtene* 10–12 (1927–1929) 280 fig. 355a.

On a Syrian connection for the Heraklion figure: Dunbabin, *The Greeks and Their Eastern Neighbors* 36; Boardman and Buchner, "Seals from Ischia and the Lyre-Player Group" 48 n. 45; Moorey and Fleming, "Problems in the Study of the Anthropomorphic Metal Statuary" 75; Verlinden, *Les statuettes* 169, accepts it as Cretan but cites as a parallel the Worcester Flute-Player generally believed to be Anatolian, which she would also make Cretan.

On music and instruments: Tölle, *Frühgriechische Reigentänze*; Wegner, *Musik und Tanz*; on bards, Hurwit, "*Thespis Aoidos*" 22–23; M. L. West, *Ancient Greek Music* (Oxford 1992).

Seals of the Lyre-Player Group: Boardman

and Buchner, "Seals from Ischia and the Lyre-Player Group."

On bronze Phoenician and Syrian lyre-players: Moorey and Fleming, "Problems in the Study of the Anthropomorphic Metal Statuary" 75; *ESA* 10 (1936) 121 fig. 39B, in Copenhagen.

For Cypriot representations and Kinyras: J. N. Coldstream, *The Originality of Ancient Cypriot Art* (Nicosia 1986) 13, figs. 41–44; S. Morris, *Daidalos and the Origins of Greek Art* 7–8.

Megiddo jug: G. Loud et al., *Megiddo* II (Chicago 1948) pl. 76, 1; Dothan, *The Philistines and Their Material Culture* 150–53, fig. 28, 1; H. Goldman, "Excavations at Gözlü Kule, Tarsus, 1935" *AJA* 39 (1935) 536–49 at 537.

S. L.

18 ENGRAVED PLATE FIBULA

Boeotian, Late Geometric, 750–700 B.C.
Height 0.067, length 0.108.
Bronze; inside edge of catchplate preserved; top edge partially broken away; bottom and outside edges entirely missing; outside bottom corner missing. Catchpin missing. Pitted surface on both sides of catchplate. Olive green patina.
Arthur M. Sackler Museum, Harvard University Art Museums, David M. Robinson Fund (1965.27).

Geometric fibulae, presumably used to secure cloth or leather garments, have been found in graves and as dedications at sanctuaries. This fine example of a Boeotian bronze plate fibula (Blinkenberg VIII), a type borrowed from Attica around the middle of the eighth century B.C., features a characteristic rectangular catchplate with exquisitely incised decoration.

The fibula was solid cast and hammered into three component parts: a paper-thin catchplate; an arched bow, slightly concave on the bottom and strongly convex on top; and a curving pin with an orthogonal top, single

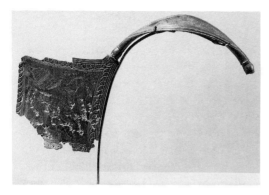

18

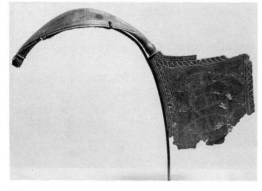

18

loop, and pointed end held in place by the up-turned bottom edge of the catchplate. The top surface of the bow is decorated with lines cut into the mold before casting. Deeply and firmly cut double borders demarcate the outline of the bow's top surface, where a spine of three shallow lines within two deeper lines runs the length of the bow from end to end. The transitions between the parts of the fibula are defined by two ovoid beads, each of which is terminated by two raised rings. Even in its fragmentary condition, the fibula is an elegant combination of swelling, curving, and flattened forms in two perpendicular planes.

One side of the catchplate depicts a tethered horse facing right with two bird companions framed by an elaborate border of double lines followed by repeating compass-drawn half circles, and finally by triple lines. The horse is shown in mixed profile and frontal

perspective, right hindquarter in front of left, and foreparts and head tilted toward the viewer. A tether trailing from the muzzle leads to a rectangular object decorated with discrete stacked zones, each divided by diagonal lines. The impression of the horse is of spirited animation with its front hooves raised off the ground and its head tossing. A bird with globular body, spindly legs, and long neck floats in the left corner above the horse and faces right. Another similar but smaller bird, facing left, perches on the groundline beneath the horse, touching the horse's underbelly with its narrow beak. Delicate incised rows create a consistent texture inside the double contour lines of the horse and birds. These are crossed by incised bands: the birds with four lines at the widest part of their bodies, and the horse with a string of diamond-shaped crossed zigzags at the middle of the neck. The upper left corner is filled by a triangle of diagonally cut lines and crossed zigzags.

The other side of the catchplate has a similarly treated triangle in the upper right corner and a nearly identical decorative frame. Enclosed are three fish facing left. Although subtle differences exist among them, they seem to be of the same species. They are seen from above in a parallel row, with diamond-shaped eyes each separated by an engraved line extending to the end of the head. All three fish have a pair of triangular fins placed symmetrically behind the head and another pair near the tail on opposite sides of the body. Contour lines are double. A band of lines divides all three fish roughly in half. More multiple lines highlight fins, tails, and the juncture between the heads and bodies. The fish appear to be swimming in unison.

On the two sides of the catchplate, the environments of earth, water, and air may represent a synopsis of the natural world. Fish occupy the elemental sphere of water. On the shields of Achilles and Herakles, water, in the form of Okeanos, circles and delimits the world. Earth, defined as the absence of water, is inhabited on the other side of the catchplate by the horse. The horse also breathes the air in which the bird travels when not on earth. The tether of the horse indicates the presence of humankind in its natural setting of earth and air.

The Boeotian epic poet Hesiod, a near contemporary of the fibula craftsman, describes essentially the same tripartite structure of the world.

> From Chaos came forth Erebus and black Night; but of night were born Aether and Day, whom she conceived and bare from union in love with Erebus. And Earth first bare starry Heaven, equal to herself, to cover her on every side, and to be an ever-sure abiding place for the blessed gods. And she brought forth long Hills, graceful haunts of the goddess-Nymphs who dwell amongst the glens of the hills. She bare also the fruitless deep with his raging swell, Pontus, without sweet union of love. But afterwards she lay with Heaven and bare deep-swirling Oceanus. (*Theogony* 123–33)

Such a cosmic world view, very similar to that of Homer, would not be out of place on the catchplates of fibulae, which accompanied the dead in burial ritual and honored the gods as dedications. Thoughts of death and of the immortal gods would naturally move beyond the here and now to larger and more universal questions.

Still, fibulae were certainly worn by the living, for whom the ordering of the world (*kosmos*), as on the catchplate, must have been of great interest. Considering that kosmos meant "the universe," "order," "good behavior," as well as "a piece of jewelry," the fibula was not a mere fashion accessory, but rather a sophisticated ontological statement.

PUBLISHED

Fogg Art Museum, Acquisitions 1965 (Cambridge 1965) 65 ill.

H.-V. Herrmann, "Geometrische Fibeln der Tübinger Universitäts-Sammlung" *Praestant Interna. Feschrift für Ulrich Hausmann* (Tübingen 1982) 248–60 at 258 n. 45.

NOTES

Similar fibulae: Cahn, *Early Art in Greece* 35–36 nos. 102–3; M. Maass, *Griechische*

und römische Bronzewerke der Antikensammlungen (Munich 1979) 64, no. 38 (Schoen Collection); Herrmann, "Geometrische Fibeln" 251 fig. 1, 257 figs. 5–7, pl. 55; Basler Kunsthandel, *Münzen und Medaillen*, Auktion 26 (October 5, 1963) no. 6 (now Walters Art Gallery).

Boeotian fibulae: Blinkenberg, *Fibules grecques et orientales*; Hampe, *Frühe griechische Sagenbilder in Böotien*; *Katalog der Sammlung antiker Kleinkunst des archäologischen Instituts der Universität Heidelberg* (Mainz am Rhein 1971); Schweitzer, *Greek Geometric Art* 205; K. De Vries, "Incised Fibulae from Boeotia" *FuB* 14 (1972) 111–12.

For a possible Bronze Age origin of the horse and bird motif: Benson, *Horse, Bird, and Man* 26ff.

Okeanos (Il.18.607); (Hes.Sc.314).

Shield of Achilles: C. V. Byre, "Narration, Description, and Theme in the Shield of Achilles" *CJ* 88 (1992) 33–42, extensive bibliography.

Hesiod's cosmology: P. Walcot, *Hesiod and the Near East* (Cardiff 1966) 41; G. S. Kirk and J. E. Raven, *The Presocratic Philosophers* (Cambridge 1966) 24–37.

Homeric cosmology: H. Philipp, "Die Kosmographie Homers" *AM* 99 (1984) 1–4.

Translation of Hesiod's *Theogony* by Hugh G. Evelyn-White (Loeb Classical Library, Cambridge MA 1914).

M. J. B.

19 PLATE FIBULA

Thessalian, Late Geometric, 725–700 B.C.
Height, 0.0662, plate height 0.0325, width 0.0435.
Bronze; pin mended; edge of catchplate chipped.
University of Missouri–Columbia, Museum of Art and Archaeology, Weinberg Fund (82.425).

The ribbed bow is formed of a tightly coiled wire decorated with a large ball and molding. The catchplate, rectangular with one contoured side, terminates in a similar molding. The plate's surface bears on both sides a finely hatched horse with pointed hooves, thin muzzle, and long ears. Hatched triangles between the animal's front and back legs and a rhomboid below its belly serve as filling ornaments. The figural panel is framed by a border of small zigzags, double semicircles, and more zigzags.

Like the styles and shapes of Late Geometric pottery, fibulae also show a broad range of regional styles. The Missouri fibula belongs to the type designated Thessalian, although so many of these have been found elsewhere, particularly in the Peloponnese, that they may have been produced in southern Greece as well. Like all fibulae, they were dress-fasteners, worn in a matching pair at the shoulders of the woolen peplos. If the orientation of the images on the plates is an indication, they were worn vertically with the plate at the top. Fibulae were also popular votive offerings and may have been given to the

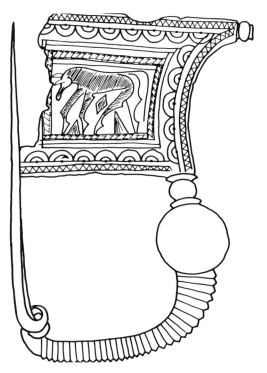

Fig. 12. Plate fibula, Museum of Art and Archaeology, University of Missouri–Columbia (19). (Drawing by John Huffstot)

deity along with garments. Excavations at the sanctuary of Artemis Enodia at Pherai discovered more than 1,800 fibulae.

Among the Thessalian fibulae, the decoration of the plate with a horse is standard and recalls the importance of horse breeding in this region of Greece. Frequently a bird appears beneath the horse; less commonly, a fish or snake shares the field (compare 18). The rhomboid ornament under the horse on the Missouri fibula is an abstract mutation of one of these creatures. Stylistically, the horses on these fibulae, with their sharply pointed hooves and angular bodies, owe little to the two-dimensional animal styles painted on pottery and much to the engraver's technique.

UNPUBLISHED

NOTES

On the Thessalian type: Blinkenberg, *Fibules grecques et orientales* 136–37, type VII 7; Kilian, *Fibeln in Thessalien* 105–37, esp.

19

119–20; I. Kilian-Dirlmeier, "Drei Kleinbronzen im J. Paul Getty Museum" *GettyMusJ*
6–7 (1978–1979) 123–30 at 123–25.
On the function of fibulae: Kilian, *Fibeln in
Thessalien* 118; K. de Vries, "Incised Fibulae from Boeotia" *FuB* 14 (1972) 111–12;
Kilian-Dirlmeier, "Drei Kleinbronzen" 125.

For similar fibulae: Cahn, *Early Art in Greece*
34–35 nos. 97–101; Kilian, *Fibeln in Thessalien* pl. 49 no. 1371, esp. pl. 50 no. 1389; D.
von Bothmer, ed., *Glories of the Past,
Ancient Art from the Shelby White and Leon
Levy Collection* (New York 1990) 96 no. 77.

S. L.

Bury me as quickly as may be, let me pass through the gates of Hades.

(Iliad 23.70–71)

THE
RITUALS OF DEATH

Two aspects of funerary practice in the
Early Iron Age are particularly revealing: the
rituals that effect the transition of life to
death and the necropolis as an urban phenomenon. Burial methods throughout
Greece from 1000 to 700 B.C. varied widely,
with various styles of inhumation and cremation rising to popularity for a brief time
or in a specific region. From the end of the
Protogeometric period a preference for inhumation gradually edged out cremation in
Attica. Amphorae served as cinerary urns
for both male and female graves, attracting
a special treatment for the vessel as if it
stood for the physical nature of the
deceased. An Early Geometric amphora
"wears" the deceased warrior's killed sword
(Fig. 13), while a Middle Geometric female
cremation in a belly-handled amphora is
accompanied by her dowry (Fig. 14), symbolized in granaries on a box (Fig. 15, compare 14). The special treatment of the
burial amphora was soon translated into a

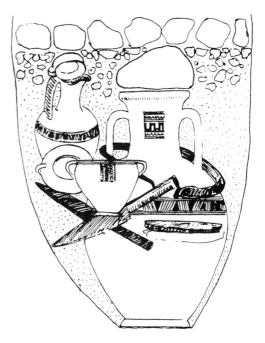

Fig. 13. Male cremation burial in the Athenian
Agora. (Reproduced by permission of American
School of Classical Studies at Athens: Agora
Excavations)

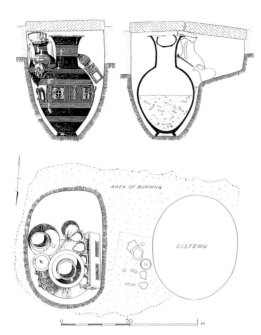

Fig. 14. Female cremation burial in the Athenian Agora. (Reproduced by permission of American School of Classical Studies at Athens: Agora Excavations)

focus on its decoration with figural scenes (**20, 25**) that may bear reference to the social rank or aspirations of the deceased.

As in other cultures, death and burial in Geometric Greece offered an important forum for reaffirming class identity and social beliefs through ritual that can be reconstructed from pottery bearing descriptive pictorial representations. An amphora from the Cleveland Museum of Art (**20**) demonstrates a typical *prothesis* (formal lying-in-state): the deceased male figure in a long robe lies on a high bier with the checkered pall raised so that we can see his body. Around it stand four women tearing their hair in lamentation; a fifth person kneels before (shown as beneath) the bed. The crowd of mourners continues on the back of the amphora's neck. Other elements of the funeral ritual can be pieced together

from related vessels. The body was carried on a wagon to the cemetery in the *ekphora* ceremony (Fig. 16), where offerings of food and drink, pottery, and sometimes weapons and personal ornaments were deposited with the dead into the grave (Fig. 17). A small Attic bowl (**21**) depicts round objects held by seated figures, which have been interpreted as clappers, rattles, water sprinklers, or pomegranates. The occurrence of this scene on vessels from grave contexts suggests a connection to rites of passage for the dead. Pomegranate vases found in many graves symbolize fertility and eternal life. An outstanding example from the Bowdoin College Museum of Art (**22**) may have contained an offering of wine or oil for the dead. A small bronze pendant of a seated figure drinking or eating is a fine example of the amulets sometimes found at the waists of skeletons, originally suspended from belts (**32**). Like the pomegranate, they seem to have symbolized fertility. One of the most enduring funerary symbols of the Aegean, the snake, achieved new life in the mid-eighth century as it became regularly integrated into the painted and plastic decorations of pottery. Moving easily between the earth and life above, snakes were both companions of the dead and protectors of the tomb. Winding around the necks and handles of amphorae they obviated the function of a central object of everyday existence (**3, 9, 20, 25**).

The range of typical grave gifts encompasses such personal effects as bronze jewelry (**30**) and necklaces of faience and carnelian beads (**31**), but most important were a variety of vessels associated with eating and drinking: the amphora whose mundane counterpart served as wine container, and the oinochoe (**33**) for decanting wine and water into cups and tankards (**34, 35, 38, 39**). A "trick vase" of three seemingly

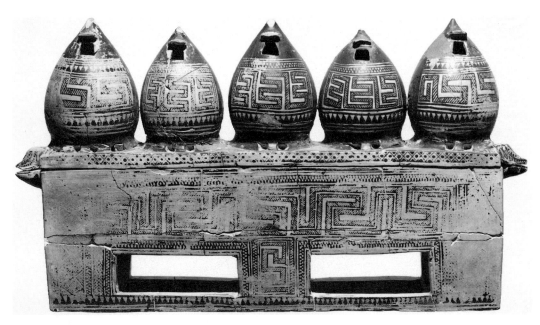

Fig. 15. Ceramic box with granary models on lid. (Photo courtesy of American School of Classical Studies at Athens: Agora Excavations)

stacked cups made a handsome gift (**23**). Such standardized grave appointments (the oinochoe **33** and the high-rimmed bowl **38** were frequently paired) recall Late Bronze Age and Early Iron Age Egyptian and Canaanite metal wine sets of bowl, jug, and strainer that were deposited in graves. The Greek drinking vessels were used for a funeral offering, perhaps a graveside meal, and for pouring wine to extinguish the pyre. By the mid-eighth century the Athenian Kerameikos cemetery was dotted with medium- to large-size amphorae and kraters and the cemetery on Piraeus street with the spectacular human-scale Dipylon amphorae and kraters (Figs. 7, 10, 16), standing as grave markers among the scattered stone markers of earlier cremation burials. The choice of the amphora and krater to monumentalize graves of high-ranking deceased individuals may relate to the importance of the ritualized drinking party, the symposium. In a broader cultural context, however, the prevalence of drinking vessels in graves

recalls the characterization of the dead as thirsty, common to Egypt, the Bronze Age Aegean, and the Near East.

Much of the meaning of funerary ritual was couched in the visual language of heroic ethos. Representations on amphorae of chariot races or processions alone or below the *prothesis* motif may refer to the games that accompanied aristocratic funerals in Homeric epic or mourners accompanying the body to the cemetery (**20, 3, 9**). For evidence of actual funeral games in Geometric Attica we have little more than the ambiguous static chariot friezes on pottery until the end of the period, when the chariot horses begin to gallop, other games join the chariotry, and Hesiod reports winning a poetry prize in the funeral games for Amphidamas. In some chariot friezes, however, warriors on foot carrying Dipylon shields (**24–25**) may refer instead to epic battle, thus connecting the deceased and his family to past heroes and reaffirming claims of rank and lineage. Round pyxides

Fig. 16. Attic krater from the Dipylon cemetery, Athens NM990. (Photo courtesy of Deutsches Archäolo-gisches Institut, Athens, neg. 75/664)

with horse figurines mounted on the lids are believed to have served as symbols of status and wealth. Examples in the exhibition illustrate the full range of types from one-horse to four-horse boxes (27–29, 82). Like the model granaries (14, Fig. 15), horse pyxides occur more frequently in women's graves than in men's and document an involvement of women in the transmission of wealth and power. In this connection it is notable that the most famous monumental grave marker of the period, amphora Athens 804 (Fig. 7), stood above the grave of a woman.

S. L.

20 NECK-HANDLED AMPHORA

Attic, Late Geometric IIb, ca. 720–710 B.C.
    Assigned to Workshop of Athens 894 by
    J. M. Cook.
Height 0.59, body diameter 0.295, foot
    diameter 0.112, mouth diameter 0.20.
Ceramic; mostly complete; upper neck
    restored from fragments, section of
    shoulder snake missing, one side of body
    quite faded.
The Cleveland Museum of Art, Purchase
    from the J. H. Wade Fund (27.6).
Columbia venue only.

The neck-handled amphora comprises an ovoid body set on a tall narrow foot with a cylindrical neck rising abruptly from the shoulder and flaring at the top. The strap handles have rolled edges flanking a flat central section. Striped plastic snakes are attached to rim, handles, and shoulder. The front neck panel containing a prothesis scene forms the vessel's decorative and symbolic focus: beneath a checkered shroud a robed man lies extended on a bier, his head resting on a pillow and his body turned so that both feet and both arms are plainly visible as well as a profile head with jutting chin. To either side two female mourners in crosshatched skirts with trailing hems tear their hair or

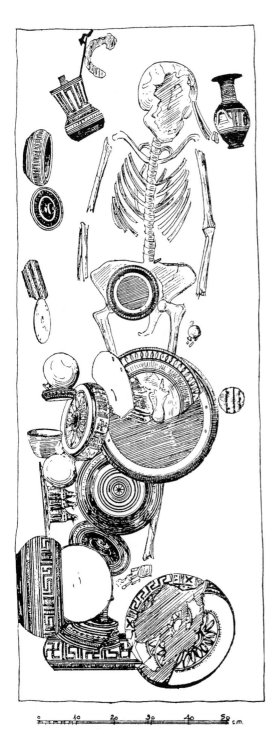

0   10   20   30   40   50 cm.

Fig. 17. *Female inhumation burial in the Athenian Agora. (Reproduced by permission of American School of Classical Studies at Athens: Agora Excavations)*

20

20, detail

touch the couch. Below the couch kneels a fifth mourner who is differentiated by a solid black robe and similarly raises hands to head. Horizontal zigzags fill the background space. A panel on the back side of the neck continues the crowd of mourning women, with six figures facing right, rendered like their companions on the front with long skirts and two or three strands of hair. Simple quatrefoils join the zigzags as filling ornaments. The remainder of the neck is decorated with bands of gear pattern, checkerboard, and hatched meander above the figural panels and horizontal zigzags below.

At the belly's greatest girth appears the usual chariot procession of two-horse chariots manned by single drivers in plumed helmets. The front and side rails of the simplified chariots rise like narrow ears from the tops of the wheels. Zigzags, quatrefoils, and an occasional bird serve as space fillers. Behind the centered chariot on the front marches a single warrior on foot armed with two spears. His torso is covered by a round shield decorated with a rosette of hatched leaves. Above the chariot frieze the shoulder carries a checkerboard zone and a winding plastic snake whose

interstices are filled with crosshatched triangles. A frieze of coursing hounds circles the lower body, framed above and below by horizontals and a band of sigmas. The foot and lowest body zone are solid.

The Cleveland amphora and its closest parallel, amphora 48.2231 in the Walters Art Gallery, are believed to have been painted by the name artist of the Workshop of Athens 894. They therefore date late in the eighth century when funerary scenes on pottery were well established. The first generations of Attic pot painters experimented on monumental vases with various details in the prothesis scenes. Family members might kneel or stand on the bier at the corpse's feet, sit on chairs, or wave branches over the deceased; cauldrons or animal offerings might appear underneath the couch. Perhaps mass-producing grave vessels for a larger clientele than that of the Dipylon Workshop, the Workshop of Athens 894 standardized the prothesis scene. It now appeared on the necks of more modest-sized amphorae, resulting in a smaller area and a simpler scheme.

The neck panels offer a glimpse into the house of the dead man on the day after his death. The women of the family have washed and dressed the body for burial and display it on a couch for friends and family to pay respects and participate in formal mourning. In Geometric scenes the corpse is covered in a shroud, nearly always a checkered cloth drawn above so as to leave the focus of the scene visible, and lies with feet to the left and pointed toward the door, ready to begin the journey to the underworld. The household, and the back of the amphora, fill with mourners, who on the Cleveland amphora happen all to be women. They rend their hair or beat their heads; Ahlberg believes that the woman kneeling beneath the bier, distinguished from the others by a black robe and different hair, represents a professional mourner. The scene recalls the return of Hektor's corpse to his house, where his people "laid him then on a carved bed, and seated beside him the singers who were to lead the melody in the dirge, and the singers chanted the song of sorrow,

and the women were mourning beside them"
(*Iliad* 24.719–22).

This expression of lament with both hands
on the head is well established in Aegean
Late Bronze Age art and indeed occurs
throughout the cultures of the eastern Mediterranean. The debt of Geometric Greek
mourning iconography to Late Bronze Age
depictions is a matter of varying opinion.
There are striking resemblances between the
Geometric prothesis scenes and Mycenaean
painted larnakes (sarcophagi) from Tanagra.
A Late Minoan III larnax with mourning
women recently found in a Cretan tomb used
from Protogeometric times to the seventh
century supports the usual proposed means
of survival of this motif: through "found"
Bronze Age artifacts that served as models for
budding Geometric artists. Those who doubt
a direct link with Bronze Age art note that
since funeral customs apparently continued
relatively unchanged throughout the Dark
Age, any new attempts by eighth-century
artists to depict their own customs would
look much like those of centuries earlier.

Certain objects, however, suggest material
continuity. Winding protectively up the
handles and around the shoulder and mouth
of the Cleveland amphora, the snake is a
well-documented funerary symbol in the prehistoric Aegean world, yet it only reappears in
Attic Geometric art in the mid-eighth-century
output of the Dipylon Workshop and becomes
fully developed in both painted and plastic
versions in the Hirschfeld Workshop. The connection of this chthonic ground-dweller with
the dead survived the Dark Age in the Greek
belief system, and artistically passed its time
on the periphery of the Greek world. In a
bothros of the Geometric sanctuary at Mi-
letus, a Mycenaean krater handle ornamented
with a dotted plastic snake was found with
Geometric sherds. A Cretan Protogeometric B
burial pithos from Fortetsa shows the old
Minoan snake goddess still alive in the ninth
century and now working for the underworld.

Mycenaean terracotta mourning figures
with hands on head similarly seem to be
ancestral to those made in Greece down into
the sixth century, particularly when attached
to the rims of vessels. Complicating the issue,
Philistine kraters from tombs of the twelfth to
eleventh centuries with terracotta mourners
fixed to the rims have convincingly been
shown to depend on similar, slightly earlier
Mycenaean lekanai known from Perati,
Ialysos, and elsewhere in the Aegean. In light
of the Philistine connections with Cyprus and
the Levantine coast, the means and place of
survival of certain Mycenaean cultural elements present a complex picture but one that
may be ultimately more plausible than theories of discontinuity and reinvention in an
isolated Greece.

PUBLISHED

CMA *Handbook* (1928) 74.

Cleveland Museum of Art Bulletin 14 (1927)
99–101.

W. Zschietschmann, "Die Darstellungen der
Prothesis in der griechischen Kunst" *AM*
53 (1928) 17–47, 37, no. 7.

J. M. Cook, "Protoattic Pottery" *BSA* 35
(1934–1935) 181.

Cook, "Athenian Workshops around 700" 144,
146, 148, pl. 21.

Davison, *Attic Geometric Workshops* 41, 144
fig. 34.

D. K. Hill, "Accessions to the Greek Collection 1960 and 1961" *JWalt* 24 (1961) 40
fig. 2.

Tölle, *Frühgriechische Reigentänze* 97 no. 327.

Coldstream, *Greek Geometric Pottery* 58 no. 6,
61, 62.

Ahlberg, *Prothesis and Ekphora* 28 no. 36, fig.
36a–d.

CVA Cleveland 1, 3–4, pls. 2, 3.1.

E. Finkenstaedt, "Mycenaean Mourning Customs in Greek Painting" *CMA Bulletin* 60
(1973) 37–43, figs. 1–2.

J. Neils, ed., *The World of Ceramics: Masterpieces from the Cleveland Museum of Art*
(Cleveland 1982) 8–9 no. 11.

Rombos, *The Iconography of Attic Late Geometric II Pottery* 82, 442 no. 164, pl. 21a.

A. P. Kazloff, *Classical Art: A Brief Guide to the Galleries* (Cleveland 1989) 2.

NOTES

Walters Art Gallery 48.2231: D. K. Hill, *JWalt* 24 (1961) 39–42, figs. 1–3; Ahlberg, *Prothesis and Ekphora in Greek Geometric Art* fig. 37a–c.

For prothesis rites: D. Kurtz and J. Boardman, *Greek Burial Customs* (Ithaca NY 1971) 58–61, 143–44.

On Bronze Age origins for Geometric funeral iconography: Benson, *Horse, Bird, and Man* esp. 88–99; Ahlberg, *Prothesis and Ekphora* 303–4; E. Vermeule, "Myth and Tradition from Mycenae to Homer" in D. Buitron-Oliver, ed., *New Perspectives in Early Greek Art* (Hanover and London 1991) 99–121.

Tanagra sarcophagi: *AAA* 3 (1970) 195–97, figs. 15–17; Sp. Iakovidis, "A Mycenaean Mourning Custom" *AJA* 70 (1966) 43–50; E. Vermeule, "Painted Mycenaean Larnakes" *JHS* 85 (1965) 123–48.

Late Minoan III A:I larnax: L. Morgan, "A Minoan Larnax from Knossos" *BSA* 82 (1987) 171–89.

On the funerary symbolism of snakes: R. Hampe, *Ein frühattischer Grabfund* (Mainz 1960) 58. *Pace* Coldstream (*Greek Geometric Pottery* 36), who finds no dotted snakes by the Dipylon Workshop, a pair of dotted serpents decorates an amphora neck fragment by the Dipylon Master, Agora P7024 (Brann, *Late Geometric and Proto-attic Pottery* pl. 14, 246).

Cretan Protogeometric snake goddess: Brock, *Fortetsa* 125–26, pls. 77, 163.

Mycenaean plastic snake: C. Weickert, "Neue Ausgrabungen in Milet" in Deutsches Archäologisches Institut, *Neue Deutsche Ausgrabungen in Mittelmeergebiet und im Vorderen Orient* (Berlin 1959) 181–96 at 191, fig. 10.

Philistine terracotta mourning figures: Dothan, *The Philistines and Their Material Culture* 237–49.

For discussion of the chariot and dog friezes, see **9** and **25**.

S. L.

21 HIGH-RIMMED BOWL

Attic, Late Geometric IIa, 735–720 B.C.
Height 0.092, width at handles 0.235, maximum diameter 0.187.
Ceramic; complete, some chips missing.
Mount Holyoke College Art Museum, South Hadley MA, Nancy Everett Dwight Fund, 1935 (B.SII.1.1935). Previously Charles T. Seltman Collection.
See Plate 12.

The bowl's tall rim carries a figural panel in which six figures sit, facing right, on cross-hatched seats with tall backs; each holds an oblong object in each hand. Checkerboard panels frame the figural zone above and below. Above the handle zone a quatrefoil lozenge is set off from the main figural zone by a vertical crosshatched lozenge chain flanked by vertical lines and crosshatched columns. The reflex handles are decorated with a dotted lozenge chain.

The iconography of this fine cup relates it to a group of vessels with similar scenes named the "Rattle Group" for the objects the figures hold. Although details differ, each vase depicts two figures seated opposite each other across a grave and wielding what have been identified as pairs of percussion instruments. It is by no means certain that these round objects with a handle and a second projection are indeed music- or noisemakers, nor does this interpretation clearly explain the consistent pattern of holding one object up and the other down. Other suggestions include distaff and spindle whorl, bronze or wood clappers, and water sprinklers in the shape of pomegranates.

On the other hand, there is little doubt that these scenes refer to a funeral ritual. In Geometric pottery bier cloths are always checkered, and checkerboard alone can denote the grave, as does the checkered rectangle that occurs between two seated figures in a number of the Rattle Group scenes. On the present cup, the predominance of this motif to surround the figures must in similar fash-

21

ion indicate the funeral setting. Since some examples replace the grave with a table and one of the sitters with a lyre-player, Cook concluded that all these scenes depict a meal following the burial of the deceased. The seated "shakers" may be making noise to exorcise evil spirits or music to accompany the meal.

Ahlberg posited the origin of the Rattle Group scenes in banqueting images on North Syrian grave stelai, in which the banqueters face each other across a table and hold pomegranates as symbols of the afterlife. Although formal similarities between the stelai and the vases are compelling, they pose the methodological problem of how motifs from the monumental art of the homebody North Syrians might have traveled to a single pottery workshop in faraway Athens, an issue that was not addressed in the study. The transfer of artistic motifs from Near Eastern art, particularly monumental media, into Greece is a recurrent problem in the study of Geometric iconography. In the case of motifs related to religious or funerary practices we might consider the implications of intermarriage between Greeks and Near Easterners. The wishes of a North Syrian spouse to have the traditional imagery of the homeland represented at his or her funeral might have led to the commissioning of such a scene. The occurrence of thirteen known examples may suggest that more than one family was involved.

If such was indeed the case, we must also ask whether these vases represent an adaptation merely of an artistic motif or of ritual itself. Most scholars have interpreted these scenes as depictions of living ritual and have used them to complete our understanding of the stages of a Geometric funeral. Since Greek custom included a funerary feast, the imported iconography was not only comprehensible to Greek eyes, but in fact was readily adaptable to local needs, as the related scenes with Dipylon shields hanging above the checkerboard warrior's grave demonstrate.

Not only is the Mount Holyoke high-rimmed bowl the only vessel of its type with this particular iconography, it is also the only high-rimmed bowl bearing a figural scene. Equally unusual is its asymmetrical abbreviation of this symmetrical scene. Two skyphoi, one in Athens and one in London, feature a similar series of figures seated on high-backed chairs and holding "rattles."

PUBLISHED

College Art Journal 22 (1962) 108, fig. 1.
Nancy Everett Dwight Foundation, 1913–1963 (South Hadley MA 1963).
S. McNally, "An Attic Geometric Vase in the Collection of Mount Holyoke College" *AJA* 73 (1969) 459–64, pl. 127.
J. C. Harris, ed., *The Mount Holyoke College Art Museum. Handbook of the Collection* (South Hadley MA 1984) 44.
Rombos, *The Iconography of Attic Late Geometric II Pottery* 284, 287, 288, 482 cat. 259.

NOTES

Studies of the Rattle Group iconography: J. M. Cook, "A Geometric Grave Scene" *BCH* 70 (1946) 97–101; Hahland, "Neue Denkmäler des attischen Heroen- und Totenkultes" 177–92; G. Ahlberg, "A Late Geometric Grave-Scene Influenced by North Syrian Art" *OpAth* 7 (1967) 177–85; Coldstream, *Greek Geometric Pottery* 71–72; Rombos, *The Iconography of Attic Late Geometric II Pottery* 283–300.
Compare a similar frieze of seated figures in individual frames on the shoulder of a jug in Boston, MFA 03.777, Hahland, "Neue Denkmäler" no. 3, pl. IX figs. 4–5.

S. I.

22 POMEGRANATE VASE

From an Attic grave, Late Geometric Ib, 750–735 B.C.
Height 0.102, diameter 0.090.
Ceramic; missing three pieces of the crenellations; minor chipping along rim of stem end.
Bowdoin College Museum of Art, Gift of

Edward Perry Warren (1915.15). Previously Sambon Collection, Lambros Collection. See Plate 6.

The pomegranate is naturalistically rendered with a globular multilobed body, a crenellated end, and a short stem with flat top and small hole. A wealth of decoration covers the small model, the body of which is divided into four decorative zones. Above the horizontally banded "foot" is a line of pendent crosshatched triangles with dots between. In the largest of the friezes, a series of metopes alternate hatched swastikas and lozenges; above them a narrower band of crosshatched triangles in panels of three fill the "shoulder" zone. The top of the object bears a band of seven striding marsh birds with crosshatched bodies. An asterisk fills the end of the stem.

An already ancient fertility symbol by Geometric times, the pomegranate, from Egypt to the Mycenaean world, from Luristan to Etruria, represented life and death, its blood-red juice a memento mori, its seeds symbolizing the promise of renewal. As one of the great universal symbols it has traveled a complicated path through artistic motifs. Vases in the form of pomegranates, however, have a more restricted life in the eastern Mediterranean, where they originated in various materials in Eighteenth Dynasty Egypt and from there spread to Cyprus and eventually to Mycenaean Greece. Cypriots are thought to have been responsible again for the reappearance of the pomegranate vase in eighth-century Greece.

Geometric pomegranate vases are numerous and vary widely both in shape, from relatively realistic modeling to simple spheres or ovoids, and in decoration. Examples with bird friezes or panels are known in Munich and in the Louvre. The Bowdoin vase is one of the earliest and finest of the Geometric form. Its date to the time of the Hirschfeld Workshop and the early creators of classic Geometric style is provided by its belonging to a group of twenty-one vessels alleged to have come from a single Attic grave, part of the original Lambros

22

Collection. The high quality of paint, careful execution of motifs, and vivid treatment of the birds all confirm this date. In fact, one of the most unusual motifs of the Bowdoin pomegranate, the panels of crosshatched triangles with dots, figures prominently as the main filling motif, along with dotted circles, of a krater in New York attributed to the work-

shop of the Hirschfeld Painter; the appearance of these designs is close enough to suggest the same hand for both vessels. Perhaps not coincidentally, along with the pomegranate the Attic grave group also included a tankard that has been attributed to the Hirschfeld Workshop. It might be assumed that the naturalistic modeling of the fruit characterizes the beginnings of this vase type. Terracotta pomegranates from ninth-to-seventh-century wells in the Samian Heraion are similarly quite realistically modeled.

The known funerary context of the pomegranate corresponds with that of the majority of Geometric pomegranate vases, which have been found particularly in children's graves. As functional vases, they might have contained oil or another liquid offering for the dead; others may simply have been a symbolic gift. A few examples have been found to contain tiny pebbles in order to function as rattles. Such evidence supports the interpretation that the figures of the "Rattle Group" scenes (see **21**) shake pomegranate-shaped rattles to provide music for the feast or to banish evil spirits. The Bowdoin pomegranate, with its tiny hole in the top, served neither as a rattle nor, probably, as an oil container. Its ultimate function was to accompany the deceased into the earth, offering symbolically both food and rebirth.

PUBLISHED

Sale catalogue of the Lambros Collection, Hôtel Drouot, Paris, June 17–19, 1912, lot 21.

Sale catalogue, *Catalogue des objets d'art, Collection of M. Arthur Sambon*, Galerie Georges Petit, Paris, May 25–28, 1914, lot 88.

B. Schweitzer, "Untersuchungen zur Chronologie und Geschichte der geometrischen Stile in Griechenland II" *AM* 43 (1918) 1–152 at 138–39, pl. 4.2.

H. E. Andrews, "Report of the Director of the Museum of Fine Arts" *Report of the President of Bowdoin College 1924–1925* (Brunswick ME 1925) 50 no. 8.

Jacobsthal, *Greek Pins* 187.

S. Charitonides, "Peline Geometrikeroias" *ArchEph* (1960) 155–64, no. 4.

K. Herbert, *Ancient Art in Bowdoin College: A Descriptive Catalogue of the Warren and Other Collections* (Cambridge MA 1964) 45–49, no. 130.

Coldstream, *Greek Geometric Pottery* 46.

Catalogue, *Aspects of Ancient Greece*, 132–33, no. 63.

M. R. Burke, ed., *Bowdoin College Museum of Art: Handbook of the Collections* (Brunswick ME 1981) 5–6, 22.

EXHIBITED

Aspects of Ancient Greece, Allentown Art Museum, Allentown PA, September–December 1979.

NOTES

On pomegranate vases and symbolism:
K. Friis Johansen, *Les vases sicyoniens* (Paris 1923) 29; Charitonides, "Peline Geometrikeroias"; S. Immerwahr, "The Pomegranate Vase: A Mycenaean-Geometric Link" *AJA* 74 (1970) 197; Muthmann, *Der Granatapfel* 39–92, esp. 60–61, 77–79.

For the Lambros grave group: Schweitzer, "Geometrischen Stile in Griechenland" 138–52, pls. I–VI.

For New York krater, Metropolitan Museum 14.130.14: Schweitzer, *Greek Geometric Art* pl. 41; Davison, *Attic Geometric Workshops* fig. 26.

Samian pomegranate: *AM* 72 (1953) Beil. 60, 1, 2; *AM* 74 (1959) Beil. 22, 1–5; Muthmann, *Der Granatapfel* fig. 44.

On pomegranate rattles: H.-G. Buchholz in Laser, *Sport und Spiel* 101–2, n. 506, 103.

Pomegranate vases with birds: Munich *CVA* 3, pl. 129.7; Muthmann, *Der Granatapfel* 61, fig. 47.

S. L.

23 TRIPLE SKYPHOS

Attic, Late Geometric, 750–725 B.C.
Height 0.128, width 0.14, rim diameter 0.09.
Ceramic; intact.
Tampa Museum of Art, Joseph Veach Noble Collection (86.20).
See Plate 5.

The single vase is formed of the profiles of three vases with one bottom and three pairs of handles. Each segment is identically decorated in three panels: a central metope filled

23

with nine dotted circles, flanked by panels with birds and star rosettes. The lip of each has horizontal bands and a row of dots. The metope system, the low body and vertical lip, the disc foot, and the slanting handles all point to a date in the third quarter of the eighth century.

With its appearance giving the illusion of three nested cups, this vase is one of the earliest examples of the uniquely Greek tradition of the "trick vase." In later centuries this term refers instead to "gag" pots, such as cups with concealed holes that spill their contents over the unwitting drinker. Single vessels made to look like several had a certain minor popularity among Attic Geometric potters and patrons and are less common later. Multiple skyphoi like the Tampa vase were probably placed in graves. Unlike the later lekythoi made with small interiors to save on burial expenses, the point of this vessel is not to "cheat" the dead with an illusion of greater expense lavished on the funeral. Since its creation no doubt posed a considerable challenge for the potter, it likely was appreciated as a tour de force, perhaps a more valuable gift for the dead than three skyphoi would have been.

PUBLISHED
Cahn, *Early Art in Greece* 45 no. 129.
J. V. Noble, "Some Trick Greek Vases" *Proc-PhilSoc* 112 (1968) 371, figs. 1–2.

Betancourt, "The Age of Homer" 9, fig. 24.
S. P. Murray, *The Joseph Veach Noble Collection* (Tampa 1985) 39 no. 2.

EXHIBITED
The Montclair Art Museum, Montclair NJ,
    May–June 1968.
The Age of Homer, University Museum, University of Pennsylvania, December 1969–March 1970.
The Joseph Veach Noble Collection, Tampa
    Museum of Art, December 1985–February
    1986.

NOTES
Parallel for the skyphos shape: Kerameikos
    376, Coldstream, *Greek Geometric Pottery*
    pl. 10b, LGIb 750–735 B.C.
Triple skyphos in Würzburg: E. Langlotz,
    Griechische Vasen (Munich 1932) pl. 4, 48;
    B. Schweitzer, "Untersuchungen zur
    Chronologie und Geschichte der geometrischen Stile in Griechenland II" *AM* 43
    (1918) 1–152 at 52 fig. 3.
Double skyphoi: from the Mount Hymettus
    Sanctuary of Zeus, M. K. Langdon, *A
    Sanctuary of Zeus on Mount Hymettos* pl.
    22, no. 273; examples in Heidelberg, *CVA*
    Heidelberg 3, 46, pl. 110.5; Mainz, *CVA*
    Römisch-Germanisches Zentralmuseum 1,
    31, pl. 12.3–4; *CVA* Louvre 1 pl. 12.3.
Six skyphoi from the Samian Heraion: *AM* 76
    (1961) pl. 33.
Multiple oinochoe: *CVA* Athens, National
    Museum 1, pl. 1.5.

S. L.

24 FRAGMENT OF A KRATER

Attic, Late Geometric I, ca. 760–750 B.C.
**Attributed to the Workshop of the Dipylon
    Master (Louvre A528).**
Height 0.09, width 0.14.
**Ceramic; fragment, figures painted with
    dark brown slip, interior painted with
    light red slip; fine, pink-beige clay with
    no inclusions.**
**Arthur M. Sackler Museum, Harvard
    University Art Museums, Transfer from
    the Department of Classics, Harvard**

24

**University, Gift of George H. Chase
(1977.216.1835).**

Preserved on the fragment are three painted
bands that separate an upper from a lower
zone of figures. In the upper zone are parts
of three warriors whose lower extremities face
to the right. The first warrior carries two
spears whose ends are seen as diagonal parallel lines. In front of each figure is a filling
ornament of a dotted ovule; other filling ornaments take the form of stacked double axes
between the warriors and solitary double axes
between the legs of the first warrior and the
spears he carries. In the lower field are the
upper parts of three warriors, two looking to
the left and one to the right. They are helmeted, as indicated by the long double
plumes that extend from their heads. Each of
these figures is separated by a double ax
design.

The relatively small fragment belongs to a
monumental krater type composed of a two-handled, cauldron-shaped bowl supported on a
tall conical foot (Fig. 16) and usually standing
more than one meter in height. The scenes
with which these impressive grave markers
were painted could have testified to the valor
of the deceased in contemporary combative
encounters if not alluding to events of the
heroic past such as those related in the *Iliad.*

Four other pieces from a pedestaled krater,
Louvre A528, have been identified as belonging to the same vase from which this fragment was broken (see 98, a similar fragment
that joins with Louvre A519). On two of the

Louvre A528 fragments an arrangement similar to that of our piece is depicted: warriors wearing double-plumed helmets stand in two zones with double axes and dotted ovules as filling ornament. One of these fragments is large enough to show us that the spear-carrying warrior on **24** probably also carried a large Dipylon-type shield and wore a sword fastened at the waist, like his counterpart in the Louvre. Additionally, this Louvre fragment shows us that the smaller figures on the lower zone of our piece were armed, at least with bows, since two of the Louvre warriors carry them. The two remaining fragments in the Louvre show all the elements of a naval confrontation: bow and stern portions of a ship are preserved, their decks occupied by warriors armed with spears, swords, and one with a bow and arrow. They are all without helmets except for one, an imposing figure who stands on the front of the ship, and he could be taken for their leader were it not for the fact that two helmetless warriors stand facing him with sword drawn and bow aimed to greet him (Fig. 18).

The artist of this vase worked closely with others whose representation of the human form, choice of subject matter, and use of an overall painted surface design with filling ornaments were inspired by, and originated with, the vase painter known as the Dipylon Master. Named from the so-called Dipylon cemetery located in the area of ancient Athens known as the Kerameikos, where many of the ceramic grave monuments credited to him were excavated, the Dipylon Master is most notable for his ambitious use of the human figure en masse on his vases. Some examples may have had more than a hundred figures included in complex compositions depicting funeral participants, chariot processions, warriors on the march, and scenes of land and naval battles. The painted compositions of the Dipylon Master and his workshop, portrayed with clear definition and economy of detail, embody the spirit of dramatic narrative so well described in the literary record by the Homeric epics.

Fig. 18. Fragment of krater from the Dipylon cemetery, Louvre A528. (Courtesy of the Musée du Louvre)

PUBLISHED
CVA, Fogg Museum and Gallatin Collections 18, pl.III,5.
Davison, *Attic Geometric Workshops* 139.
Coldstream, *Greek Geometric Pottery* 31.

NOTES
Attributed to the Workshop of the Dipylon Master (Louvre A528): Davison, *Attic Geometric Workshops* 139.
For Louvre A528: CVA, Louvre III, 8, pl. 7, nos. 1, 6–8; E. Kunze, "Disiecta membra attischer Grabkratere" *ArchEph* (1953–1954) 166–67; Schweitzer, *Greek Geometric Art* 44, fig. 14.
For the Dipylon Master and his Workshop: Coldstream, *Geometric Greece* 110–14; Coldstream, *Greek Geometric Pottery* 29–41; Schweitzer, *Greek Geometric Art* 38–45.
For the pioneer works (monumental krater, N.Y. 34.11.2, and a skyphos, Eleusis 741) that anticipate the iconography of the Dipylon Master and his Workshop: Coldstream, *Geometric Greece* 110, 137 nos. 3, 5.

For funeral ritual depicted on vases: Ahlberg, *Prothesis and Ekphora*.

For the Dipylon Master's linear decoration: Coldstream, *Greek Geometric Pottery* 35–37, and for his figural style 37–39.

A. J. P.

25 NECK-HANDLED AMPHORA

Attic, Late Geometric IIb, 720–700 B.C.

Height 0.472, maximum diameter 0.246, lip diameter with snake 0.197.

Ceramic; mended from numerous pieces; one handle and body fragment just above foot restored; paint worn in places.

University of Missouri–Columbia, Museum of Art and Archaeology (58.3). According to the dealer, found in a village twenty miles from Athens on the way to Sounion.

The neck-handled amphora has a well-balanced profile of swelling body and slightly concave neck. A plastic snake decorates the outside of the rim. Bands of decoration cover the vessel from foot to lip, with triple horizontal lines separating each ornamental frieze. In the main figural zone, the upper belly, a frieze of charioteers parades to the right, each chariot pulled by two horses and driven by an unarmed figure. Alone among the chariots stands a single warrior on foot, set beneath one handle. He wears a Dipylon body shield and carries two spears. Friezes of running dogs at shoulder and lower belly frame the main zone. The neck provides a second focus of figural ornament in a panel filled on either side with five male figures facing right, each grasping the sword at his waist with both hands. Subsidiary ornamentation is limited to bands of crosshatched triangles, zigzags, and vertical strokes.

The Missouri amphora is so similar to an example in Münster as to be by the same hand. The artist's distinctive style shows affinities with major Attic workshops. The overall scheme of a sedate chariot procession on the amphora belly with a running-dog frieze above or below is standard for the Workshop

of Athens 894, which seems to have adopted the dog frieze from the Workshop of Athens 897. The Missouri artist's human figures are characterized by beaky noses, the absence of chins, single-plumed helmets, short torsos and massive thighs, and oddly pointed heels. Horses' tails hang to the groundline, while their feet and legs are sufficiently detailed to include two toes and fetlocks. Among the numerous parallels for the running-dog motif in Attic painting, none has quite the same combination of blunt muzzles, single ears, and dewclaws on the legs, although their bulky bodies resemble the dogs of the Workshop of Athens 897. The artist confines himself to chevrons and Ms as filling ornaments among the human figures and longer zigzags among the dogs, a starkness that suggests a date in the Late Geometric IIb period, 720–700 B.C.

From Protogeometric times the neck-handled amphora was used to hold a man's cremated ashes, while a belly-handled type held women's burials. Although there is no direct reference to the deceased or his rites on this grave vessel, the funerary theme is evoked by the modeled snake around the rim, a chthonic symbol that provides a link with the underworld.

The chariot frieze around the belly is a standard element on amphorae made for funerary purposes. Whether the scene is meant to represent a procession to the battlefield or to the cemetery is unknown. A clue may lie in the Dipylon warrior tucked under the preserved handle; the same figure is visible on one side of the Münster amphora. The single warrior on foot among the vehicles is in fact a recurrent image among chariot amphorae. It is unlikely that these standing warriors were simply space-filling remedies for the artists' poor planning, since methods for precise measurement and spacing around the circumference of a vessel had been worked out since Protogeometric times. More plausibly, such figures were planned from the outset, either to facilitate the spacing of the lengthy chariot groups or to provide a fuller iconographic

25

context. Described by Homer and commonly found on the battle scenes of Geometric art, the Dipylon shield is thought to have been a memory preserved in epic from the Bronze Age and used by artists to evoke a heroic atmosphere. Recent studies have noted that it often seems to have been used to distinguish its bearer from other figures in a scene. Standing alone among the chariot-mounted warriors, he may have represented a heroic ancestor of the deceased.

The neck panel of processing swordsmen is highly unusual. A similar scene encircles the shoulder of an oinochoe. As warriors on foot, and shown shieldless in the act of pulling sword from scabbard, they might have served as the shorthand rendition of a great fighting force. An amphora neck panel in Tübingen featuring a procession of warriors with both swords and upright spears has been seen as representing the high social rank of the deceased. Another explanation is suggested by a lidded krater on the belly of which a similar procession of swordsmen is led by a man playing a lyre. If correctly interpreted as a sword dance, this scene would offer interesting evidence of an early ancestry for the armored dances of Archaic and Classical Greece. The Münster amphora offers support for a ritual interpretation. Its neck panels contain processing men who seem to hold a three-pronged object that Wegner interprets as a bronze or wood instrument and links to funerary ritual.

The running-dog frieze frequently includes the dogs' quarry, a rabbit or fox. When the frieze contains only dogs, as on this amphora, it still functions as *pars pro toto* for the hunt formula and subtly continues the themes of heroism and war. Through a symbolism already traditional in Bronze Age art, the image of animal predation, whether dogs and rabbits or lions and deer, expresses the valor and pathos of war and death and contextualizes human conflicts within the larger rhythms of nature. (See also the comments under 11.) Some scholars believe the dog was a symbol of death in early Greek art, an interpretation that would account for the popularity of the running-dog motif on Attic Geometric funerary pottery. In the *Odyssey* dogs are aristocratic symbols, corresponding to horses in the *Iliad*; perhaps this meaning pervaded the artistic imagery as well. The occasional Mycenaean custom of burying a man's hunting dog and sometimes even his horse with him provided companionship and symbolized the activities of his life. The regular presence of these two animals in Geometric funerary amphorae must serve the same function.

UNPUBLISHED

NOTES

M. Wegner, "Spätgeometrische Amphora in Münster" in P. Zazoff, ed., *Opus Nobile. Festschrift zum 60. Geburtstag von Ulf Jantzen* (Wiesbaden 1969) 172–80, pl. 29, 1–2.

On the Workshops of Athens 894 and Athens 897: Davison, *Attic Geometric Workshops* 41–48, figs. 33–36, 40–46; Cook, "Athenian Workshops around 700" 144–49; C. Brokaw, "Concurrent Styles in Late Geometric and Protoattic Vase Painting" AM 78 (1963) 63–72; Coldstream, *Greek Geometric Pottery* 58–64, 77–81.

On gender-related amphora shapes: Coldstream, *Greek Geometric Pottery* 39.

On the Dipylon shield used to characterize its bearer: Snodgrass, *An Archaeology of Greece* 151–53.

For Dipylon warriors inserted among chariot friezes: Rombos, *The Iconography of Attic Late Geometric II Pottery* 136 n. 87; E. Rystedt, "Die Wagenfriese der attischen geometrischen Keramik und die Frage ihrer Ablesung" OpAth 18 (1990) 177–83.

For an oinochoe with swordsmen: *Münzen und Medaillen* Auktion 22 (May 13, 1961) no. 103, pl. 29; Tölle, *Frühgriechische Reigentänze* 88 no. 147.

For the Italo-geometric lidded krater: *Münzen und Medaillen* Auktion 26 (October 5, 1963) pl. 15, no. 54.

26

For the amphora in Tübingen: H. Bloesch,
ed., *Greek Vases from the Hirschmann Collection* (Zurich 1982) 10–11, no. 1; Rombos,
*The Iconography of Attic Late Geometric II
Pottery* 149.

For evidence of the pyrrhic dance in Geometric art: A. Kaufmann-Samaras, "A propos
d'une amphore géométrique du Musée du
Louvre" *RA* (1972) 23–30.

On the meaning of the hunt: Vermeule,
*Aspects of Death in Early Greek Art and
Poetry* 84–93.

On the dog as a symbol of death: Bevan,
*Representations of Animals in Sanctuaries of
Artemis* 332–33.

S. L.

26 FLAT PYXIS

Attic, Middle Geometric II, ca. 775–760 B.C.
Height with lid 0.184, body height 0.114,
maximum diameter 0.245, lid diameter
0.179, base diameter 0.172.
Ceramic; complete, repaired.
The Detroit Institute of Arts; Founders
Society Purchase with funds from the
bequest of Dr. Lester W. Cameron (65.82).

The flat "sugar-bowl" type of pyxis features
a strongly curving body with an inset rim to
hold a lid smaller in diameter than the box
itself. On the flat lid the handle consists of a
ridged shaft surmounted by a tiny reproduction of the pyxis including the sort of conical

handle often found on this pyxis type. Two pairs of holes are aligned on the edge of the lid and the rim of the body. The decoration recalls the tradition of early Attic Geometric pottery that used a single large motive, here a hatched meander, in the main decorative zone. In the hands of the classic Late Geometric painters this treatment gave way to the popular square metope system. Above and below the meander, bands of dogtooth, zigzag, and chevrons, interspersed with triple horizontal lines, fill the remaining space on the body. From rim to center, the lid is ornamented with concentric bands of dogtooth, dots, and zigzag. The miniature pyxis features a chevron frieze and the standard bands around the cone handle. Beneath the lid an X is painted near one of the small holes.

The flat pyxis is an innovation in Athens around 850 B.C., based perhaps on a combination of influences from the Mycenaean "powder pyxis," Protogeometric pyxides, and even wooden boxes. There is no consistent development of the type, and many of the features of the Detroit pyxis are present in the earlier Middle Geometric I phase, including the tiny pyxis handle, the conical knob, and the holes intended for suspension of the vessel. The dating of the Detroit pyxis as Middle Geometric II is suggested by its size, which surpasses pyxides of the ninth century.

By far the majority of preserved pyxides have been found in graves, although ancient repairs indicate their use during the owner's life, perhaps as jewelry or toiletry containers. At burial they may have contained other, now lost, items, such as food offerings. It has long been observed that pyxides usually appear in graves that can be identified by other finds (such as jewelry and hydriae) as those of women. A recent comparison by Bohen of anthropological evidence from a number of Protogeometric through Late Geometric graves with the presence or absence of pyxides, however, reveals a nearly even distribution between male and female graves in

Protogeometric and Middle Geometric, with a clear rise in pyxis occurrence only in Late Geometric female graves.

PUBLISHED
Cahn, *Early Art in Greece* 40–41, no. 115.
W. G. Moon, *Greek Vase-Painting in Midwestern Collections* (Chicago 1979) 2–3, no. 1.

EXHIBITED
Greek Vase-Painting in Midwestern Collections, The Art Institute of Chicago, December 1979–February 1980.

NOTES
On the type: Coldstream, *Greek Geometric Pottery* 23; Bohen, *Die geometrischen Pyxiden* 27–40, esp. 35–38.
Similar pyxides: Kübler, *Die Nekropole des 10. bis 8. Jahrhunderts* pl. 53, 5714a; M. Collignon and L. Couve, *Catalogue des vases peints du Musée National d'Athènes* (Paris 1904) pl. 14; Cahn, *Early Art in Greece* 41, no. 116; CVA Munich 3, 26–27, pl. 127.1, 3; CVA Scheurleer 1, pl. 2.2; British Museum 1313.11–13.2, Jacobsthal, *Greek Pins* pl. 165.
As sex-linked grave gifts: Young, *Late Geometric Graves and a Seventh Century Well in the Agora* 18; Desborough, *Protogeometric Pottery* 105; Bohen, *Die geometrischen Pyxiden* 7–8, 125–27.

S. L.

27 HORSE PYXIS

Attic, Middle Geometric II, 800–775 B.C.
Height 0.21, diameter 0.256.
Ceramic; repaired from numerous fragments, tail broken off horse.
Museum of Fine Arts, Boston; Catharine Page Perkins Fund (97.359).

Belonging to the earliest phase of the horse pyxis, the Boston vessel has a strongly curving profile with the point of widest diameter above the center of the body; the lid is flat. The pyxis body features a simple large hatched meander as its principle decoration.

27

A band of dogtooth just above the foot and a dense zigzag are both framed by pairs of horizontal lines. Both a horse and a banded conical knob ornament the lid, the surface of which bears another dogtooth and a gear pattern in concentric bands around the horse. The central "tondo" has a crosshatched triangle to either side of the horse. The horse has a mostly black body with a reserved underside. The face has dotted-circle eyes and a crisscross representing a bridle on the muzzle; two chevrons framed above and below by horizontals cover the chest; a hatched line runs from mane to tail. On the underside a central tondo of reserved cross with stacked chevrons in the quadrants is ringed with thin lines, a gear pattern band, two solid broad bands, and a ring of parallel strokes interrupted by Xs.

Representing one of the five initial workshops of horse pyxides, the Boston vase is the namepiece of the Workshop of Boston MFA 97.359, to which six examples have been assigned. Two pieces from the Kerameikos have been attributed to the same hand as the Boston artist. The horses of this workshop are characteristically short-legged and very curvy, with a great arch under legs and belly and a fluid countercurve from head to back and up over the flank.

Contemporary with the Detroit pyxis (26), the Boston example demonstrates the origin of the horse pyxis in the standard flat pyxis form. The bodies of both vessels are of a similar strongly rounded wall with small and distinct ring base. As the Boston vessel shows, the customary conical knob of the standard pyxis lid is retained when horses first appear on the lid. The decorative treatment of the Detroit and Boston pyxides also betrays their close relationship, not only in the focus on a dominant meander, but also in the halftone effect created by the use of closely spaced narrow bands of ornament. The idea of placing a horse over the knob on a pyxis lid may have been related to the urge to distinguish certain individuals by introducing painted figures on their funerary vessels at about this same time.

PUBLISHED

A. Fairbanks, *Catalogue of Greek and Etruscan Vases* (Museum of Fine Arts, Boston) I (Cambridge MA 1928) 83 pl. 24, no. 278.

G. H. Chase, *Greek and Roman Antiquities. A Guide to the Classical Collection* (Boston 1950) 14 fig. 9.

C. C. Vermeule, *Greek, Etruscan, and Roman Art. The Classical Collections of the Museum of Fine Arts, Boston* (Boston 1963, 1972) 30 fig. 20.

CVA Louvre 16, 19, under pl. 21.

Ashmead and Phillips, *Classical Vases* 23, under no. 20.

F. Hiller, "Nochmals zu den Lanzenschwingern Olympia B 1701 und B 1999" AA (1977) 149–59 at 152.

Maass, *Die geometrischen Dreifüsse von Olympia* 107, n. 15.

M. Brouscari, "Collection P. Canellopoulos: vases géométriques" BCH 103 (1979) 430–55 at 446, n. 53.

Zimmermann, *Les chevaux* 289 n. 171, 290 n. 176.

Bohen, *Die geometrischen Pyxiden* 36, 51–53, 145, pl. 37, 1.

NOTES

On the Workshop of Boston MFA 97.359: Bohen, *Die geometrischen Pyxiden* 51–53.
Related pyxides: Kübler, *Die Nekropole des 10.*

bis 8. Jahrhunderts pl. 54, 5716c; AD 17 (1961–1962) pl. 34a; CVA Karlsruhe 1, B 2688, pl. 4.3.

S. L.

28 HORSE PYXIS

Attic, Late Geometric Ia, 760–750 B.C.
Height 0.140, body height 0.059, diameter 0.209, lid diameter 0.184.
Ceramic; complete, broken and mended.
Museum of Art, Rhode Island School of Design, Providence, Gift of Mrs. M. S. Danforth (37.022).

The main zone of the Providence pyxis body features a series of broad panels of confronted marsh birds with hatched bodies alternating with rectangular metopes containing either dotted tangential circles or quatrefoils. No two panels are exactly alike. The bird pairs flank outline crosses and outline leafrosettes; multiple zigzags fill the space behind each bird. The underside of the box contains a large quatrefoil of triple outline leaves with four smaller leaves between them; into the interstices project sets of chevrons from the circular border.

Surmounting the pyxis lid are two plastic horses above a simple cylindrical knob. Solid painted horse bodies contrast with reserved heads and necks on which are painted eyes, bridles, a hatched mane-to-tail stripe, a large asterisk on the outer side of the necks, and dappled strokes on the inner side. Most distinctive is an outline fish painted on the lid at the side of either horse. Concentric bands of decoration on the flat lid include angle hatching, chevrons, and dots.

The presence of fish beside the horses appears on at least nine other two-horse pyxides. On the basis of their formal homogeneity they have been grouped as the products apparently of a single source (but by more than one artist), nicknamed the Fish Workshop. The lid of the Providence pyxis displays the basic characteristics of this group: besides the fish, the horse type with modeled ears

28

and broad reserve necks with "brands." The complexities of defining workshops are demonstrated by the box decoration, the compositional scheme of which is better paralleled in a pyxis in Cambridge, Fitzwilliam Museum 84, which belongs to another pyxis workshop.

The significance of the fish beneath the horses is unknown. They apparently do not represent the "signature" of a particular artist or workshop, since the styles of pyxides so decorated vary too widely and some of them lie outside the oeuvre of the Fish Workshop. The connection between horse and fish seen here recalls the most popular imagery of Argive Geometric pottery, where their relationship might have characterized the physical juxtaposition of sea and pastureland of the horse-breeding Argolid (compare 90). Alterna-

tively, it has been seen as symbolic of Poseidon, or as a reference to the annual Argive sacrifice to that god that involved driving a horse into the sea. The purely Athenian tradition of the horse pyxides requires a local explanation for the horse-fish connection. The combination of horses, birds, and fish on this pyxis is reminiscent of the elemental scheme of earth, air, and water reflected in the poetry of Homer and Hesiod and popular particularly in the fibula art of central Greece (see 18, 81).

PUBLISHED

E. Robinson, *Rhode Island School of Design Museum Notes* 27 (1939) 20 fig. 2.
Ashmead and Phillips, *Classical Vases* no. 21.
Bohen, *Die geometrischen Pyxiden* 63, Workshop X, 7; pl. 37, 5.

NOTES

On the Fish Workshop: Bohen, *Die geometrischen Pyxiden* 63–66.

Pyxis Fitzwilliam 84: Bohen, *Die geometrischen Pyxiden* 71, Workshop XII, pl. 38, 2.

On the joint representation of horses and fish: Courbin, *La céramique géométrique de l'Argolide*; Boardman, "Symbol and Story in Geometric Art"; S. Langdon, "The Return of the Horse-Leader"; P. Courbin, "La signification du géométrique Argien" 55–64 in *Polydipsion Argos* (BCH Suppl. XXII 1992).

On the date of the Providence pyxis: Ashmead and Phillips, *Classical Vases* no. 21.

S. L.

29 HORSE PYXIS

Attic, Late Geometric II, 735–720 B.C.

Box height 0.081, diameter 0.312, lid height 0.142, diameter 0.314.

Ceramic; box broken and mended, section of wall and small area of bottom restored in plaster and painted; lid also broken and mended, horses reattached and heads extensively restored.

University of Missouri–Columbia, Museum of Art and Archaeology, Gilbreath-McLorn Museum Fund (92.1 a, b). Previously in a French private collection.

See Plate 3.

The pyxis bottom features a central star pattern with eight rays and a chain of tangential dots, around which radiate sixteen crosshatched leaves and an outer ring of tangential dots. Small rosettes lie between the tips of the leaves. A triglyph-metope design decorates the pyxis wall. The metopes carry checkerboard patterns alternating with hatched swastikas with zigzags between the arms. Triglyphs are formed by triple vertical lines-flanking a crosshatched panel. The lid is simpler with, from rim to center, concentric rings of vertical strokes alternating with Xs, rosettes alternating with zigzags, a tangential dot chain alternating with large and small dots,

and a ring of small dots. Surmounting the lid are four horses with solid black bodies. A continuous row of dots runs from top of mane to bottom of tail, with another row of dots at the bases of the necks. The faces are marked with an X on the muzzles and dots for eyes.

Numerous details of this pyxis reveal it to be a product of the Workshop of Agora P4784, a group apparently based in Athens, but whose pyxides were popular in nearby Anavysos as well. First identified by Young in 1939, this workshop is responsible for more than forty known horse pyxides, the largest number preserved from any single artistic hand or group. Its production extended over several decades from ca. 750 to 720 B.C., with the Missouri pyxis belonging to the later years. This pyxis is particularly close to other examples of this workshop in Copenhagen and Athens, with which it shares the arrangement of swastika panels in which the arms touch the frame and zigzags fill the interstices.

The tondo on which the horses stand sinks toward the center, where a small hole is bored. Found on numerous other horse pyxides, this arrangement must have accommodated a libation to be collected in the pyxis for the deceased.

UNPUBLISHED

NOTES

On horse pyxides in general: J. Bouzek, "Die attisch-geometrische Keramik im Nationalmuseum im Prag und in den anderen Tschechoslowakischen Sammlungen, Anhang I, Zu den Pyxiden mit Deckelpferden" *Sbornik historicky* (1959) 131–36; Bohen, *Die geometrischen Pyxiden*, on the Workshop of Agora P4784, 66–70.

Workshop first identified: Young, *Late Geometric Graves and a Seventh Century Well in the Agora* 91–92, no. XVIII 6.

Compare CVA Copenhagen 2, National Museum 4741, 52–53, pl. 71.4a–b; Kerameikos Inv. 338, Kübler, *Die Nekropole des 10.*

29

29

bis 8. Jahrhunderts pl. 59; Athens, Hadrian's Library 1669, Bohen, *Die geometrischen Pyxiden* pl. 38, 1; art market, Basel, *Münzen und Medaillen* Auktion 60 (1982) no. 5.

S. L.

Sometime around 800 B.C. an Athenian potter, acting either on commission or on personal initiative, attached a clay horse to the lid of a standard flat pyxis that was destined to be buried with other grave offerings and began a century-long fashion among well-to-do Athenians. The form underwent only one important change over the next few decades—the accumulation of up to four horses on the lid; there were never more than four and, in the

Late Geometric period, rarely as few as one or two. The majority of these vessels went into the graves of women, where they are thought to have held food or liquid offerings and, occasionally, small personal items for the deceased. They have been found laid next to the head or hand of the skeleton, and in one case the body was arranged with one hand reaching inside the horse pyxis.

Scholars have proposed that the horses on the lid represent, *pars pro toto*, a chariot, their variations in number corresponding to painted chariot teams on pottery ranging from one to four horses. The aristocratic associations of the high-maintenance horse and chariot, the rich contents of the graves in which they occur, and the limited popularity of this fashion among all the known Athenian Geometric graves indicate that the horse pyxis was an important emblem of status, perhaps a direct reference to the property and rank of the owner's family. Developing more or less from the time the ceramic granary models (14) disappear, these pyxides may have served a similar symbolic function, with the boxes likewise representing the dowry chest with lid decoration that proclaims the father's and husband's affluence and role in community affairs. The specific number of horses included may not signify much, since on more than one occasion pyxides with different numbers of horses have been found in a single grave.

Recent scholarship has emphasized the socioeconomic significance of these objects and usefully compared their occurrence and decline with other status symbols in eighth-century Athens. It is important to recall, therefore, that to their contemporaries horse pyxides certainly carried other meanings as well. Although ancient repairs of some examples seem to indicate their use in life as well as in death, the horse iconography may have been guided as much by the pyxides' ultimate destination below ground as by their aristocratic associations. Two of the earliest known pyxides, both from graves in the Kerameikos cemetery, present single horses flanked by a pair of plastic spotted frogs, a motif rare in

Geometric art but familiar from Egypt and the Near East. The frogs' apparent mass regeneration from pure mud each spring offered an obvious funerary symbol. Often painted on the undersides of these pyxides or added in plastic on the lid, the snake with its observable comings and goings from the earth was a much more successful chthonic symbol in Greece; it pervades Geometric funerary pottery. The connection of horses with death and the underworld can be traced back to iconography and ritual practices of the Late Bronze Age. In the simplest interpretation, the high status connoted by horse and chariot suggests that their deployment in a funerary context conferred honor on the deceased. In the early Iron Age the horse appears along with other motifs such as snake, bird, frog, and solar forms, which cautions against too narrow an interpretation of symbols. The horse and the horse-and-chariot may also have carried implications of the journey of the dead.

The exhibition includes four examples of horse pyxides, one with each of the four different numbers of horses, representing the full chronological and stylistic range of such vessels (27–29, 82).

NOTES

General discussions of horse pyxides: Bouzek, "Die attisch-geometrische Keramik"; Smithson, "The Tomb of a Rich Athenian Lady" 96; Bohen, *Die geometrischen Pyxiden* 5–12; J. Bouzek, review of Bohen in *Gnomon* 64 (1992) 273–74.

On funerary associations of the horse: Benson, *Horse, Bird, and Man*; Goodison, *Death, Women, and the Sun* 151–53.

S. L.

30 JEWELRY GROUP

Probably northern Greek, Late Geometric or Subgeometric, mid-eighth to seventh century B.C.

Ring dimensions: diameters 0.019–0.022, band widths 0.001–0.013; fibula length 0.051.

30

Bronze; objects largely intact, missing small
  chips; fibula .18 lacks part of catchplate.
University of Missouri–Columbia, Museum
  of Art and Archaeology, anonymous gift
  (90.116.1–3, 6, 8–16, 18). Purchased in
  Thessaloniki, 1931.

The objects pictured here are believed to
have composed a single grave group of bronze
jewelry. Five of the rings (90.116.1–3, 6, 8) are
simple flat bands of sheet bronze with one
end overlapping the other. All bear incised
tremolo decoration, the curving zigzags made
by rocking a tool from side to side. The simplest ring is decorated with only a broad
tremolo zigzag, the most elaborate with a
bisected row of tremolo lozenges bordered at
top and bottom. Similar bronze rings found
near the head in burials at Vergina indicate
their use as hair ornaments as well as finger
rings. A second type, represented by seven
rings, is narrower and made of thin bronze
strips, usually triangular in section. Four of
these have incised tremolo lines.

A third type of ring (90.116.16) consists of a
wire coiled in five loops with the ends terminating in spirals. This ring type occurred first
in the Submycenaean period, when the spiral
ornamentation popular in Europe began to
enter Greece. These rings remained fairly
common in Greece into the eighth and sev-

enth centuries, when they spread into Peloponnesian sanctuaries as votive offerings.

The plate fibula has an arched bow with a
single spring at either end and a triangular
catchplate. A type widespread in the Balkans
and less common in Greece, it appeared
infrequently in contexts from the late eighth
to early seventh century, and more often in
the seventh and sixth centuries. Also belonging to this jewelry group are an Attico-Boeotian
fibula with a double bow and four additional
rings illustrated here; their fragile condition
prevented their inclusion in the exhibition.

Grave groups of bronze jewelry comprising,
like this one, finger rings, hair rings, and fibulae belong to a long tradition of adornment
for burial that dates from the outset of the
post-Mycenaean era in Greece and lasts down
to the sixth century. This conservatism in
dress fashion typifies the culture of northern
Greece and the Balkans. Fashions in fibulae
and other ornaments changed more steadily
in central and southern Greece under the
influence of luxury goods and styles from
the East.

UNPUBLISHED

NOTES
For the first type of ring: Bouzek, *Graeco-
  Macedonian Bronzes* 127, group A, common
  in graves of the Chauchitsa cemetery.

For the second type of ring: M. Andronikos, *Bergina* I (Athens 1969) 240–41, fig. 81; Bouzek, *Graeco-Macedonian Bronzes* fig. 39:9 from Vergina; Philipp, *Bronzeschmuck aus Olympia* no. 534, pl. 42.

For the third type of ring: Bouzek, *Graeco-Macedonian Bronzes* 129, type C, pl. 39:8; V. R. d'A. Desborough, "The Greek Mainland, c. 1150–c. 1000 B.C." *PPS* 31 (1965) 224.

On tremolo patterns: Jacobsthal, *Greek Pins* 209; *BSA* 31 (1930–1931) 34, fig. 14, 35 n. 3; J. Boardman, *Excavations in Greek Emporio, Chios, 1952–1955* (BSA Supplement 6, London 1967) 212; *BSA* 64 (1969) 146 n. 27; Philipp, *Bronzeschmuck aus Olympia* nos. 745, 755.

For the first fibula type: Blinkenberg, *Fibules grecques et orientales* 80, no. 4, fig. 70; Bouzek, *Graeco-Macedonian Bronzes* 132–33; D. Gergova, *Früh- und altereisenzeitliche Fibeln in Bulgarien* (Prähistorische Bronzefunde XIV, 7, Munich 1987) 41–43, type B1,2 (variant delta).

Grave groups: *ArchDelt* 36 (1981) [1989] pl. 5, Geometric period grave in Tragana; J. Bouzek, "Addenda to Macedonian Bronzes" *Eirene* 18 (1982) 44 fig. 2.1–12, 6th c. grave between Kavalla and Drama; *BSA* 23 (1918–1919) 21 fig. 12, early 6th c. grave near Aivasil in Macedonia.

S. L.

31 BEADS

Vrokastro, Chamber Tomb I,
Protogeometric, ca. 925–875 B.C.
Faience beads, maximum length ca. 0.032; carnelian beads, largest diameter ca. 0.018.
Faience and carnelian; intact, faience beads on modern string.
The University Museum, University of Pennsylvania (MS 4755 and MS 4767; Neg. #S4–140823 and S4–140825). From Candia Museum through E. Dohan 1912.

The eighty-three faience beads represent three common forms: elongated, flat disk, and

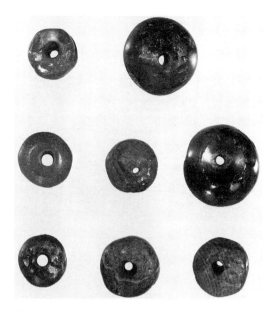

31

spherical. The eight carnelian beads are all spherical.

Simple faience and carnelian beads of the types represented here changed little in form over time and are best dated by associated finds. Chamber Tomb I at Vrokastro was used to house at least six burials, five adult cremations and an inhumed child, ranging from the tenth to early ninth centuries as the pottery and other finds demonstrate. During this time the tomb accumulated an abundance of grave goods, including over thirty-five vases, a bronze rod tripod, a gold ring, bronze fibulae, a number of faience seals and two hundred and fifty beads, and "masses" of iron tools and weapons. The richness of Tomb I might suggest that, just as in the Bronze Age, these chamber tombs were the resting places of the highest ranking families, were it not for the fact that other chamber tombs at Vrokastro and elsewhere in Crete are in general modestly appointed.

These faience beads are certainly an import from the eastern Mediterranean, where small items of faience were used for barter. After the widespread use and local manufacture of faience in Bronze Age Greece and Crete, its disappearance in the early Dark Age marks a

31

technological loss. The distribution of this material in Greece reveals a gap between the eleventh and late tenth centuries, when it is again known from Athens, Tiryns, Asine, and Lefkandi, but primarily from Crete, and in these cases seems to be imported. Faience seals and beads occur in more than half the Vrokastro chamber tombs, attesting a local availability of these inexpensive but attractive

trinkets. The later bone enclosures at the site contain no faience except for a single tiny bead.

Carnelian, a hard stone of the quartz family, was also a material not locally available whose technique required specialized skill. The stone is native to Egypt, western Asia, and India, as well as parts of Europe, making the source of the carnelian beads at Vrokastro and Fortetsa difficult to assess. Like the faience, the beads testify to a greater network of contacts from which Crete benefited.

PUBLISHED
Hall, *Vrokastro* 123–39, esp. 136–37, pl. XXXV.

NOTES
Dating Tomb I: Coldstream, *Geometric Greece* 281.

Faience: from Athens, Smithson, "The Tomb of a Rich Athenian Lady"; from Tiryns, *AM* 78 (1963) 36–37, 42, Beil. 3, 1; from Asine tomb 1970.15, *Asine* II, fasc. 4, pt. 1, 16, 18, fig. 24; from Lefkandi, Popham and Sackett, *Lefkandi* I 218, pls. 218–21, 233.

Faience in Iron Age Crete: Brock, *Fortetsa* 208; *BSA* 55 (1960) 134, pl. 39.

Carnelian beads in Crete: Brock, *Fortetsa* 209; see generally, J. Ogden, *Jewellery of the Ancient World* (London 1982) 105–8.

S. L.

32 PENDANT WITH SEATED FIGURE

Northern Greek, Late Geometric, ca. 700 B.C.
Height 0.127.
Bronze; stem broken and repaired.
Walters Art Gallery, Baltimore (54.2473).

The ornate bronze pendant features a figure perched atop a knob-covered rod. The miniature anthropoid figure squats on a small flat base. The legs are drawn in toward the body and the arms are raised to the face, with elbows resting on knees. The peculiar head curves forward from the neck with a slight bulge suggesting hair at the nape. The head is marked by a projecting muzzlelike

32

tical lines and voids. Figure and base rest upon a short strut, beneath which hangs a staff terminating in another strut with a rounded bottom. The shaft is studded with eight sets of four rounded knobs that project at regular intervals.

Until recently similar pendants were conventionally called "jug-stoppers," from Jantzen's clever explanation of their unusual form in which cording wrapped around the shaft allowed them to function as corks. Excavated examples found at the waists of skeletons have demonstrated instead their use as belt pendants. Scores of preserved examples show a stylistic evolution of the figure from relative naturalism to extreme abstraction; the Baltimore pendant belongs early in the series, which begins around 700 B.C. The broad distribution of the type throughout Thessaly, Macedonia, and eastern Albania, with relatively few known Peloponnesian examples, indicates an origin in northern Greece.

Interpretation of the object is more difficult than identification of its function. The small sitters seem to have been derived from the somewhat earlier Peloponnesian bronze seated figurines found exclusively in sanctuaries. Best exemplified in the fine Baltimore sitter (80), the ancestors were equally ambiguous in their activity, and usually seem to hold an object to their mouths. A clue to their meaning may lie in the fact that in several of the most naturalistic rod pendants the shaft was broken away and the remaining figure was saved and buried with the dead. It may be concluded that the rod pendants served an amuletic function, embodying in the strange eating figure a symbol of nourishment, fertility, and regeneration appropriate for a grave as it was earlier for a votive offering.

The peculiar form of the knob-covered rod, challenging to cast in bronze, probably derives from related Balkan and Thracian bronze pendants with only one or two rows of "buttons." With its simian-looking figure perched on top, however, the fully evolved rod pendant resembles a highly stylized Tree of Life.

face around which the hands are wrapped. A thickening between the hands suggests an object held to the mouth. The compact figure offers a strikingly abstract composition of ver-

PUBLISHED

Hesperia Art XLIII (1966) no. A 30.

D. K. Hill, "When the Greeks Began on Bronzes" *Bulletin of the Walters Art Gallery* 21, 3 (1968).

Betancourt, "The Age of Homer" 6, no. 7.

EXHIBITED

The Age of Homer, University Museum, University of Pennsylvania, December 1969–March 1970.

NOTES

On the pendant type: U. Jantzen, "Geometrische Kannenverschlüsse" *AA* (1953) 56–67; Schweitzer, *Greek Geometric Art* 160–61; Bouzek, *Graeco-Macedonian Bronzes* 76–86; Kilian, "Trachtzubehör der Eisenzeit" 114–15, pl. 96 type 1; Vickers, "Some Early Iron Age Bronzes from Macedonia" 17–19, n. 7; Kilian-Dirlmeier, *Anhänger in Griechenland* pls. 61–73, esp. no. 1174; S. Langdon, "From Monkey to Man" 413–15.

S. L.

33 LARGE OINOCHOE

Attic, Late Geometric II, 735–720 B.C.
Height 0.429, maximum diameter 0.276.
Ceramic; complete, mended from fragments.
University of Missouri–Columbia, Museum of Art and Archaeology (60.19).

The globular body sits on a low ring base, with a tall narrow neck and trefoil lip. The strap handle extends from lip to shoulder and is vertically divided by grooves into three segments. Separated by groups of two or three horizontal lines, the decorative bands are, from foot to lip: crosshatched triangles, checkerboard, zigzag, hatched double leaves with crosshatched triangles in the interstices, blind lozenge chain, hatched simple meander, blind lozenge chain, dotted snake with crosshatched triangles and pair of mastoi (or relief nipples), zigzag; on the neck: bird frieze, blind lozenge chain, hatched snake meander, blind lozenge chain, chevrons. The handle decoration consists of a vertical lozenge chain flanked on either side by vertical lines and diagonal strokes.

This vessel is derived from a giant meter-high oinochoe type apparently monumentalized for funerary use by the Dipylon Master. The type was continued on a more moderate scale by numerous workshops from 750 to 720 B.C. The painter of the Missouri oinochoe shows both an awareness of the Dipylon tradition and an interest in independent trends. The use of the lozenge chain to separate wider zones was favored by the Dipylon Master, as were the row of leaves below the midpoint of the vase, the use of a checked zone, and the resistance to dividing the shoulder zone into metopes, a system found in nearly every later large oinochoe. Similar in decoration and shape are two oinochoai in Basel and Athens, both attributed to the Lambros Workshop, whose style is characterized by the use of dotted bird friezes, metopes, and dotted lozenge chains. Lacking all three of these features, the Missouri oinochoe is therefore not of this group, but shares with it the dotted serpent on the shoulder and the hatched snake meander on the neck.

A common element of these large oinochoai is the pair of breastlike mastoi high on the shoulder. Found in Attic pottery mainly on oinochoai and small cups, they date well back into the Early Geometric period. Whether or not their origin lies in a life-giving symbolism, their survival into Late Geometric may be tied to practicality. Absorbed into the general decorative composition, they offer a convenient brace for the hand when pouring from the heavy container.

Despite the oinochoe's precise and elaborate decoration, certain details hint at the encroaching debasement of the motifs and indicate a date slightly later than that assigned to the Lambros group (750–735 B.C.). These include the omission of dots from the lozenge chain, the line of hatched triangles without a corresponding set above, and the filling of checkerboard squares with round dots.

UNPUBLISHED

33

NOTES

For the Basel oinochoe: Basel Historisches Museum, *AM* 43 (1918) pl. 2, 2; Schefold, *Meisterwerke griechischer Kunst* no. 42; Davison, *Attic Geometric Workshops* 63, fig. 86; Coldstream, *Greek Geometric Pottery* 44, no. 2; *CVA* Basel 1, pl. 2.

For the Athens oinochoe (NM 178): M. Collignon and L. Couve, *Catalogue des vases peints du Musée National d'Athènes* (Paris 1904) pl. 13, 238; *JdI* 14 (1899) 211, fig. 87; Davison, *Attic Geometric Workshops* 3, fig. 85; Coldstream, *Greek Geometric Pottery* 44, no. 3.

Related oinochoai: in Mainz, *CVA* Römisch-Germanisches Zentralmuseum 1, 23–24, pl. 8.1–2; in Copenhagen, NM 9361, *CVA* Copenhagen 1 pl. 72,2.

On the mastoi: Courbin, *La céramique géométrique de l'Argolide* 470–71.

For the funerary significance of the snake, see **20**.

S. L.

34 TANKARD

Attic, Late Geometric Ib–IIa, 750–725 B.C.
Height with handle 0.175, maximum diameter 0.121, mouth diameter 0.107.
Ceramic; lip and handle fragments restored.
University of Missouri–Columbia, Museum of Art and Archaeology (57.2).

Variously labeled by different scholars as mug, olpe, mug-olpe, jug, and tankard, this vessel type developed in the Middle Geometric period as a variant of the small mug. Characteristically, the lip is clearly articulated and taller than the rounded body, while the handle is taller yet, attached by a strut to the body and arching high above the rim. On the Missouri tankard a well-preserved glossy black slip presents the decorative scheme. The body of the mug has a solid black-slipped bottom, four horizontal bands, and elongated dots connected by tangents; the bottom of the lip has a row of dots between triple horizontal lines; the main lip panel features a triglyph and

34

metope frieze with a large hatched swastika in the central metope, flanked by a marsh bird facing to the center in each side metope. The bird panels have dot rosette, dotted line, and swastika filling ornaments. Triglyphs are composed of vertical lines flanking a vertical zigzag. The handle is decorated with horizontal lines alternating with a large and a small X. The vessel is datable no later than 725 because the body diameter outspans the rim diameter and the lip/body junction is relatively well defined.

The tankard attained great popularity in the Late Geometric period, when it was used particularly for funerary purposes and may have been produced in sets for funerary meals. Excavations at Spata in Attica found a tankard in every grave of this period. The grave of a rich woman in the Kerameikos cemetery had no fewer than nine. Similar to the Missouri mug, although by a different hand, is a tankard in a German private collection. An identical twin to the German example, now in Copenhagen, was produced by the same artist.

The swastika motif, which appears at both large and small scale on the Missouri tankard, was employed sporadically on Early and Middle Geometric pottery before it entered the repertoire of Geometric ornamentation on a regular basis in the eighth century. Scholarly consideration of this motif has led in two directions. To some it is pure ornament, a native Greek invention independent of its other appearances in the ancient world. In this light it might be a variation on the meander, whose sudden popularity is linked to its ability to fill the square spaces of the new metopal system of Late Geometric I pottery. Similarly, Benson thought it a geometricized floral ornament.

Swastikas also occur, however, as filling motifs in close association with both birds and horses. Earlier views, such as those of Schweitzer and Roes, granted it a broader context within prehistoric Indo-European sun symbolism. Bouzek, however, has pointed out that the original meaning of the swastika outside Greece had waned by the Geometric period. Reminiscent of this older view is a recent study by Goodison that connects the swastika with other sunlike motifs in funerary contexts.

PUBLISHED

Illustrated Museum Handbook (Columbia MO 1982) 19, no. 47.

NOTES

On the type in general: Coldstream, *Greek Geometric Pottery* 23, 47, 86, pl. 10j.

Young, *Late Geometric Graves and a Seventh Century Well in the Agora* 89 fig. 60,1, 88 fig. 59, shows the tankard from Agora grave XVIII in situ beside the head of the skeleton.

Spata graves: *ArchDelt* 6 (1920–1921) 131–38.

B. von Freytag, "Ein spätgeometrisches Frauengrab vom Kerameikos" *AM* 89 (1974) 1–25, esp. 11 no. 6 with additional bibliography.

Similar examples: Joslyn Art Museum 1963.479, *Greek Vase-Painting in Midwestern Collections* 2–3, no. 3; *Hesperia* 30 (1961) no. 2, pl. 16, L20; Kübler, *Die Nekropole des 10. bis 8. Jahrhunderts* pl. 111, inv. 363, gr. 21; Young, *Late Geometric Graves and a Seventh Century Well in the Agora* 89, grave XVIII, no. 1, p. 110; *AA* (1992) 404 no. 6, fig. 6a–d; *CVA* Copenhagen, National Museum 2, 52, pl. 70.13.

The swastika as ornament: Courbin, *La céramique géométrique de l'Argolide* 476; J. Bouzek, *Homerisches Griechenland im Lichte der archäologischen Quellen* (Prague 1969) 143; Benson, *Horse, Bird, and Man* 27–28.

As sun symbolism: A. Roes, "Les ex-voto de bronze de l'époque géométrique" *RA* (1970) 195–208 at 201; Schweitzer, *Greek Geometric Art* 27; Goodison, *Death, Women, and the Sun* 126–38.

S. L.

35 TANKARD

Attic, Late Geometric Ib–IIa, 750–725 B.C.
Height 0.162, rim diameter 0.110.
Ceramic; intact except for small chip on lip.
The University Museum, University of Pennsylvania, Gift of John F. Gunmere (75.8.1, Neg. #S8–97518).

The neatly painted tankard has a broad, low swelling body tapering in an unbroken contour to a tall neck with flaring rim. The strap handle, connected by one strut, rises well above the rim. Decoration from bottom to top consists of horizontal bands separating decorative bands of vertical lines in groups of four, chevrons, dots, and, in the main neck frieze, crosshatched gadroons in panels separated by narrow hatched triglyphs. The handle is ornamented by a star and Xs in a vertical column.

The gadroon, formed by pushing out the convex vessel wall in a vertical oval molding, derives from a metalworking technique. Greek potters first began to imitate this technique on ceramic shapes in Middle Geometric I, creating a fair imitation of metal vessels much less costly for the patron. By Late Geometric Ib a painted version of gadrooning, which

35

translates into a tongue pattern filled with either chevrons or crosshatching, became popular on drinking vessels, while real gadroon forms in ceramic continued briefly. If the ceramic version with real gadrooning seemed an odd marriage of ceramic and metal techniques, the use of two-dimensional painted gadroons on concave rather than convex portions of the pot, as in this tankard, defies logic altogether and suggests that the original point of the motif has been forgotten. The loss of the Mycenaean tradition of metal vessel manufacture during the Dark Age meant that Geometric potters were influenced not by native Greek models but by the foreign vessels of bronze, gold, or silver that were worked with gadroons in several Near Eastern regions in the early first millennium.

PUBLISHED
Catalogue, *Aspects of Ancient Greece*, 12 no. 2.

EXHIBITED
Aspects of Ancient Greece, Allentown Art Museum, Allentown PA, September–December 1979.

NOTES
For tankards with gadroons: Würzburg K49, *JdI* 74 (1959) 65 figs. 5–6; Young, *Late Geometric Graves and a Seventh Century Well in the Agora* 102, fig. 72, no. XXV3; *CVA* Brussels 3, 3, pl. 2.13.
For tankards with lancet-shaped gadroons: *CVA* Michigan 1, pl. 12.3; *CVA* Leipzig 1, pl. 17.3–4; *ArchEph* (1898) pl. 4 no. 8 (from Eleusis).

S. L.

36 FENESTRATED STAND

Attic, Late Geometric I, 760–735 B.C.
Height 0.23, mouth diameter 0.104, diameter at bottom of feet 0.165.
Ceramic; restorations on mouth and a section of one leg.
Phoebe Hearst Museum of Anthropology, University of California at Berkeley, gift of Mrs. P. A. Hearst (8/3353). Purchased in Athens in 1901.

Tapering from bottom to top, this unusual vessel support rests on six rectangular legs. A square window perforates the cylindrical midsection above each leg and a narrower neck is topped by a concave lip. Reddish glaze covers the surface in a variety of ornamentation, from bottom to top: checkerboard patterning on the legs; hatched peaked triangles on the ring connecting the legs; birds in the panels between windows; zigzag on the ring above; neck zone with a series of metopes, one containing a grazing deer, the other four alternating a hatched rosette and a lozenge with checked center; above, a ring of hatched triangles and lip band of connected blobs.

The grazing deer featured in a panel on the front of the stand is a fixed iconographic type first used by the Dipylon Master around 760 B.C. Standing with head lowered to the ground, the husky Berkeley deer is surrounded by a line of dots and two asterisks. The

36

"K-headed" deer is known from other Attic vessels, and its unusual appearance alone in a panel has been linked with a series of oinochoai attributed to the Dipylon Workshop. Like the equally "fixed" representations of couchant goats, grazing deer appear suddenly in Late Geometric I Attic art without any stylistic relation to previous Greek animal representations. There is no reason to doubt that both images entered Greek workshops from the Near East by way of ivories, seals, and metalwork. Strikingly similar grazing deer are featured on ninth- and eighth-century ivory plaques from Arslan Tash, Samaria, Nimrud, and Assur. Because the motif appeared more or less simultaneously in Attica on gold bands and pottery of the Dipylon Workshop, it is uncertain in which craft the motif was first taken up. It provides an interesting illustration of the active give-and-take among artisans of different media at this time.

In addition to these Eastern borrowings in Greek art, the Berkeley stand also demonstrates connections with the Cyclades. Melian fenestrated stands developed in the Late Geometric apparently under Attic influence, as evidenced by the form of their broad necks. While the Attic type continued to reflect more or less faithfully its metal prototype through the representation of legs with narrow struts, the Melian stands favor the perforation of the wall with multiple windows, a construction that quickly abandons its metal origins. In its decorative treatment and specific motifs the Berkeley stand demonstrates an Attic provenance, while its construction, unparalleled in the Attic type, may betray an influence from the Cyclades.

A similar Attic stand of Late Geometric Ib date excavated in a grave in Corinth indicates how these objects were used; it holds a tankard of the same type as **34, 35,** and **46,** creating an elegant presentation of a drinking vessel for the graveside ceremony.

PUBLISHED
CVA California 1, 10–11 no. 2, pl. I.2a–d.
Davison, *Attic Geometric Workshops* 74,
    fig. 107.
Rombos, *The Iconography of Attic Late Geometric II Pottery* 55, 417 cat. 39.

NOTES
On the Oinochoe Workshop: Davison, *Greek Geometric Workshops* 73–74.
On the origin of the deer motif: Carter, "The Beginning of Narrative Art in the Greek Geometric Period" 40–41.
Stand with tankard from Corinth grave: *Hesperia* 1 (1932) 63, fig. 9.
On Melian stands: H. Smith, *CVA California 1* cites extensive bibliography; Coldstream, *Greek Geometric Pottery* 183 and n. 5; Melian stands with goats and birds in London and Paris, Coldstream pl. 39a–d; E. Pottier, *Les vases antiques du Louvre* I (Paris 1897) pl. 19.

S. L.

37

37 FIGURAL STAND FOOT

Attic, Middle Geometric II, 800–760 B.C.
Height 0.095, width at top 0.050, width at
**   bottom 0.060, thickness 0.011.**
Ceramic; fragment preserves one foot of a
**   pot stand, with breaks at bottom right**
**   corner and along top edge.**
Royal Ontario Museum, Toronto (957 × 245).

The rectangular, slightly splaying foot preserves a scene of two dueling swordsmen bordered by double lines. Clad only in crested
helmets, the pair face each other in nearly
perfect symmetry. They are shown in the
height of action with their legs braced; each
grasps the crest of the other with one hand
while thrusting a sword with the other hand
down at his opponent's thigh.

A second foot from this same stand is preserved in Athens. A study of their break patterns reveals that they belonged to a
fenestrated stand, originally with four feet.
As an Attic fenestrated stand this perforated
form, typically Cycladic, would have been
unusual. An equally rare complete example of
this type is the Berkeley Attic stand (**36**). The
Athens-Toronto stand is unique in providing a
field for human-figured scenes. The Athens
fragment preserves in entirety the dueling
scene, which differs from the Toronto piece in
that the combatants do not touch each other's
crests, the artist having neglected to paint
their forearms.

The later Middle Geometric date for the
stand comes not from its form, but from its
attribution by Coldstream to the same artist
as the New York krater 34.11.2, a vessel decorated with a magnificent ship scene (Fig. 10).
The figures on the Toronto stand are therefore ancestral to the great Dipylon Workshop
and show the already classic body construction of triangular torso, long legs with heavy
thighs, and a small head with long pointed
chin. The Toronto duelists belong to a still
exclusive club of Middle Geometric human
figures. The complete symmetry of the figures' composition, a scheme that can deaden
a scene of high action, here detracts nothing
from the intensity of the moment since the
outcome remains undetermined.

The attribution to this early artist may aid
in our understanding of the scene. Duels are
extremely rare in Attic art outside the larger
battlefield panoramas of the Dipylon kraters
and amphorae. On a kantharos in Copenhagen two pairs of duelists appear amid
scenes of boxing, dancing, and lion mauling
and have accordingly been thought to refer to
funeral games or a secular sporting event.
Two warriors facing each other across the
inverted body of a third, deceased(?) figure on
the Boston oinochoe (**99**) may enact a duel as
well, although there is no swordplay. Since
there is no evidence besides the ambiguous
chariot scenes on neck-handled amphorae for

actual funerary games in eighth-century Attica, it would be perverse to look for such a reference in single duels. Secular sporting events, which would have included boxing and wrestling and were perhaps more akin to festival activities like the Olympic games, are represented only in Late Geometric II. As for the artist's better-known work, the New York krater, it is interesting to note that two dueling scenes nearly identical to this one appear onboard the ships. The early date of the work and the artist's position as creator of the first epic-looking battle scenes recommend that the sword combat on the stand fragment be read as a duel excerpted from the chaos of the battlefield, much as Homer organized the Trojan War into encounters between heroes. Although Benson has noted striking Bronze Age parallels for the symmetrical duel motif, others have drawn attention to such Near Eastern sources as a ninth-century relief from Tell Halaf.

PUBLISHED

A. Cambitoglou, "Two Fragments of a Geometric Stand in Toronto and Athens" *AJA* 64 (1960) 366–67.

Coldstream, *Greek Geometric Pottery* 26, 28 n. 2.

Benson, *Horse, Bird, and Man* 100, pl. XXXVII, 3.

Ahlberg, *Fighting on Land and Sea* 49 nos. 1, 2, fig. 47.

S. Marinatos, "Kaineus (Caeneus): A Further Link between the Mycenaean and the Greek Worlds" in *The European Community in Greek Prehistory* (Totowa NJ 1971) 53–56 at n. 4.

Ahlberg-Cornell, "Games, Play and Performance" 62 fig. 12.

Rombos, *The Iconography of Attic Late Geometric II Pottery* 425 cat. 114.

NOTES

On the stand foot Athens NM 17384: CVA Athens 2, 11 no. 2, fig. 3, pl. 14.2; Schweitzer, *Greek Geometric Art* 174

fig. 102; Benson, *Horse, Bird, and Man* pl. XXXVII, 4.

The New York krater, Metropolitan Museum 34.11.2: Schweitzer, *Greek Geometric Art* pl. 34; Benson, *Horse, Bird, and Man* pl. XXXVII, 2a–b.

For dueling scenes in Attic art: Schweitzer, *Greek Geometric Art* 174–75; Ahlberg, *Fighting on Land and Sea* 76–77; Ahlberg-Cornell, "Games, Play and Performance" 59–61; Rombos, *The Iconography of Attic Late Geometric II Pottery* 209–14.

On Near Eastern sources for the motif: Ahlberg, *Fighting on Land and Sea* 76–77, esp. the orthostate from Tell Halaf, fig. 68.

S. L.

38 HIGH-RIMMED BOWL

Said to be from Athens, Late Geometric IIa, ca. 735–720 B.C.

Height 0.093; diameter 0.20.

Ceramic; intact; minor scratches and abrasions on the exterior; deep scratches inside.

The Art Museum, Princeton University, Museum purchase (y1929–19).

Bowls such as this, with a shallow body, tall straight rim, horizontal ribbon handles, and a ring foot, are peculiar to Athens. They apparently functioned as pyxides, as many excavated examples are equipped with a conical lid. Coldstream dated the earliest examples to Late Geometric Ib and traced their origin to the Dipylon Workshop, where potters combined a low, skyphoid body with the high rim of a lekaina. By Late Geometric II they were much more common, apparently replacing the flat-bottomed pyxis. This vase, with a somewhat taller base ring than most Late Geometric Ib examples and a slightly concave rim, should perhaps be assigned to Late Geometric IIa. In Late Geometric IIb examples, the rim slopes outward and the foot increases in height to become a fenestrated stand, a

38

process that continues in Protoattic examples, when the stand became taller than the bowl.

The clay is a fine buff yellow. The painted decoration is fired black on one side, red on the other (and on most of the bottom). The decoration is in four superimposed bands framed by horizontal stripes. Circling the rim is a broad band of hatched meanders in a simple key pattern. Below this, on the lower rim, is a narrower band of compass-drawn circles with dotted centers, linked by sloping lines. On either side of the bowl, between the handles, is a broad panel of stacked zigzags flanked by paired metopes: one containing a water bird, the other zigzags. Around the lower body, framed by triple stripes, is a band of black ovals linked by curving lines. A broad, solid stripe circles the reddish foot, the underside of which is decorated with concentric circles. A row of dots on the resting surface of the foot is largely effaced. The interior is glazed black except for the upper rim, a reserved dot in the center, and a single reserved stripe. A stripe circles the reserved rim, and above this are groups of short, vertical stripes. The outsides of the handles are decorated with a row of tall water birds, separated by hatched triangles and rows of dots. The curved flanges of the handles are striped on the inside.

The decoration combines both common and atypical elements, the latter including the double row of ornament on the rim and the birds on the handles. In many cases, the rim decoration is disposed in a series of metopes containing rosettes, swastikas, short meanders, or checkerboards. In cases where a continuous band circles the rim, motifs include water birds, gazelles, chevrons, meanders, and cross-hatched triangles ("wolf's teeth").

UNPUBLISHED

NOTES

For the development of the shape: Coldstream, *Greek Geometric Pottery* 34, 48–49, 86, pls. 10g–h (LGIb), 12e and 15e (LGIIa), and 15m (LGIIb).

For the shape of the Princeton bowl: *CVA Munich* 3, pl. 122, 1–2; *AD* 22 (1967) B pl. 79d for shape.

Other examples of the type: C. S. Sweet, "Six Attic Vases in the San Francisco Bay Area" *CSCA* 2 (1969) 271–84 at 272–73; *CVA Robinson Collection* 1, pl. 10, 1–3; *CVA Cambridge* 1, pl. 1, 14; *CVA Copenhagen* 2, pl. 71, 1; *CVA Madrid* 1, pl. 1, 6; *CVA Geneva* 1, pl. 5, 3–4; *CVA Univ. Vienna* 1, pl. 4, 1; *CVA Munich* 3, pl. 122, 3.

J. M. P.

39

39 SKYPHOS

Attic, Late Geometric I, ca. 750 B.C.
Height 0.095, maximum diameter 0.14.
Ceramic; mended from fragments.
Museum of Art, Rhode Island School of
    Design, Providence, Anonymous gift in
    memory of C. A. Robinson, Jr. (83.025).

Representing one of several varieties of the
drinking cup form in Late Geometric Athens,
this elegant skyphos is an exceptionally fine
example of the potter's art as well as that of
its meticulous painter; the two may have been
the same person. Set on a small round base,
the low body rises broadly to its maximum
diameter, above which point it is abruptly
constricted with a tall, offset lip tapering up
to a straight rim. Ribbon handles enhance the
cup's low, compact form while offering a com-
fortable fingerhold to the drinker. The precise
ornamentation recalls the sober tradition of
Middle Geometric painting while it hints at
the growing profusion of new designs entering
Late Geometric art. The body up to the bot-

tom of the handles is solid glossy black. The
main decorative zone begins abruptly, without
the "softening" effect of three horizontal lines
that will soon become the rule in Attic painting. A short hatched meander is the central
focus, separated from multiple zigzag columns
by vertical triglyphs. A zigzag band decorates
the handles and a dotted lozenge chain the
tall lip.

The Providence skyphos is a rare example
of the transitional Middle Geometric skyphos
developing from its low, broad form into the
high-rimmed bowl (compare 38). The present
example retains the reflex ribbon handles and
solid black lower body of the Middle Geometric II skyphos while deepening the bowl and
raising the lip. Coldstream attributed these
changes to the Dipylon Workshop, whose profound impact on Athenian pottery traditions
included the invention of a number of new
vase types as well as its well-known experi-
mentation with figural themes. Few of the
extant Late Geometric I skyphoi demonstrate
as does this fine vessel the careful mainte-

nance of Middle Geometric aesthetic and technical standards during the more or less radical refurbishing of traditional forms that occurred in Late Geometric I.

PUBLISHED

Rhode Island School of Design Museum Notes 70 (1983) 9.

NOTES

On high-rimmed bowl development: Coldstream, *Greek Geometric Pottery* 34.

Similar transitional skyphoi: Kübler, *Die Nekropole des 10. bis 8. Jahrhunderts* pl. 90 no. 840, pl. 94 nos. 826, 827 still with a low lip; pl. 97 no. 328; AD 18 (1963) B pl. 40a–b.

S. L.

For always in time past the gods have shown themselves clearly to us, when we render them glorious grand sacrifices.

(*Odyssey* 7.201–2)

RELIGION
AND THE RISE OF SANCTUARIES

The collapse of the Mycenaean palaces, with the consequent dispersal of cult apparatus and personnel, guaranteed some discontinuity during the Dark Age in both location and nature of the Olympian cults. While uninterrupted occupation from the Bronze Age appears likely at a number of Geometric religious sites, their continuous use for religious purposes is difficult to establish. At sites such as Kalapodhi, where the stratigraphic sequence is unbroken, the religious function in Late Helladic remains undemonstrated. More frequently met is the problem of demonstrating early Dark Age occupation at sites where both Mycenaean and Geometric cult activities are clear, such as at Delphi and Samos. This pattern appears throughout Greece but can be variously interpreted: were the eleventh- and tenth-century offerings simply of an ephemeral nature, leaving few traces in the archaeological record, or had a dislocated population abandoned its traditional sacred sites? Although excavations in Greece continue to fill in missing pieces, the pattern of discontinuity remains the norm.

The emergence of the Olympian cults together with the founding of great sanctuaries was one of the most important legacies of the Geometric period. From the eleventh to the eighth centuries all the major sanctuaries and many minor ones were founded or reoccupied. During this period these sacred sites, including the great Panhellenic foundations of Olympia and Delphi, bore little physical resemblance to the artistic and architectural centers they would become in later times. Most sanctuaries were simply open-air places of worship with an altar and no substantial architecture. With time and use the sanctuaries accumulated masses of bronze and pottery votive offerings, their spiritual atmosphere enhanced by the stark juxtaposition of gifts to the gods displayed in a powerful natural setting. Beginning in the eighth century at

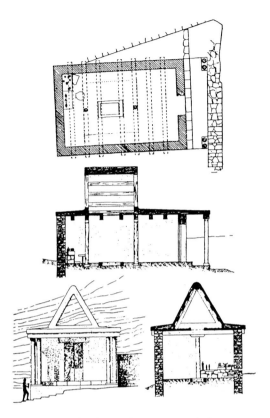

Fig. 19. Temple plan and reconstructed elevation of the temple of Apollo at Dreros. (Reproduced by permission of École Française d'Archéologie, Athens)

a few sites like Dreros and Samos, the early Iron Age saw the development of the temple into a freestanding unit housing a cult statue and votive offerings, with architectural forms as diverse as the cults that adopted the idea (Fig. 19). Traditional views that derived the origin of the Greek temple from the Mycenaean megaron or other native Helladic architecture are now undergoing revision by studies that emphasize the debt of the single-room naos within a temenos to North Syrian and Phoenician temples. The recent discovery of two successive Phoenician-plan temples founded ca. 925 B.C. at Kommos on Crete's southern coast gives new context to the early occurrence of tem-

ples at Dreros and Prinias whose bench-lined plans are paralleled in the Levant. Forms of worship developed along new patterns. Periodic religious festivals initiated the Olympic, Pythian, and other games, which included the performance of poetry. Perhaps most important to the developing Iron Age society, the great Panhellenic sanctuaries offered meeting places for Greeks from all cities, fostering a cultural unity that shaped their artistic, political, and literary, as well as religious, traditions.

The post-Mycenaean reconstitution of the Olympian cults appears to have been a piecemeal mixture of half-remembered official rituals and folk beliefs; the result was a complex and essentially new collection of old gods. These Iron Age cults emerged from the synthesis of Helladic tradition, Near Eastern influence, and responses to contemporary social needs. These diverse sources survived in the images of the deities and the gifts they received. Religious art in the Geometric period early developed an iconography for votive offering, particularly in small-scale sculpture, but was slow to depict the gods—a reluctance perhaps related to the scarcity of Mycenaean deity representations. It would be going too far to suggest that the first artistic depictions of the gods in Geometric times were influenced by Homer's memorable characterizations. Yet the urge to depict the gods may have arisen from the same need to formalize the Greek pantheon felt by Homer and Hesiod late in the period.

The sources for these first depictions are diverse and can be seen in a small number of bronze votive figurines. A male figure with arms outstretched (40) revives the Bronze Age pose signifying epiphanic appearance, which during the Dark Age continued to exist in Crete and Cyprus. In Minoan and Mycenaean art it characterized gods, in particular female deities. In Geo-metric sculpture it may have become a ges-ture of prayer, an enactment of the desired result of invoking the divine. Its reintroduc-tion into the Greek mainland probably came from Crete, along with the inspiration for bronze votive sculpture. A bronze divine couple, perhaps Zeus and Hera (41), demon-strates another source of models for divinity representations. The pair may have been patterned after a Syrian type of divine cou-ple (42) but appears rendered with charac-teristic Greek apparel.

The votive figurines follow the develop-ments of cults and the needs of worshipers: they are not a reliable guide to lost cult images of perishable materials, which must have existed during at least the latter stages of the Geometric period when the first temples were built. A Cretan terracotta votive tray (43) depicting a nature goddess with wild goats combines Near Eastern ele-ments and Minoan tradition. The narrow, rigid figure standing on a small base may embody some dim reflection of these lost statues.

The forms of worship changed considera-bly in the early Iron Age, as seen in both the cult paraphernalia and the subjects of votive offerings. A curious composite vase or kernos (44) from Cyprus bears multiple cups and an attached bull's head; the liba-tion was collected in the cups and poured out through the bull's mouth. This early example marks the important role of Cyprus in preserving Bronze Age religious traditions, as it links the Aegean and Cypri-ot kernoi of the Late Bronze Age with the multiple vessel adopted into certain Greek cults in the eighth century. Vessels of vari-ous types have been found in abundance at many sanctuaries and attest to the impor-tance of meals in religious ceremonies (45–46). These were often subsequently broken

so that no further use could desecrate them.

Votive offerings often referred to ritual and to celebration of the divine. A bronze Cretan male figure with arms clasped near his waist (47) and another male figure seat-ed with hands to his head (48) exemplify worshipers in poses of devotion. Aside from prayers, the most important element in Olympian worship was animal sacrifice. Sac-rificial victims may have been symbolized in small bronze figurines that were left to com-memorate a specific event. Four sheep con-nected on a plaque (49) and a small ram (50) depict favorite animals for sacrifice. A statuette of a man gently leading a ram (51), once attached to a rein guide, recalls the importance of the sacrificial animal's docile behavior in effecting a successful offering. Dancers on painted pottery sherds (52–53) and a tiny bronze flute-player (54) evoke the music and dances central to every festival at a Greek sanctuary.

Bronze figurines of animals may have referred to the personal concerns of the worshiper or have been meant simply to please. The small bronze horses (55, 92–97) are too ubiquitous in Greek sanctuaries to have reflected the aristocratic status of their donors; more likely the horse's aristocratic symbolism simply made the animal the gift of choice for the gods. Figurines of birds and deer (56–58) depict the frequent object of prayers by invoking the divine protection of animal life and hunter's luck. Other typi-cal offerings to the Olympians include mas-sive incised armbands (59) and ritual belts enhanced by a wealth of incised decoration (60). Such large items of personal adorn-ment, like the giant fibulae found at some sanctuaries, might even have graced the arm or robe of a wooden cult statue. Bronze was an important new medium for votive offerings on the Geometric Greek

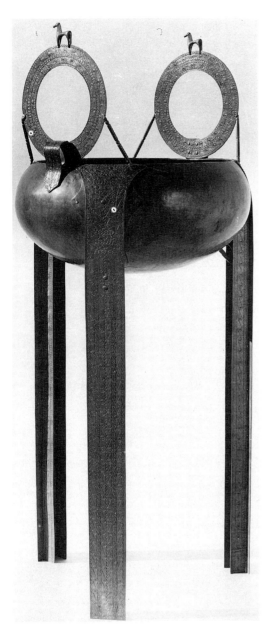

Fig. 20. Reconstruction of a bronze tripod from
Olympia. (Photo courtesy of Deutsches Archäologisches Institut, Athens, neg. 74/115)

mainland and illustrates another Iron Age
cult practice without Mycenaean Bronze
Age precedent. A striking phenomenon is
the mass dedication of bronze objects by
the hundreds and even thousands at many
sites, which accompanied the rediscovery of

connections to sources of copper and tin
during the Dark Age.

An event of profound importance for the
development and diffusion of early Greek
culture was the foundation of the Olympic
games. Traditionally established in 776 B.C.,
these games formalized the competitive
nature of Greek society. Their transformation from a small local religious festival to
an event of unprecedented Panhellenic
scope had profound consequences for later
generations. The most important prize
awarded to Olympic athletes was a bronze
tripod cauldron, which would have been
dedicated to Zeus and left in the sanctuary.
Tripods came to be made on enormous
scale, standing as tall as five feet (Fig. 20).
With roots in simple portable braziers and
cooking pots of Mycenaean households, various preserved examples trace the tripod's
diffusion from Greece to Cyprus through
the hands of Mycenaean refugees, and from
Cyprus back to the Iron Age Greek mainland. An eleventh-century terracotta tripod
vessel stand from Cyprus with painted
human figures in probable ritual scenes (61)
is modeled on an earlier bronze type that
had become a precious rarity by that time.
A Geometric Greek cast-bronze tripod
handle from Praisos on Crete (62) is close
in style to typical mainland tripods of the
eighth century. Like the drinking vessels
that were enlarged to mark aristocratic
graves, the tripod was a mundane domestic
object that Geometric artists monumentalized to suit a newly symbolic status. It
exemplifies the tendency of this Dark Age
culture to adapt its modest resources and
material traditions to the needs of a developing society with heroic aspirations.

S. L.

40 STANDING MAN

**Peloponnesian, Late Geometric,
750–700 B.C.**

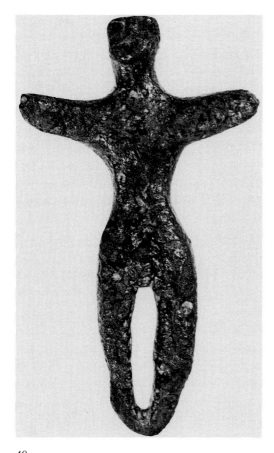

40

Height 0.061, width at arms 0.035, head
  diameter 0.001.
Bronze, mottled dark green patina; intact.
Museum of Art, Rhode Island School of
  Design, Providence, Gift of John Maxon
  (61.083).

The small figure stands rigid with its arms
outstretched to the sides from a short torso
and curving very slightly to the front. The
stocky neck rises into a flat-topped head with
narrow face; the eyes are rendered as shallow
depressions. The simple tubular body and
limbs lack articulated joints and modeled contours. A small phallus is roughly indicated in
a projecting lump. The feet are joined in a
rounded V.

The modest Providence figurine plays a role
in the complicated history of the gesture of
outstretched arms. Its great antiquity gives

this gesture the force of a sacred sign of divinity, designating a deity's sudden epiphany. Its
earlier Aegean career involved a slightly different pose; instead of the widespread arms of
the Providence bronze, Minoan goddesses
raised their forearms vertically with palms
opened flat. The gesture became especially
important in Late Minoan III when it enhanced the sacred presence of the terracotta
poppy and bird goddesses of Gazi and Karphi;
it continued in Subminoan and Protogeometric terracotta figures. Evidence is ambiguous
as to whether this was also a pose for mortal
prayer in Minoan iconography. Although a
scene on a gold ring shows a tiny deity hovering above a group of women whose arms
stretch up toward it, this pose never became
one of the traditional gestures of salutation
rendered in Minoan bronze votive figurines.
Only in the Protogeometric period does the
epiphany gesture make a sudden appearance
in Cretan bronze sculpture, at which time it
is no longer certain that all Cretan votive
bronzes represent worshipers and not gods.
Unlike the continuity exhibited in Crete, in
Greece the Mycenaean employment of this
gesture in a variety of handmade and wheelmade terracotta figurines, with examples
known from Mycenae, Tiryns, and Aegina,
seems to cease after about 1200 B.C.

By the seventh century the gesture of
upraised arms, although not common, is again
fully integrated into Greek religious iconography where examples reveal that it signifies
divinity. The reintroduction of the gesture
into Greece, however, still poses questions.
Early depictions of this pose in Iron Age
Greece occur in a number of simple terracotta
and bronze figurines at Olympia, among which
the Providence figure stylistically and thematically belongs. At least two different series of
these male figures are represented, one that
includes upraised arms and a pointed cap or
helmet, and another that depicts the figures in
a cruder style with arms simply outstretched.
The Providence bronze is related to the latter
group.

Karageorghis has demonstrated that during

the Dark Age the pose was maintained for
female terracottas in Cyprus, where it had
been introduced from Crete in the early eleventh century. His conclusions find the pose
reintroduced into Greece by Cypriot influence through wheelmade figures in Samos
and Rhodes. There are, however, earlier
instances of the gesture in Geometric Greece.
A remarkable figure painted on an Argive jug
standing with arms raised at the elbows, fingers outstretched to show open palms, is
dated to the early eighth century. In view of
the earlier reappearance of the gesture in
small votive figurines at Olympia that demonstrate affinities with bronze Cretan figures,
primacy must be given to Crete as a source
for the pose. The possible role of Near Eastern art further complicates the picture. A
bronze matrix from Tell Halaf attests to the
epiphany gesture in Syria; significantly, the
figure in this position is male.

As in the Bronze Age evidence, it is not
always clear whether a figure in this pose is
mortal or divine. It is the most common attitude for prayer in the epic poems, as in *Iliad*
15.368–71 when Nestor and the Achaeans
pray: "and to all of the gods, uplifting their
hands each man of them cried out his prayers
in a great voice, and beyond others Gerenian
Nestor, the Achaians' watcher, prayed, reaching out both arms to the starry heavens."
Without any attributes but his standard Geometric nudity, the Providence bronze could
represent either an early depiction of Olympian Zeus or his fervent worshiper. Mitten has
discussed the difficulty of dating these stylistically unsophisticated figures. Without strati-
graphical evidence to support an earlier date,
they are safely set into the Late Geometric
period, when the popularity of bronze figurine dedication at Olympia was at its greatest.

PUBLISHED
Mitten, *Classical Bronzes* 22–23, no. 5.

NOTES
On the epiphany pose: S. Alexiou, "He
    Minoike Thea meth'Upsomenon Cheiron"

CretChron 12 (1958) 179–299; R. V. Nicholls,
    "Greek Votive Statuettes and Religious Con-
    tinuity, c. 1200–700 B.C." in *Auckland Classi-
    cal Essays to E. M. Blaiklock* (Auckland 1970)
    1–37, esp. 4–7, 17–18, 21–22; V. Karageorgh-
    is, "The Goddess with Uplifted Arms in
    Cyprus" *Scripta Minora* (1977–1978) 5–45.
7th c. examples of the pose: terracotta plaque
    from the Athenian Agora, Nicholls, "Greek
    Votive Statuettes" pl. 4c; Boeotian amphora,
    Hampe, *Frühe griechische Sagenbilder in
    Böotien* pl. 17 lower; relief pithos from
    Thebes, K. Schefold, *Frühgriechische Sagen-
    bilder* (Munich 1964) pl. 12.
Painted goddess on Argive jug: H. Palaeolo-
    gou, "Un vase géométrique figuratif d'Ar-
    gos" *Études Argiennes* (BCH Suppl. VI
    1980) 75–84.
Matrix from Tell Halaf: M. von Oppenheim,
    Tell Halaf IV (Berlin 1962) pl. 129, no.
    84a–b.
Figures with outstretched arms from Olympia:
    E. Kunze, "Zeusbilder in Olympia" *AuA* 2
    (1946) 95–104; A. Furtwängler, *Die Bronzen.
    Olympia Ergebnisse* IV (Berlin 1890) nos.
    234–38, 240, 241, 261; E. Kunze, *OlBer* VII
    (Berlin 1961) 138–41; E. Kunze, "Kleinplas-
    tik aus Bronze" *OlBer* VIII (Berlin 1967)
    213–24; Schweitzer, *Greek Geometric Art*
    figs. 117–23; W.-D. Heilmeyer, *Die Frühe
    Olympische Tonfiguren* (OlForsch VII,
    Berlin 1972) 32–34, nos. 201–2, 204, pls.
    26–30.

S. L.

41 PAIR OF DEITIES

**Possibly Cretan, Late Geometric, 750–700
B.C.**
Height 0.08.
**Bronze, dark green patina; figures broken at
the legs and mended.**
**Museum of Fine Arts, Boston, Gift of
Leslie Hastings, Esq. (63.2755). Acquired
in the nineteenth century by the Hastings
family.**
See Plate 2.

Sharing a small base, the divine couple

41

stand side by side, leaning slightly backward with their inner arms across each other's backs in a pose both companionable and powerful. The man wears a broad belt and a helmet that curves back in a point; his outer arm is outstretched, the serrated palm open. His counterpart wears a round cap or polos with a brim marked by a groove; her right hand clasps her pellet breast from below. Both faces are sketched with a simple pinched profile and indented mouths and eyes. Their lower bodies continue the same abstract form, as cylindrical bars flattened at the bottom where they are joined on an oblong base.

This remarkable statuette hints at the complexities surrounding the origins of Greek bronze sculpture. Since its initial publication

by Palmer it has sometimes affectionately, sometimes seriously, been called "Zeus and Hera," an understandable tendency since they alone of the Olympian gods compose a regular "consort" pair in the early Greek artistic repertoire. As a joined male and female pair in bronze, the Boston statuette is unique in Geometric art, although a late seventh-century wood sculpture of Zeus (securely identified by his eagle) with Hera from the Samian Heraion provides a close iconographic parallel and supports the identification of both these *hieros gamos* couples as the head Olympians.

Perhaps because of this iconography the Boston bronze has always been assumed to originate in Olympia or at least the Peloponnese, yet the pair has no close stylistic relatives there. Despite their unique style—the rodlike bodies, vertically pinched faces, and irregular base form—they look comfortably at home in eighth-century Greece. The man's backward-curving headgear is worn by numerous Geometric bronze figures, looking sometimes like a crested helmet and sometimes, as here, like a floppy felt cap, although the figure's abstract style does not permit such a literal interpretation. His belt, horizontally divided by two grooves, is also standard gear among Geometric figurines, particularly those who wear a back-curving helmet. His outflung arm recalls the "epiphany" gesture of the early male bronze series at Olympia and one in particular from the Athena Chalkioikos sanctuary at Sparta. The appliquéd breasts of his companion resemble those of Cretan Geometric figurines. Her rounded cap is not precisely matched on any other Geometric bronzes but must be a variation of the polos. This millinery attribute, her gesture to her breast, and his arm pose all signify that the couple are divine.

Although the work is thus demonstrably Geometric Greek, its similarity to Levantine bronze deity pairs has been noted and some sort of remote influence commonly assumed, much as a North Syrian Astarte type stands behind the famous ivory female figurines from a Dipylon grave and the Near Eastern "smiting

god" figurines are vaguely ancestral to the
spearbearers of Geometric art. The difficulty
for the Boston pair is that the Near Eastern
joined bronzes that apparently inspired it are
as much as a millennium too early and,
unlike the "smiting gods," have not been
found outside their homelands. A near parallel
to the Boston bronze is a North Syrian joined
pair in the Ashmolean Museum of Middle
Bronze Age I–IIA date. Perhaps helping to
close this mysterious chronological gap is a
deity pair in the Louvre from Cyprus, plausibly dated to the twelfth century.

Crete, rather than Olympia, might have
been the original home of the Boston couple.
A bronze figurine in Berlin dated to Protogeometric provides a good parallel with its similarly rodlike body. Although its provenance is
not secure, its traditional attribution to Crete
reasonably arises from its affinities with other
Cretan Protogeometric bronzes. It is also
indisputably based on a North Syrian type. A
late Geometric bronze pair of male figurines
cast side by side on a rectangular base from
Kato Syme Viannou was likely influenced by
the Syrian pairs, some of which comprise two
male figures; there is no mainland parallel for
such pairs of Geometric figures, either male
or female. The presence of North Syrian
metalsmiths working on Crete in the ninth
century is attested to by the strong artistic
influence of that culture in bronze shields
and related objects. It therefore comes as no
surprise to find their influence shaping the
design of certain types of local votive
figurines.

If the Berlin figurine and other orientalizing Cretan bronzes were made for the private
use of immigrant Syrians, the same cannot be
true of the Boston couple with their Greek
accoutrements. The image of a (divine?) male
figure and his consort was firmly entrenched
in Cretan art by the eighth century, but not
on the Greek mainland until the seventh. A
Late Geometric funerary tripod pithos from
Knossos bears a *hieros gamos* scene: she wears
a polos and veil(?), he a curving pointed helmet. A terracotta couple from the Patsos

Cave, reported by Sir Arthur Evans, stand
with their arms around each other's shoulders
in a pose reminiscent of the twelfth-century
Cypriot bronze in the Louvre. The little Boston sculpture, perhaps indeed representing
Zeus and Hera, may thus attest to the adaptation of an old Bronze Age formula of a god
with his divine consort to the needs of a
developing religious iconography in the Iron
Age Aegean.

PUBLISHED

H. Palmer, *BMFA* 56 (1958) 64–68, figs. 1–3.
C. C. Vermeule, *MFA Annual Report* 1958,
    33.
FA 13 (1958) 87, no. 1370.
Boardman, *The Cretan Collection in Oxford*
    78 n. 2.
C. C. Vermeule, *MFA Annual Report* 1963, 37.
Himmelmann-Wildschütz, *Bemerkungen zur
    geometrischen Plastik* 18 n. 3.
Klearchos 29–32 (1966) 221.
Mitten, "The Earliest Greek Sculptures in the
    Museum" 11–12, fig. 11.
AJA 74 (1970) 108.
Comstock and Vermeule, *Greek, Etruscan and
    Roman Bronzes in the Museum of Fine
    Arts, Boston* 4, no. 2.
Vermeule, *Götterkult*, pl. VIIId.
C. Rolley, review of Comstock and Vermeule,
    AJA 78 (1974) 98–99 at 99.
Fittschen, *Untersuchungen zum Beginn der
    Sagendarstellungen* 133 no. GP1.
M. B. Comstock and C. C. Vermeule, *Sculp-
    ture in Stone: The Greek, Roman, and
    Etruscan Collections of the Museum of Fine
    Arts* (Boston 1976) 117.
Verlinden, *Les statuettes anthropomorphes cré-
    toises* 168.
A. Kossatz-Deissmann, "Hera" *LIMC* IV
    (1988) 1, p. 683 no. 197.
C. Reinsberg, *Ehe, Hetärentum und Knaben-
    liebe im antiken Griechenland* (Munich
    1989) 25–26, fig. 2.

NOTES

Wooden Zeus and Hera from Samos:
    P. Demargne, *Aegean Art: The Origins of
    Greek Art* (London 1964) fig. 498.

42

On headgear: Rolley, *Monuments figurés, les statuettes de bronze* 34.

On Near Eastern joined figurines: Negbi, *Canaanite Gods in Metal* 4–7; Seeden, *The Standing Armed Figurines in the Levant* 16–17.

Ashmolean bronze 1912.973: Negbi, *Canaanite Gods in Metal* pl. 4, no. 9; Seeden, *Standing Armed Figurines* pl. 10 no. 32; Moorey and Fleming, "Problems in the Study of the Anthropomorphic Metal Statuary" 83 no. 4 and pl. XXI, 4.

Cypriot version: Courtois, *RDAC* (1971) pl. VII; Negbi, *Canaanite Gods in Metal* pl. 4 no. 11 (printed backward), with an excessively early date based on typology rather than style.

Cretan Protogeometric bronze figure, Berlin 8071: Naumann, *Subminoische und protogeometrische Bronzeplastik* pl. 27, P19; Verlinden, *Les statuettes anthropomorphes crétoises* pl. 81 no. 203a.

Male pair from Kato Syme Viannou: A. Lembessi, "A Sanctuary of Hermes and Aphrodite in Crete" *Expedition* 18, 3 (1976) 2–13 at 4, fig. 4.

For North Syrian artisans in Crete: Dunbabin, *The Greeks and Their Eastern Neighbors* 36–37; Boardman, *The Greeks Overseas* 56–60; Coldstream, *Geometric Greece* 100.

On deity pairs in early Greek art: Fittschen, *Untersuchungen zum Beginn der Sagensdarstellungen* 132–42.

For the Knossosian pithos: *BSA* 29 (1927–1928) 240 no. 38, pl. 11, figs. 10, 11, pls. 12, 13; Beyer, *Die Tempel von Dreros und Prinias* A with bibliography and new reconstruction, cat. 48, pl. 34, 1.

For terracotta couple from the Patsos Cave: Boardman, *The Cretan Collection in Oxford* 77 fig. 34c, suggests a LMIII date.

S. L.

42 PAIR OF DEITIES

Levantine, Early Iron Age, 1000–700 B.C.
Height 0.071.
Bronze; intact.
Arthur M. Sackler Museum, Harvard University Art Museums, Louise M. Bates and George E. Bates Collection (1992.256.61).

The pair share a single base, standing with their outer arms extended forward and their inner arms laid across each other's backs with hands on shoulders. By their tubular body construction and short legs they seem to wear robes; a thick belt around each waist is apparent on the back. Little distinguishes one from the other except the headgear of the left figure, which is slightly more conical. Their heads are long with applied pellet noses and eyes; their mouths are indented and their ears crudely modeled.

The Harvard bronze has stylistic affinities with the faces and generally rodlike body construction of two such pairs in the Ashmolean Museum dated Middle Bronze Age I–IIA. Among the joined figurine pairs from the

Levantine coast, the sex is often not clearly indicated, but when it is the couple are usually a male and a female. Sometimes the male is taller; sometimes he wears a pointed headdress in contrast with his consort's bare head or rounded cap. More fully detailed versions of the Middle Bronze Age depict the male armed with a dagger or other weapon. Negbi has identified these couples as a Syrian war god and his consort, a goddess of fertility, but this broad identification has been challenged by Moorey, who observed that they have no clear divine attributes and may well represent worshipers.

Although the theory is clearly not without problems, it is likely that similar paired figurines served as the model for the bronze couple in Boston, **41**. The same motif appears in Italic bronzes and terracottas in the eighth century and perhaps attests to a new version of the old image traveling under Phoenician passport. A much-discussed Egyptianizing Phoenician bronze deity pair in the Louvre has recently been redated from the fourteenth or thirteenth century to the eighth to fourth centuries on the basis of the chariot they stand in. Recent research has only begun to deal with the identification of Phoenician bronze figurines.

UNPUBLISHED

NOTES

For the type: Negbi, *Canaanite Gods in Metal* 4–7, esp. pl. 4, nos. 9, 10; Seeden, *The Standing Armed Figurines in the Levant* 16–17; Moorey and Fleming, "Problems in the Study of the Anthropomorphic Metal Statuary" 69, pl. XXI, 4 and 5; example in H. Bossert, *Altsyrien* (Tübingen 1951) pl. 158 center.

For Italic examples: *Prima Italia* (Rome 1981) 30 no. 3, 31 no. 4; *Cronache di Archeologia e Storia dell'Arte dell'Università di Catania* 7 (1968) 16–17, 72–73; sale catalogue, Sotheby's (New York), December 2, 1988, no. 259.

On Phoenician bronzes and the Louvre chariot group: M. A. Littauer and J. H. Crou-

wel, "A Bronze Chariot Group from the Levant in Paris" *Levant* 8 (1976) 71–81; Moorey and Fleming, "Problems in the Study of the Anthropomorphic Metal Statuary" 75–76; A. Spycket, *La statuaire du Proche-Orient ancien* (Leiden 1981) 428–29.

S. L.

43 TRAY WITH RELIEF DECORATION

Cretan, Late Geometric, ca. 750 B.C.
Diameter 0.25, height 0.035.
Ceramic; cracked at upper edge; restored lower left area includes part of animal, small section of skirt, and corner of base.
University of Missouri–Columbia, Museum of Art and Archaeology (73.212).

The tray is circular with convex profile, constricted rim, and two horizontal handles. Two holes pierce the rim directly above the figure. The surface is covered in dark brown slip. Moldmade relief decoration features a standing female figure facing left in a long decorated robe and tall polos, with narrow chevron-patterned wings rising from her shoulders. Her thin arms project from the garment and hang against her sides. She stands on a small rectangular base. Her feet are not visible. Along either side appears a kneeling agrimi goat with head turned back. Four large flowers faintly visible in cream-colored slip on the background surround the figure, while two crossed circles frame her head. The robe is decorated with an X on the bodice crossing between two dots, probably breasts; a central vertical panel of dotted tangent circles adorns the skirt.

With roots in the Minoan past, this female figure demonstrates an important revival of the Bronze Age *potnia theron*, or "Mistress of Animals," in the early Iron Age. Accompanied by animals and vegetation, she symbolizes divine control over wild nature. The Bronze Age *potnia* took different guises as revealed in various accompanying animals. Specifically, this figure with agrimia accords with Minoan representations that have been interpreted as "the Mistress of Wild Goats," a goddess per-

43

haps worshiped on mountaintop shrines. Goat
horns found in the shrines at Vrokastro and
Dreros reflect the importance of the goat in
Cretan cult. The winged and polos-clad Mistress of Animals seen here is a short-lived
phenomenon, arriving into Cretan art under
oriental influence in the ninth century, as
seen especially on Knossos pithos T.107.114,
and gone by the early seventh century, as
shown by the wingless goddess on a large burial pithos from Arkades. Although it is impos-

sible to name the Minoan *potnia theron,* or
even to determine whether she is one or
many, this Geometric goddess may be Artemis, protector of the wild animal world.

The Missouri figure is thoroughly Cretan
and owes nothing to mainland Geometric
style or iconography, which was slow to depict
deities, particularly in vase painting. The goddess's attire, from the rectangular skirt with
central decorative panel to the shawl-like
outer garment around her torso and her tall

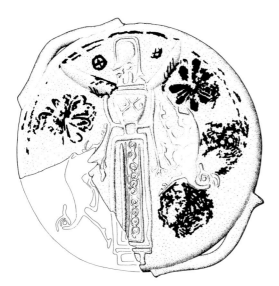

Fig. 21. Cretan votive tray, Museum of Art and Archaeology, University of Missouri–Columbia (43). (Drawing by John Huffstot)

polos, is the canonical Cretan fashion of the early Iron Age. Best known in the Late Geometric female sphyrelata from Dreros and in Daedalic figures such as the limestone Auxerre statuette, this clothing actually dates back to the Protogeometric period, as the Knossos pithos with a goddess on a wheeled platform and the Fortetsa pithos 1440 with the so-called snake goddess reveal.

The tray is difficult to date. In style, iconography, and composition its figure has much in common with the goddesses of the Protogeometric B pithoi and the female figures on an Early Geometric bronze belt from Fortetsa. The rosettes with arcaded outlines that give the tray an "orientalizing" look actually begin in Early Geometric. The base on which the goddess stands and her angular profile are paralleled on a Late Geometric pithos from Fortetsa on which a male and female figure face each other. A date in the mid-eighth century may not be far off.

The moldmade figural decoration makes this vessel unique and may reflect the influence of the important local Knossian tradition of figured metalwork. Similar ceramic trays with reflex handles occur in pairs at Fortetsa

from Protogeometric B to Late Geometric phases. The Fortetsa trays all come from grave contexts, but they may be related to a much broader class of offering trays used in sanctuary contexts, including the Idaean Cave and the Samian Heraion. The Missouri tray may originally have been a votive offering, filled with fruit or suspended in a shrine in honor of the goddess.

PUBLISHED
Apollo 93 (March 1971) 74 (ill.).
E. Bielefeld, *Kunstwerke der Antike*, Galerie für Griechische, Römische und Byzantinische Kunst (Frankfurt 1972) no. 1.
"Acquisitions 1973" *Muse* 8 (1974) 9.
Beyer, *Die Tempel von Dreros und Prinias* A 53, 57, 157–59 no. 61, pls. 38, 1 and 39, 1.
N. Reed, "A Daedalic Sampler" *Muse* 15 (1981) 60–62, figs. 4, 5.
Illustrated Museum Handbook (Columbia MO 1982) 20, no. 48.

NOTES
For the shape: trays at Fortetsa, Brock, *Fortetsa* 45 no. 422, 47 no. 446, 165, pl. 148 nos. 422, 446 esp.; dated by Coldstream, *Greek Geometric Pottery* 243. Fortetsa tray inv. 446, possibly datable to Middle Geometric, is nearly identical to the Missouri tray in size and profile.
For *potnia theron*: Spartz, *Das Wappenbild des Herrn und Herrin der Tiere*; Nilsson, *The Minoan-Mycenaean Religion* 352–60, 507; C. R. Long, *The Ayia Triadha Sarcophagus* (SIMA XLI, Göteborg 1974) 55–57 for the Goddess of Wild Goats; B. C. Dietrich, "Some Light from the East on Cretan Cult Practice" *Historia* 16 (1967) 385–413, esp. 403. Compare a Cypriot goddess of goats, J. M. Webb, "A Cypriote Caprid Goddess?" *RDAC* (1988) pt. 1, 275–79.
Protogeometric pithos from Fortetsa Tomb P: Brock, *Fortetsa* 125–26 no. 1440, pls. 77i–ii, 163; Coldstream, *Greek Geometric Pottery* pl. 51g.
Protogeometric cremation pithos from Knossos, T.107.114: J. N. Coldstream, "A Protogeome-

44

tric Nature Goddess from Knossos" *BICS* 31 (1984) 93–103; W. Burkert, "Katagogia-Anagogia and the Goddess of Knossos" in *Early Greek Cult Practice* 81–87.

Geometric pithos from Fortetsa with deity pair, Herakleion Museum inv. 6391: H. Payne, "Early Greek Vases from Knossos" *BSA* 29 (1927–1928) 240 no. 38, pl. 11, 10–11, 12–13; reconstruction, Beyer, *Die Tempel von Dreros und Prinias* A pl. 34, 1.

Bronze belt from Fortetsa Tomb P with three figures: Brock, *Fortetsa* 134–35 no. 1568, pl. 168; Beyer, *Die Tempel von Dreros und Prinias* A pl. 46, 1.

7th c. "Mistress of Animals" on a pithos from Arkades: *ASAtene* 10–12 (1927–1929) 330 fig. 431; Beyer, *Die Tempel von Dreros und Prinias* A pl. 38, 2.

Votive trays: Idaean cave, I. Sakellarakis, "Some Geometric and Archaic Votives from the Idaian Cave" in *Early Greek Cult Practice* 173–92 at 191 figs. 32–34; Samian Heraion, Coldstream, *Geometric Greece* fig. 82b; *BSA* 31 (1930–1931) 29 n. 4; K. Friis Johansen, "Exochi, ein frührhodisches Gräberfeld" *ActaArch* 28 (1957) 1–192 at 139–42.

S. L.

44 KERNOS

Cypriot, Cypro-Geometric I, 1050–950 B.C.
Height 0.113.
Ceramic; cups broken off and reattached; missing part of bull's right horn.
The Metropolitan Museum of Art, The Cesnola Collection, purchased by subscription, 1874–1876 (74.51.659).

The White-Painted I annular vase has three vessels and an animal protome attached at the four quadrants; a basket handle rises from behind the head to the opposite side. The bull's head is painted white with pierced muzzle, eyes, and horns articulated in black and a decorative lozenge on its forehead. Around the ring, which is painted solid except for the reserved top, sit three one-handled cups glazed black inside and decorated with a thin band outside the lip and a wavy band on the body. The stemmed feet and area of attachment of cups to ring are also covered in black. The handle is ornamented with alternating horizontal bands and dotted lozenge chains and a bisected vertical panel of crosshatching.

Cult vessels of this type were created for the performance of ritual libations in such a way that a liquid poured into the attached cups entered the hollow ring and could be poured out through the bull's mouth. Kernoi first appeared simultaneously in Cyprus and Palestine in the Early Bronze Age, although many scholars believe they originated in Cyprus. Based on a frequently cited ring kernos in the Museum of Fine Arts, Boston, earlier scholarship on the type assumed the Mycenaeans adopted the vessel from the Cypriots and added the bull protome, which subsequently became standard in Cypriot kernoi. The Boston vessel has recently been attributed to Cyprus rather than Mycenaean Greece, however, leaving only one example from Mycenae of certain Greek provenance. The importance of the kernos in Cypriot and Philistine cults is evidenced by its continued production throughout the twelfth and eleventh centuries in both areas. In Cyprus kernoi were manufactured without interruption into the Geometric period.

While kernoi are found at Philistine sites primarily in settlements, usually in cult contexts, in Cyprus they occur in tombs. The embellishment of the ring with bull and goat protomes, miniature cups, pomegranates, and birds adapted the cult object to funerary use. The fertility symbolism of these elements found the vessel a niche in Greek sanctuaries in the eighth century, probably arriving via Cypriot influence first on Samos where the earliest examples appear in the third quarter of that century. In Geometric mainland sanctuaries they acquire a new significance in the cults of certain goddesses, particularly Hera and Demeter. Examples of ring kernoi from the Samian Heraion, Eleusis, and Perachora support a variety of protomes and miniature vessels.

The Metropolitan ring kernos inherits the bull's head protome of the Late Cypriot III kernoi. Its narrow muzzle corresponds with a slightly later example from Lapithos Tomb 401 rather than the flaring trumpet muzzle that became increasingly common. The simple cups, unusual among Cypriot kernoi, which employed miniature amphorae as the standard vessel attachments, support its early date. Their high feet were replaced by low or flat bases after the mid-tenth century. The monochrome treatment of the ring is paralleled in a Cypriot Protogeometric kernos from Lapithos Tomb P.74.

PUBLISHED

Myres, *Handbook of the Cesnola Collection* 68 no. 522, ill.

H. Payne, *Necrocorinthia* (Oxford 1931) 296.

Demetriou, *Cypro-Aegean Relations in the Early Iron Age* 41, 105 nn. 13, 14 (LCIII date).

RDAC (1990) 92.

NOTES

Similar kernoi and general discussions: A. Pieridou, *O Protogeometrikos Rythmos en Kypro* (Athens 1973) pl. 24; A. Pieridou, "Kypriaka Teletourgika Angleia" *RDAC* (1971) 18–26; Gjerstad, *The Cypro-Geometric, Cypro-Archaic and Cypro-Classical Periods* fig. 15, 2; Demetriou, *Cypro-Aegean Relations in the Early Iron Age* 41–42.

Philistine kernoi: H. G. May, *The Material Remains of the Megiddo Cult* (Chicago 1935) 17–18, pl. XVI; Dothan, *The Philistines and Their Material Culture* 222–24.

45

8th and 7th c. kernoi from Samos: *Samos* V
(1968) pl. 47, 48:281; *AM* 76 (1961) Beil. 24–
34; from Eleusis: *AM* 23 (1898) 304.

Parallels for cups: Karageorghis, *Palaepaphos-
Skales* pl. XXIX, White-Painted I cups from
Tomb 44.

Kernoi from Lapithos Tombs 401 and P.74:
Pieridou, "Kypriaka Teletourgika Angleia"
no. 20, pl. XI, 1–2, and no. 16, pl. X, 2.

S. L.

45 SKYPHOS

Attic, Late Geometric, ca. 750–735 B.C.
Height 0.065, maximum diameter 0.143.
Pottery; complete, mended from several
fragments.
University of Missouri–Columbia, Museum
of Art and Archaeology (60.23).

The broad low cup has a short, slightly
everted rim, a flat base, and two handles set
at a sharp angle. The central zone is reserved
with a single horizontal line above and two
below. The central panel features a serpent
bordered by dots with zigzags in its curves.
Vertical strokes line the handles.

Although the panel with serpent is not
uncommon on Attic skyphoi with high vertical rims and horizontal ribbon handles, the
short rim and round handles of this example
point to an earlier date. A similar shape is

found in a skyphos from Kerameikos Grave
50, dated transitional Late Geometric Ia–Ib,
ca. 750.

Skyphoi decorated with serpents have been
found in both sanctuaries and graves, but the
image is usually associated with funerary contexts. The dotted serpent is an innovation of
Attic Late Geometric I painters, and was
quickly adopted by major workshops as well as
by painters outside the classical tradition. Perhaps not coincidentally, plastic snakes on the
handles of funerary amphorae begin at the
same time, around 750. The association of
this chthonic symbol with the dead reaches
back into the Bronze Age and persists in the
historical period; however, its continuity
through the Dark Age in Greece cannot yet
be demonstrated (see also **20**).

The skyphos is the standard Greek drinking
cup from Protogeometric to Hellenistic times.
The very high proportion of skyphoi and
other vessels appropriate for drinking found in
Geometric sanctuaries has raised much discussion about the importance of drinking rituals
in religious activity. Yet this high proportion is
true of all known Geometric shapes. The
scarcity of plates and low dishes in this period
suggests that skyphoi and other cups were
used for eating as well as drinking.

UNPUBLISHED

NOTES

For similar decoration: M. K. Langdon, *A Sanctuary of Zeus on Mount Hymettos* 57, skyphos H 295 cat. 212, pl. 18, here dated MGII; skyphos in Agora grave D16:3, *Hesperia* 19 (1950) pl. 104b, dated by Young to the late 8th c., by Coldstream to LGIIa; skyphos with high rim and ribbon handles, *JdI* 14 (1899) 215 fig. 100; *CVA* Sweden 3, Göteborg, Public Collections 53, pl. 17.1 (GA 1648) and pl. 17.2 (GA 1649).

For similar shape: skyphos 1301 from Kerameikos Gr. 50, Kübler, *Die Nekropole des 10. bis 8. Jahrhunderts* pl. 97, dated second quarter of 8th c.; dated by Coldstream, *Greek Geometric Pottery* 46.

On the snake motif: Young, *Late Geometric Graves and a Seventh Century Well in the Agora* 217; Coldstream, *Greek Geometric Pottery* 36.

Attic or Atticizing skyphos with similar decoration: *ClRh* III (1928) 133, fig. 125.

S. L.

46 TANKARD

Attic, Late Geometric Ib–IIa, 750–725 B.C.
Height 0.176, mouth diameter 0.10.
Ceramic; intact, some surface wear.
Yale University Art Gallery, Gift of Rebecca Darlington Stoddard, 1913 (1913.55).

The high-handled tankard is, in shape and decorative scheme, closely related to the Missouri tankard (**34**). Its solid black lower body creates a visually stable base corresponding to the thickened lower wall and bottom of the vessel. To avoid a harsh contrast between the decorative zone and the solid one, the artist provides a transition of fine banding. The decorative patterns begin at the handle level with a row of false spirals, above which are a blind lozenge chain and more thin bands. The neck zone features three metopes separated by vertical chevrons. On the sides the panels enclose a long-legged marsh bird surrounded by four dot rosettes. Opposite the handle, the central metope has as an ornamental motif a fringed circle surrounding a false-spiral ring.

This latter motif began in Late Geometric I when the metope system was adopted by a number of workshops and artists were presented with the problem of finding motifs suitable for framing. They invented some new ornaments, like the quatrefoil, and used existing repetitive elements singly, like the bird. Even more revealing of the conservative nature of Geometric tradition, artists adapted continuous forms, in this case the false-spiral chain, to the square field. The resemblance of this circular ornament to a sunburst probably did not escape the artist's eye, and it is often used in proximity to birds, as on this tankard.

Its use as a grave gift was not the exclusive context for this type of drinking vessel. Excavated examples occur in religious settings as well, as at the sanctuary of Zeus on Mount Hymettus, where similar tankards are among the most common vessel types found in the dump of old votive offerings that were periodically cleared off the altar.

The long-necked water bird is a favorite Geometric ornament whose application to pottery varies from the purely decorative to the symbolic. It is particularly popular on drinking vessels, perhaps because of the bird's connection with water and moisture. This connection carries religious content as well. As personification of water and hence fertility, the water bird is a frequent attribute of female deities, making a regular appearance as a bronze votive offering (**58**) and as a decorative motif on other votive objects.

PUBLISHED

Baur, *Catalogue of the R. D. Stoddard Collection* 49 no. 55, fig. 11.

Matheson Burke and Pollitt, *Greek Vases at Yale* 10 no. 10.

NOTES

For tankards in general, see notes under **34**.

Similar tankards: *JdI* 14 (1899) 209 fig. 81; *AM* 89 (1974) pl. 6, no. 7; M. K. Langdon, *A Sanctuary of Zeus on Mount Hymettos* pl. 21 no. 247.

46

On the fringed false-spiral circle: Davison, *Attic Geometric Workshops* 15 fig. B14; Coldstream, *Greek Geometric Pottery* 50.

On the significance of water birds: C. A. Christou, *Potnia Theron* (Thessaloniki 1969) 69; E. Bevan, "Water-Birds and the Olympian Gods" *BSA* 84 (1989) 163–69.

S. L.

47 MALE FIGURINE

Cretan, Late Geometric, ca. 700 B.C.
Height 0.082.
Bronze, dark brown patina; intact.
University of Missouri–Columbia, Museum of Art and Archaeology, Gift of Mr. J. Lionberger Davis (69.950).

Wearing a simple belt and beretlike cap, the nude male figure stands taut with knees flexed, arms clasped to his sides with elbows bent and hands curled in fists in front of him. His large head is strongly defined. A groove sets off the cap above large circular ears. Large hollow eyes and a broad incised mouth dominate the square face; a small, pointed nose and lightly modeled cheekbones further detail the face. The body reveals much less surface articulation. The flat torso tapers from square shoulders to narrow waist. Buttocks, thighs, and phallus are briefly and vaguely rendered. Lower legs receive more detailed treatment, the calves swelling naturally to protruding anklebones and flat feet with notched toes. Despite uneven execution, the figure's overall impact is energetic and surprisingly naturalistic.

The Missouri bronze is best understood as part of a Cretan tradition of bronze votives representing worshipers that stretched without interruption from the beginning of the second millennium to the seventh century B.C. The style and proportions of these figures changed by the end of the new palatial period, reflecting the loss of the Minoan naturalistic canon. The Missouri figure's proportionately large head and ears, his hollowed eyes, and his square jaw are typical of the early Iron Age,

as are several other features. Very rare in Bronze Age art, his nudity is a hallmark of Protogeometric and Geometric sculpture on both Crete and the Greek mainland. The beretlike cap is a sure guide to the figure's Geometric date and Cretan origin. Appearing first on such Cretan Protogeometric bronzes as a male figurine excavated at Kato Syme, and continuing on belted figures through the Geometric period, this particular headgear is unknown on the Greek mainland. It may have distinguished the identity or status of the wearer in some way.

Despite these new elements, the Missouri votary's pose connects him to the age-old traditions of worship on Crete. Although the flexed-knee stance is yet another Iron Age innovation common to Geometric period sculpture everywhere, the arm gestures of post-Minoan votive figurines undergo not so much an outright change as a slow erosion of the former precision and exuberance of the Minoan worshipers. The holding of both fists clenched before the chest is a pose long known in Minoan art, denoting a gesture of worship or reverent salutation alternate to the more standard fist on the brow. From Protogeometric through Geometric and into the Daedalic style this gesture persists with increasing vagueness as the Minoan ritual heritage breaks up under the pressure of Iron Age changes.

As a votive offering, this small bronze may have been given to a deity in one of several different contexts. The standard types of sacred places in Crete—open-air, cave, and bench shrines, the latter evolving into the earliest Cretan temples—continued to attract bronze human votive figurines into Geometric times. In such settings figurines of bronze and terracotta have been found in situ on altars and benches or tucked among rocks in caves. The Missouri bronze plays a modest but not insignificant role in reflecting the changes in Cretan religion in the early Iron Age. Archaeological evidence from all over Crete indicates a gradual shift of emphasis in the post-palatial age from the old Minoan

47   47

goddesses to the male and female deities worshiped in Greece. With its emphatically Iron Age appearance and only the lingering trace of traditional Minoan gesture, the Missouri worshiper addresses the new era in Cretan religion.

PUBLISHED
S. Langdon, "A Votive Figurine from Early Crete" *Muse* 25 (1991) 21–29.

NOTES
For similar figurines: Naumann, *Subminoische und protogeometrische Bronzeplastik,* from Patsos Cave, Heraklion Inv. 208 pl. 31, P26; Verlinden, *Les statuettes anthropomorphes crétoises* British Museum Inv. 1930.6–17.1 pl. 83, 211; Boardman, *The Cretan Collection in Oxford* 120–21 from Agiou Giorgiou Papoura, Ashmolean Museum AE16, pl. XLIV, 523; from Afrati, F. Halbherr, "Unknown Cities at Hagios Ilias and Prinia" *AJA* 5 (1901) 395–96, fig. 6.
For capped figures: Protogeometric male figure from Kato Syme, *Prakt* (1976) pl. 222c; Geometric figures from Patsos Cave, Hagia Triada, and Kato Syme, Naumann, *Subminoische und protogeometrische Bronzeplastik* pl. 31 P26, pl. 32 P28; *Prakt* (1977) pl. 215a; *Ergon* (1977) 179 fig. 118; *Ergon* (1981) fig. 114.
On sacred places in Crete: G. C. Gesell, *Town, Palace, and House Cult in Minoan Crete* (SIMA LXVII, Göteborg 1985); S. Marinatos, "Le temple géométrique de Dréros" *BCH* 60 (1936) 214–85; A. Lembessi and P. Muhly, "Aspects of Minoan Cult. Sacred Enclosures" *AA* (1990) 315–36; Beyer, *Die Tempel von Dreros und Prinias A.*

S. L.

48 WEEPING MAN

Peloponnesian, Late Geometric, 750–700 B.C.
Total height 0.050, base 0.023 x 0.017, length of lug 0.002.
Bronze; intact; surface generally smooth except pubic area, inside of thighs, and

48

upper surface of base between the legs; generally dark brown, with extensive mottling of dark red patina and lesser patches of green.
Arthur M. Sackler Museum, Harvard University Art Museums, David M. Robinson Fund (1981.41).

This figurine has many characteristics that associate it with other examples of the seated figurine type exemplified by the Baltimore bronze (80), yet differs from them in significant ways that merit careful attention. From either side, the figure can be seen as a scalene triangle. The shape is repeated in patterns of positive and negative space formed by the angles and extensions of the arms and legs, as well as by the voids between the extremities, trunk, and base. The triangular patterns visible in the open spaces of the composition recall the punchwork designs common on Geometric period animal figurine bases, especially those from the Laconian bronze workshop, and may provide a clue to the origins of this figurine whose provenance is otherwise unknown.

A smooth, undulating line runs from the crown of the head down the back to the buttocks where it continues along the edge of the base to the front before turning up to the knees, and down again to the hip flexors. The figure and its base are cast as one piece. The base is undecorated, with a small lug projecting from the underside at the rear. Whereas most seated figures rest on a chair or a stool above the base, indicating personal ease and an air of deliberation, this man is positioned directly on the ground. Where his buttocks and the base meet, the bronze is seamless with no continuation of the edge of the base, which can otherwise be observed on its forward and side rims. The unarticulated feet, set in front of the figure, curve inward flush with the leading edge of the base. The effect is of constriction and containment, making the base a tiny ovoid island scarcely sufficient to accommodate its human burden. The weight of the composition is concentrated in its lower half, from the waist of the figure downward.

Most Geometric seated figures feature exaggeratedly elongated limbs that curve far out into space before turning to the head, in the case of the arms, or to the base, in the case of the legs. The Harvard figurine is realistically proportioned; the flaccidly modeled limbs give a gravid, meaty impression, quite different from the airy tectonics generally characteristic of this figurine type. The chest rises at the breastbone and then tapers inward to the genital area, which is only roughly indicated. This indeterminate sexual definition is unusual in Geometric period male figurines; many of the seated figurines are clearly ithyphallic. In this case, the artist may have meant to indicate both a physical and a psychological impotence.

The legs and arms are characteristically positioned with the elbows counterpoised against the knees. The figure is noteworthy for the tight retraction of the extremities toward the trunk so that from both the front and the

side the composition seems enclosed and self-contained. Both arms point to the smooth, featureless head: the left hand curves inward to meet and merge with the left cheek, while the right hand, set slightly higher than its counterpart, curves forward in a blunt fist that presses against the right cheek. The blank face repels us, but the hands draw us back. Instead of holding some exotic object, as is common in this figurine type, these hands hold the head itself, which, lacking the expressive instruments of eyes or mouth, conveys all the more strongly a sense of woeful, interior preoccupation. In this context, the gesture of the right hand may be seen as wiping away tears.

Such a gesture appears in the *Iliad* (2.266–70) in a memorable scene of public humiliation endured by the fool and braggart Thersites at the hands of Odysseus. Having spoken out of turn and berated his betters in public council, he is beaten by Odysseus for his rudeness, whereupon "he doubled over, and a round tear dropped from him, and a bloody welt stood up between his shoulders under the golden sceptre's stroke, and he sat down again, frightened, in pain, and looking helplessly about wiped off the tear-drops." The association between weeping and sitting down is repeated in other Homeric scenes such as *Iliad* 1.348–51, where no less than Achilles himself "weeping went and sat in sorrow apart from his companions beside the beach of the grey sea looking out on the infinite water."

Whether the Harvard man represents Thersites or Achilles is impossible to say. If it is Thersites, in the *Iliad* his humiliation and weeping occasion laughter among the Greeks (2.270), so this figurine could have been interpreted as enjoyably humorous rather than as an emblem of shame or an object for solemn contemplation. Certainly its value to its owner, either as a pendent or as a stationary piece of art fixed on a concave base by its shallow lug, must have been considerable given its careful and intricate execution in bronze. We are reminded of the "zanes" stat-

49

ues at the sanctuary of Olympia, which, in a later time, commemorated cheaters at the games in the same heroic—and ironic— metal.

PUBLISHED

P. R. S. Moorey and H. W. Catling, *Antiquities from the Bomford Collection* (Oxford 1966) 62 no. 310, pl. 28.

S. Langdon, "From Monkey to Man" fig. 8.

NOTES

For twelve examples of the seated figurines: S. Langdon, "From Monkey to Man" 408–13; see also Mitten and Doeringer, *Master Bronzes from the Classical World* 32, no. 9.

On positive and negative space in seated statuettes: Schweitzer, *Greek Geometric Art* 159–61, pls. 197–9; M. True, "Seated Man" in Kozloff and Mitten, eds., *The Gods Delight* 49–51.

On parallels to the simian belt amulet figures: True, "Seated Man" 50; S. Langdon, "From Monkey to Man" 413–15.

On Egyptian and Near East influence on early Greek seated figures: P. Kranz, "Frühe griechische Sitzfiguren: zum Problem der Typenbildung und des orientalischen Einflusses in der frühen griechischen Rundplastik" *AM* 87 (1972) 1–55, pls. 1–24.

On the "zanes" statues at Olympia: Pausanias, *Guide to Greece* 5.21.2ff.

T. A.

49 GROUP OF FOUR SHEEP

Late Geometric, ca. 700 B.C.
Height 0.045, width 0.07.

Bronze, dark green patina; intact.
Museum of Fine Arts, Boston, Samuel Putnam Avery Fund (58.1189).

Four bleating sheep with modeled ears and indented eyes stand side by side on a rectangular frame bisected by a crossbar. A T-shaped extension projects from the back of the frame. The simplicity of the modeling makes the assignment of date or place of origin difficult, and attribution may depend more upon theme than style.

Despite the regular practice of sacrificing sheep to the Olympian gods, figurines of sheep are surprisingly rare among the great numbers of Geometric bronze and terracotta votive animals. Individual bronze sheep have been found at Delphi and possibly at Tegea; terracotta sheep at Olympia, Tegea, and Kombothreka may date as early as Late Geometric. This paucity speaks against them as commemorating real sacrifices. These four sheep more likely were intended to symbolize an entire flock, over which the worshiper requested divine protection. Even without an accompanying shepherd they recall a small bronze group of four sheep with their herder in the National Museum in Palermo. In Greece the sculptural theme of a man herding one or more animals is known only at Delphi, where it appears in a series of men and rams on bases that might all have once been fixed to a utensil or vessel (see 51). At least one of the three pairs from Delphi topped a rein guide mounted on a staff.

Outside Greece a close parallel from Luristan might explain the odd form of the Boston group. A bronze belt buckle from Amlash consists of four sheeplike quadrupeds standing abreast on a flat rectangular framework of approximately the same dimensions as the Boston piece; a T-shaped strut extends behind it. Lacking the front crossbar to provide an opening for a leather or cloth strip, the Boston group cannot function in the same way as the Luristan buckle. The connection with a Luristan object is supported by the form of the Delphi rein guides, which is believed to have originated in the Luristan area and earlier in Hittite culture. Like the Amlash buckle, whose animals might have served to indicate the wealth of the wearer, the unusual Boston quartet may also have expressed something of the magnitude of the flock the worshiper owned.

PUBLISHED

C. C. Vermeule, *MFA Annual Report* 1958, 31.

C. C. Vermeule, "Greek, Etruscan and Roman Bronzes Acquired by the Museum of Fine Arts, Boston" *CJ* 55 (1960) 193–94, fig. 1.

FA 15 (1960) no. 671.

Mitten, "The Earliest Greek Sculptures in the Museum" 10–11, fig. 10.

Comstock and Vermeule, *Greek, Etruscan and Roman Bronzes in the Museum of Fine Arts, Boston* 6, no. 4.

F. Hiller, "Beobachtungen zur Form der spät-geometrischen Plastik" *JdI* 94 (1979) 18–31 at 29 n. 30.

Heilmeyer, *Frühe Olympische Bronzefiguren* 183 n. 223.

Rudolph and Calinescu, eds., *Ancient Art from the V. G. Simkhovitch Collection* 82, under no. 55.

NOTES

Sicilian group: Palermo, Museo Nazionale 8232, C. A. Di Stefano, *Bronzetti Figurati del Museo nazionale di Palermo* (Rome 1975) 60, no. 100; D. G. Mitten, "Man and Ram: A Bronze Group of Geometric Style in the Fogg Art Museum" in *Essays in Honor of Dorothy Kent Hill*, ed. Diana M. Buitron et al., *JWalt* 36 (1977) 31–36 at 35 n. 6; La Rosa, *Cronache* (1968) 22, pl. VIII.

Rein guide from Delphi: Rolley, *Monuments figurés, les statuettes de bronze* 56 with further bibliography in n. 3; *Syria* (1932) 227–29, 321–26.

Amlash buckle: Paris, Hôtel Drouot, *Bronzes antiques de la Perse. Collection Jean Paul Barbier, Geneva* (Paris 1970) no. 157, 120.

For a Caucasian pin with three rams abreast: Jacobsthal, *Greek Pins* 54, p. 245.

S. L.

50

50 RAM

Central Greek or Thessalian, Late Geometric, ca. 700 B.C.
Height 0.029, length 0.038.
Bronze; intact.
Museum of Art, Rhode Island School of Design, Providence, Gift of Mrs. Celia Robinson Stillwell (84.065).

Like other bronze figures in the exhibition, the slender ram figure captures not the reality of the animal but a graceful abstraction of its form. It is rendered in the simplest of styles, with narrow torso and limbs that taper to rounded feet. The neck also tapers to a blunt ovoid head whose only details are a pair of long horns that curve forward the length of the muzzle and low swellings that suggest ears. A straight tail hangs behind. There is no support under the feet, but a vertical hole cast through the torso likely attached the figure to a suspension cord.

Unusual among the Geometric bronze figurines, a vertical hole through the body occurs in ten bronze animals from the sanctuary of

Artemis Enodia at Pherai and in single examples from Elateia, Delphi, and the Ptoion. Two of those from Pherai are rams, probably of local manufacture. Of a different style, which has been related to Corinthian work, although not necessarily produced in the Corinthia, are a ram from Delphi, a pierced ram of unknown provenance in the Benaki Museum, and a ram in the Walters Art Gallery. Its suspension hole ties the Providence ram to a production and use area in central Greece and Thessaly.

Pierced bronze animal figurines have been found only at sanctuaries, but similarly pierced bird figurines found in graves suggest that the animals were intended as dress ornaments or jewelry pendants and worn in everyday life before being offered in a sanctuary.

51

PUBLISHED
Rhode Island School of Design Museum Notes
    71 (1984) 8.

NOTES
On bronze pendant animals: Kilian-Dirlmeier, *Anhänger in Griechenland* 186–88, pl. 59 esp. nos. 1128, 1129; ram on cage pendant, pl. 34, 654.
Rams: from Delphi, Rolley, *Monuments figurés, les statuettes de bronze* 81 no. 120, pl. 21; of unknown provenance, Kilian-Dirlmeier, *Anhänger in Griechenland* pl. 59, 1128; Walters Art Gallery 54.2383, AJA 59 (1955) pl. 29, fig. 6; see also three rams on a Caucasian Iron Age pin, Jacobsthal, *Greek Pins* pl. 245.

S. L.

51 YOUTH AND RAM

Magna Graecia, Late Geometric, early seventh century B.C.
Total height 0.065, length 0.054, width 0.034, base approximately 0.030 x 0.030, length of visible iron dowel 0.012.
Bronze; intact, with brown corroded iron dowel between ram and upper surface of base; smooth dark brown surface overall with patches of green and red patina;

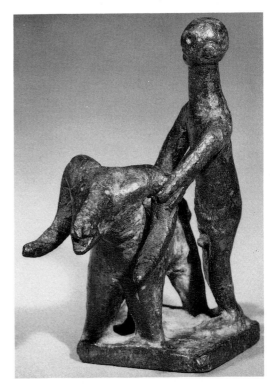

51

trapezoidal base with undecorated, slightly corroded underside; two small modern test holes from atomic absorption analysis on forward underside of base.
Arthur M. Sackler Museum, Harvard University Art Museums, David M. Robinson Fund (1970.26).

The ram is thick and bulky, evoking its heavy wool and musculature, while its long, forwardly curving horns convey its potency. Its elongated, triangular face features a high nasal ridge extending from between the horns to the end of the muzzle. The ram's mouth is open as if emitting a bleat, perhaps as the animal sights the altar in a sanctuary where it is to be offered in sacrifice. The eyes and nostrils are indicated by precisely impressed dots. The squat, stubby legs taper abruptly into the trapezoidal base that it shares with its human attendant and against which it seems to brace itself.

The left horn of the ram is held firmly by the three-fingered left hand of the supplely modeled, youthful male figure at its side. The youth's right hand, with all the fingers fully articulated, pulls against the right flank of the ram, steadying and straightening it into the frontal plane of the composition. The effort of controlling the struggling animal is expressed in the torsion of the youth's shoulders, back, and hips and by the uneven distribution of his weight: forward on the bent left leg, with the straight right leg impelling him from behind. Both feet are planted flat on the base.

The ceremonial nudity of the youth suggests a depiction of sacrifice rather than a genre scene from the daily life of a shepherd. His slender form is played off against the heavy maturity of the ram, which stands nearly waist-high to him. While the animal is oriented along vertical and horizontal planes, indicating power and control, the youth is turned in a three-quarter view and slanted off the vertical plane, indicating that his aspiration to dominance is in doubt. In a similar bronze group from Delphi, both figures stand on strongly vertical axes, illustrating the Homeric value of *kosmos*: the orderly accomplishment of right action. The Delphi group exudes an air of calm inevitability; the sacrificial ram, knee-high to its attendant, stands as quietly as a dog brought to heel. The mature status of the otherwise nude human figure from the Delphi group is clearly indicated by a heavy belt around his waist. The Harvard youth, not yet master of the task before him, lacks this emblem of status and achievement (see **60**). The struggle of his ram to escape its fate, and the struggle of the youth to insure that fate, suggest impending disorder and a dramatic threat to the values of *kosmos*.

The attenuated, perpendicular column of the young man's neck leads to another focal point of this group: his face, with its far-off gaze. The head is round and smooth; the nose and ears are shallowly modeled, and the eyes are impressed dots. But the slitlike mouth is open and animated, and the chin, though subtly rendered, is clearly defined. The apparently sketchy features are solemn and convey a compelling sense of immediacy. The youth looks diagonally to his right over the back of the ram into the distance. The direction and intensity of his gaze imply another plane of reference that, while not formally expressed in the plastic medium of the figurine group, is nevertheless an intentional and complementary component of the total composition.

As a rule in the arts of the Geometric period, especially in vase painting and epic composition, all subjects are placed in a uniform visual and perceptual foreground without dimensional depth. The inclusion by this artist of an implied, invisible element, spatially removed from the group composition yet nevertheless integral to it, is a daringly sophisticated device amounting to the achievement of visual perspective. The viewer, standing at a distance, is the object of the youth's intense gaze. The culturally and emotionally informed response of the viewer across open space completes the group, giving it purpose and context. This artistic device, involving an invisible but complementary element in a work of plastic art, parallels the recitation of Homeric epic, which achieved full poetic and musical realization only in performance before an audience.

Statuette groups of a man or youth with a ram are known from many parts of the early Greek world. The example presented here is remarkable for the liberties taken by the artist with the frontal and profiled views preferred in Geometric period art, for its implied visual reference point as an unexpressed element of the formal group composition, and for the emotional realism of the scene.

PUBLISHED

Sale catalogue, Sotheby's (London), November 27, 1969, lot 180 (ill.).

D. G. Mitten, "Man and Ram: A Bronze Group of Geometric Style in the Fogg Art Museum" in *Essays in Honor of Dorothy Kent Hill*, ed. Diana M. Buitron et al., *JWalt* 36 (1977) 31–36.

NOTES

On the sacrifice of a black ram to Pelops at Olympia: Pausanias, *Guide to Greece* 5.13.2.

Man with ram at Delphi: Rolley, *Monuments figurés, les statuettes de bronze* 53–54, pl. XII 42, 44.

On the Homeric ideal of order in Geometric period artistic canons: Hurwit, *The Art and Culture of Early Greece* 71–124.

On the concept of an implied audience for Homeric epic: J. M. Foley, *Immanent Art: From Structure to Meaning in Traditional Oral Epic* (Bloomington IN 1991) 42–45.

T. A.

52 FRAGMENT OF A KRATER

Argive, from the Heraion, Late Geometric II, ca. 725–700 B.C.
Attributed to the Dance Painter.
Height 0.08, width 0.105.
Ceramic; fragment, figures painted with dark brown slip, interior painted with

52

Fig. 22. *Krater C229 from Argos, with panels of dancing women, represents the shape and decorative organization by which the Harvard fragment 52 can be reconstructed. (Photo courtesy of École Française d'Archéologie, Athens)*

brown slip; the fine clay fabric with no inclusions is pink-beige in color.
Arthur M. Sackler Museum, Harvard University Art Museums (1954.33).

The three women depicted on the fragment, framed by painted bands of lines and horizontal zigzags, would have been a focal point of figural decoration on the shoulder of a particular type of large bellied krater, made with flat stirrup handles joined to the vase at the lip and sides. A complete example was excavated in the North Cemetery at Corinth, and it has been determined to be of Argive manufacture and exported to that site.

These seemingly stationary and static women, facing to the right with joined hands that hold branches between them, are actually meant to be viewed as participating in a line dance. They wear long peploi gathered around their wasplike waists by two long girdle cords that flare out to the right, indicating the direction the women face on this and other examples. Vertical columns of stacked chevrons, painted in an abbreviated manner with quick, single brush strokes, fill the remaining space between the dancers.

After the figural compositions of man, horse, and fish, the second main theme of the Argive artist is that of dancing women. They are usually shown in isolated groups of three or four, sometimes accompanied by a male figure who dances at the end of the line procession or holds the hand of the last woman dancer. Rarely these dancing women are joined by a man leading a horse (see **53**). In earlier depictions, the women's peploi are decorated with hatching or lozenge nets and they move with more animation in the figure field. At a later date, as here, their peploi are painted in unpatterned silhouette.

The artist of this fragment, named the Dance Painter from the subjects he depicted, utilized the krater shape for his representations of these women. This theme first appeared in Argive ceramic decoration on the krater Argos C210, where women dance in panels beneath other panel compositions that feature horse-leaders. During this period, depictions of dancing women were popular in the Peloponnese, not only in Argos but in Laconia and Arcadia as well. On the Late Geometric ceramics of Attica, they appear on amphorae, hydriae, and tankards. The hydriae, decorated with plastic snakes, may hint at the chthonic significance of these dancers, as do the branches, perhaps of myrtle, that they hold. In the Argive representations, dancing women on these vases may be interpreted as depicting the religious rites performed as part of funerary ritual. It is significant that three of the four works attributed by Coldstream to the Dance Painter come from graves where they may have been intended to accompany the dead in the after-

life. Such dancing scenes persist on pottery until early in the seventh century B.C. and the Protoattic period, where they appear on the neck of the hydria from Analatos, by the painter of the same name.

PUBLISHED
Tölle, *Frühgriechische Reigentänze* 45, no. 115, pl. 24c.
Coldstream, *Greek Geometric Pottery* 140, no. 2.
L. J. Siegel, "An Argive Dancer at Columbia University" *AJA* 81 (1977) 363–65 at 364.

NOTES
On the Dance Painter: Coldstream, *Greek Geometric Pottery* 140–41, pl. 30 a–b.
For dancing women on Argive ceramics: Waldstein, *The Argive Heraeum* II 114, pl. LVII, 15–19; Coldstream, *Greek Geometric Pottery* 140–41, pl. 30 a–b; Schweitzer, *Greek Geometric Art* 162–63, figs. 21–22, pl. 74; Coldstream, *Geometric Greece*, 141–42, fig. 46e.
For the krater with stirrup handles, Corinth T2545, from Grave 47 of the North Cemetery at Corinth: T. L. Shear, "Excavations in the North Cemetery at Corinth in 1930" *AJA* 34 (1930) 411, fig. 5; R. S. Young, *Corinth XIII* (Princeton 1964) 35–36, 45–46, pl. 9; J. L. Benson, review of Young, *CP* 61 (1966) 271; Coldstream, *Greek Geometric Pottery* 140–41, no. 3, pl. 30 a–b; Schweitzer, *Greek Geometric Art* pl. 74.
For dancing women accompanied by male figures: Waldstein, *The Argive Heraeum* II, pl. LVII, 17, 19; Courbin, *La céramique géométrique de l'Argolide* pl. 147.
For krater Argos C210: Courbin, *La céramique géométrique de l'Argolide* pls. 41–42; Coldstream, *Greek Geometric Pottery* 141.
For Late Geometric Attic dancing women, Workshop of Athens 894: Coldstream, *Greek Geometric Pottery* 59–60, pl. 11d, f.
For the Analatos Painter hydria: Schweitzer, *Greek Geometric Art*, pls. 52–55.

A. J. P.

53

53 FRAGMENT OF A CUP

Argive, from the Heraion, Late Geometric
    II, ca. 725–700 B.C.
Height 0.037, width 0.072.
Ceramic; fragment, figures painted in dark
    brown slip, interior painted with dark
    brown slip; the fine clay fabric with no
    inclusions is pink-beige in color.
Arthur M. Sackler Museum, Harvard
    University Art Museums, Gift of Miss B.
    J. Kahnweiler (1935.35.17).

The fragment belongs to a shallow cup
with an offset lip, a small vessel that could
have had horizontal rolled handles, like a skyphos, or vertical strap handles that would
identify it as a kantharos shape. The lip of
the cup is defined with painted vertical lines
and a reserve line that separates it from the
figural field below.

The figure scene combines two of the most
popular themes of the Argive artist: a horse
accompanied by a man, the horse-leader, also
known as the "master of horses," and a line
of dancing women who join hands and hold
branches between them (see 52). In this unusual combination of the two types, the horse-
leader joins in at the end of the line dance as
he holds the hand of the last woman with his
left hand while leading the horse with his
right. Subsidiary decoration fills the spaces of
the figure field: stacked chevrons between the
bodies of the figures, and pendants, indicated
by quickly painted dabs, between the heads of
the figures and the branches. A pendant triangle hangs between the horse's head and

that of his leader, and part of a corner panel
is preserved just behind the horse's head and
above its back. Another object, the edge of
which can just be seen, filled the space
beneath the horse's belly.

The painting on this piece is done in a
manner noted by Coldstream as the Miniature Style, to which he attributes works by
the Verdelis Painter. Although this piece is
not by that painter, it is executed in a minute
and sketchy technique that shows a relationship to his work. In the Miniature Style, linear draftsmanship is carried to its limits and
the anatomy of the figures is stylized, reduced
enough to be conveyed with a single brush
stroke. The filling ornament is light and simple, barely conveying what it might represent
at larger scale. This minimalist style may be
the Argive artist's reaction to the finely produced miniature work being developed by
Corinthian artists, obsessed with the fastidious
details that would become one of the hall-
marks of Protocorinthian ceramic production.

The unusual theme of dancing women and
horse-leaders represented together also occurs
on a large, stirrup-handled krater, Argos C210,
which is also one of the earliest representations of dancing women. Unlike the depiction
on the Harvard fragment, the horse-leader
and women are separated by panel compositions that enclose them and make their direct
contact an impossibility. On two other fragments from the Argive Heraion, dancing
women are represented with male figures at
the end of their line. Early in the seventh
century men and women continue to participate in line dances, as depicted on the hydria
by the Analatos Painter, where six male and
four female dancers, segregated by gender,
join hands and hold branches between them
as they approach a central male figure who
strums on a lyre. This depiction of dance and
music could have a mythological significance
if the lyre-player is seen as Apollo. More likely, it may be an attempt to portray a scene
from the real world, the ritual lamentation
and funeral rites being performed for the
deceased. A similar interpretation could be

inferred from the action depicted on the Harvard cup fragment. If not, perhaps a religious celebration or a festival is depicted that would take note of the Argolid's riches, represented by the horse, an embodiment of real and symbolic wealth in the Geometric period. Whatever the scene on this cup meant to its Argive owner, it is clear that both men and women took part in the ritual performance of these dances.

PUBLISHED

Tölle, *Frühgriechische Reigentänze* pl. 24b.

NOTES

For cup shapes of the type from which this piece may have come: Courbin, *La céramique géométrique de l'Argolide* pl. 54 (C3959), pl. 57 (C871).

For the horse-leader and master of horses: Schweitzer, *Greek Geometric Art* 62–63; S. Langdon, "The Return of the Horse-Leader" 185–86.

For Miniature Style and Verdelis Painter: Courbin, *La céramique géométrique de l'Argolide* pl. 58 (C20, C22); Coldstream, *Greek Geometric Pottery* 135–36, pl. 29a, b, c.

For the object represented beneath the horse on this fragment, maybe a fish (see **90**) or a rounded, hump-shaped structure: Courbin, *La céramique géométrique de l'Argolide* pl. 65 (C1146), a skyphos with offset lip and horse-leader panel.

For Argos C210, see under **52**.

For dancing women and heraldic horse-leader compositions: Courbin, *La céramique géométrique de l'Argolide* pls. 41–42.

For men at the end of the women's line dance: Waldstein, *The Argive Heraeum* II pl. LVII, 17–19; Courbin, *La céramique géométrique de l'Argolide* pl. 147.

A. J. P.

54 SEATED FLUTE-PLAYER

Macedonian or Thessalian, Late Geometric to Subgeometric, late eighth to seventh century B.C.

Height 0.032, base diameter 0.017.

54

Bronze, pale green patina; base broken on figure's left side.
Sol Rabin Collection, Los Angeles.
Previously Leon Pomerance Collection.

Perched on a stump, the tiny figure sits hunched over with elbows against his knees intently playing a long flute that he holds to his mouth. Details are minimal. The figure wears a flat belt visible only on his back. His hair is indicated by vertical striations, his eyes by indentations in his planar face. His feet and stump are attached to a base in the form of a Boeotian shield, hollowed underneath.

Although a seated flute-player must have been a ubiquitous sight in Greek towns and sanctuaries, the artist of this miniature musician rendered his theme not from nature but from art. Several Subgeometric bronze figurines play double pipes, but this is the only known example of a flute-player. Without an existing prototype in sculpture or painting from which to work, the artist of this bronze adapted a seated type known from Peloponnesian sanctuaries (see **80**) and from subsequent pendants in which a tiny abstract figure with hands to mouth sits atop a knob-covered rod (see **32** and related **48**).

Stylistic details identify our flutist as originating in northern Greece, most likely in Thessaly. Body proportions and anatomical treatment are much like those small figures who sit with hands on knees as the finials of cage pendants. An example in the Metropolitan Museum has vertically striated hair and a simple belt incised only on the back. A female figure seated on a bench in a Swiss private collection must be broken from the largest known example of a cage pendant; it also has the hair striations, planar face, and wiry arms of the flute-player.

Throughout eighth-century Greece the importance of music in both religious and secular life gave rise to one of the most popular themes in art, that of men and women dancing to the tune of a pipes- or lyre-player. In central and southern Greece the theme appears in vase painting, particularly in Argive art, as on sherds **52–53**. In the north, where pottery lacks a figural tradition, the theme is supplied by this small bronze figure. It was most likely carried to or made in a sanctuary like Pherai or Philia.

PUBLISHED

Brooklyn Museum, *The Pomerance Collection of Ancient Art* (Brooklyn 1966) 79 no. 89.
Small Sculptures in Bronze from the Classical World, ed. G. K. Sams (Chapel Hill NC 1976) no. 7.
S. Langdon, "From Monkey to Man" 408 n. 5.

EXHIBITED

Age of Homer, University Museum, University of Pennsylvania, December 1969–March 1970.
Small Sculptures in Bronze from the Classical World, Chapel Hill, 1976.

NOTES

Bronze seated pipes-player figurines: from Kameiros, British Museum 64.10–7.3, S.

Langdon, "From Monkey to Man" 408, 413 fig. 11; G. Ortiz Collection, most recently Rudolph and Calinescu, eds., *Ancient Art from the V. G. Simkhovitch Collection* 82 no. 55; an odd figure in Brussels may not be Greek, Tölle, *Frühgriechische Reigentänze* pl. 27a.
Bronze figurines with Boeotian-shield bases: Sparta and Olympia birds, lion, Dörig, *Art antique* no. 108; pair of lions, Stathatos Collection, H. Stathatou, *Collection Hélène Stathatos* III (Strasbourg 1963) 91–92 no. 22, pl. 12; birds, Kilian-Dirlmeier, *Anhänger in Griechenland* pl. 56 nos. 1049–51.
Bronze cage pendants: Richter, *Handbook of the Greek Collection* 22, pl. 13c; Bouzek, *Graeco-Macedonian Bronzes* 74–75; Kilian-Dirlmeier, *Anhänger in Griechenland* pl. 28 nos. 542–46.
Female figure on a bench: Rudolph and Calinescu, eds., *Ancient Art from the V. G. Simkhovitch Collection* 78–79, no. 52.
On the aulos: Tölle, *Frühgriechische Reigentänze*; Wegner, *Musik und Tanz* 19–22.

S. L.

55

55 HORSE FIGURINE

Arcadian, Late Geometric, 750–725 B.C.
Height 0.087, length 0.07, base 0.068 x
0.032.
**Phoebe Hearst Museum of Anthropology,
The University of California at Berkeley,
Gift of Mrs. P. A. Hearst, 1901 (8–74).**

The Berkeley horse captures the stability
and strength that Geometric artists strove to
express in their bronze horse statuettes.
Although it is thought to have originated in
Arcadia, its style fuses elements known from
several regions of Greece. Influenced by the
bronze horses of Laconia to the south, its
base is decorated with two rows of triangular
perforations and a projection for the tail. Also
Laconian are the general proportions of short
neck, short trunk, long legs, and an overall
orthogonal construction. The rounded muzzle
and the arching profile of legs and belly are
typical of bronze horses of the Argive plain to
the northeast. The stylized knobs of knees
and hocks at the same level recall Corinthian
works. Combining the best of the great
regional styles, the result is a rigid and powerfully built figure with a strong presence. Its
attribution to an Arcadian workshop relies on
its affinities with a number of horses excavated at Tegea.

It has been remarked that a purely Arcadian horse is impossible to find, that is, one
devoid of the influence of any other regional
style. Instead, borrowed elements in various
combinations made for widely varied Arcadian
productions, as demonstrated by the remarkably different appearances of the Baltimore
(95) and Berkeley horses. This phenomenon
may seem surprising for an area as isolated as
mountainous Arcadia but can be attributed to
the existence in the region of one of the
major routes across the Peloponnese to Olympia. Consequently, Arcadian bronzeworkers
found their greatest market, outside their own
sanctuaries, at Olympia, where they could
take advantage of the mix of artistic styles
being produced there.

As for the great popularity of the horse as a
votive offering in Arcadian sanctuaries, it may
be unnecessary to look as far away as the
votive practices at Olympia. Predominant in
Arcadian cults are divine associations with the
horse, among them those of Poseidon Hippios
and Demeter at Lykosoura, Demeter Melaina
and Despoina at Phigaleia, and Demeter
Erinys at Thelpusa.

Freestanding bronze horse figurines like the
Berkeley example were dedicated at nearly
every known Geometric sanctuary and comprise the majority of all known Geometric figurine types. The large landholdings necessary for
the costly maintenance of horses made them
an obvious elite symbol. A long-established
iconography from the Bronze Age, however,
gave the horse more than a merely societal
significance. Its power and nobility, expressed
in the bronzeworkers' finest language, made
the horse a gift pleasing to the gods. Often
considered to have been the "signatures" of
aristocrats visiting sanctuaries, the horse offerings range in quality from artistic masterpieces to comically inept efforts and terracotta
knockoffs, suggesting that all levels of society
participated in their symbolism.

PUBLISHED
D. H. Amyx, "Geometric Platform Bronzes"
    AJA 53 (1949) 147–48.
Selection 1966 (Berkeley 1966) 13–15, no. 18.
Mitten and Doeringer, *Master Bronzes from
    the Classical World* 37, no. 18.
N. Himmelmann-Wildschütz, "Geometrisches
    Bronzepferdchen in Bonn" AA (1974) 550
    n. 17.
Zimmermann, *Les chevaux* 95 no. 74, 104, pls.
    20, 74.

EXHIBITED
Master Bronzes from the Classical World, The
    Fogg Art Museum, Cambridge MA,
    December 1967–January 1968, City Art
    Museum of Saint Louis, March–April 1968,
    The Los Angeles County Museum of Art,
    May–June 1968.

NOTES
On Arcadian horse style: Zimmermann, *Les
    chevaux* 100–102 and esp. 102–6 on

"Tegean" type; M. Weber, "Eine arkadisch-geometrische Bronzegruppe" *StädelJb* 1 (1967) 8–17; U. Sinn, "Ein Fundkomplex aus dem Artemis-Heiligtum von Lusoi im Badischen Landesmuseum" *Jahrbuch der Staatlichen Kunstsammlungen in Baden-Württemburg* 17 (1980) 25–40; Heilmeyer, *Frühe Olympische Bronzefiguren* 99–109; Voyatzis, *The Early Sanctuary of Athena Alea at Tegea* 127–38.

Related horses from Tegea: *BCH* 45 (1921) 345 fig. 6 no. 9; Zimmermann, *Les chevaux* nos. ARC 52, 53, 59, 70, 71, 73, pls. 19–20.

On Arcadian cults: Schweitzer, *Greek Geometric Art* 158–59; M. Jost, *Sanctuaires et cultes d'Arcadie* (Paris 1985); Voyatzis, *The Early Sanctuary of Athena Alea at Tegea*; Bevan, *Representations of Animals in Sanctuaries of Artemis* 195–97, 213.

For the significance of bronze horse dedications and their bases: Amyx, "Geometric Platform Bronzes" 147–48; most recently Zimmerman, *Les chevaux* 314–18, with further bibliography.

S. L.

56

56 DEER

Probably Laconian, Late Geometric, 750–725 B.C.
Height 0.068, length of base 0.035.
Bronze, dark green patina; tip of right ear broken.
Walters Art Gallery, Baltimore (54.2382).

The graceful young animal leans back on long legs with a somewhat startled air. Perched atop a narrow neck, its head is a simple cylinder with slightly bulbous muzzle and tall alert ears. Thin legs, square in section, rise in an arching contour to triangular shoulders and flanks, leaving little corporeal mass. A short, perky tail extends in back. Small sharp projections indicate knees and hocks. No incised details interrupt the smooth polished surface. The rectangular base is perforated with two rows of triangles and divided lengthwise underneath with two raised lines.

The Baltimore deer finds stylistic parallels among few other deer figures, the closest being a bronze fawn in a Swiss collection. Comparisons with horses suggest that the origin for the splendid finish, "arrested" stance, cylindrical head, and abstractly knobby legs of the Baltimore animal can be found in Laconian work. An examination of Laconian deer and stags shows a greater stylistic range than occurs among horses. A deer on a rectangular base from the sanctuary of Artemis Ortheia lacks the fine articulation of head and legs and the unifying contour of the Baltimore fawn. Laconian deer and stags dedicated at Olympia, on the other hand, show a closer relationship with horses in their angular profile and orthogonal construction centered on a short rod torso and broad neck and flanks.

The Baltimore animal is possibly intended as a fawn. Like the suckling fawn of the well-known Boston group and the small bronze in the Menil collection (**85**), the enormous ears of this animal seem intended to characterize it as very young.

PUBLISHED
D. K. Hill, "Six Early Greek Animals" *AJA* 59 (1955) 40 no. 2, pl. 29, figs. 4–5.

Herrmann, "Werkstätten geometrischer Bronze-
  plastik" 21, n. 14.
Bulletin of the Walters Art Gallery, 18, 2
  (1965) 4.
Mitten, "The Earliest Greek Sculptures in the
  Museum" 18 n. 23.
Zimmermann, *Les chevaux* 170, n. 406.

EXHIBITED
The Age of Homer, University Museum, Uni-
  versity of Pennsylvania, December 1969–
  March 1970.

NOTES
Deer in Swiss private collection: Schefold,
  Meisterwerke griechischer Kunst 129 no. 62.
Laconian horse parallels: Zimmermann, *Les
  chevaux* for legs pl. 33, 116; pl. 34, 124; pl.
  35, 138 and 140; pl. 36, 147; for profile and
  stance pl. 37, 167.
Laconian deer: Dawkins, *The Sanctuary of
  Artemis Orthia at Sparta* pl. 76m; Heilmey-
  er, *Frühe Olympische Bronzefiguren* pl. 68,
  507 and 507a.
Similar bases: Heilmeyer, *Frühe Olympische
  Bronzefiguren* pl. 67 no. 506; Zimmermann,
  Les chevaux pls. 76–77.
Boston fawn and doe group but cf. Perachora
  deer with large ears: Heilmeyer, *Frühe
  Olympische Bronzefiguren* 88 fig. 3, NM
  16 162.

S. L.

57 STAG

Late eighth century B.C.
**Height 0.054, length 0.045, base 0.035 x
0.025.**
Bronze; complete, gash in underside of base.
**The Art Museum, Princeton University, Gift
of Frank Jewett Mather, Jr. (y1946–93).**

Standing erect on a rectangular base, the
stag holds his antlered head proudly alert. The
small modeled antlers and ears and deeply
indented eyes define his head. The contour of
his high-arching rump continues down to the
shoulders and back up the neck to the head.
This profile, combined with straight, slightly

57

splayed legs, has been cited in identifying the
bronze as an Arcadian product. Numerous
examples of deer and stags from Arcadian
sanctuaries show them to have been an unusually popular theme among Arcadian
votives. Yet their attenuated forms correspond
so little to the Princeton animal that another
origin is equally plausible. Close stylistic parallels are found among animals from the Argive
Heraion, a site that has produced two deer
figurines. The solid base of the Princeton
stag, its underside decorated with chevrons
and a meander in relief, recalls supports
under Argive animals and Arcadian figures
under Argive influence. While the patterns on
the base find numerous parallels among
Argive figurines, its bisection into two different designs is unusual.

The ubiquitous bronze animal figurines
from Greek sanctuaries raise a central question: were they dedicated because they were
considered appropriate for the deity of the
place, or did they embody the worshiper's
concerns? The distribution of figural types
over time suggests that in certain cases their
connections with specific deities developed

only in the Archaic period. Thus the deer became the special animal of Artemis as huntress and was one of her chief attributes in Archaic and Classical art. As her sacred animal, deer lived protected in the precincts of some of her sanctuaries, while at others they were sacrificed live at the altar.

However, sanctuaries not only of Artemis but also of Hera, Apollo, and Athena have yielded figures of stags, deer, and fawns from the eighth century. The importance of hunting for sustenance at that time must have made the fertility of wild animals and hunter's luck matters to be taken to the gods. Votive offerings representing these concerns, such as the Princeton stag, the Baltimore deer (56), and the Harvard fawn (86), would have accompanied prayers to whatever deity was the most readily accessible.

PUBLISHED

Record of the Art Museum, Princeton University 6, 1 and 2 (1947) 8.

Mitten and Doeringer, *Master Bronzes from the Classical World* no. 24.

Zimmermann, *Les chevaux* 108 n. 145, 112 n. 180.

EXHIBITED

Master Bronzes from the Classical World, The Fogg Art Museum, Cambridge MA, December 1967–January 1968, City Art Museum of Saint Louis, March–April 1968, The Los Angeles County Museum of Art, May–June 1968.

NOTES

Arcadian provenance for this deer: Zimmermann, *Les chevaux* 108 n. 145.

Arcadian deer figurines: Voyatzis, *The Early Sanctuary of Athena Alea at Tegea* pls. 74–76.

Similar deer: Waldstein, *The Argive Heraeum* II (Cambridge 1905) pl. 73 no. 19.

Different styles: from Tegea, Ch. Dugas, "Le sanctuaire d'Alea Athena de Tegée avant le IVe siècle" *BCH* 45 (1921) 335–435, no. 13; from the Ptoion, NM 10853, Heilmeyer,

Frühe Olympische Bronzefiguren 91 fig. 4; from Olympia, Heilmeyer pl. 68, 507a.

Bases: Waldstein, *The Argive Heraeum* II pls. 72 and 73, esp. bisected bases 12 and 13.

Deer representations at sanctuaries: Bevan, *Representations of Animals in Sanctuaries of Artemis* 389–93.

S. L.

58

58 BIRD FIGURINE

Northern or Central Greek, Late Geometric, ca. 700 B.C.

Height 0.054, length 0.077, body width 0.025.

Bronze, dark reddish brown patina; intact except for tip of left foot; both feet slightly bent.

Museum of Art, Rhode Island School of Design, Providence, Museum Works of Art Fund (54.198).

The plump water bird has a nearly spherical body from which a flat spatulate tail and slender neck rise at the same angle from back and front. The small head with pellet eyes has an upturned beak that parallels the curled feet. A large transverse hole perforates the hollow body, leaving a raised rim around each opening. A suspension loop on a stem extends from the back.

The enormous variety of Geometric bronze birds includes several variants constructed with large spherical body and small appendages representing head, feet, and tail. To preserve the striking silhouettes, wings are never portrayed. The majority of examples of the same type as the Providence bird have come from Macedonian graves as personal ornaments worn by the deceased. A closely similar waterfowl was found in a grave at Oresani, Macedonia, together with several bronze beads and two other pendants that might have hung on a necklace. The nearest parallel for the Providence bronze, although somewhat larger, is a bird from a grave at Radanje, Macedonia. These birds follow the pattern of other Macedonian and Thessalian bronzes documenting their use in graves in northern Greece and sanctuaries in southern Greece. An example from Olympia was found in the stadium fill where many bronze votive offerings were dumped. Another in the Vathy Museum came from the Samian Heraion. The relatively low technical quality of the Olympian and Samian birds has been taken to indicate copies of the north Macedonian type.

The satisfying plumpness of the Providence bird, the finest example of its type, was achieved by the difficult technique of hollow-casting. As Mitten suggested, the perforation of this example was probably produced by means of a ceramic plug inserted into the wax model, which could be removed after casting. The purpose of the hole is unclear. Since its rims do not show the same signs of wear as the suspension loop, it was not an alternate means of suspension. Nor was it necessary for successful hollow-casting; other hollow-bodied birds were made without perforations. Scientific examination of a particularly elaborate example of ca. 750–700 B.C. has revealed more complex casting and repair techniques than had hitherto been suspected for this early date.

The Providence bird belongs to a great family of bronze bird pendants popular in Hallstatt, Caucasian, and Villanovan cultures as well as Greek; they probably were all ultimately related. This broader context as well as their known use as personal adornment caution against interpretations that refer specifically to Greek iconography. Along with other Macedonian bronze beads and pendants, these plump, perforated water birds seem to have been derived from the Caucasus, where bronze jewelry belonged to the realm of magic and offered protection to the wearer. In northern Macedonia this function may have fostered the enormous popularity and bewildering variety of bronze pendants. As they traveled south and were deposited in sanctuaries rather than graves, this original significance may have become a distant echo.

PUBLISHED
Mitten, *Classical Bronzes* 26–27, no. 7.
Kilian-Dirlmeier, *Anhänger in Griechenland* 143 no. 804, pl. 45.

NOTES
On Geometric bronze bird pendants: Bouzek, *Graeco-Macedonian Bronzes* 13–23; Kilian-Dirlmeier, *Anhänger in Griechenland.*
For the variant and its find contexts: Bouzek, *Graeco-Macedonian Bronzes* 20–21, group C; Kilian-Dirlmeier, *Anhänger in Griechenland* 142–44, pls. 44–45; Oresani bird, 111 no. 615, 142–43 no. 799, pl. 45; Kilian, "Trachtzubehör der Eisenzeit" 95 pl. 57.
Hollow-casting of bronze birds: Mitten, *Classical Bronzes* 26, 28 nn. 12, 14, 15; H. Lechtman, *Art and Technology, a Symposium on Classical Bronzes* (Cambridge 1970) 14–22.
On the magical significance of Macedonian bronzes: D. Metzler, "Zum Schamanismus in Griechenland" *Antidoron. Festschrift für Jürgen Thimme zum 65. Geburtstag* (Karlsruhe 1982) 75–82; Bouzek, *Graecolatina Pragensia* 11 (1987) 98–99.

S. L.

59 ARMBAND

Said to be from Olympia, Late Geometric, ca. 700 B.C.

Maximum diameter 0.162, maximum height 0.05.

Bronze; intact, possibly bent, some surface wear.

University of Missouri–Columbia, Museum of Art and Archaeology (64.3).

59

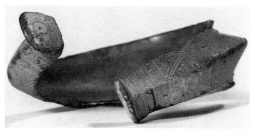

59

The large curving armband is solid cast and triangular in section with a ridge along the center and smaller ridges on the outer edges. The squared endplates are decorated with one large central and two (originally four) small stamped concentric circles. Incised decoration of the band is restricted to the ends: an X design of stamped dots on either side of the center rib, and two bands of incised herringbone and zigzag bordered by two incised lines and one dot-line.

The type represented by the Missouri bronze is dated ca. 700 B.C. and appears to have originated in southeast Albania and spread out from the Illyrian-Macedonian region to the Chalkidike. Greek sites where these have been found include Olympia, Dodona, Delphi, Kedros near Philia, and an unknown provenance in Boeotia. Like other Macedonian bronzes, these are found in grave contexts in northern areas and in sanctuaries when they occur in Greece, fitting the Geometric period pattern of offering exotic or foreign objects to the gods rather than adopting them into current fashion. The armbands seem too stylistically consistent with the core group of northern examples to suggest any local Greek manufacture of these items, and the Missouri ornament should be considered an import from a Macedonian or Balkan source. The closest parallel for the Missouri armband is the elegant example from Prilep in western Macedonia. Their massive scale and impressive weight must have made them seem especially appropriate gifts for the gods.

It is unknown to whom this armband was dedicated at Olympia, where a number of gods were worshiped. Throughout Greek history a general pattern finds more jewelry dedicated to female than to male deities, although personal ornaments found at the Dictaean Cave, Delphi, and the Amyklaion among other early sanctuaries of male gods must have been dedicated to those deities.

PUBLISHED
Münzen und Medaillen, Basel, Auktion 26 (October 5, 1963) no. 5.
Bouzek, *Graeco-Macedonian Bronzes* 126 no. 14.

EXHIBITED
Jewelry of the Ancient Mediterranean, The California Palace of the Legion of Honor, San Francisco, December 1969–February 1970.

NOTES
General discussions of the type and examples: Bouzek, *Graeco-Macedonian Bronzes* 124–26 type D 2, fig. 40, pls. 29–30; Kilian, "Trachtzubehör der Eisenzeit" 109, 131, pls. 1, 60, 61 no. 4 (Prilep example), 86 type 2; Philipp, *Bronzeschmuck aus Olympia* 207 nos. 765, 766, pls. 13, 48. These sources have extensive bibliographies of parallel bracelets found in Greek and northern sites.
Also: A. de Ridder, *Les bronzes antiques du Louvre* (Paris 1913–1915) II, pl. 91, 2195;

60

Schefold, *Meisterwerke griechischer Kunst*
fig. 68–69; Cahn, *Early Art in Greece* nos.
104, 105.

S. L.

60 ENGRAVED BELT

Thessalian, Late Geometric, 725–675 B.C.
Height 0.052, total length 0.887.
Bronze, greenish gray patina; intact with five
vertical cracks.
Arthur M. Sackler Museum, Harvard
University Art Museums, Gift of Robert
A. Kagan (1986.384).
See Plate 10.

The bronze belt is solid cast and hammered,
with a unique program of incised decoration
on its two surfaces. The thin band is widest at
front center, whence it tapers gradually toward
two finial terminations. These finials link
two flattened ovoid beads of decreasing size,
between two serrated cylinders. The convex
arc of the top edge is slightly more pronounced than that of the bottom.

Although the belt shares typological features with Thessalian and Boeotian armbands
dating to the late eighth to early seventh centuries, its extraordinary decoration and large
size set it apart and suggest that an armband
workshop was commissioned to produce a
deluxe belt. The inwardly curving ends hint
that it once may have been held in a coil in
the manner of an armband, and then perhaps
uncoiled in antiquity or more recently, resulting in multiple cracks. However, a coil config-
uration would have obscured the exquisitely
balanced and coordinated decoration. The
artifact is best explained as a belt that took its
form from an armband type.

The decorative program of the belt exhibits
precision and technical mastery and connotes
prearrangement. On the surface facing the
viewer, nine enclosed zones of measured
width are bracketed by a chain of hatched
diamonds giving way to finely cut vertical
lines. The entire design is circumscribed by
two double borders, between which are
engraved repeating concentric half circles rendered with the aid of a compass. Two horse
and bird groups and compass-drawn wheel
compositions alternate with groups of vertically banded zones, the bands being distinguished by changing ornamental treatments.
The confronting horse and bird groups are
remarkable for their meticulous execution.
They are most unusual for being positioned
on inverted groundlines. The overall design
presents a succession of paired zones around
a central banded zone. Read linearally, the
sequence ends at the center of the composition and then is reversed. This sequence
(*abcdedcba*) is in fact the visual equivalent of
"ring-composition," a technique characteristic
of Homeric epic and of the *Iliad* in particular.

Total symmetry, however, is upset by the inverted horse and bird groups.

The opposite side of the belt employs a similar framework. Loosely rendered pairs of lions, deer, and fish, all subjects of similes in the *Iliad*, interchange with vertically banded zones punctuated by compass-drawn concentric half circles. The selection and placement of the animal pairs frustrate any sense of logical order and seem improvised.

The two sides of the belt are united by a common decorative framework and contrasted by how that framework is filled. The alternation of zones is reversed, so that a banded zone on one side aligns with a representational zone on the other. Integral to this schema is a calculated interplay of balanced opposites. Sequential order on one side is set against an improvised arrangement on the other, the reasoned world of humankind (domesticated horses) against instinctive nature (lions, deer, and fish). As in the *Iliad*, opposing themes and patterns are brilliantly integrated and harmonized within a structure that is simultaneously formulaic and improvisational.

The practice of bracketing zones of representational or abstract motifs between zones of grouped vertical bands, reminiscent of the metope and triglyph arrangement of a Doric temple, was popular on painted Attic Late Geometric pottery. The incised decorations on the catchplates of late eighth-century Thessalian fibulae provide the closest stylistic parallels to the decoration of the Harvard belt (compare **19**).

In a wider context, belts are a pervasive attribute of the hero in Greek literature and art of the Geometric and Orientalizing periods. In the *Iliad*, belts protect heroes from death in battle, distinguish king from commoner, are exchanged as gifts of guest-friendship, and are worn by boxers, charioteers, and wrestlers. Eighth- and seventh-century figures in Greek art, cast in bronze, engraved on sheet bronze, sculpted in marble, and painted on pottery, represent belted but otherwise nude male figures, many engaged in various heroic activi-

ties. By contrast, belted female figures of the same period are clothed.

Belts were dedicated at major Greek sanctuaries in Asia Minor and on the mainland during the eighth and seventh centuries, a further indication of the value attached to them on both sides of the Aegean. Belt dedications are well attested to on Chios and Samos, where ancient sources state that groups of rhapsodes were devoted to the tradition of Homer. At Olympia, belt dedications ended just when articles of hoplite armor began to appear in the seventh century, evidence in the material record of the transition from the heroic oikos to the developing polis.

PUBLISHED
Sale catalogue, Sotheby's (London), December 14–15, 1981, lot 295 (ill.).

NOTES
Further discussion: M. J. Bennett, "The Belted Hero in Early Greece" (Ph.D. diss. Harvard University, forthcoming).

Thessalian armbands and fibulae: Kilian, *Fibeln in Thessalien.*

Boeotian armbands: Philipp, *Bronzeschmuck aus Olympia* nos. 756, 757, with extensive bibliography; *Ergon* (1989) 44–45 fig. 44.

Ring composition: J. L. Myres, "Homeric Art" *BSA* 45 (1950) 229–60; C. Whitman, "Homer and the Heroic Tradition" (Cambridge MA 1958) 249–84; A. B. Lord, *Epic Singers and Oral Tradition* (Ithaca NY 1991) 32.

Similes: W. C. Scott, *The Oral Nature of the Homeric Simile* (Leiden 1974).

Metope and triglyph decoration: Coldstream, *Geometric Greece* 114.

Homeric belts: H. Brandenburg, *Mitra, Zoma, Zoster* (ArchHom I, E, Göttingen 1977) 119–43.

Belted bronze statuettes: A. Fürtwangler, *Die Bronzen und die übrigen kleineren Funde von Olympia* (Berlin 1890); E. Kunze, "Kleinplastik aus Bronze" *OlBer* VII (Berlin 1961) 141–51; W.-D. Heilmeyer, "Wagenvotive" *OlBer* X (Berlin 1981) 59–71; Rolley, *Monuments figurés, les statuettes de bronze.*

61

61

Belt dedications: W. Kasper, "Die buckelver-
zierten Bleche Olympias" (diss. Munich
1972); B. Fellmann, *Frühe Olympische Gür-
telschmuckscheiben aus Bronze* (OlForsch
XVI, Berlin 1984); J. Boardman, "Ionian
Bronze Belts" *Anatolia* 6 (1961) 179–89; U.
Jantzen, *Ägyptische und orientalische Bronzen aus dem Heraion von Samos* (Samos
VIII, Bonn 1972).

Belt pendants: S. Langdon, "From Monkey to
Man" 414, nn. 24–26.

Important references to belts in the *Iliad*:
4.132–35; 5.539, 615, 857; 6.219; 7.305; 10.77;
11.234–37; 12.189; 14.214–17; 17.519, 578;
20.414; 23.127–31, 683, 710.

M. J. B.

61 FIGURED TRIPOD

Cypriot, Cypro-Geometric I, 1000–950 B.C.
Height 0.178, diameter 0.147.
Ceramic; broken in several places and
repaired; decoration partially effaced and
repainted.
The Metropolitan Museum of Art, The
Cesnola Collection; purchased by
subscription, 1874–1876 (74.51.437).

The stand's three straight legs support the
tapering ring body with everted rim. Figural

scenes in matte black and red paint decorate
two of the legs; the third has geometric
designs. On one side, a man strides to the
right carrying a branch or plant and flanked
by two small quadrupeds, probably goats. The
figure's torso is formed by a tapering hatched
rectangle. His profile face features a single
large reserved dotted eye; his hair sprouts in
strands from the back of his head. In the second scene a man, apparently the same one,
stands between two black fish. He holds an
oblong object to his face. His action has been
interpreted as sniffing a flower; more likely,
given his aquatic companions, he is blowing a
conch shell. Abstract decorations of checkerboard and crosshatched lozenges and triangles
fill the remaining surfaces.

Such tripods were used to support a round-
bottomed vessel such as a bowl or krater. A
one-piece krater on tripod stand from Kouklia-
Evreti Tomb 14 and an eleventh-century one-
piece tripod amphora from Kouklia-*Skales*
Tomb 81 provide schematic parallels. The
Metropolitan tripod is an imitation in clay of
a late thirteenth- to early twelfth-century cast-
bronze tripod. The relation of our stand to its
metal prototype is manifest in such details as
the loops attached to the arches between
each leg, where "danglers," usually bronze
buds and pomegranates, hang in the metal

versions. The relief or *ajourée* zigzag that decorates the ring top of many bronze-cast tripods is recalled in the lozenge band around the top of the stand.

The Metropolitan tripod is unique among clay tripods for its figural decoration; even the related bronze versions do not carry figural decoration on the legs. For the source of the iconography we must turn to the bronze four-sided stands that were made in the same workshops as the bronze tripods and offered the artist greater scope for figural scenes on their four rectangular panels. Combined elements of Aegean, Cypriot, and Levantine tradition make up the iconography of these stands, with the Aegean influence often predominant. The closest parallel for the plant-bearer and fish-companion of the Metropolitan tripod is a much-illustrated stand from Episkopi now in London. On each side appears a tree at the left toward which a man approaches bearing an offering (in one case a pair of fish). The grouping of man with fish, tree, and goats on the present stand recalls the Aegean cosmological scenes found in Bronze Age and early Iron Age art particularly on Crete. Aegean affinities are also detectable in the heraldic symmetry of the goats and the fish in each scene. Triton shells, both real and manufactured of stone or faience, appear regularly in religious contexts in the Aegean and Cyprus. A Late Minoan III seal from the Idaean Cave shows a figure in a pose nearly identical to the tripod figure blowing or perhaps pouring a libation from a triton shell beside an altar. The great antiquity of the ritual use of tritons is attested to by the recent excavation at Kissonerga-*Mosphilia*, Cyprus, of a Chalcolithic ritual deposit containing a triton inside a building model accompanied by numerous figurines.

The Metropolitan tripod is datable to the later phase of Cypro-Geometric I by the figure style, which parallels a plate from Kouklia-*Skales*, and also by shape comparisons with tripods from excavated graves at Lapithos, Kaloriziki, and Kouklia-*Skales*. Made perhaps as much as two centuries after the cast tripods it imitates, the Metropolitan tripod belongs to a trend that replaces with clay copies the dwindling numbers of precious bronze tripods that had been preserved as heirlooms. Consequently, its figural decoration also continues Late Bronze Age Aegean iconography, perhaps revitalized through Cretan connections in the eleventh century when it is thought the bronze heirloom tripods were distributed into the Aegean region through Crete.

While there can have been no direct influence from this tripod, a close parallel exists in an equally rare Attic figural clay stand of similar form found in the Kerameikos. Dating to ca. 730 B.C., it features a man fighting a lion on each leg and a warrior frieze on its ring. Part of a general phenomenon of Cyprus preserving elements of Mycenaean heritage through the Dark Age, tripods like this one made forms as well as figures available for later Greek artists to revive.

PUBLISHED

Cesnola, *Cyprus* pl. XLIV.

Cesnola, *A Descriptive Atlas of the Cesnola Collection* II pl. CXXXIII, 984.

M. Ohnefalsch-Richter, *Kypros, the Bible, and Homer* (London 1893) 458 and pls. XCVII, 4 and CLVI, 4.

M. Hoernes, *Urgeschichte der bildenden Kunst in Europa* (Vienna 1915) 601, fig. 180.

W. Deonna, "Les origines de la répresentation humaine dans l'art grec" *BCH* 50 (1926) 319–82 at 343 fig. 9.7, figure reprinted in Benson, *Horse, Bird, and Man* fig. 1.

Myres, *Handbook of the Cesnola Collection* 67, no. 513, ill.

H. T. Bossert, *Altsyrien* (Tübingen 1951) fig. 248.

Catling, *Cypriot Bronzework in the Mycenaean World* 214 n. 2.

Karageorghis and Des Gagniers, *La céramique chypriote de style figuré* 100, IX.4.

J. Karageorghis, *La grande déesse de Chypre et son culte* (Lyon 1977) 168.

Gjerstad, *The Cypro-Geometric, Cypro-Archaic and Cypro-Classical Periods* fig. XXIV, 8.

Karageorghis, *Palaepaphos-Skales* 124 n. 142.
Iacovou, *The Pictorial Pottery of Eleventh Century B.C. Cyprus* 27, 40, 41, 55, 56, 62, 72, fig. 33.

NOTES

Generally on Aegean clay tripods: Catling, *Cypriot Bronzework in the Mycenaean World* 213–17; Iacovou, *The Pictorial Pottery of Eleventh Century B.C. Cyprus* 40; Demetriou, *Cypro-Aegean Relations in the Early Iron Age* 27–30.

On date of the stand: Iacovou, *The Pictorial Pottery* 27; Karageorghis, *Palaepaphos-Skales* 124 n. 142.

Parallels: Karageorghis, *Palaepaphos-Skales* T. 49 pl. LXXXVI, T. 67, pl. CXXX.

On the heirloom theory: H. Catling, "Workshop and Heirloom: Prehistoric Bronze Stands in the East Mediterranean" *RDAC* (1984) 69–91.

For iconography: Boardman, *The Cretan Collection in Oxford* 46–47, no. 217, fig. 21; S. Langdon, "The Return of the Horse-Leader" 190–94.

For the religious use of tritons: Idaean Cave seal, Nilsson, *The Minoan-Mycenaean Religion* 153 fig. 61; C. Baurain and P. Darcque, "Un triton en pierre à Malia" *BCH* 107 (1983) 3–73; E. Peltenburg, "The Beginnings of Religion" in *Early Society in Cyprus* 108–26 at 120.

S. L.

62 RING HANDLE OF A TRIPOD CAULDRON

Found 1894 in Praisos, Crete, Late Geometric, eighth century.
Diameter 0.241, height 0.1967.
Bronze; broken and repaired; large missing section restored in lead.
The Metropolitan Museum of Art, Gift of the Archaeological Institute of America, 1953 (53.53).

The circular cast handle is flat in section with simple molding on inner and outer rims. An openwork dogtooth design decorates the

62

flat surface between the rims. A pair of small rivets remains on a solid section of the ring. Approximately one-fourth of the handle is missing. Halbherr interpreted the pair of rivets near the break as evidence of an ancient repair.

The handle segment was found in the temenos area on Acropolis III at Praisos in eastern Crete. Originally settled as a refugee haven in remote hill country at the end of the Bronze Age, the site later developed into a thriving Archaic city-state. Given this Cretan provenance, we may reconstruct the original appearance of the tripod from which the handle comes on the basis of parallels from the Idaean Cave, Arkades, Palaikastro, and Kato Syme. The "Idaean type" is characterized by the openwork dogtooth handles and is found on most Cretan tripods. Horses or birds may sit on top of the handle, although the Metropolitan example preserves no such evidence. Cretan tripod legs tend to have a rectangular form and simple vertical fillet decoration.

The development of the bronze tripod and its changing role in Greek consciousness are fairly well documented. Prior to its symbolic use, the tripod-cauldron's essential function was for the cooking of food; its three legs enabled it to stand over a fire, and the ring-handle form allowed a pole to be passed through for lifting the vessel off the fire. Precisely how and when the tripod's status grew from lowly domesticity to gift for the gods are not completely understood but likely occurred in the context of festival activities that included feasting and games at sanctuaries. Contemporary painted scenes show contests of skill being waged over a tripod, an association that echoes the awarding of tripods as prizes for games in Homeric epic.

Although predecessor Mycenaean bronze tripod-cauldrons were known on Crete, as in the example from Zapher Papoura, the Geometric tripod attained stature and ornamentation on the mainland before being introduced to Crete in the eighth century. The greatest numbers of Cretan fragments come from the Idaean Cave and Palaikastro, both sanctuaries of Zeus. An identification of Cretan Zeus with his Olympian cult may have been the tripod's passport into Crete, although Maass's survey of deities known to have received tripod offerings cautions against an association between the object and any single god.

Geometric Cretan art tends to be strongly orientalizing; in form and decoration the bronze tripods reflect, unusually, a purely native Greek mainland tradition. Whether the function and symbolic content of the object in its Cretan home corresponded equally to mainland usage in less certain. Its connection with athletic victory may have been less important on Crete, where representations of tripods in other media focus on their oracular associations. A painted Late Geometric terracotta shield from Fortetsa depicts a figure holding thunderbolts and striding toward a tripod; beneath the tripod a head is seen eerily emerging from the ground. The scene has been interpreted as a divine epiphany of Zeus in association with his oracular cults. A bronze mitra from Axos shows apparently another epiphany pictured as a head above a shield arising from a tripod cauldron, an image reminiscent to some of mantic Apollo. The tripod in Cretan art and perhaps in its role in the Zeus cults of the Idaean Cave and

Palaikastro represented purification and oracular power.

PUBLISHED

F. Halbherr, "American Expedition to Krete under Professor Halbherr" *AJA* 9 (1894) 543.

F. Halbherr, "Report on the Research at Praesos" *AJA* 2d ser. 5 (1901) 383, fig. 12.

R. C. Bosanquet, "Excavations at Praesos I" *BSA* 8 (1901–1902) 231–70 at 259.

Benton, "Evolution of the Tripod-lebes" 93, under type B (d).

Richter, *Handbook of the Greek Collection* 26, n. 29, pl. 17f.

F. Willemsen, *Dreifusskessel von Olympia* (OlForsch III, Berlin 1957) 47.

M. Maass, "Kretische Dreifüsse" *AM* 92 (1977) 33–59 at 47 n. 45.

NOTES

On Cretan tripod types: Benton, "Evolution of the Tripod-lebes" 119; Willemsen, *Dreifusskessel von Olympia* 57, 175–76; Coldstream, *Geometric Greece* 283; Maass, "Kretische Dreifüsse."

Tripod parallels: from Palaikastro and Praisos, S. Benton, "Bronzes from Palaikastro and Praisos" *BSA* 40 (1939–1940) 51–59, pls. 21–22, pl. 32 no. 1; Maass, "Kretische Dreifüsse" no. 36, fig. 2, pl. 24.

From Idaean Cave: Ashmolean Museum AE 24, 1894.139, Boardman, *The Cretan Collection in Oxford* 79, 86–87 cat. 377, pl. XXVII; Coldstream, *Geometric Greece* 282, fig. 90d; Maass, "Kretische Dreifüsse" nos. 37–38, fig. 2, pls. 24–25.

Zapher Papoura tripod: *Archaeologia* 59 (1905) 433, fig. 38 and pl. 89; A. Evans, *The Palace of Minos at Knossos* II (London 1928) 629, 634 fig. 398.

On the origins and function of the tripod-cauldron: Benton, "Evolution of the Tripod-lebes"; Maass, *Die geometrischen Dreifüsse von Olympia* 1–4.

Tripods in Cretan art: terracotta shield, Brock, *Fortetsa* no. 1414, pl. 107; Axos mitra, *ASAtene* 13–14 (1930–1931) pl. XIII; D. Levi, "Gleanings from Crete" *AJA* 49

(1945) 270–329 at 293–313; C. Picard, "Apollon sur la mitra d'Axos" in *Studies Presented to David Moore Robinson* I, ed. G. E. Mylonas (St. Louis 1951) 655–63; D. Levi, "Postilla sulla mitra di Axos" *PP* 7 (1952) 41–47.

For connections of tripods with sacrifice and regeneration: also W. Burkert, *Homo Necans* (Berkeley 1983) 83–130, esp. 100–101; R. C. Bosanquet, "Dicte and the Temples of Dictaean Zeus" *BSA* 40 (1939–1940) 60–77.

S. L.

Much did I suffer and wandered much before bringing
all this home in my ships when I came back in the eighth year.
I wandered to Cyprus and Phoenicia, to the Egyptians,
I reached the Ethiopians, Eremboi, Sidonians,
and Libya where the rams grow their horns quickly.

(Odyssey 4.81–85)

GREECE
AND THE GREATER WORLD

The nearly complete isolation of Greece from the rest of the world in the Dark Age meant above all a severance from external sources of metals. It was this need for bronze and gold that finally compelled Greeks in the ninth century into maritime exploration and renewal of contact with their foreign neighbors. By the mid-eighth century the pressures of repopulation and perhaps also famine added incentives to colonize new land. Confronting the world as traders and as settlers, the Greeks found in these experiences much to excite the imagination and to incite anxiety (Fig. 23). The krater scenes of fighting on ship or shore may reveal the sometimes hostile nature of Greek encounters with the greater world (Figs. 10, 18). By the end of the eighth century Greek culture was thoroughly infused with the borrowings from the world outside. In addition to the importation of metals and luxury items came the more subtle influences, by firsthand experience or second-

hand account, of the Phoenician alphabet, Egyptian "monumentality," Near Eastern myth, poetry, and exotic deities. The fact that these influences helped to shape the developing hellenic culture is undeniable; the extent to which this occurred has been controversial. The objects assembled here—Phoenician, Cypriot, Etruscan, Luristan, and Balkan—bear thematic and stylistic relations to Geometric Greek art and represent different sorts of foreign contact: imports, exports, direct and indirect imitations of foreign objects, the influence of Geometric Greek style on other cultures, and the work of Greek colonists under local foreign influence.

Led by the same adventurous Euboeans who penetrated early into the eastern Mediterranean (see 71), the search for external sources of metals prompted the first Greek colonists to venture west, settling in Ischia and the coast of Italy by the mid-eighth century. Half a century later the impact of

Fig. 23. Shipwreck scene on a krater from Pithek-
oussai. (Reproduced by permission of the Swedish
Institute, Rome)

Greek art combined with local Italic traditions to create a geometric figural style variously labeled "Italo-Geometric" or Etruscan. An olla with an abduction scene (63) and a standed krater (64) both bear the stamp of Attic, Euboean, and Argive Geometric painting in their style and iconography, particularly the latter in scenes of horse-taming. Their shapes are more firmly grounded in local Italic pottery traditions. The lower half of a Protocorinthian lekythos (65) with a wolf chasing two horses and a bird humorously approaching a griffin-protome cauldron shows the continuation of purely Greek work in the Italian colonies, reflecting the new wave of orientalizing influence that heralds the demise of Geometric art.

Some types of Geometric objects were so widely spread throughout Greece, the Adriatic, and the Balkans that it is difficult to determine where they originated. The spectacle fibula and the bronze armbands, found in a great variety of sizes and forms, are well-known examples of such objects (59, 66). Baltic amber beads found in Greek graves reflect the continuation of ancient trade routes through central Europe and down the Adriatic (67) and suggest the means by which the bronze jewelry forms also traveled.

The role of Cyprus in preserving Mycenaean traditions and reintroducing them to Greece is illustrated by objects of funerary and cult function. The tenth-century duck vase (68), much like those found at Lefkandi in Euboea, bears the imprint of Cypriot bird vases. The kernos (44) and ceramic tripod (61), both objects from Cypriot graves, fostered new forms of votive objects in Geometric Greece. Figural representation, richly explored by Mycenaean artists and potters, nearly vanished during the early Dark Age in Greece but found continuous expression in Cyprus. The offering scenes on the Cypriot ceramic tripod (61) and the large figure-eight body shield on an amphora fragment (70) preserved elements of Aegean pictorial tradition. A Euboean pendent semicircle skyphos found its way to Cyprus through trade or immigration (71). The type is the most widespread of all Greek pottery exports, found from Sicily to Syria, and enables us to trace Greek activity in the Mediterranean region. A Cypriot cup (72) bearing a Phoenician inscription painted before firing suggests both the source of the Greek alphabet and the means by which it may have been introduced into Greece, perhaps through Cypriot intermediaries as well as Phoenician.

Despite the evidence of early trade connections with the Levant by the Euboeans, Phoenicia first came to Greece rather than vice versa. Recent finds have identified Phoenician unguent and faience factories on several Aegean islands, Phoenician temples on Crete, and Phoenician-influenced cult activity at Sparta. The resulting imprints on Greek art, religion, commerce, and material resources are still being assessed. In the exhibition, Levantine influence can be found in the gold earrings with granulation (13), the horse-taming skyphos (10), the bronze lyre-player (17), and the ritual scenes of a funerary cup (21). A Phoenician scarab seal found inside a Late

63

63

Geometric skyphos in an Athenian grave documents the special regard given foreign exotica, and perhaps the amuletic function of seals as well (73–74). Remarkably similar is a seal found recently at Lefkandi. A small seal of the Lyre-Player Group (75) may have been manufactured in Cilicia for the Greek market; the majority of such seals have been found in children's graves at Pithekoussai. Like the pair of deities imitating Syrian prototypes (41–42), a type of Geometric bronze warrior derives from the widely disseminated Near Eastern smiting god statuettes (76–77).

Nomadic Asian cultures, masters of bronzeworking and small-scale portable art, present an incompletely understood influence on Geometric Greek art. Luristan art exemplifies the broader scope of an "Animal Style" artistic tradition that characterizes much of Europe and Asia throughout the second and early first millennia. For all the complexity of their sources, Greek Geometric art and Homeric epic similes owe something to this background as well as to orientalizing influences. Buried in the animal images of predator and prey (7, 11) are the remnants of Bronze Age animal style. Yet the abstraction of the Luristan idol standard (78) is of an essentially different

nature from that of Greek Geometric art. Bronze objects from Luristan appear with some frequency in Greek sanctuaries as votive dedications and also seem to have had an impact on the production of Greek votive objects. Small bronze pendants of birds and abstract ornaments may have decorated horse bridles and clothing in their native western Asia and seem to have influenced favorite votive types found especially in Thessalian and Macedonian sanctuaries (32, 58).

S. L.

63 STAMNOID OLLA

Italo-Geometric (early Etruscan), ca. 700–680 B.C.
Height 0.216, diameter 0.232.
Ceramic; large chip missing from foot; chipping around root of one handle; gash in bird on Side A; some paint loss, particularly on the bull.
The Art Museum, Princeton University, Museum purchase, John Maclean Magie and Gertrude Magie Fund (y1965–205).
See Plate 8.

A shape believed to originate in Etruria, the stamnoid olla has a globular body, collar-like mouth, and two horizontal handles set obliquely on the shoulder. Lidded Greek vessels of related shape are usually classed as globular pyxides, and this Italic vase may also have functioned as a pyxis.

The clay is a pale orange-red, with decoration in a reddish brown slip. The foot, inner neck, and outside of the handles are solid in color. The lower body is filled by parallel stripes; three more stripes circle the mouth. Both figure scenes are framed by groups of seven or eight vertical stripes. These are connected above and below the handles by groups of three to four horizontal lines, creating small side panels. In the panel below one handle is a bull or cow, with curved horns, long slender body, and curly tail. A row of dots in a reserved band runs the length of the animal's body, which has zigzags and rows of dots beneath and in front of it. The opposite panel contains zigzags and dots.

On Side A, a tall man reaches out to touch or grab the head of a shorter woman, standing at left. Both figures have wasp waists, triangular trunks, outlined heads with crude but sinuous profiles, and long wavy hair. The woman is identified as female by a long dress with wavy folds. The man, apparently nude, has large thighs and short shanks; his penis is clearly indicated. Both of his eyes are crowded into the near side of his head. The painter showed his impatience with the confining groundline by placing the man's feet among the stripes below; the woman's feet were simply omitted. The woman turns her face away from her assailant. Her right arm is only partially represented, being cut off by the panel's border, but she raises her left hand to touch the man's breast, perhaps in supplication. The single stroke emerging from her mouth is possibly a mistake. The action is observed by a male on horseback at right, who uses both hands to steady himself on his mount. He is smaller than the man at center and either is a boy or, more likely, was simply reduced by the artist to make him fit comfortably within the panel. The long-legged water bird standing between the horse and the taller man is a common decorative filler on Geometric vases in both Italy and Greece

(e.g. 74). Zigzags and rows of dots fill the rest of the space around the figures.

On Side B a man stands with his right hand at the head of a horse; no rope is represented, but he is clearly holding it by a lead or bridle. Below the horse is a large fish decorated with vertical and horizontal stripes. Like its counterpart on Side A, the horse has long slender legs, a mane of stiff perpendicular strokes, and a reserved eye. The spreading of the forelegs shows he is more restless than the other horse, in need of calming. The man is drawn like the larger male on the front, with two exceptions: a vertical stripe reinforces the isolation of the eyes on one side of the face, and three small reserved circles on the waist probably indicate a belt. As on side A, zigzags and rows of dots fill the space around the figures. Above the back of the horse is a large crosshatched meander, and below the horse's head is a vertical column of crude, hatched lozenges.

The vase was previously assigned to a Greek workshop in Argos, on the basis of Argive examples of related shape with a wealth of linear ornament and the same odd combination of a fish beneath a horse. As was first suggested by Dyfri Williams, however, the vessel must have been made in Italy. A series of such ollas were produced in the seventh century in Southern Etruria, at sites such as Cerveteri and Veii. This example is of particular importance not only for its figure decoration, which may well have been based partially on Argive models, but also for its place at the head of the series of stamnoid ollas. A date soon after 700 B.C. is suggested by both the shape and the decoration. The collar is taller and the globular body wider and more depressed than in later examples. The outlining of the figures' heads, a precocious feature reminiscent of the early Protoattic style, is somewhat at odds with the triangular torsos and the purely Geometric motif of the hatched meander. The austere linear ornament is a common feature of Early Protocorinthian vases exported to Italy at the beginning of the seventh century. Although rare on Italo-Geometric vases, the few known examples of figure scenes tend to be large in relation to the rest of the vessel and not confined to narrow friezes or small metopes; an example is the famous Shipwreck Krater from Pithekoussai (Fig. 23).

Jones suggested the scene on Side A might represent the abduction of the young Helen by Theseus. The two horsemen would thus be Helen's brothers Kastor and Polydeukes— the Dioskouroi—come to fetch her home to Sparta. The problems with this interpretation include the fact that the horsemen are on different sides of the vase, that neither seems particularly bellicose, and that the subject might be considered unlikely for an Etruscan vase painter of this period. Theseus turns up early in Greek art as the slayer of the Minotaur, but very seldom as the abductor of Helen, although her rescue by the Dioskouroi was represented on the seventh-century Chest of Kypselos, seen at Olympia by Pausanias (V.19.2–3). The scene on Side A seems to tell a story, but we cannot be certain if it is a Greek or an Italian one. The central male has a heroic air, and the aggressive gestures and the turning away of the woman point to a rape or abduction rather than a more tender encounter such as Theseus and Ariadne, or Menelaos and Helen. Of possible relevance is an Attic Late Geometric krater in London with a male and female about to board a ship, interpreted by some as the departure of Theseus and Ariadne from Crete, by others as the elopement of Paris and Helen; the woman, though grabbed by the wrist, may be boarding of her own will. The Homeric poems were brought to Italy by Greek traders and colonists, and Etruscan artists were representing identifiable episodes by the middle of the seventh century. If the subject of the Princeton vase is the abduction of Helen not by Theseus but by Paris, the relative insignificance of the rider is more readily explained: he is a henchman rather than a rescuer. Perhaps in seventh-century Italy, Helen was credited with being forcibly abducted rather than an active party to elopement.

Like the bull beneath the handle, the scene on Side B probably has no connection with that on Side A. The so-called horse-leader motif is relatively common in Geometric art. On Late Geometric pottery at Argos a fish is also commonly present, often directly beneath the horse. The meaning of this motif is much debated, some seeing the horse-leader as Poseidon, god of both horses and the sea, others preferring a more general reference to horse-raising aristocrats and seaborne trade.

PUBLISHED

F. F. Jones, "A Greek Pot of the Geometric Period" *Record of the Art Museum, Princeton University* 26, 1 (1967) 4–12.

Betancourt, "The Age of Homer" 12 (ill.).

Archaeology 23 (1970) 53 (ill.).

Ahlberg-Cornell, "Games, Play and Performance" 62 n. 25.

EXHIBITED

The Age of Homer, University Museum, University of Pennsylvania, December 1969–March 1970.

NOTES

For an overview of Italo-Geometric pottery: F. Canciani in *La ceramica degli Etruschi* ed. M. Martelli (Novara 1987) 9–15, 65–80, 242–54.

For 7th c. Etruscan orientalizing pottery: Martelli, *La ceramica degli Etruschi* 16–22, 81–96, 255–68.

For the Etruscan origin of stamnoi: C. Isler-Kerenyi, "Stamnoi e stamnoidi" *NumAntCl* 5 (1976) 33–52.

For an Argive krater of related shape, with linear decoration and a horse-leader on one side: Courbin, *La céramique géométrique de l'Argolide* pl. 36 (C.1017).

For the horse-leader motif: Argive, Courbin, *La céramique géométrique* 397–413, 480–82, pl. 28; S. Langdon, "The Return of the Horse-Leader"; Attic, Coldstream, *Greek Geometric Pottery* pl. 13e–f.

For fish on 7th c. Etruscan pottery: R. Dik, "Un oinochoe ceretana con decorazione di pesci" *Meded* 43 (1981) 69–81.

For the stamnoid olla in Etruria: S. Stuart Leach, *Subgeometric Pottery from Southern Etruria* (SIMA-PB 54, Göteborg 1987) 79–91, 111–14, pls. 57–67; Martelli, *Ceramica degli Etruschi* 83, fig. 28.4.

The figure style is without exact parallels; cf. the dancers on an oinochoe in London (British Museum 49.5–18.18): J. N. Coldstream, "A Figured Oinochoe from Italy" *BICS* 15 (168) 86–96; Canciani, *Ceramica degli Etruschi* 80, 255–56, no. 25; the musician and acrobats on an amphora in the Fujita collection (on loan to Würzburg, inv. ZA 66): Martelli, *Ceramica degli Etruschi* 92 and 262–63, no. 38.

For the Shipwreck Krater from Pithekoussai: S. Brunnsåker, *OpRom* 4 (1962) 165–242; G. Buchner, "Figurlich bemalte spätgeometrische Vasen aus Pithekussai und Kyme" *RM* 60–61 (1953–1954) 39–47, pls. 14–16.1.

For Theseus in early Greek art: K. Schefold, *Frühgriechische Sagenbilder* (Munich 1964) 37–40; J. Neils, *The Youthful Deeds of Theseus* (Rome 1987) 17–23; Fittschen, *Untersuchungen zum Beginn der Sagendarstellungen* 161–68.

For a possible depiction of Theseus, Helen, and the Dioskouroi on a Protocorinthian aryballos (Louvre CA617): Schefold, *Frühgriechische Sagenbilder* 39, fig. 9; Neils, *Youthful Deeds of Theseus* 20–21, pl. 1, fig. 2.

For the Geometric krater in London (BM 1899.2–19.1): A. S. Murray, "A New Vase of the Dipylon Class" *JHS* 19 (1899) 198–201, pl. VIII; Coldstream, *Geometric Greece* 353–55, fig. 112b.

J. M. P.

64 STANDED KRATER

Said to be from Vulci, Italo-Geometric, ca. 710 B.C.

Height 0.37, width at handles 0.447.

Ceramic; edge of foot repaired, with some restoration; considerable surface wear, particularly on bowl.

Tampa Museum of Art, Gift of Mr. and Mrs. Charles W. Sahlman (91.26)

Although resembling a two-piece dinos and stand, the vessel is actually a type of standed krater, with a broad bowl, bulbous midsection, and hollow, trumpet-shaped foot. The clay is a fine buff yellow, with decoration in slip, fired black to reddish brown. Inside, the upper half of the bowl is glazed and the reserved lower half is decorated with broad concentric stripes. The exterior from rim to foot is covered with geometric and figural decoration. The double-arched handles are striped and crosshatched. A lozenge-chain appears on top of the rim, with a band of zigzags along the outer edge. Around the foot and midsection are bands of metopes containing rosettes and birds accompanied by leaves, zigzags, and triangles, bordered above and below by rows of crosshatched triangles. Metopes on the lower part of the bowl contain checkerboards alternating with reclining foals or fawns.

On the upper body, the isolation of figures in metopes is abandoned on the obverse in favor of a continuous frieze. Three male horsemen ride to the right, each holding reins in his left hand and a crop in the right. At either end of the cavalcade is a riderless horse. The horses have long thin legs and spikey manes, while the riders are distinguished by triangular crosshatched torsos. The background is a welter of filling ornaments—birds, triangles, leaves, and "windows." Similar filling ornament surrounds the figures on the reverse, where there are two more horsemen, in this case confined to metopes on either side of a broad central panel framed by vertical bands of solid and reserved lozenges. In the center, a pair of horses face each other over a low, tablelike object, probably a manger. Below the manger is yet another of the ubiquitous long-necked birds.

The decoration, which lacks any native Italian or orientalizing elements, is close in both style and iconography to Euboean Late Geometric pottery. The metopes, horses and riders, reclining foals, as well as the birds,

64

checkerboards, rosettes, and triangles are found on pottery not only from Euboea but also from the earliest colonies in Italy, Pithekoussai and Cumae, founded in the third quarter of the eighth century by Greeks from Chalkis and Eretria. The shape of the vessel, however, is unlike any from Euboea or its colonies; in fact, although the decoration is not orientalizing, the shape recalls the oriental bronze cauldrons found in rich Italian tombs of the early seventh century, such as the Barberini and Bernardini Tombs at Praeneste and the Regolini-Galassi Tomb at Cerveteri. These imported cauldrons, ringed with lion or griffin protomes and supported on conical stands,

were probably brought from North Syria, either by Phoenician traders (also present at Pithekoussai) or by Greeks from the emporium at Al-Mina, where Euboean merchants were well established. Similar stands have been found at Olympia. Most of the stands are topped by a flowering capital with a bulb-like calyx, similar to but less prominent than the bulb on the Tampa vase. The latter also differs in having a more trumpet-shaped foot and a broader and shallower bowl.

At least four similar kraters with related decoration are known. Two have been attributed by Williams to the same painter as the Tampa vase, thought to be an immigrant

Euboean artist working at Vulci in the last decade of the eighth century. Colonna attributes to the Tampa artist a vase of related shape in the Villa Giulia, a "holmos," long said to have been found at Cerveteri. Isler makes the Tampa krater (64) the earliest known product (ca. 710) of a Vulcian workshop in which he identifies the influence, if not the actual presence, of vase-painters from Argos. Its motifs, however, are equally at home in the Euboean repertoire, and there is no other evidence for an Argive presence in Etruria in the late eighth century.

As in Greece, the horses and riders on the Tampa krater may indicate that the owner was an aristocrat of the local horse-owning class, the Vulcian counterparts to the *Hippobatai* of Euboea. The horses at the manger are not tethered, like many horses on contemporary Greek vessels, but face each other in the same manner as some of their Greek counterparts. Whatever meaning the motif held for the Euboean painter, we may wonder if his Etruscan patron interpreted it in the same way.

As for the shape, Colonna is right in de-emphasizing the connection with oriental cauldrons, pointing instead to a development from the holmos and from earlier stands of black impasto, so-called *calefattori*, with bulbous necks and bowl-like mouths. Apparently, a few potters at Vulci were inspired by the earliest imported cauldrons to create a new type of vessel incorporating elements from both the bronzes and the native holmos, drawing as well upon the local tradition of hammered bronze amphorae and Italic copies of imported bronze stands, like that from the Artiaco Tomb at Cumae. This new type of standed krater was short-lived, yielding in the early seventh century to the more versatile two-piece holmos-and-cauldron, several of which, with griffin protomes on their impasto bowls, continue to draw inspiration from the imported cauldrons.

PUBLISHED

Summa Galleries, Inc., Catalogue 4, *Ancient Vases* (Beverly Hills 1978) no. 15.

G. Colonna, "Parergon, A proposito del frammento geometrico dal Foro" *MEFRA* 92 (1980) 603, pl. 4.

H. P. Isler, "Ceramisti greci in Etruria in epoca tardogeometrica I. Cratere geometrico in una collezione ticinese" *NumAntCl* 12 (1983) 26, no. 1.

D. Williams, "Greek Potters and Their Descendants in Campania and Southern Etruria, ca. 720–630 B.C." in *Iron Age Artefacts in the British Museum* ed. J. Swaddling (London 1986) 300, n. 42.

J. G. Szilagyi, "La pittura etrusca figurata dell'etrusco-geometrico all'etrusco-corinzio" in *Atti del II Congresso Internazionale Etrusco* II (1989) 613ff.

L. Donati, "Rappresentazione etrusche della capra e del cervo di tipo 'scita'" *ArchCl* 43 (1991) 922, no. 2; 924, fig. 3; 927–28.

NOTES

For Italo-Geometric pottery: Å. Åkerström, *Der geometrischen Stil in Italien* (Lund 1943); more recently F. Canciani, in *La ceramica degli Etruschi* ed. M. Martelli (Novara 1987) 9–15, 65–80, 242–54.

For Euboean Late Geometric pottery: Coldstream, *Greek Geometric Pottery* 189–95, pl. 41; Coldstream, *Geometric Greece* 192–95; J. Boardman, "Euboean Pottery in East and West" *DialArch* 3 (1969) 85–101.

For the pottery of Pithekoussai and Cumae: G. Buchner, "Scavi nella necropoli di Pithecusa" *AttiMGrecia* 1 (1954) 3–19; G. Buchner, "Figurliche bemalte spätgeometrische Vasen aus Pithekussai und Kyme" *RM* 60–61 (1953–1954) 37–55; G. Buchner, "Pithekoussai: Oldest Greek Colony in the West" *Expedition* 8:4 (Summer 1966) 4–12; Coldstream, *Geometric Greece* 225–33; D. Ridgway, in *Greek Colonists and Native Populations*, ed. J. P. Descoeudres (Oxford 1990) 61–72.

For horse symbolism: S. Langdon, "The Return of the Horse-Leader"; horses with a manger, Courbin, *La céramique géométrique de l'Argolide* pls. 31, 34 (C.738); H.-P. Isler in *Greek Vases from the Hirschmann Collec-*

tion ed. H. Bloesch (Zurich 1982) 14–15, no. 3; Coldstream, *Greek Geometric Pottery* pl. 8d.

For oriental bronze cauldrons with conical stands in Italy: Coldstream, *Geometric Greece* 361–66; A. Rathje in *Italy before the Romans* ed. D. and F. R. Ridgway (London 1979) 158–65; L. Pareti, *La Tomba Regolini-Galassi del Museo Gregoriano Etrusco* (Vatican City 1947) pl. 39, no. 303; C. D. Curtis, "The Barberini Tomb" *MAAR* 5 (1925) pls. 27.2, 28, no. 80, and pls. 29–31, no. 81.

Other standed kraters of this type: Art Institute of Chicago 1985.627, L. Berge in *Daidalikon: Studies in Memory of Raymond V. Schoder, S.J.* ed. R. F. Sutton (Wauconda IL 1989) 46–51, pls. 8–11a; *Münzen und Medaillen* Sonderliste U (Basel 1984) 6–7, no. 6; Vulci, Museo Archeologico 98857, Canciani in *La ceramica degli Etruschi* 72 and 248–49, no. 13.

A related standed bowl from Narce in the University Museum, Philadelphia: *Etruscan Pottery: The Meeting of Greece and Etruria* (exhib. cat. Dickinson College, Carlisle PA 1984) 31 no. 14.

For immigrant Greek potters and vase painters in Etruria: M. Torelli, "Greek Artisans and Etruria" *ArchNews* 5:4 (Winter 1976) 134–38; D. Ridgway in *Papers in Italian Archaeology I: The Lancaster Seminar* (BAR Suppl. Series 41, Oxford 1978) 121–28; E. La Rocca, "Crateri in Argilla Figulina del geometrico recente a Vulci" *MEFRA* 90 (1978) 465–514; Isler, "Ceramisti greci in Etruria in epoca tardogeometrica" 9–47, 26–28 and 41.

For the holmos in the Villa Giulia: Coldstream, *Geometric Greece* 232, fig. 76b; Colonna, "Parergon" 598–601, pls. 1–3; Canciani, *Ceramica degli Etruschi*, 71, fig. 12.

For the relationship between calefattori, holmoi, and standed kraters: G. Colonna, "Un tripode fittile geometrico dal Foro Romano" *MEFRA* 89 (1977) 471–91; Colonna, "Parergon."

For the Artiaco Tomb: G. Pellegrini, "Tombe

greche Archaiche e tomba greco-sannitica a tholos della necropoli di Cuma" *MonAnt* 13 (1903) 204–94 esp. 251 fig. 27; I. Strom, *Problems concerning the Origin and Early Development of the Etruscan Orientalizing Style* (Odense 1971) 146–49, fig. 79.

For a hammered bronze amphora: *StEtr* 37 (1961) pl. 38d.

For 7th c. impasto protome-cauldrons: A. Pasquier, *The Louvre: Greek, Etruscan and Roman Antiquities* (London 1991) 58; M. Torelli, *L'arte degli Etruschi* (Bari 1985) fig. 35; *Acta Hyperborea* 1 (1988) pl. 7; *Münzen und Medaillen* Sonderliste U (Basel 1984) 9 no. 10.

J. M. P.

65 CONICAL LEKYTHOS-OINOCHOE

Said to be from Cumae, Early Protocorinthian, ca. 700 B.C.
Height 0.092, base diameter 0.164.
Ceramic; missing neck and part of shoulder.
The Metropolitan Museum of Art, Rogers Fund, 1923 (23.160.18).

The flat-bottomed vessel has a conical body with steep and gently rounded profile; missing are a long narrow neck with trefoil mouth and vertical strap handle. The Detroit lekythos-oinochoe (89) is similar, with a somewhat lower body. The body of the Metropolitan vase preserves three bands of ornament. The lowest is occupied by a sinuous black snake with added white dots and a triangular head; groups of five sigmas fill the interstices. The central figural zone presents a cacophony of animal life. Its focus is two galloping horses pursued by a wolf who leaps, claws extended, at the tail of the hindmost horse. With a small fish above and a large fish below the body of each animal, the horses appear to be bounding over the sea. Dotted reserved eyes lend the horses desperation, the wolf and fish immediacy. The scene takes place in no real space, for the two ends are linked. Before the front horse struts a large long-legged bird with wing and tail unfurled and beak open in

65

65

65

apparent animated communication with the griffin protome of a standed cauldron. A second griffin head opposite seems to watch the predation beyond. The cauldron is covered in tiny white dots, perhaps intended to suggest a scaly body, thus animating not just the pro-

tomes but the entire object, or perhaps meant to imitate hammer marks on metalwork. Above the figural zone is a band of pendent tasseled crosshatched triangles between rosettes. A swastika decorates the bottom of the vessel.

The small vase presents a miniature cosmos: creatures of sky, sea, and earth are represented, as well as those of the civilized human sphere (the domesticated horses) and its opposite (their wild predator). Both the fantastic and the manmade appear in the griffins who grow out of a cauldron. This exuberant painting style, which has little regard for geometry but a real feeling for coloristic effects and animating detail, is characteristic of the vase painting of Cumae, where imitations of Corinthian pottery can be difficult to distinguish from the imports. The shape is Corinthian, and the subsidiary ornaments—dotted snake, spiral hooks, and star rosettes—are recent arrivals by 700 B.C.

In Corinth and the regional workshops operating under its influence, orientalizing art arrived in full force by the end of the eighth century. Heralded in realistic detail on this vase, the griffin-head cauldron was just starting to replace the tripod cauldron in sanctuaries across Greece and in tombs in Italy. Greek and Italian potters quickly adapted this new fashion from the Near East to their craft, as the standed krater from Tampa (64) shows. The oriental bronze cauldrons were often decorated with friezes that assembled different species of animals and fantastic creatures together. Under the spell of these oriental bestiaries, Corinthian painters departed from the traditional Geometric Greek one-species friezes. The Metropolitan oinochoe demonstrates not just new motifs but also the new technique of incision, used to articulate the eyes of the griffins and horses; from this time on its application to silhouette shapes will begin to revolutionize Greek painted pottery.

PUBLISHED
G. M. A. Richter, "Early Greek and Etruscan Vases" *BMMA* 19 (1924) 98, fig. 3.

E. B. Stebbins, *The Dolphin in the Literature and Art of Greece and Rome* (Menasha WI 1929) 97.

G. M. A. Richter, *Handbook of the Classical Collection* (New York 1930) 59, fig. 36.

M. Robertson, "Excavations in Ithaca, V" *BSA* 43 (1948) 47.

Richter, *Handbook of the Greek Collection* 35, pl. 23a.

R. Hampe, *Ein frühattischer Grabfunde* (Mainz 1960) 55–57, figs. 40–42.

W. L. Brown, *The Etruscan Lion* (Oxford 1960) 9, pl. 5, b–1.

T. J. Dunbabin, ed., *Perachora* II (Oxford 1962) 22, 36, 43.

Coldstream, *Geometric Greece* 365, fig. 114.

Catalogue, *Aspects of Ancient Greece*, 120–21, no. 57.

R. Hampe and E. Simon, *The Birth of Greek Art* (New York 1981) 159–60.

H. C. Ebertshäuser and M. Waltz, *Vasen, Bronzen, Terrakotten des klassischen Altertums* (Munich 1981) 39–40, fig. 42.

A. Dierichs, *Das Bild des Greifen in der frühgriechischen Flächenkunst* (Münster 1981) 40.

Catalogue, *Animal Style on Greek and Etruscan Vases*, 14, no. 2.

Rombos, *The Iconography of Attic Late Geometric II Pottery*, 255–56.

EXHIBITED

Aspects of Ancient Greece, Allentown Art Museum, Allentown PA, September–December 1979.

Animal Style on Greek and Etruscan Vases, Robert Hull Fleming Museum, Burlington VT 1985.

NOTES

For similar shape: F. Johansen, *Les vases sicyoniens* (Copenhagen 1923) pl. VIII, 5; E. Gabrici, "Cuma" *MonAnt* 22 (1913) pls. 34, 2; 36, 1 and 3; 37, 1–3; 38, 1–2.

The bird-and-cauldron motif: on an aryballos from Corinth now in Berlin, Johansen, *Les vases sicyoniens* pl. V, 6a.

On standed cauldrons with griffin protomes:

U. Jantzen, *Griechische Griefenkessel* (Berlin 1955); U. Jantzen, "Greifenprotomen vom Samos. Ein Nachtrag" *AM* 73 (1958) 26–49. For bibliography on oriental bronze cauldrons and on pottery from Cumae, see also notes under standed krater **64**.

S. L.

66

66 SPECTACLE FIBULA

Northern Greek, ca. 700 B.C.
Length 0.145, width 0.064.
Bronze; intact, dark brown patina.
University of Missouri–Columbia, Museum of Art and Archaeology (61.29).

The fibula consists of a single length of heavy wire, rhomboidal in section, twisted into a figure eight in the middle, formed into two spiral disks, and ending in a pin at one end, a clasp at the other.

The spectacle fibula originated in central Europe before 1000 B.C. and there enjoyed a remarkable vogue of over five centuries. It entered Greece through Macedonia from the Balkans, apparently as early as the ninth century, where it appears first in Macedonian graves, especially those of women. The inhabitants of Vergina were particularly fond of the type; over 150 such fibulae were found during excavation of the graves there. The fact that the spectacle fibulae were found in Macedonia with other Balkan objects may indicate a movement not just of fibulae but of their wearers as well. By the eighth century this fibula form had spread to southern Greece primarily through dedications in sanctuaries. The Argive Heraion, Olympia, Sparta, Lousoi, and Tegea have all produced examples. These sanctuaries have yielded a remarkable version of the form rendered in bone and ivory.

Five main types and twenty subtypes of the spectacle fibula have been distinguished. Distribution patterns suggest that in the Balkan regions, particularly in Croatia, Serbia, and Bosnia-Herzegovina, different subtypes were worn by different "tribal groups," revealing an urge for differentiation that now seems an ironic echo of contemporary events. Of the several types and subtypes that enjoyed popularity in Greece, the form of the Missouri fibula with rhomboidal section and figure-eight center is the earliest.

PUBLISHED

M. Glascock, T. G. Spalding, J. C. Biers, and M. F. Cornman, "Analysis of Copper-based Metallic Artifacts by Prompt Gamma-Ray Neutron Activation," *Archaeometry* 26 (1984) 96–103.

EXHIBITED

Jewelry of the Ancient Mediterranean, The California Palace of the Legion of Honor, San Francisco, December 1969–February 1970.

NOTES

Blinkenberg, *Fibules grecques et orientales* 255, type XIV a.

J. Alexander, "The Spectacle Fibulae of Southern Europe" *AJA* 69 (1965) 7–23, type I; finds in Greece, 21.

E. Bielefeld, *Schmuck* (ArchHom I, C, Göttingen 1968) 49–51, fig. 6n.

Kilian, "Trachtzubehör der Eisenzeit" 106–7, pls. 77, 78.

Kilian, *Fibeln in Thessalien* 147 (Brillenfibeln B II d).

Philipp, *Bronzeschmuck aus Olympia* 295–96, no. 1069.

M. Andronikos, *Bergina* I (Athens 1969) 227–30.

For bone and ivory examples: T. J. Dunbabin, ed., *Perachora* II (Oxford 1962) pls. 183–85.

S. L.

67

67 SIX BEADS

Geometric to early Archaic, eighth to early sixth century B.C.

Maximum dimensions: (90.117.1) 0.041; (.2) 0.021; (.3) 0.024; (.4) 0.023; (.5) 0.022; (.7) 0.033.

Dark red translucent amber; friable patination over all surfaces; .4, .5, .7 slightly chipped.

University of Missouri–Columbia, Museum of Art and Archaeology, anonymous gift (90.117.1–5, 7). Purchased by donor in Thessaloniki, 1931.

All now reduced to rough forms, the beads vary in shape including one oblong, one round, one rectangular, and three biconical. All but the large biconical bead are pierced.

Probably once belonging to a single necklace, these beads represent the commodity of one of the longest-established trade routes into Greece. In both the Bronze and Iron ages, Baltic amber entered Greece by a route through central Europe to the head of the Adriatic and then down the Illyrian coast. This pattern apparently continued unbroken in the Dark Age in Italy and the Balkans, but in Greece a gap between finds of the eleventh century in Metaxata and Lakkithra on Kephallenia and the ninth century on Tenos has not yet been bridged. The distribution of amber finds at early Greek sites includes nearly all the important sanctuaries (Delos, Ephesos, the Idaean Cave, Lindos, Olympia, Perachora, Pherai, Samos, and Sparta), many islands, and graves around Greece, East Greece, and Greek South Italy. It has been noted that the route from Macedonia to East

Greece and the islands matches that of the legendary Hyperboreans who sent sacred offerings by relay to Delos.

Because of its magnetic properties, amber was prized for its amuletic and medicinal value in addition to its attractive appearance. Particularly in Etruria amber was employed for charms and apotropaic pendants, while in Greece, where the decorative aspect was perhaps its primary attraction, it was used mainly for jewelry and decorative inlays. Homer's references to amber illustrate its glamour and desirability. The suitor Eurymachos attempts to win Penelope with "an elaborate necklace of gold, strung with bits of amber, and bright as sunshine" (*Odyssey* 18.296). The Phoenician who arranged the kidnapping of the boy Eumaios used a gold and amber necklace to distract the servant women in his father's house (*Odyssey* 15.460).

UNPUBLISHED

NOTES

On ancient amber: D. Strong, *Catalogue of the Carved Amber in the Department of Greek and Roman Antiquities* (London 1966); C. W. Beck, "Amber in Archaeology" *Archaeology* 23 (1970) 7–11; Z. Bokowski, "Critically about the So-Called Amber Route in the Odra and Vistula River Basins in the Early Iron Age" *Archaeologia Polonia* 28 (1990) 71–122.

On distribution of amber finds: Strong, *Catalogue of the Carved Amber* 21–23; I. Sakellarakis, "Some Geometric and Archaic Votives from the Idaian Cave" in *Early Greek Cult Practice* 187.

On the Hyperborean route: Herodotus, *Histories* 4.33; Strong, *Catalogue of the Carved Amber* 9.

For amber beads in northern Greek Geometric contexts: Vickers, "Some Early Iron Age Bronzes from Macedonia" fig. V, from Potidaea in a Geometric period group; Strong, *Catalogue of the Carved Amber* 41, no. 3, pl. 1, from Potidaea; Popham and Sackett, *Lefkandi* I 223, in EGII and MGI

tombs; *BSA* 26 (1923–1925) 24, from Chauchitsa, Macedonia; N. Vulić, "Ein neues Grab bei Trebenischte" *ÖJh* 27 (1932) 37, no. 48, fig. 62 and Vulić, "Neue Gräber in Trebenischte" *ÖJh* 28 (1933) 182–83, from 7th c. graves at Trebenischte.

On amber in Crete: N. K. Sandars, "A Minoan Cemetery on Upper Gypsades: The Amber Beads" *BSA* 53–54 (1958–1959) 237–39.

S. L.

68

68 DUCK VASE

Possibly Greek, Late Protogeometric, 950–900 B.C.
Height 0.176, length 0.203, depth 0.097.
Ceramic; beak restored, surface worn.
Arthur M. Sackler Museum, Harvard University Art Museums, Bequest of David M. Robinson (1960.262).

The deep-bellied bird balances on two broad, flat feet, the left set slightly forward of the right. The wide handmade body swells at midpoint and curves in quickly to a flat back, on which are set a basket handle and a tubular spout with flaring rim. In profile the ridged back is horizontal, extending behind into a flat tail and rising vertically in front to a small beaked head. Two small round indentations on either side of the head represent eyes and ears; a small hole pierces the base of the neck in front. The entire vase is covered in a solid, streaky black slip.

A vase type with very old roots in the Bronze Age, perhaps beginning in Early Bronze Age Crete, the bird vase soon appeared in the Cyclades and Cyprus, where it flourished in the Late Bronze Age (although perhaps not without a break) and particularly in the Iron Age. Greece has produced several examples of Late Helladic IIIC and Protogeometric date, including vases from Athens and Achaea and, most important for understanding 68, from Lefkandi, where four examples were found in graves. A Late Protogeometric bird vase from Lefkandi closely resembles the Harvard duck, while Submycenaean and Early Protogeometric examples from the site may track the development of a local form, although they differ somewhat from the later version. No good parallel from Cyprus exists for the Harvard vase, but one from a Lapithos tomb of Late Cypriot IIIB1 (1100–1050 B.C.) with feet and a basket handle (but no spout) might provide a missing link. The relationship of Achaean duck vases with Cypriot, Attic, and Euboean examples is not fully understood. The deep-bellied Achaean forms with small heads and flat splaying struts seem related to the Late Protogeometric Lefkandi and Harvard vases with their distinctive feet. An unpublished duck vase in the Buffalo Museum of Science is quite similar to the Harvard vase, but with a third leg and painted decoration, and probably came from the same source. The separated basket handle and spout of these two examples may have developed in Greece out of the Late Helladic IIIC combination of handle and spout, or may have been worked out in Cyprus, as seen in the Lapithos vase.

Even without a precise parallel, a Cypriot inspiration for this bird vase appears reasonable. Dating around 900 or a little earlier, the Lefkandi duck is contemporary with several signs of that site's renewed contact with Cyprus: an imported Bichrome flask was found in the same tomb, the famous terra-

cotta centaur (Fig. 3) exhibits possible links to Cypriot work, and the bronze foundry at Lefkandi was most likely supplied with Cypriot copper. Although Desborough believed the earlier Protogeometric duck vase from Lefkandi was made locally, he suggested the late tenth-century bird was an import of unknown origin. The type is undocumented elsewhere, but its unusual solid body, similar to that of the Harvard vase, seems anticipated in the mostly dark ground Early Protogeometric example from the site. Future research may yet discover a Euboean home for this type.

All duck vases from Greece and the Aegean come from tomb contexts, which may attest to their special significance. It has been suggested that as migratory birds with seasonal departures and returns and an intimate connection with water, ducks were symbols of rebirth and fertility and therefore appropriate gifts to send with the dead into the earth. The Harvard vase, unlike some of the other bird vases, is made for pouring. As water could symbolize the underworld for the Greeks, so the duck may have provided the ideal instrument for a libation of water or wine for the dead.

PUBLISHED

CVA Robinson Collection, Baltimore MD 1, 11, no. 11, pl. I.11 (published as Cypriot Middle Bronze Age; its provenance, given as "from Cyprus," may be conventional).

H. Bossert, *Altsyrien* (Tübingen 1951) 14 no. 199 (ill.).

NOTES

On bird vases: R. V. d'A. Desborough, "Bird Vases" *CretChron* (1972) 245–77; V. Karageorghis, *Nouveaux documents pour l'étude du bronze récent à Chypre* (Paris 1965) 224 n. 4; Demetriou, *Cypro-Aegean Relations in the Early Iron Age* 47–51.

LHIIIC bird vases in Greece: Achaea, E. Vermeule, "The Mycenaeans in Achaia" *AJA* 64 (1960) 1–21 at 11–12 nos. 44, 45, pl. 4 figs. 30, 31; *ADChr* 25 (1970) pl. 185a; Lefkandi, Desborough, "Bird Vases" 255 no.

46, 257 no. 56; Popham and Sackett, *Lef-kandi* I pl. 254 a–b.

EPG and LPG Lefkandi askoi: Desborough, *The Greek Dark Ages* 50 pl. 4D; *Archae-ology* 25 (1972) 18; Popham and Sackett, *Lefkandi* I 344, pl. 254 c–d.

Lapithos example: M. Ohnefalsch-Richter, *Kypros, the Bible, and Homer* (London 1893) 425, pl. 98, 6.

On symbolism: M. Yon, "Ducks' Travels" *Acta Cypria. Acts of an International Congress on Cypriote Archaeology Held in Göteborg on 22–24 August 1991* (SIMA-PB 107, Jonsered 1992) pt. 2, 394–407.

S. L.

69

69 AMPHORA NECK WITH PICTORIAL DECORATION

Cypriot, Cypro-Geometric III, 850–750 B.C.
Height 0.15, width 0.253.
Ceramic; fragment preserving part of neck and shoulder.
The Metropolitan Museum of Art, The Cesnola Collection; purchased by subscription, 1874–1876 (74.51.5862).

The neck fragment of a White-Painted III–IV amphora is divided into decorative panels by triple vertical lines framing stacked cross-hatched lozenges. Only part of the panel to the left is preserved. On a broad horizontal band at the shoulder junction stands a fantas-tic quadruped. From tiny multitoed feet, its black legs broaden to the shoulder. The body is ornamented with a harlequin suit of loz-enges. Attached directly to the body without benefit of neck, the head consists of enor-mous open tooth-lined crescent jaws, from which juts a large upward-curving tongue. At the back of the jaws a vertical line sets off the rest of the head, mostly filled with a great circular eye. The animal's rigid stance and open jaws render it ferocious.

The only previous discussion of this sherd identified the animal as a wild boar, but lack-ing tusks and a recognizable snout it seems more plausibly a lion. In contrast to Greek Geometric art, the lion is rarely found among Cypriot Geometric and early Archaic vase painting motifs. When it does occur, however, it roars with toothy jaws agape and curving tongue protruding, much as our beast. The present example shares several features with Greek Geometric lions, including a hatched torso (to indicate mane) at a time when most figures are solid silhouettes. Although it is possible that lions still lived in Attica in the eighth century and certainly in the areas neighboring Cyprus, the Geometric artists seem to have imitated art rather than life. Their models were the ubiquitous lions that decorated Near Eastern seals, bronze bowls, and jewelry, in fact the whole spectrum of portable art. It is easy to see how the abstracted tufts of the mane, often rendered in Syrian and Neo-Hittite art as overlapping triangles or lozenges, could have become in Cypriot hands a harlequin coat. A spirited lion on a Late Geometric amphora excavated at Pithekoussai, not dissimilar to the Cypriot beast, attests to the image further west. The rarity of the beast in Cypro-Geometric art indicates that Cyprus was not particularly involved in its transmission farther west to Greece. Rather, in comparing the Cypriot lion with the Attic type, represented here on pitcher-olpe **79**, we see the simultaneous adoption of this motif in two different geo-metric artistic traditions. Although much dis-cussion on the meaning of the lion as a popular Greek motif has turned on its possible symbolism of death, the scarcity of lions in Cypriot art suggests no such interpretation for that island.

PUBLISHED

Karageorghis and Des Gagniers, *La céramique chypriote de style figuré* pt. 1, 59, pl. 217, XXI.1.

NOTES

Cypro-Geometric lions on a WPIII amphora: Karageorghis and Des Gagniers, *La céramique chypriote de style figuré* pls. 142–43, XIV.1.

On lions in Greek Geometric art: Carter, "The Beginning of Narrative Art in the Greek Geometric Period" 43–44; Rombos, *The Iconography of Attic Late Geometric II Pottery* 185–208.

Near Eastern lions: H. Frankfort, *The Art and Architecture of the Ancient Orient*, 4th ed. (Harmondsworth 1970) 293 fig. 341, 326 fig. 388; G. Markoe, *Phoenician Silver Bowls from Cyprus and the Mediterranean* (Berkeley 1985) 39–41.

Boeotian(?) amphora from Pithekoussai: *AR* (1970–1971) 63 fig. 1.

S. L.

70 AMPHORA NECK WITH PICTORIAL DECORATION

Cypriot, Cypro-Geometric III, 850–750 B.C.
Height 0.118, width 0.279.
Ceramic; fragment preserving neck from shoulder junction to rim.
The Metropolitan Museum of Art, The Cesnola Collection; purchased by subscription, 1874–1876 (74.51.5861).

This large White-Painted III amphora bears on its neck figural scenes in panels. Two panels are partially preserved, separated by double vertical lines framing a crosshatched column. The top and bottom of the neck are bordered with thick black bands. In the panel to the right stands a figure whose body is formed of two rounded segments covered with a lozenge net pattern, a horizontal band at his waist. Facing left, the man carries a spear across his shoulders, supported by his hands. From the back of his head fall several strands of hair. The extremely clumsy figure style turns his head into an outline blob filled with a dotted circular eye. The arms are carelessly drawn, with the left much larger than the right.

The other panel preserves two figures and the arms of a third. Rendered with silhouette bodies and outline heads, the figures are engaged in an unusual scene. Facing left, a standing figure holds a long staff or pole on his shoulders with both hands. A smaller figure on his right seems to collapse, his knees sharply flexed and his body bent back. On the left and just visible beside the break, the upraised arms of a third figure seem to hold a cup aloft in one hand while the other hand touches the tip of the pole.

Following the pattern of Cypriot figured pottery, the two panels are not necessarily thematically related. The unmistakable spear borne by the figure in the first panel designates him as a warrior. His unusual apparel recalls the so-called figure-eight type of body shield known in Mycenaean art, although its recurrence in Cypriot Iron Age art is difficult to explain. An earlier parallel may be provided by a human figure whose body is apparently concealed by a large oval shield on a Late Cypriot IIIB Proto-White-Painted pyxis. A seventh-century terracotta Cypriot figurine with a peculiar shield like an elongated figure eight has been connected with the Bronze Age type, and an early tenth-century bronze warrior figure from Megiddo Stratum VB carries a tiny figure-eight shield. If the Metropolitan figure does indeed wear a body shield, then the strands of hair might have been intended as a plumed helmet.

The two preserved figures of the other panel were suggested by Karageorghis and Des Gagniers as a dancing man and a shepherd carrying a staff. This perplexing scene might be clearer if it is assumed to relate to the adjacent one. It then becomes a

70

fight scene in which the fully preserved figure
holds his spear aloft like his companion in the
other panel, while a comrade or foe collapses
beside him. Yet without the other panel nothing in this scene inherently suggests warlike
activities. No one wears a shield or helmet,
and the polelike object has no spearhead.

The figure offstage to the left hints of
another possible interpretation. The visible
hands holding a cup and the dark mass above
and behind them are of a larger scale than
the other two figures. It is not difficult to
complete the scene as Odysseus driving a
stake into the eye of the sitting, drinking
giant whose raised hands ineffectively ward
off the blow, much as on the famous Protoattic Eleusis amphora neck. In this restoration,
the hapless central figure represents one of
Polyphemus' victims. Two major considerations caution against such an interpretation. A
narrative scene would be remarkable among
the generic and symbolic scenes of Cypriot
Iron Age pictorial vases. Moreover, at ca. 750
B.C. this image would predate all other repre-

sentations of the Homeric story. On the other
hand, an early Cypriot narrative vase would
not be unique. A Cypro-Geometric IB plate
from Kouklia-*Skales* Tomb 58 contains several
figures that can plausibly be understood as
Herakles and Iolaos fighting the Hydra, datable close to 950 B.C., much earlier than the
next known occurrence of this scene on a
Boeotian fibula. The outline-style "frog-
headed" figures with small silhouette bodies
and rubbery limbs appear early in Cypriot
painting and persist into the seventh century,
as for example the man boarding a ship on a
White-Painted IV jug. A later dating for the
Metropolitan fragment, making it dependent
on the fixed iconography of the early seventh-
century Polyphemus scenes, corresponds with
developments in the subject matter of Cypro-
Archaic I painting, which began to reflect the
impact of epic poetry.

Although these early narrative scenes lack
indisputable Mycenaean precedents, it is generally agreed that Cypriot pictorial imagery on
pottery developed primarily as an amalgama-

tion of Mycenaean, Levantine, and native Cypriot elements, with Mycenaean traditions frequently prevailing. It is more circumspect to conclude that the scene combines elements unique in Cypriot pictorial practice in such a way as to suggest a narrative interpretation.

PUBLISHED

Karageorghis and Des Gagniers, *La céramique chypriote de style figuré* pt. 1, 34 no. 3, pt. 2, 99, IX.3.

NOTES

LCIIIB PWP pyxis: Iacovou, *The Pictorial Pottery of Eleventh Century B.C. Cyprus* 71 cat. no. 15, figs. 34 and 36; E. S. Sherratt, "Immigration and Archaeology: Some Indirect Reflections" in *Acta Cypria. Acts of an International Congress on Cypriote Archaeology Held in Göteborg on 22–24 August 1991* pt. 2 (SIMA-PB 107, Jonsered 1992) 316–47 at 334–35. It has also been identified as the figure's awkwardly rendered body.

Terracotta figurine: S. Hiller, "Mycenaean Traditions in Early Greek Cult Images" in *The Greek Renaissance of the Eighth Century B.C.* 91–99, at 98 fig. 14.

Bronze warrior from Megiddo: R. S. Lamon and G. M. Shipton, *Megiddo* I (Chicago 1939) pl. 89, 2–3.

Eleusis amphora and other 7th c. representations of the Polyphemus story: G. E. Mylonas, *Protoattikos amphoreus tis Eleusinos* (Athens 1957); K. Schefold, *Myth and Legend in Early Greek Art* (New York 1966) pls. I, 16; P. E. Arias and M. Hirmer, *A History of Greek Vase Painting* (London 1962) 274, pl. 13; P. Courbin, "Un fragment de cratère protoargien" *BCH* 79 (1955) 1–49, figs. 1, 3, 4, pl. 1; B. Schweitzer, "Zum Kraker des Aristonothos" *RM* 62 (1955) pl. 40, 1; Fittschen, *Untersuchungen zum Beginn der Sagensdarstellungen* 192–93 (SB 111–14).

Herakles plate: Karageorghis, *Palaepaphos-Skales* pl. LXXXVII, fig. CXII; Iacovou, *The Pictorial Pottery of Eleventh Century B.C. Cyprus* 27 cat. no. 33, figs. 77–78.

Cypriot WPIV jug with ship: Karageorghis and Des Gagniers, *La céramique chypriote* pt. 2, 122–23, IX.2; also pt. 1, 112 for epic influence on 7th c. Cypriot pottery iconography.

S. L.

71

71 PENDENT SEMICIRCLE SKYPHOS

Euboean, from Cyprus, Middle Geometric, 800–750 B.C.
Height 0.078, rim diameter 0.115, foot diameter 0.053.
Ceramic; complete, reconstructed from several fragments; fine, pink-orange fabric with no inclusions, covered with pale orange slip; pairs of drilled holes along breaks mark sites of ancient repair.
Arthur M. Sackler Museum, Harvard University Art Museums, Alpheus Hyatt Fund (1953.116).

This two-handled bowl, with offset lip and low ring foot, is a vessel that functioned as a cup and was commonly used for drinking liquids. Its interior is painted with a dark orange slip except for a small circle in the center and a reserve band on the lip. The exterior is completely painted except for the area beneath the handles and the two reserved panels on either side of the cup, each of which is decorated with two sets of intersecting pendent semicircles made with a multiple brush. The reserve fields between the handles of this skyphos remain standard for the depiction of figures, animals, and geometric ornament on cups from Middle to Late Geometric periods, and even beyond into Corinthian and Attic black-figure production.

The skyphos shape must have been quite practical in its service, to judge from the long time of production for the type, ca. 900–725 B.C., and the extent of its findspots in the Mediterranean region, from Cyprus and Syria in the east to Italy and Sicily in the west. This small drinking cup is related to the relatively larger krater (4) and continues the development in decoration and form of this earlier type which, in turn, drew its inspiration from Mycenaean prototypes. Like its ancestral krater, this skyphos is of Euboean manufacture, as is evidenced by lack of mica in the clay fabric. Additionally, the slipped surface may mark it as a product of Lefkandi in Euboea, which produced mostly slipped vessels.

This particular skyphos is significant because of its Cypriot provenance. It was probably brought there from Euboea by enterprising Greeks who were expanding their influence by trade contacts and permanent settlements throughout the Mediterranean at this time. Excavations at Lefkandi have suggested that, besides Thessaly and the Greek islands, Euboea was a center for production of these skyphoi, and examples from Lefkandi can be found to parallel the Harvard skyphos in both shape and decoration.

The cup must have been a prized possession to its original owner, for it shows signs of its repair in antiquity. Holes were drilled along the edges of the fragments on this cup to receive staple-shaped pieces of lead or bronze that, when fixed into the holes and clamped, would have held the pieces securely together. Pine pitch could have then been applied to the seams, thereby making the vase water-tight and restoring it to use.

PUBLISHED

G. M. A. Hanfmann, "On Some Eastern Greek Wares Found at Tarsus" in *The Aegean and the Near East. Studies Presented to Hetty Goldman* 173, 179, fig. 16.

H. W. Catling, "A Pendent Semicircle Skyphos from Cyprus and a Cypriot Imitation" *RDAC* (1973) 181, no. 13.

E. Gjerstad, *Greek Geometric and Archaic Pottery Found in Cyprus* (Stockholm 1977) 24, no. 22.

Kearsley, *The Pendent Semi-circle Skyphos* 19, no. 34, 79–81, 99–100, 106, 121, 123.

NOTES

For the date of this piece: Kearsley, *The Pendent Semi-circle Skyphos* type 5, 128.

For the life span of the pendent semicircle skyphos: Desborough, *Protogeometric Pottery* 193.

For a comparative piece with discussion of the type: Desborough, *Protogeometric Pottery* 180–94, pl. 25c, B711.

On the pendent semicircle skyphos and its relationship to Mycenaean prototypes: Kearsley, *The Pendent Semi-circle Skyphos* 109–14.

A Euboean parallel: Boardman, *The Greeks Overseas* 41, fig. 13.

Repairs on ancient vases: J. V. Noble, *The Techniques of Painted Attic Pottery* 2d ed. (London 1988) 174–75.

A. J. P.

72 CUP WITH PHOENICIAN INSCRIPTION

Cypro-Archaic I, seventh century B.C. (Like tripod 61, Cesnola's *Atlas* names Idalion as the provenance; Myres, *Handbook of the Cesnola Collection* xv–xvi, however, cautions against accepting Cesnola's designations. In recent literature only Masson and Sznycer have repeated his claim.)
Height 0.197.
Ceramic; repaired from fragments.
The Metropolitan Museum of Art, The Cesnola Collection; purchased by subscription, 1874–1876 (74.51.1001).

The unusual Bichrome IV jar combines a

72

72, *detail*

stamnoid body with a flaring pedestal foot.
Dense ornamentation in white, black, and red
gives a tapestry effect. The foot is solid with
pairs of reserve bands near the edge and near
the body. The reserved lower body is framed
by a solid wide band up to the carination.
Between the goat-head handles extends the
decorative zone: a crosshatched lozenge
between two halves of the same ornament,
the interstices filled with checkerboard. Vertical lines and lozenge chain frame this zone
on either side. Alternating thin and broad
bands fill the shoulder to the rim. On the

reserved lower body against the black band appear the four painted letters of the Phoenician inscription.

First read as "RGMN," the inscription seems to record a personal name, although the unusual forms of the first and last letters have proved controversial. Masson and Sznycer suggest the reading of "RGM" to construct a name such as "Rêgêm." Because of the similarity of the paint with the adjacent decoration, the inscription seems to have been drawn before the decorative band was added, which covers the top of the last letter. It was perhaps made to order for a Phoenician who was living on Cyprus. Although a number of earlier Phoenician inscriptions are known from Cyprus, this jar illustrates one circumstance in which the Phoenician alphabet first became familiar to Greek eyes, by marking ownership of an object. Claiming property was also one of the earliest uses to which the Greeks put their new skill, although the prevalence of hexameter verses among the first recorded Greek inscriptions shows that recording ownership was neither the only use nor necessarily the impetus that led to the adoption of an alphabet.

The complexity of alphabetic writing, particularly to an illiterate culture, presupposes that not labeled objects but sustained contact between teachers and pupils was required for the Greeks to acquire this skill. Coldstream and others have noted that the introduction of the alphabet must have occurred in a place where Greeks and Phoenicians were living together. Cyprus, with one Phoenician and several Greek communities established at various sites by the late ninth century, is a possibility, although evidence of Greeks living in close proximity with the Phoenician settlers at that time remains to be found. Recent studies have begun to examine the role of Euboea in the adaptation of the alphabet to Greek use.

PUBLISHED

Cesnola, *Cyprus* 68, pl. 10, no. 9.

Cesnola, *A Descriptive Atlas of the Cesnola Collection* II, 1047 (inaccurate drawing gives it human-headed handles); III, CXXIII, 21.

S. Reinach, *Gazette archéologique* 8 (1883) 329–30, pl. 54.

I. H. Hall, "Some Phoenician Inscriptions in New York" *Hebraica* 2 (1885–1886) 7.

G. Perrot and Ch. Chipiez, *History of Art in Phoenicia and Its Dependencies* 267 fig. 203.

Myres, *Handbook of the Cesnola Collection* 101 no. 775, 521.

Gjerstad, *The Cypro-Geometric, Cypro-Archaic and Cypro-Classical Periods* fig. XXXII, 8.

O. Masson and M. Sznycer, *Récherches sur les Phéniciens à Chypre* (Geneva 1972) 112–13, pl. XIV, 1–2.

Peckham, *Phoenician Scripts* 17.

NOTES

On the transmission of the alphabet: A. Huebeck, *Schrift* (ArchHom III, X, Göttingen 1979) 73–100; J. N. Coldstream, "Greeks and Phoenicians in the Aegean" in Niemeyer, *Phönizier im Westen* 261–72; A. Johnston, "The Extent and Use of Literacy" in *The Greek Renaissance of the Eighth Century* B.C., 63–68, esp. 66–68; Powell, *Homer and the Origin of the Greek Alphabet*; further discussed in *Cambridge Archaeological Journal* 2 (1992) 115–26.

For a Euboean connection: Powell, *Homer and the Origin of the Greek Alphabet*.

J. Ray, *Cambridge Archaeological Journal* 2 (1992) 120 asks whether it was not the Phoenicians but another Semitic group whose language provided the model for the Greeks.

S. L.

73 SCARABOID SEAL

Levantine, late eighth century B.C.
Height 0.028, length 0.048, width 0.038.
Whitish green basalt; intact, some flaking of stone.
Arthur M. Sackler Museum, Harvard University Art Museums, Bequest of David M. Robinson (1960.628).

The Egyptianizing scaraboid seal displays a

73

73

frontal bearded face on the back where a scarab is usually depicted. A symmetrical composition of a winged scarab surmounted by two falcons and a pair of maat feathers comprises the intaglio seal on the underside. The carving, particularly on the underside, is delicate. A hole has been drilled lengthwise through the seal's center for a string or metal fitting.

This scaraboid seal has an unusual combination of Egyptian motifs on the underside and, on the back, the bearded face motif

common in the region of Palestine. A number of scaraboid seals decorated with such faces have been found in excavations in Israel. The best example, dated between the thirteenth and eighth centuries B.C., now in the possession of the Israel Department of Antiquities, comes from the site of Acco.

The imagery on the underside of the Harvard seal, however, is more closely connected to eighth- and seventh-century Phoenicia than to Palestine. The intentionally archaizing motifs are borrowed from Egypt, from the time of Tuthmosis III in the Eighteenth Dynasty (ca. 1567–1320 B.C.). The royal cartouche has been dropped, and the individual elements have been symmetrized with no legible hieroglyphic meaning.

This seal was found inside Geometric skyphos 74 in a tomb southeast of Athens. It is an early import from the Levant into Athens after almost four centuries of severed trade relations between Greece and the Near East. A similar seal of about the same date but of cruder workmanship, inscribed with its owner's name, Kreontidas, was found in a Greek tomb on the island of Aegina.

Although seals in the Near East were often used for administrative purposes related to the seal impressions, this imported Egyptianizing scarab seal appears to have performed an amuletic or religious function.

PUBLISHED

D. M. Robinson, "The Robinson Collection of Greek Gems, Seals, Rings, and Earrings" *Hesperia* Supplement 8 (1949) 310–11, pl. 40, no. 7.

G. M. A. Hanfmann, *The David Moore Robinson Bequest of Classical Art and Antiquities: A Special Exhibition* (Cambridge MA 1961) 10, no. 32.

EXHIBITED

The David Moore Robinson Bequest of Classical Art and Antiquities, Fogg Art Museum, Harvard University, May–September 1961.

NOTES

For scaraboids from the Levant: *Les Phéniciens et le monde méditerranéen*, exhibition

74

catalogue (Brussels and Luxembourg 1986);
G. Hölbl, *Ägyptisches Kulturgut im Phöni-
kischen und Punischen Sardinien* (Études
préliminaires aux religions orientales dans
l'empire Romain, Leiden 1986) 164–337.

On the Acco seal: R. Giveon, *The Impact of
Egypt on Canaan* (Orbis Biblicus et Orientalis 20, Freiburg Schweiz and Göttingen
1978) 90–98, no. 48.

For scarab seals from the time of Tuthmosis
III: B. Jaeger, *Essai de classification et data-
tion des scarabées Menkhéperrê* (Orbis Biblicus et Orientalis, Series Archaeologica 2,
Freiburg and Göttingen 1982).

On connections between Greece and the
Near East: Boardman, *The Greeks Overseas*
35–109, esp. 71, ill. 57.

On the Kreontidas Scarab Seal: J. H. Middle-
ton, *The Engraved Gems of Classical Times
with a Catalogue of the Gems in the Fitzwilliam Museum* (Cambridge 1891) 14–15,
pl. 1, no. 4.

M. H. F.

74 SKYPHOS

Attic, from a tomb southeast of Athens,
Late Geometric I, 750–735 B.C.
Height 0.082, rim diameter 0.132.

Ceramic; mended, restored and repainted;
buff-colored fabric decorated with dark
brown slip, interior slipped with a reserve
band.
**Arthur M. Sackler Museum, Harvard
University Art Museums, Bequest of
David M. Robinson (1960.281).**

The low, wide body of the vessel is decorated with a panel between the handles that
has been sectioned into three metope shapes,
each set off by three vertical painted lines.
The decorative scheme is the same for both
sides of the cup. In the central panel is
painted a four-leafed rosette, whose leaves are
hatched with diagonal lines; four triangle
shapes between the leaves are attached to the
edges of the field. Each side panel has a
painted bird facing toward the central panel;
these have solid-painted heads, necks, and
jointed legs, with reserve bodies decorated
with hatching. The field decorations that surround them vary slightly, but both birds have
a swastika painted above them. The other
motifs include, in the left panel, a dot rosette
and a vertical row of dots extending down
from the bird's beak and, in the right panel, a
ring of dots filling the space in front of the
bird's neck. Around the cup, painted beneath

the handles, are three lines and a solid painted base. Both the lip and handles are decorated with a row of dots and horizontal lines.

Cups like this shallow skyphos have earned
the name "bird bowls" from the animals
depicted in the decorative panels between the
handles and from their low, open shape,
which is bowl-like. When it was found, report-
edly in a grave, this particular example contained inside it the carved sealstone scarab
73. Both pieces attest to the relative affluence
of the Late Geometric period in Attica. Cup
shapes are now more finely potted, thinner
walled, and with a smooth transition from lip
to curving body and base, the foot of which
has now disappeared, absorbed into the simplicity of this new vase profile. The serpentine, flat ribbon-handle on this cup is less
common than the more simple rolled handles
and also contributes to its added sophistication. The trade contacts that brought the
imported carved sealstone to Attica were well
established and also brought carved ivory and
decorated gold fillets from trading centers in
the eastern Mediterranean. The Harvard sealstone and skyphos, well-made pieces, were
probably enjoyed by their owner in life and
could have been given as grave gifts to the
deceased to be used in the hereafter. The
ability of the living to provide such fine gifts
to dispose at the burial is testimony to a certain amount of expendable wealth available to
the population of Attica at this time.

The closest parallel for the Harvard bowl is
a "bird bowl" (Kerameikos 376, from Grave
24) from the excavations of the Kerameikos
cemetery. The decoration and shape of the
two pieces are virtually the same, except that
the Kerameikos piece has rounded serpentine
handles, a slightly higher lip, and the artist
used a simple dotted circle as filling ornament
for the three metopes on the cup's sides.

PUBLISHED
D. M. Robinson, "The Robinson Collection of
    Greek Gems, Seals, Rings, and Earrings"
    Hesperia Supplement 8 (1949) 310–11,
    pl. 40, 7a.

G. M. A. Hanfmann, *The David Moore Robinson Bequest of Classical Art and Antiquities:
A Special Exhibition* (Cambridge MA 1961)
10, no. 32.

EXHIBITED
*The David Moore Robinson Bequest of Classi-
cal Art and Antiquities,* Fogg Art Museum,
Harvard University, May–September 1961.

NOTES
For Kerameikos 376: Kübler, *Die Nekropole
des 10. bis 8. Jahrhunderts* 226, pl. 97; Coldstream, *Greek Geometric Pottery* 48–51, pl.
10b; Coldstream, *Geometric Greece* 112–13,
fig. 34b.

A. J. P.

75

75 SEAL WITH PIPES-PLAYER

Cilician, 750–700 B.C.
Dimensions 0.0159 x 0.0126 x 0.0079.
Pale green serpentine; intact.
**University of Missouri–Columbia, Museum
of Art and Archaeology, Weinberg Fund
(92.2).**

The green serpentine scaraboid with plain
back is pierced lengthwise. Standard for the
group to which this seal belongs, the image is
incised in a linear outline style. Within a
framing line a standing figure holds a double
pipe with both hands. He wears a long robe
with the skirt rendered in vertical lines. At
his waist a slanting line indicates a sword or

dagger. Facing the figure stands a large bird with raised hatched wings. The illustration shows a modern impression on the right.

This small seal belongs to a large group of stone scaraboids produced in the Near East but valued by Greeks as amulets and exotic offerings for their gods. Generally known as the Lyre-Player Group after one of their most common motifs, these seals with simple linear figures have been found in large numbers in Greek sanctuaries and were once thought to be of Greek, specifically Rhodian, manufacture. The fundamental study by Boardman and Buchner, however, traced their style and iconography back to Neo-Hittite art and concluded that they were produced in Cilicia on the south coast of Asia Minor. A special market was apparently found for them by the Euboean Greeks, who distributed them to western colonies in Ischia and Etruria, where they are found in the graves of infants and children, placed around the neck as a protective amulet. Many of the seals show signs of wear, indicating that they were carried by adults as well. In Greece and the Aegean islands, lyre-player seals were dedicated to the gods and may not have borne the same amuletic value as they did for the western Greeks.

The Missouri seal represents an excerpt from larger banqueting scenes that often appear on similar seals and are generally popular in oriental art. These scenes ordinarily include a seated figure approached by standing musicians playing the lyre, the pipes, and the tambourine. Meaningless to the Greek audience, the full image was never adopted into Greek art. Nevertheless, the popularity of Near Eastern seals in Greece, where seals were a novelty at this time, is one way in which other orientalizing motifs entered Late Geometric art. The earliest representations of the double pipes, or *aulos*, in Greek art occur around 700 B.C. and likely indicate when the instrument itself came into Greece from the east.

This is the only known seal on which the piper appears alone, with the bird. The pairing of lyre-player and bird is the standard version of this seal group, and the bird is occasionally replaced by a sphinx. The significance of the bird is unknown. Boardman and Buchner ruled out the likelihood that the lyre-player was a deity accompanied by his bird familiar, since there is no known corresponding eastern or Greek god. The same reasoning must apply to the pipes-player as well. Yet the image of musician and bird was not entirely foreign to the Greek viewer. Bronze Age representations of bards, such as the banquet scene of the Pylos "Orpheus" fresco and a Late Minoan III pyxis from Kalamion, included an accompanying bird, which might have symbolized the music or poem, or the performer's muse.

PUBLISHED
Frank Sternberg AG, Zurich, *Auktion* XXV (November 25–26, 1991) no. 680.

NOTES
On the Lyre-Player Group in general: Boardman and Buchner, "Seals from Ischia and the Lyre-Player Group"; E. Porada, "A Lyre Player from Tarsus and His Relations" in *The Aegean and the Near East. Studies Presented to Hetty Goldman* 185–211.

Examples of seals with pipes-players: Boardman and Buchner, "Seals from Ischia" 33 no. 103 from Kameiros, 34 no. 115 from Tarsus, 41 nos. 161–62 in collections.

Oriental banquet scenes: relief from Karatepe, H. Frankfort, *The Art and Architecture of the Ancient Orient*, 4th ed. (Harmondsworth 1970) figs. 360–61; ivory box from Nimrud, fig. 370; bronze bowl found at Olympia, fig. 390.

Early representations of the *aulos* in Greek art: Tölle, *Frühgriechische Reigentänze* 72–73, Beilage V, 41–49.

Pylos fresco: M. Lang, *The Palace of Nestor at Pylos in Western Messenia* II. *The Frescoes* (Princeton 1969) 79–80, pl. 125.

LMIIIB pyxis from Kalamion: *AAA* 2 (1969) 365, fig. 2; *AAA* 3 (1970) 111, figs. 1–2; S. Marinatos and M. Hirmer, *Kreta, Thera,*

und das mykenische Hellas (Munich 1976)
pl. 128.

S. L.

76 SMITING GOD

Levantine, twelfth to tenth century B.C.
Height 0.102.
Bronze; intact.
Arthur M. Sackler Museum, Harvard
    University Art Museums, Louise M. Bates
    and George E. Bates Collection
    (1992.256.80).

76

The slender striding figure raises his right
hand beside his head and extends his left forward at waist level. He wears a simple kilt
and a tall Egyptian white crown. Although
proportions are generally naturalistic, anatomy
is simplified with little modeling. Most
detailed is the face, with indented eyes, modeled lips, and projecting ears and nose. The
right fist is clenched and pierced to hold a
weapon, now lost. The left hand is open; a
shield might originally have been attached to
the forearm. Fingers of both mittenlike hands
are indicated by light incisions. Short pegs
extend beneath the feet. The figurine's proportions and head are reminiscent of bronzes
found in the Obelisk Temple court and other
deposits at Late Urban Byblos. Although
these involve somewhat greater naturalism
and detail than the Harvard figure exhibits,
they share a stylistic type that continues into
the second half of the second millennium.
The legs set one before the other occur in
these later figures. The unusual open flat
palm may indicate the presence of a shield
rather than a second weapon; never common,
shields are a late attribute to appear on smiting figures. Examples are found on two
bronzes from Megiddo (dated by the exca-
vators to ca. 1050–1000 and 1350–1200 respec-
tively) and an imported figurine from Delos
(fourteenth to thirteenth century).

The Harvard figurine belongs to a type of
bronze figure based upon the traditional
Egyptian image of the pharaoh smiting his
foes. Manufactured in great quantities for
votive offerings in the Middle and Late
Bronze Age Levant, such figurines have been
interpreted as a Syrian deity, most likely
Reshef or Baal. Despite their derivation from
the divine Egyptian ruler and their function
in religious contexts, the identification of
these warriors as divinities lacks unequivocal
support from inscriptions. A recent study
has called into question our acceptance of
this interpretation for all armed figures in
striking pose, suggesting that they must have

represented the spectrum from mortals to priests, kings, and gods. Variations in attributes offer clues to interpretation, and the Egyptian white crown worn by the Harvard figure seems more often to designate a divinity than a mortal on inscribed stelae and probably on metal figurines as well.

The appearance of Near Eastern bronze smiting figures in the Late Bronze Age and early Iron Age Aegean and their influence on Greek Geometric figurines are frequently acknowledged but far from understood. The figurines found in the Aegean tend to be earlier than the contexts in which they are found and are often difficult to assign a place of origin. Those from Late Bronze Age or Submycenaean contexts, such as Mycenae, Phylakopi, and possibly Tiryns, had no discernible local impact since the Mycenaeans did little with bronze sculpture. Imported smiting figurines in post–Bronze Age Greek contexts, including Delos, Lindos, Samos, and Thermon, are commonly considered to be survivors. Iron Age smiting figures are rare in the Near East but are documented in a bronze from Megiddo Stratum VB and a Cypriot warrior from the Samian Heraion. From the eighth century the type, known through heirlooms or contemporary imports, apparently served as models for the similar warrior figures encountered on Geometric Greek tripod handles and used as independent votive offerings, such as the Menil figurine, 77.

UNPUBLISHED

NOTES

Parallels: Seeden, *The Standing Armed Figurines in the Levant* pl. 94, nos. 1652–53 from Byblos, pl. 104 nos. 1736–37 from Megiddo, pl. 113 no. 1813 from Delos.
On Near Eastern bronze smiting figures: D. Collon, "The Smiting God: A Study of a Bronze in the Pomerance Collection in New York" *Levant* 4 (1972) 111–34; Negbi, *Canaanite Gods in Metal* 30–41; Seeden, *Standing Armed Figurines*; Moorey and Fleming, "Problems in the Study of the Anthropomorphic Metal Statuary."

On Near Eastern smiting figures in the Aegean, see under 77.
For the problem of Phoenician bronzes and Iron Age smiting figures: Moorey and Fleming, "Anthropomorphic Metal Statuary" 73–76; A. Spycket, *La statuaire du Proche-Orient ancien* (Leiden 1981) 426–30; O. Negbi, "Evidence for Early Phoenician Communities on the Eastern Mediterranean Islands" *Levant* 14 (1982) 179–82.

S. L.

77 HELMETED WARRIOR FIGURINE

Thessalian, Late Geometric, 725–700 B.C.
Height 0.092.
Bronze, gray-green patina; intact.
The Menil Collection, Houston. Photo by Paul Hester, Houston.

The nude male figure stands with feet slightly apart, right arm raised and left hanging at his side. His rolled and pierced right hand once brandished a spear in attack position; his left arm, which tapers to the end without an articulated hand, may once have held a shield. Set on an elongated neck, the large head bears a modeled face with projecting nose, lips, and chin and deeply indented eyes. The sides of the head are flattened into large, pierced ears. He wears on his head a helmet with a pointed crest turned backward. The simple tubular torso widens to the hips and legs, which, typical of Geometric sculpture, exhibit well-articulated knees and calves, roughly formed phallus, and flattened feet. Rivet holes in his feet show that he was originally fixed to something else, perhaps a tripod handle or wooden base, while a suspension hole at the base of his helmet gives an alternate means of display.

The figure style, particularly the elongated neck and the oblong, flattish face with roughly modeled features, indicates a northern Greek origin. Closely similar figures include an unpublished example in the Volos museum and a warrior from Philia now in Copenhagen. Two of four bronze warrior figures on display in the Volos museum also have rivet holes in their feet; it is possible they were originally attached to a tripod handle.

Of all Geometric bronze figurines the standing armed warrior who brandishes a spear in his right hand was the most frequently represented and widely distributed type. Spearbearers graced the handles of tripods and stood alone as independent offerings. In view of the variety these figures display there is no reason to assume that all require the same interpretation. Those attached to tripods usually had forward-curving headgear and often a belt; free-standing warriors might sport "fore-and-aft" or, less commonly, backward-curving helmets. While some of the tripod warriors can be demonstrated to lead a horse with their left hand, other bronzes figures occasionally carry shields on the left arm; at least one also wears a sword.

The meaning of the figures might vary with regional and cultic custom. At Olympia, where there existed a tradition of a helmeted "Zeus Areios" type and "epiphany" figures in similar headgear number among the earliest bronzes, a warrior might represent a god. At Delphi, the source of the greatest number of striding and standing warriors, the figures may refer either to Apollo's warlike aspect or to the heroic but mortal worshipers who consulted the oracle before heading into the unknown dangers of battle or colonizing expeditions. Other examples come from Philia, Dodona, Thebes, and the Athenian Acropolis; outside Olympia, the Peloponnese is not strongly represented by this type, although most of the tripod handles bearing figures have been attributed to Argive manufacture. Perhaps more meaningful than the association with cult is the tripod context in which many warrior figures were deployed as spearbearer and horse-leader. In view of their customary belts, as a recent study suggests, these particular figures might represent heroes of the type met on the battlefields of the *Iliad*. Unbelted warriors like the Menil figure likely represent mortal worshipers who left images

77

of themselves, thus heroically characterized, before their gods.

The figure's nudity is a new feature of Greek art in the Iron Age; although it may have been influenced by Near Eastern representations, it must carry a special meaning in its Greek context. The extreme rarity of female warriors in Geometric art suggests that phallic representations of this theme intended more than the simple gender identification that nude painted figures entail. In Homeric epic nakedness implies dishonor, vulnerability, or death. The regularity of nude representations in Geometric art therefore attests to the early existence of different kinds of nudity in Greek culture. The nudity of a heroic warrior is apotropaic and must symbolize his valor and perhaps even divine favor.

The ancestry of Geometric spear-bearing bronze warrior figurines in Near Eastern "smiting gods," exemplified here in **76**, has been much noted. Since the warrior with right arm raised is an established iconographic type in eighth-century Greek bronze sculpture but not in painting, it is fair to assume its ultimate derivation from the widely distributed Near Eastern bronzes, many of which have been found in the Aegean. The relationship, however, is complicated by the lack of synchronicity between the Syrian and Canaanite bronzes and their eighth-century Greek offspring. Were the Geometric artists modeling their heroes on foreign "heirlooms" accidentally found in Mycenaean contexts? Such circumstances may explain the cache of fourteenth-century objects, including a Syrian "smiter" and a Mycenaean ivory, that was buried in the eighth century under the Artemision at Delos, and the rescue and reuse of one of two imported thirteenth-to-fourteenth-century bronze smiting figures from a collapsed shrine at Phylakopi in the eleventh century. Or were the Greek bronzeworkers better acquainted with the offerings of faithful Near Eastern travelers and traders who carried their gods with them to dedicate at such sanctuaries as Samos and Lindos? The further identification of Phoenician and other eighth-century Near Eastern bronzes undertaken in recent studies may help to clarify our understanding of the sources of Geometric sculpture.

PUBLISHED

Hoffmann, *Ten Centuries That Shaped the West* 152–53, no. 72.

EXHIBITED

Ten Centuries That Shaped the West: Greek and Roman Art in Texas Collections, October 1970–July 1971.

NOTES

Parallels: bronze warrior from Philia, Volos Museum, *AD* 19 (1964) 247, pl. 291a; bronze allegedly from Philia, Ny Carlsberg Glyptothek I. N. 3311, F. Johansen, "Graeske Geometriske Bronzer" *MedKøb* 38 (1982) 77 fig. 6.

For belts, see **60** and M. Bennett, "Homer, Belted Heroes, and Asia Minor" [abstract] *AJA* 97 (1993) 317.

On nudity in Greek art: L. Bonfante, "Nudity as a Costume in Classical Art" *AJA* 93 (1989) 543–70.

On the problem of Near Eastern smiting figures in the Aegean: J. Vorys Canby, "Some Hittite Figurines from the Aegean" *Hesperia* 38 (1969) 141–49; J. Bouzek, "Syrian and Anatolian Bronze Age Figurines in Europe" *PPS* 38 (1972) 156–64; W. Burkert, "Rešep-Figuren, Apollo vom Amyklai und die 'Erfindung' des Opfers auf Cypern" *Graz-Beitr* 4 (1975) 51–79; J. D. Muhly, "Bronze Figurines and Near Eastern Metalwork" *IEJ* 30 (1980) 148–61; Moorey and Fleming, "Problems in the Study of the Anthropomorphic Metal Statuary" 74–75; C. Rolley, "Un dieu syrien à Thermon" *BCH* 108 (1984) 669–70; H. Gallet de Santerre, "Les statuettes de bronze mycéniennes au type dit du 'Dieu Reshef' dans leur contexte égéen" *BCH* 111 (1987) 7–29.

On bronzes from the Delos deposit: J. Tréheux and H. Gallet de Santerre, "Dépôt égéen et géométrique de l'Artémision à Délos, V. Objets de bronze" *BCH* 71–72

(1947–1948) 221–38 no. 76 pl. 39, 1–4; See-den, *The Standing Armed Figures in the Levant* 127 no. 1813, pl. 113.
Phylakopi bronzes: C. Renfrew, "The Mycenaean Sanctuary at Phylakopi" *Antiquity* 52 (1978) 7–15; C. Renfrew, *Archaeology of Cult: The Sanctuary at Phylakopi* (BSA Supplement 18, London 1985) 302–10, pls. 67–70.
On Iron Age smiting figures from the Near East, see 76.

S. L.

78 IDOL STANDARD

Luristan, ninth to eighth century B.C.
Total height 0.221, finial height 0.120.
Bronze; intact except for small hole in base of neck of one animal.
University of Missouri–Columbia, Museum of Art and Archaeology (77.32.a, b).

The highly decorative standard features two feline beasts holding aloft a human head in their joined front paws. Typical of Luristan style, the elements are segmented and greatly abstracted so that it is difficult to distinguish human anatomy from animal. Surmounting the piece is a narrow head with bulging eyes outlined by brows that continue down into the prominent nose; round cheeks are framed by spiral-form ears or hair. A molding on top of the head matches one on the bottom of the finial. The sex of the figure is indeterminate. A relief spiral ornaments the front of the neck as well as the animals' shoulders and haunches. The strongly arching necks of the felines project directly from the center, their upturned heads formed with flattened muzzles, protruding eyes, and small ears. A raised oval with horizontal striations centered on the human form between the animals renders their joined claws, as does a smaller version at their rear feet. Their bodies are bound together by a wide vertically grooved girdle. From the pair of round haunches extend tails that hang down, swirling in a countercurve to the odd stance of the legs. The function of

78

the object is unknown, aside from its use as terminal on top of a hollow bottle-shaped support. The support shown with it is said to belong.

Formally related to the well-known Luristan rampant animal finials and Master-of-Animal standards, the type represented by the Missouri bronze has been termed "idol standards" by Muscarella. The type is thought to form an intermediate or transitional link between the other two groups, introducing the human element through the isolated head, which soon develops into the more fully formed and active master of animals. It is not, however, clear that the detached head of the idol standards plays the same beast-dominating role as his later counterpart. While the meaning of these objects is unknown, speculation has focused on religious content. Certainly the combination of frontal staring face and beasts of prey was intended to ward off evil, although any further significance is unclear. The traditional but discredited identification of these groups with Gilgamesh still occasionally occurs in the literature on these standards. The finials and standards have been found in tombs, but from the lack of recorded findspots for them it is not known whether they could also have been dedicated in shrines and used in houses.

The style of the Missouri standard and other Luristan bronzes reveals an abstraction of nature into geometric forms that yields a distinctly different effect from that of contemporary Greek work. Circles, spheres, spirals, and undulating curves in the standard are subject to the rule of symmetry and dominant axes. Unlike the schematic organic constructions of Greek Geometric art, these forms are fractured and their surfaces obscured by minute ornamentation, resulting in a restless and incorporeal image. The portable, nomadic animal style of art to which the Luristan bronzes belong has been described through the lens of shamanism, as seeking a spiritual reality independent of the visible world. The shifting, unstable patterns and surfaces of nomadic

art stand in strong contrast with the stability and essential anthropocentrism of such urban cultures as Greece.

The worlds of Greece and Luristan touched from time to time, at first with small impact on one another. In the eighth century the travel of objects seems to have been primarily one-directional, with Luristan bronzes and other portable art disseminated perhaps from the North Syrian coast at the end of the trade route through Assyria to Luristan. Small numbers of Luristan objects filtered into Greek sanctuaries, such as a Luristan finial at the Samian Heraion, dedicated perhaps as curiosities. Both cultures, however, responded to their exposure to the same ancient traditions of the Near East by transforming borrowed imagery into culturally coherent art. So the beast-mastering image known throughout the Near East appears fragmented in this standard and in an essentially organic form in the Mistress of Animals of the Cretan tray (**43**).

PUBLISHED
"Acquisitions 1977" *Muse* 12 (1978) 6 (ill.).

NOTES
P. R. S. Moorey, *Catalogue of the Ancient Persian Bronzes in the Ashmolean Museum* (Oxford 1971) 148–53, nos. 172, 173, 175, pls. 33–34.

O. W. Muscarella, *Bronze and Iron. Ancient Near Eastern Artifacts in the Metropolitan Museum of Art* (New York 1988) 146–47, nos. 225–27.

On finds from Luristan in Greek sanctuaries and Iranian influence on Greek art: H.-V. Herrmann, "Frühgriechischer Pferdeschmuck vom Luristantypus" *JdI* 83 (1968) 1–78; O. W. Muscarella, "The Archaeological Evidence for Relations between Greece and Iran in the First Millennium B.C." *JANES* 9 (1977) 31–57; I. Kilian-Dirlmeier, "Fremde Weihungen in griechischen Heiligtümern vom 8. bis zum Beginn des 7. Jahrhunderts v. Chr." *JRZM* 32 (1985) 215–54.

S. L.

And as when a master craftsman overlays gold on silver,
and he is one who was taught by Hephaistos and Pallas Athena
in art complete, and grace is on every work he finishes.

(Odyssey 6.232–34)

THE
REBIRTH OF GREEK ART

The ways in which the Greeks represented and interpreted their world through consciously selected artistic styles and themes tell us as much about the culture as do the primary contexts in which the objects were used, which are examined in the preceding sections.

The term *Geometric* as a label for this period derives from the characteristic geometrical approach to the decoration of pottery in these centuries. Although the term was coined at the turn of our century, it retains an apt emphasis. The design aesthetic based on an underlying mathematical structure that emerged in the Protogeometric period and persisted to 700 B.C. has been taken to reflect a meaningful cultural response to the insecurities of a dark age; its passwords are order, control, and predictability. This decorative system is characterized by a highly formalized and rational organization of controlled and measured pattern sensitive to the fundamental struc-ture of the vessel. Its repetition of motifs marshaled into metopes and bands expresses a new sense of measure and order that may have been psychologically satisfying to the descendants of a collapsed society.

The Meaning of Geometric Style

Geometric art is a triumph of analytic design achieved at a time when the Greeks were first exploring the nature and possibilities of the alphabet. The individual motifs of the vases have been characterized as the irreducible building blocks of a greater whole, much like the similes of epic poetry and the letters of the new alphabet. In sculpture as well as painting, each figural form encases the inner reality of its subject through reduction to essential elements; the result is denaturalized, generic, ideal, and thereby the more strongly expressive. Some of the finest artworks in the exhibition

serve to demonstrate the principles of Geometric style.

Geometric art is usually defined and
judged on the basis of works created at the
mid-eighth century, typically a vessel like
the splendid amphora Athens 804 (Fig. 7).
Such a monument attests to the ultimate
goals of the Geometric potter and painter:
it reveals an intimate art of minute detail,
precise brush stroke, and an almost unbelievable accuracy of planning and measurement in two-dimensional enhancement of
the solid vessel form. A comparison of earlier and later works, however, suggests a
changing rather than a static ideal. While
the decoration of the Middle Geometric
amphora (2) is so minimal that its effect is
entirely to enhance the vessel's structure,
the large pitcher-olpe by the Lion Painter
(79) from the end of the period documents
the near abandonment of structure for an emphasis on its charming painted bestiary.
This interest in motif, particularly in assem-
bling a cosmic collection of living and
abstract elements, as seen in fibulae 18 and
81, pyxis 82, pitcher 83, tripod 61, and lekythos 65, is sometimes overlooked in charac-
terizing the period chiefly by its classic
style.

In their best small-scale bronze sculptures
the Greeks could capture the complexity of
the third dimension, resulting in an "accidental" naturalism that, combined with the
essentially abstracted human form, yielded
striking results, as in the seated figure from
the Walters Art Gallery (80). At other times
the sophistication of the abstract form gives
way to a desire for added detail, as in the
small struggling pair of bird and man (100)
and the bronze lyre-player and companion
(101), who ingenuously tell us much about
the important role of epic and lyric
performance.

The Role of Artistic Personality

In Geometric art already by about
760 B.C. an interest in the individual can be
detected in the emergence of recognizable
artistic hands and workshops. This emergence of artistic personalities sets the Greek
tradition in pronounced contrast with the
anonymity of Near Eastern art.

Seated figure 80 may be cited as the best
proponent of Geometric sculptural style, yet
its sophistication is not typical. Bronze
sculpture was first and last a votive medium, concerned with subject matter rather
than execution, which makes such a masterpiece all the more provocative: one feels in
the Baltimore bronze the presence of the
artist rather than that of the dedicant. No
other work has been attributed to the
exceptional artist of the seated figure,
although the bronze-master whose hand is
recognizable in a number of animal statuettes, particularly deer, is represented by
two small fawns (85–86). The oeuvre of the
"Master of the Boston Deer and Fawn,"
named for the famous group in the Museum of Fine Arts, Boston (Fig. 24), reveals a
probably Boeotian artist fluent with other
regional styles who specialized in small
sculptures of wild animals created with delicacy and humor. It becomes surprisingly
easy to begin to think of the artist as a not-
quite-nameless individual (Fig. 25).

It seems almost absurd to speak of specific artistic hands and influences in the
relentless anonymity of repeating patterns
and established compositional formulas. Yet
a number of artistic personalities have been
identified through distinctive compositional
schemes and details of execution, as in the
Workshop of Athens 894, represented here
by amphorae from Richmond (3), Buffalo (9),
and Cleveland (20), or by a "signature"
motif, as in the Birdseed Painter and work-

Fig. 25. *Geometric bronzesmith statuette, Metropolitan Museum of Art, 42.11.42 (Photo courtesy of the Metropolitan Museum of Art, Fletcher Fund, 1942)*

Fig. 24. *Deer and fawn statuette from Thebes. (H. L. Pierce Fund, courtesy Museum of Fine Arts, Boston)*

shop represented by a large pitcher (83) and a standed bowl (84).

The complex counterpoint of the conservative tradition of Geometric art and the innovations provided by individual artists propelled Greek art through profound developments in two centuries. The Late Geometric I monumental scenes (24, 98) are full of personality and achieve something new only by breaking the rules of a conservative geometric style to introduce irregularities, asymmetries, and the urge to explain what is happening to small dabs of paint deployed on the pot.

The Meaning of Regional Styles

The regional stylistic diversity of eighth-century Geometric pottery and bronzes stands in marked contrast with the relative unity of the preceding Bronze Age. In earlier periods the rise of local styles coincided with times of invasion, conflict, and breakdown in communications. Despite the improving communications and the rising prosperity of the Late Geometric period, the general homogeneity of art from ca. 1000 to 750 B.C. gradually yields to a marked parochialism in the productions of various centers. Gathered here in contrast to the largely Attic style represented in the exhibition are closely contemporary Late Geometric vessels from the Cycladic Islands (87), Crete (88), Corinth (89), the Argive plain (90 and see Fig. 26), and Boeotia (91). Underlying reasons for growing regionalism can be traced to the self-identity of the emerging poleis.

Bronze horse figurines of Laconian, Messenian, Arcadian, Aetolian, Thessalian, and Argive styles (92–97) represent an equally varied stylistic spectrum. Their function as votive figurines creates a complex phenomenon. Like vases, the different horse styles can be associated with specific regions, including even Thessaly and Macedonia, where poleis were slow to develop. The archaeological evidence for on-site bronze-casting at Olympia and other sanctuaries suggests that bronzeworkers established themselves there and made available horses that could evoke the home regions of individual dedicants. Such a picture of stylistic pluralism corresponds with the competitive trends in early Greek society. The presence of multiple bronze workshops operating simultaneously at major sanctuaries seems ironically to have led to a gradual blending of styles. Naturally, it is fair to ask whether this is an accurate accounting of the situation, based as it is on the assumption that eighth-century Greeks were closely attuned to stylistic nuances, or whether the process of artistic apprenticeship itself helped create a certain homogeneity of style.

From Geometry to Poetry

The evolution of the Geometric artistic style from abstract design to figural subject and narrative concept can be traced in a steady development extending from the tenth to the eighth centuries. From a twentieth-century viewpoint the idea of depicting a specific myth or Homeric reference seems a logical extension of an increasingly varied figural style, yet it is a matter of continuing debate at what point such a notion occurred. Some scholars are quick to discover specific Iliadic episodes among such battle scenes as that from which 98 comes. Yet from a pragmatic viewpoint we must also consider the accessibility of epic in the eighth century. Boardman offers a sobering but plausible view: "No Attic Geometric artist had ever read or heard recited a single line of Homer."

A fragment of a monumental funerary krater (98) joins with a large section in the Louvre illustrating a battle scene that is at once generic and episodic, thus raising the question of the influence of Homeric epic on pictorial art. An oinochoe (99) with three warriors, one dead and two fighting, has been interpreted both as a shorthand version of a Homeric struggle to claim a body (either generic or Priam and Achilles) and as a specific myth (Aigisthus and Klytemnaestra). A remarkable bronze group (100) depicting a heroic struggle between a tiny man and a formidable bird, in which the latter is clearly winning, looks humorous to modern eyes, and this may have been the artist's intention. It probably records the first artistic depiction of the annual battle of the pygmies against migrating cranes, the sort of folktale by which lands lying far beyond the experience of eighth-century Greeks were characterized by Homer and by later poets and historians. The contemporary appearance of this theme in Homer and in art is significant. Like the bronze singer with his companion (101) it records the beginning of the profound interdependence of Greek art and epic subject matter that points the way beyond Geometric style.

S. L.

79 PITCHER-OLPE BY THE LION PAINTER

Attic, Late Geometric, ca. 730–700 B.C.
Height 0.522, mouth diameter 0.26, body
    diameter 0.352.
Ceramic; excellent condition; a single
    fracture around lower part of neck; three
    mended breaks in handle; small plaster
    infill in rim to right of handle; a few
    rubbed places on painted decoration.
Arthur M. Sackler Museum, Harvard

79, detail

79, detail

University Art Museums, Francis H. Burr Memorial Fund (1950.64). From Walter Ephron Gallery, New York City. See Plate 16.

The vase, with its concave neck sitting atop a generously swelling ovoid body, rests on a ring foot, hollow beneath. The high vertical handle rises to a point ca. 0.03 meter above the rim, then curves straight down to join it; two cylindrical struts anchor it to the back of the neck. Except for the black-painted area around the foot and lowest part of the body, the pitcher-olpe is completely covered by an intricate network of lateral bands of painted ornament. The neck and body feature a program of major and subordinate sequences of ornamental elements. The three principal zones (in the middle of the neck, on the shoulder next to its junction with the neck, and encircling the widest part of the body) consist of alternating metopes within which rosettes, lozenges, swastikas, and other geometric motifs alternate with panels that contain animals and birds. These major lateral bands are framed by lesser zones of continuous meander. The meander band encircling the flaring lip just below the rim forms a sort of cornice for the entire vessel.

The ornamental system is further divided by thin bands of continuous lozenges, a continuous frieze of four rows of dots disposed in alternating fashion, a "bird file," and, on the lower part of the body, a zone of tiny triangles with tendril points and a lowest band of upright oval lozenges with central dots. All these zones, major and minor alike, are further framed and separated by groups of horizontal lines.

The central figural panel on the neck features a lion. Panels on the shoulder contain two large-eyed grazing deer, a pair of long-necked confronted birds, and a pair of confronted kneeling goats. Around the body, panels include two standing horses facing right and two lions facing right. On the shoulder and body zones, the animal panels occur in alternating positions above and below each other, except for the right-hand lion on the body, which appears almost directly beneath a left-facing grazing deer. Small stylized birds appear frequently in the design scheme as well. A continuous file of birds with long curved necks beside vertical columns of minute dots encircles the upper neck. In addition, tiny birds appear as filling ornament in the figural and swastika panels. The handle, consisting of a broad strap band flanked by two relief fillets, bears a vertical serpent with birds among its curves and delicate dot-rosettes. The badly abraded top of the handle appears to carry a single small swastika.

The painted brushwork on this vase shows a vigorous sure hand at work. This individual was termed the "Lion Painter" or "Lion Master" by Kahane; his known work was expanded and revised by Cook, Davison, and Coldstream. By the time of Coldstream's study in 1968, the Lion Painter's oeuvre numbered six vases: three round-mouthed pitchers, including the Harvard example, two kotylai, and a standed bowl. Coldstream has characterized him as a mannerist working at the beginning of Late Geometric IIb, perhaps ca. 720–710 B.C., speaking of him as a principal figure in the disintegration of linear ornament in the vase painting of Athenian Late Geometric II times, with easily recognizable features, such as his massive, narrow-waisted two-legged lions, his use of the double-ax motif, and his treatment of square metopelike panels. Coldstream considers the Harvard vase to be early in this painter's work before his drawing and his systems of ornament fell apart. However, close examination of this vase suggests a revision of this judgment, revealing an artist who not only filled every available space with painted ornament but who also, at least on this vase, combined everything into a harmonious whole.

This vase is an unusually large example of a shape peculiar to Athenian Late Geometric II pottery: the round-mouthed pitcher, or "pitcher-olpe," as Davison calls it. These vases are usually provided with low conical lids, sometimes surmounted with elaborated knobbed handles. A smaller form of round-mouthed pitcher with flat bottom, almost a mug, also exists within the same time range. Neither form, however, survives into the earliest phases of Protoattic pottery manufactured at the beginning of the seventh century B.C. Rather than serving to contain or pour liquids, large vases such as this would have functioned as prestige items for display and deposit in funerary ceremonies, and perhaps in some cases as grave markers or monuments as well. While the antecedents and origins of these pitchers are still not known, they show close resemblances to late Phrygian painted and monochrome one-handled round-mouthed jugs of the late eighth century B.C. from Gordion, as well as some bronze examples. Whatever their origins, such large pitchers provided an attractive alternative, or fashion, for a generation of Late Geometric town and country Athenians who prized impressive funerary pottery, but examples less expensive than the great "Dipylon" amphorae and kraters of Late Geometric I. Why they ceased being made

and used must be connected with the causes for the marked decline both in quality and in quantity of cultural remains in Attica during the first half of the seventh century B.C.

PUBLISHED

P. Kahane, "Die Entwicklungsphasen der attisch-geometrischen Keramik" *AJA* 44 (1940) 464–82 at 479–80, 482, pl. XXVII, 3 (then in the art market; attribution credited to E. Kunze).

Cook, "Athenian Workshops around 700" 143–44.

Davison, *Attic Geometric Workshops* no. 1, fig. 30.

C. Brokaw, "Concurrent Styles in Late Geometric and Early Protoattic Vase Painting" *AM* 78 (1963) 65, n. 5, 66; Beil. 29, 1.

Coldstream, *Greek Geometric Pottery* 73 (XV.1), 74.

K. Kübler, *Die Nekropole des späten 8. bis frühen 6. Jhr.* (Kerameikos VI, 2, Berlin 1970) 581, no. 82; 10, 11, 12, 13, 14, 17–19, 20, 45, 56, 63 n. 189, 80.

D. G. Mitten and A. Brauer, *Dialogue with Antiquity* (Harvard University Art Museums, Cambridge MA 1982) no. 4.

Rombos, *The Iconography of Attic Late Geometric II Pottery* no. 264, 485.

NOTES

On the "Lion Painter": Coldstream, *Greek Geometric Pottery* 73–74, 331 chart.

On the "pitcher-olpe" shape: Davison, *Attic Geometric Workshops* 10, fig. a; 12.

For resemblances of the pitcher-olpe with Phrygian ceramic and metal shapes: R. S. Young et al., *Three Great Early Tumuli* (Gordion I, Philadelphia 1981) 34–35 (general remarks), examples pls. 16 D–F, 17 A–F, 88 E. Two Near Eastern (Phoenician?) bronze round-mouthed jugs from Lefkandi, *BSA* 77 (1982) 239, fig. 8, pl. 20, 31.

On Attica in early 7th c.: R. Osborne, "A Crisis in Archaeological History? The Seventh Century B.C. in Attica" *BSA* 84 (1989) 297–322.

D. G. M.

80

80 SEATED MAN

Allegedly found in the Alpheios Valley in
  Elis, Late Geometric, 750–700 B.C.
Height 0.072.
Bronze, dark green patina; surface
  extensively pitted, front leg of stool
  broken and reattached.
Walters Art Gallery, Baltimore (54.789).
  Purchased in 1925.

The figure sits on an arched stool set upon
a T-shaped base; his feet meet the ends of

the crossbar. His arms curve out from his
shoulders to hold, with elbows perched on
knees, an ovoid object against his nose. The
figure's anatomy is utterly simple. Elongated
wiry arms and legs, their diameters scarcely
changing between trunk and hand or foot,
extend from a narrow torso that widens from
the center to shoulders and hips. Genitals are
marked. The head is defined by a distinct
ridge separating brow and ears from cranium;
the rounded face features indented eyes, a long
vertical nose, and a prominent chin. Short
grooves mark fingers at the ends of the attenuated arms, and feet are not rendered at all.

This well-known bronze represents for
many the essence of Geometric sculptural
style. The simplicity of its subject—a seated
man holding an object—gave the artist an
opportunity to explore composition and style
in terms of the utmost reduction of nature to
geometry while still leaving room for minor
articulating details. The result is a closed,
symmetrical form in which the composition's
vertical lines are met by diagonals and curves
to lead the eye fully around the sculpture's
three dimensions and through its surprising
depth. Its linearity finds balance in the triangular and rectangular masses of space its
forms delimit. A date in the later eighth century is demanded by its conceptual sophistication, almost mannerist, and the technical
daring of its slender elements.

So perfect and timeless is the resulting
image that not even placing it in its context
within a standardized bronze votive figurine
"type" diminishes its unique aesthetic
achievement. A dozen examples from such
diverse findspots as Olympia, Sparta, Tegea,
Eretria, Kameiros, and central Italy display
variations on the seated theme. Some hold
objects or only their hands to their mouths;
others sit in a relaxed attitude with their
hands on their knees or face (compare 48).
Those that like the Baltimore sitter grasp an
object have elicited interpretations of their
activity as drinking from a flask or skin, playing a musical instrument, sniffing a bud, and
most recently, blowing a conch shell (a sugges-

tion that recalls ancient Aegean religious tradition as in **61** but finds no corroborating Geometric period evidence). That the figure is not simply a musician working an ill-defined instrument is supported by the series of rod pendants (for example **32**) topped by tiny sitting figures that look like distant cousins of the Baltimore man, although lacking stool and "instrument." Originating about the time the series of larger independent sculptures ends, these seem to represent a popular spin-off, a personal amulet version of the seated votive figures.

Among the seated figures the Baltimore bronze is by far the finest work; Schweitzer and Jantzen in fact believed that it was the prototype on which all others were based. It should instead be seen as the most fully developed and originally interpreted of the series. Many of the more pedestrian examples have distinctly simian proportions and shape of head and recall the Egyptian-derived amulets of squatting baboons widespread along the paths of Phoenician travel, an appearance even more strongly evoked in the seated pendant figures. Sitting figurines with known provenance cluster in the lower Peloponnese, where stylistic connections support a Laconian origin of the type. It is probably no coincidence that Sparta was an important entry point for Near Eastern ivories and iconography in association with the Artemis Ortheia cult, in which setting one of these seated figures was found.

The artist of the Baltimore bronze created an original from the raw materials of a standardized votive type and the unlimited potential of an abstract sculptural style. After nearly sixty years of study, the small man retains his mystery.

PUBLISHED

BSA 35 (1934–1935) 116.

E. Buschor, *Die Plastik der Griechen* (Berlin 1936) 8.

D. K. Hill, *Catalogue of the Classical Bronze Sculpture in the Walters Art Gallery* (Portland ME 1949) 77 no. 167, pl. 36.

E. Homann-Wedeking, *Die Anfänge der griechischen Grossplastik* (Berlin 1950) 15–16, 24.

U. Jantzen, "Geometrische Kannenverschlüsse" *AA* 68 (1953) 63 n. 4.

L. Alscher, *Griechische Plastik* I (Berlin 1954) 21–22, fig. 16.

Himmelmann-Wildschütz, *Bemerkungen zur geometrischen Plastik* 11, figs. 51–53.

R. Lullies in Schefold, *Die Griechen und ihre Nachbarn* 160, pl. 8a–c.

D. K. Hill, "When the Greeks Began on Bronzes" *Bulletin of the Walters Art Gallery* 21, 3 (1968).

Mitten and Doeringer, *Master Bronzes from the Classical World* 32 no. 9.

Rolley, *Monuments figurés, les statuettes de bronze* 43 n. 4.

W. Fuchs, *Skulptur der Griechen* (Munich 1969) 246, fig. 268.

Schweitzer, *Greek Geometric Art* 160, pl. 199.

F. Canciani, "Scimmie a Creta" in *Antichita Cretesi. Studi in Onore di Doro Levi* I (Catania 1973) 107–10 at 109 and n. 28.

F. Canciani, "Due bronzetti della Collezione Pansa nel Museo Archeologico Nazionale di Chieti" *PP* (1975) 232–39 at 234 and n. 12.

Vickers, "Some Early Iron Age Bronzes from Macedonia" 25, n. 41.

Kilian-Dirlmeier, *Anhänger in Griechenland* 206, n. 18.

G. Ortiz in *Hommes et dieux de la Grèce antique* 203–5 under no. 124.

J. Bouzek, "Addenda to Macedonian Bronzes" *Eirene* 18 (1982) 35–59 at 51.

Floren, *Die geometrische und archaische Plastik* 58, pl. 5, 6.

M. True in Kozloff and Mitten, eds., *The Gods Delight* no. 1, 48–51.

S. Langdon, "From Monkey to Man."

Voyatzis, *The Early Sanctuary of Athena Alea at Tegea* 110–15.

EXHIBITED

4000 Years of Modern Art, Walters Art Gallery, Baltimore, 1953, no. 15.

Master Bronzes from the Classical World, The Fogg Art Museum, Cambridge MA,

December 1967–January 1968, City Art
Museum of Saint Louis, March–April 1968,
The Los Angeles County Museum of Art,
May–June 1968.

*The Gods Delight. The Human Figure in
Classical Bronze,* The Cleveland Museum
of Art, The Los Angeles County Museum
of Art, The Museum of Fine Arts, Boston,
November 1988–July 1989.

NOTES

For a catalogue of related Geometric seated
figures: S. Langdon, "From Monkey to
Man" 408–11.

On the origin of the type: Schweitzer, *Greek
Geometric Art* 160; S. Langdon, "From
Monkey to Man" 421–22; Voyatzis, *The
Early Sanctuary of Athena Alea at Tegea*
113–14; see P. Kranz, "Frühe griechische
Sitzfiguren" *AM* 87 (1972) 1–55 for a differ-
ent view.

For Phoenician influences in Laconia: E. L.
Marangou, *Lakonische Elfenbein und
Beinschnitzereien* (Tübingen 1969); P. Cart-
ledge, *Sparta and Laconia: A Regional History 1300 to 363 B.C.* (London 1979); J. B.
Carter, *Greek Ivory-Carving in the Orientalizing and Archaic Periods* (New York 1985);
J. B. Carter, "The Masks of Ortheia" *AJA*
92 (1987) 355–83; S. Langdon, "From Monkey to Man" 421–24.

S. L.

81 ENGRAVED BOW FIBULA

**Central Greek, Late Geometric,
750–700 B.C.**

Height 0.17, width 0.10.

**Bronze, ruddy dark green patina; missing
small pieces from top edge of bow and
three corners of the catchplate; one side
uniformly rough, with bright bronze
patches showing through and incision
somewhat obscured by accretions.**

**Arthur M. Sackler Museum, Harvard
University Art Museums, Ancient Art
Acquisition Fund through the generosity
of Walter and Ursula Cliff (1986.655).**

81

See Plate 7.

The form and decorative technique of the
bronze fibula clearly associate it with Attica.
Distinctively Attic is the use of rocked zigzags
and delicate punch marks to create textured
contour lines. However, the central disk motif
on both sides of the fibula bow recalls the
elaborate radiate disks depicted on Boeotian
bow fibulae. Boeotia may be the source for
the motif, but it is more plausible that this
fibula was an ancestor of the Boeotian
examples.

The solid-cast and hammered fibula incor-
porates flat areas of sheet bronze with ovoid
and cylindrical forms in a satisfying structural
whole. The shape is dominated by the large
crescent bow, arched strongly on the top and
more subtly on the bottom. The catchplate
and pin are extensions of the narrow ends of
the bow, each separated from the bow by
beaded transitions. The pin forms a double
loop and projects to a tapering point secured
by the catchplate's folded edge.

The better preserved side of the bow displays a symmetrical composition within an
elaborate border of tremolo lines framing a
zigzag along the upper edge of the bow and
linked diamonds along the bottom edge.
Enclosed by the border is a central disk composed of two compass-drawn circles, one
twice the size of the other. The smaller circle
is repeated seven times within the larger: one
is concentric; the other six are radially positioned at measured intervals between the center of the design and its outer perimeter.

The intersection of these circles forms a six-petaled rosette within the smaller concentric circle. These petals are filled with punch marks, as are sections of the six radially arranged circles. Single punch marks occur between the rosette petals.

The rest of the decoration on the bow is executed with very fine punch marks. Pairs of birds, horses, and fish symmetrically flank the central disk. The birds and horses face toward the disk while the fish are positioned in the opposite direction. The birds appear above the horse's heads. A single rein linking the horses' muzzles follows the bottom edge of the disk. A border similar to that of the bow also frames the catchplate, which contains a horse confronting what appears to be a fish.

The scene on the bow bears a remarkable resemblance to these passages from the Homeric hymn to Helios:

> Son of Earth and starry Heaven. . . . As he [Helios] rides in his chariot, he shines upon men and deathless gods, and piercingly he gazes with his eyes from his golden helmet. Bright rays beam dazzlingly from him, and his bright locks streaming from the temples of his head grace-fully enclose his far-seen face: a rich, fine spun garment glows upon his body and flutters in the wind: and stallions carry him. Then, when he has stayed his golden-yoked chariot and horses, he rests there upon the highest point of heaven, until he marvelously drives them down again through heaven to Ocean. (3.8–16)

The succession of paired fish, horses, and birds traces an arc culminating with the radiate disk. Just as Helios rests at the highest point of heaven in the hymn, the disk is rendered roughly at the highest apex within the crescent of the bow. The sequence, whether read from left to right or right to left, ends with the central focus of the disk.

If the disk represents Helios, the birds, horses, and fish can be explained as environmental stages through which the sun-chariot must pass in its trajectory from one horizon, to the zenith of the sky at noon, and down again to the far horizon. Helios rises from Okeanos (the fish) toward heaven (the bird) to

its highest point (the central disk), whence the sequence is reversed. On the catchplate below, the horse and fish, perhaps standing for earth (Gaia) and water (Pontus) respec-tively (see 18), embody the temporal realm.

Accretions obscure much of the decoration on the other side of the fibula. What can be seen suggests a similar if not identical composition.

Bow fibulae are known in far fewer num-bers than plate fibulae. Most excavated exam-ples are from graves. The designation refers to the distinctive crescent shape, a broad thin plate continuous and in the same plane with the pin and catchplate. The type may be traced back to Lefkandi, where graves dated to the last quarter of the ninth century B.C. have yielded a similar form. One unusually rich grave in the Kerameikos cemetery (grave 41) contained four bow fibulae and a plate fibula fastened one to another like the links of a chain. In the late Geometric period, Boeo-tian craftsmen begin to produce bow fibulae with minimal catchplates and complex figural decoration.

UNPUBLISHED

NOTES
D. von Bothmer, ed., *Glories of the Past: Ancient Art from the Shelby White and Leon Levy Collection* (New York 1991) 97 no. 78.

Bow fibulae: Lefkandi, *Archaeology* 25 (1972) 18; Attica, Kübler, *Die Nekropole des 10. bis 8. Jahrhunderts* 235–36, pls. 159–61; Boeotia (in Berlin) A. Furtwängler, "Erwerbungen der Antikensammlungen in Deutschland. Berlin" AA 9 (1894) 115–16, nos. 1–2, fig. 2; Hampe, *Frühe griechische Sagenbilder in Böotien* 98, nos. 60–62a–b, fig. 1 pls. 4–5; E. Reisinger, "Geometrische Fibeln in München" *JdI* 31 (1916) 288–305, pls. 17–18; H. B. Walters, *Catalogue of the Bronzes, Greek, Roman, and Etruscan, in the Depart-ment of Greek and Roman Antiquities, Brit-ish Museum* (London 1899) 372–74, nos. 3204–5, figs. 85–88; B. Schweitzer, *Herakles,*

82

*Aufsätze zur griechischen Religions-und
Sagengeschichte* (Tübingen 1922) figs. 30–31;
K. Schefold, *Frühgriechische Sagenbilder*
(Munich 1964) pl. 6a.
Translation of the Homeric hymn to Helios:
H. G. Evelyn-White (Loeb Classical Library,
Cambridge MA 1914).
Sun symbols: Goodison, *Death, Women, and
the Sun* esp. ch. 3; N. Yalouris, "Das Akro-
ter des Heraions in Olympia" *AM* 87 (1972)
93–98.

M. J. B.

82 HORSE PYXIS

Attic, Late Geometric Ib, 750–735 B.C.
Height 0.208, widest diameter 0.318, lip
   diameter 0.28, base diamete· 0.292.
Ceramic; repaired from numerous fragments.
The Museum of Fine Arts, Houston, Gift of
   Miss Annette Finnigan (acc: 37.17).

The three-horse pyxis has a gently rounded
profile between flat bottom and nearly flat
lid. Surrounded by rings of parallel strokes
and false spiral, the three horses have dark-
ground bodies with reserved areas allowing
painted details: painted ears, dotted circle
eyes, angled lines along the muzzles, false
spiral around the necks, hatched lines from
mane to tail. Each of the outer horses has
concentric circles on its outer flank. On the
pyxis body two pairs of metopes contain confronted grazing deer; a third pair flanks a
water bird. The other metopes enclose
hatched swastikas; narrow panels of stacked
Ms separate the metopes. A dotted lozenge
chain circles the top of the body. The underside has a central quatrefoil of double outline
leaves surrounded by triple bands, a false
spiral ring, and a ring of hatched leaves with
crosses between.

The animals in metopes on the pyxis body are unusual in this vessel type but not unique. A pyxis in the Louvre has standing long-horned goats, and another in Berlin features horses with birds; birds alone are much more common, as in the Providence pyxis, **28**. A pyxis by the same painter is Cambridge **84**, which lacks grazing deer but has water birds identical to the one on the Houston pyxis.

The Houston pyxis offers a direct comparison of plastic and painterly animal forms. Formed by single precise brush strokes, the extremely attenuated anatomy of the deer reduces shoulders to a semicircular blob, legs to pins, and head and neck to a long S-curve, resulting in an impressionistic rendering. The stocky lid horses, on the other hand, are built of clay elements pinched, rolled, and pressed together. The deer and horses share cylindrical trunks and straight limbs but little else. The formal gulf between the husky three-dimensional horses and the calligraphic two-dimensional deer distinguishes the hands of potter and painter and points up essential differences in media. The differing approaches also warn us against assigning stylistic correspondences and variances a chronological value.

PUBLISHED

Hoffmann, *Ten Centuries That Shaped the West* 308–10, fig. 149 a–b.

Bohen, *Die geometrischen Pyxiden* 71–72, fig. 20d, pl. 38, 3.

Rombos, *The Iconography of Attic Late Geometric II Pottery* 423 cat. 98, pl. 3b.

EXHIBITED

Ten Centuries That Shaped the West: Greek and Roman Art in Texas Collections, October 1970–July 1971.

NOTES

For the function and significance of horse pyxides, see **29**.

Animal metopes on horse pyxides: CVA Louvre-16, 18–20, pl. 21.1–2 (A 567); Berlin Staatliche Museen, V.I.3143.1, *Führer durch die Antikenabteilung* (1968) 35; Bohen, *Die geo-metrischen Pyxiden* pl. 38, 2 and 5; CVA Cambridge 1, 2, pl. I.19a–b.

S. L.

83 PITCHER

Attic, Late Geometric IIa, 735–720 B.C.
Height 0.467, height to rim 0.422, maximum diameter 0.241, base diameter 0.113.
Ceramic; top of handle and small areas of lip and neck restored.
Indiana University Art Museum (66.10).
Photograph by Michael Cavanagh, Kevin Montague.

The pitcher is constructed with a low center of gravity, its broad ovoid body resting on a low conical foot. The vessel achieves its greatest diameter high on the body and then curves rapidly to the shoulder and the base of the neck. Almost equal in height to the body, the tall neck follows a slightly concave profile and widens to a flaring mouth. The strap handle rises from the shoulder and arches high above the rim, where it is attached between two plastic snakes. Connected to the middle of the neck by a strut, the handle curves inward to parallel the neck's graceful contour.

The neatly executed decoration in reddish brown glaze develops from foot to rim. A row of dots rings the foot below a solid lower body. Triple horizontal lines separate the bands of ornament: a frieze of two-legged birds, each with a row of dots in front; zigzag; a decorative zone at the widest diameter with metopes, each occupied by a horse and two birds, alternating with panels of stacked zigzags; zigzag; crosshatched triangles standing on their apices; outlined crosshatched triangles. The neck is symmetrically treated with minor zones of zigzag and checkerboard above and below the main ornament, a complex hatched meander. The handle features a dotted serpent on the flat center between outer ribs; the neck panel underneath is reserved, with two large painted Xs.

The birds and horses punctuate the

83

rhythms of this lively vessel. In the metopes and the frieze the birds stand stiff-legged, tails curving down, necks arched back, and heads held horizontal. Each metope contains a horse tethered to a tiny manger on the panel's "wall," with two birds perched on its back. Dotted lines of seeds rise to the chins of both horses and birds. Standing on curving hooves the horses are lean and linear, with bulk only at their flanks and shoulders. The series of six horse panels terminates in a small metope to the right of the handle containing a single heron, its long legs flexed at the knees and the neck and tail forming graceful counter-curves. The heron is a charming surprise and probably appears here because the artist left no room for a full horse metope.

The monumental version of a pitcher was invented by the Dipylon Master, whose group produced examples as tall as 0.77 meters. The form soon settled down to the more modest but still impressive size of the Indiana pitcher. Rather too large to function easily for pouring liquids, the vessels were created for funerals, as the plastic snake of the Indiana example demonstrates, and held food and drink for the deceased. By 735 B.C. the large pitcher enjoyed such a vogue that for a time it replaced the amphora as the grave vessel of choice. About this time the bird motif also acquired new popularity, appearing sometimes as subsidiary ornament, sometimes as the only living creature represented, and usually deployed in long files around the body. The chief proponent of this idea, dubbed the "Birdseed Painter," added a line of dots or seeds extending at an angle from the chin of one bird to the tail of the next, with a second line behind each bird's feet. Birds and bird-seed soon constituted a regular fad in Athens, used not just by the Birdseed Painter but also by many of his contemporaries.

The Indiana pitcher is probably not by the Birdseed Painter but is close enough in style to be attributed to the Workshop. It shares the Painter's distinctive use of the compli-cated hatched meander as the primary neck ornament and the plastic snakes; it lacks his

hallmark "wolf's tooth"—interlocking rows of crosshatched triangles always set directly below the rim. In shape and ornament the Indiana pitcher resembles pitchers in Toronto and New York assigned to the Birdseed Painter. Close stylistic correspondences between the Indiana pitcher and one in a Portuguese private collection suggest a single artistic hand. Two other vessels in the exhibition, the Princeton high-rimmed bowl (38) and the Yale standed bowl (84), also participate in the birdseed fad.

PUBLISHED

J. Langdon-Mastronarde, "An Attic Late Geo-metric Pitcher from the Birdseed Painter Workshop" *Indiana University Art Museum Bulletin* 1 (1977) 6–13.

NOTES

On the Birdseed Painter and Workshop: Davison, *Attic Geometric Workshops* 55–62; Coldstream, *Greek Geometric Pottery* 67–70.
Parallels: Toronto C.201, Davison fig. 72; New York, Metropolitan Museum 41.11.4, Davison fig. 73; Private Collection, Portugal, Langdon-Mastronarde, "An Attic Late Geometric Pitcher" fig. 9.

S. L.

84 STANDED BOWL

Attic, Late Geometric II, ca. 720 B.C.
Height 0.119, mouth diameter 0.179.
Ceramic; broken and mended, surface worn in places.
Yale University Art Gallery, Gift of Rebecca Darlington Stoddard, 1913 (1913.58).

The bowl's conical stand is perforated by ten small rectangular windows; between them are panels decorated by checkerboards and large Xs. Above a row of tangent dots, the handle zone carries a frieze of water birds with diagonal lines of dots leading from the chin of one to the back of the next. Broad panels of hatched meander are flanked above the handles by panels containing a reclining goat and checkerboard pattern. The handles carry a single row of dots.

84

Standed bowls developed in Late Geometric II out of the high-rimmed bowl (see **21** and **38**), which had replaced the flat pyxis (see **26**). The Yale bowl can be placed early in the series by its still nearly vertical rim and relatively low foot with many windows; a little later, fewer windows and a slanted rim become the norm. The development of fenestrated stands on bowls reflects the widespread popularity of tall stands for vases displayed at the funeral pyre, perhaps because the added height and "presentation" offered greater pomp and visibility.

Like the Princeton high-rimmed bowl with birds parading along the ribbon handles (**38**), the appearance here of a bird-and-birdseed frieze reflects, if not the workshop of the Birdseed Painter, at least the contemporary popularity of the motif made famous by that artist.

PUBLISHED
Baur, *Catalogue of the R. D. Stoddard Collection* 50 no. 58, fig. 11.
Matheson Burke and Pollitt, *Greek Vases at Yale* 7 no. 11.

NOTES
On the development of the form: Coldstream, *Greek Geometric Pottery* 86.
Standed bowl with horse in panel above the handle: Kübler, *Die Nekropole des 10. bis 8. Jahrhunderts* pl. 122 inv. 313; Coldstream, *Greek Geometric Pottery* pl. 15m.
Parallel: Standed bowl with bird-and-birdseed panel, *JdI* 14 (1899) 215 no. 102.
Similar shape: *JdI* 14 (1899) 214 fig. 96; *AD* 22 (1967) B pl. 88a.

S. L.

85 FAWN

Boeotian, Late Geometric, 750–700 B.C.
Height 0.04, length 0.035.
Bronze; intact.
The Menil Collection, Houston; Photograph by Paul Hester, Houston. Formerly in the collections of Captain E. G. Spencer-Churchill and George Ortiz.

The Menil fawn evokes the grace and fragility of a young deer. The minute creature stands on the thinnest of legs that widen

85

slightly at haunches to join the slender trunk. Overly large ears on the small blunt head enhance the animal's attenuated proportions. A short pointed tail flips up in back. Concentric punched circles with central points enliven the surface by providing eyes as well as a dappled coat, with one on each leg and two on either ear. Two tiny nostrils are punched in. The four feet merge into the corners of a thin rectangular base, decorated underneath with a double raised frame. A short suspension chain remains attached to a ring around the fawn's trunk.

This sensitively portrayed animal has been attributed to the Master of the Boston Deer and Fawn, one of the best-loved works of Geometric sculpture (Fig. 24). The Menil fawn closely resembles the deer of that masterpiece, from her distinctive proportions and silhouette to the inaccurate but expressive treatment of her anatomy. Just as the male deer's antlers serve to balance and augment the complex composition in Boston, so the exaggerated ears of the Menil fawn, the bulkiest part of the minute creature, offer a steadying mass and accentuate the figure's delicacy.

Remarkably, several other works by this artist have been recorded; in fact the number has grown from the four noted in the original

identification by Ortiz, expanded by Mitten, to thirteen in the most recent compilation by Zimmermann. Fawns at Harvard (86), Copenhagen, Karlsruhe, and London and a dog in Berlin are among the known works. The attribution of so many bronzes from a single artist of this early period is unparalleled, and their preservation may indicate a particular admiration for these works in ancient times. Although specific findspots are lacking for most of the pieces, a Boeotian provenance has been accepted for the group. Three came from the same female grave at Kamilovrisi, an unusual context for bronze figurines. The namepiece is said to be from the Theban Kabeirion. Aside from bull figurines of a different style from the Kabeirion, there exist few other indisputably Boeotian Geometric bronze figures on which to build a definition of local style. The works by the Master of the Boston Deer and Fawn reveal Corinthian influence in their punched circle decoration and their sharp fetlocks, features also strongly present in the bronze sculpture of neighboring Thessaly. How much these endearing deer and fawns of the Master reflect individual genius and how much local style remains to be sorted out.

PUBLISHED
Hoffmann, *Ten Centuries That Shaped the West* 148–49, no. 69.
Zimmermann, *Les chevaux* 241 n. 185.

EXHIBITED
Ten Centuries That Shaped the West: Greek and Roman Art in Texas Collections, October 1970–July 1971.

NOTES
On the Master of the Boston Deer and Fawn: Mitten, "The Earliest Greek Sculptures in the Museum" 12–16; Coldstream, *Geometric Greece* 206; Zimmermann, *Les chevaux* 241 n. 185 with complete list and bibliography.
On the problem of Boeotian style: Zimmermann, *Les chevaux* 240–41, who attributes

most of the animals from the Ptoion and
Elateia to other regions.
For discussion of deer representations as
votive offerings, see 57 and 86.

S. L.

86 FAWN ON RECTANGULAR BASE

Boeotian, Late Geometric, 750–700 B.C.
Height 0.04; length 0.05, base 0.03 x 0.017.
Bronze; tail broken away; body surface
smooth with patches of dark green and
red patina; bronze disease damage on
middle right side of base; corrosion on tip
of muzzle.
Arthur M. Sackler Museum, Harvard
University Art Museums, David M.
Robinson Fund (1966.108).

86

86

Attributed to a Boeotian workshop, this
delightfully conceived miniature fawn may be
part of a larger ensemble, perhaps by the
Master of the Boston Deer and Fawn as originally defined by Ortiz. The left legs are mark-
edly thicker than those on the right, which
may indicate a preferred profile with the animal facing to the right. The alert, somewhat
oversize head with its pricked-up ears is set at a
diagonal to the short neck, while the strongly
horizontal back leads to a short tail, now broken off. The face is thrust forward in a manner suggesting curiosity mixed with caution.
The pronounced, spurlike hocks accentuate
the adolescent quality of the legs that splay
out to the four corners of the base. Each
upper leg is stamped with a circle containing
a central point, the two designs on the left
being somewhat more visible than their counterparts on the right. The underside of the partially corroded base is decorated by inset
concentric rectangles. The inner rectangle is
slightly off center.

Figurine representations of both domestic
and wild animals were dedicated in quantity
at Geometric period sanctuaries throughout
Greece. Domestic animals were the most popular subjects, reflecting their importance in
an economy that was based on agriculture

and animal husbandry throughout the period.
Only at the Arcadian sanctuary of Athena
Alea at Tegea did bronze votives in the form
of deer outnumber all other animal representations. We do not know if figurines of wild
animals and domestic animals served the
same purposes. Images of domestic animals
may have encouraged their patron divinities
to increase the animals' numbers for the satis-
faction of human appetites and for the
requirements of sanctuaries for sacrificial victims. Figurines of deer, however, may have
been created for more complex purposes.
Deer were sacred to the goddess Artemis,
who both protected and hunted them, and
figurines of deer are numerous at her sanctuaries. However, in the Geometric period, the
relationship between the deer and Artemis
was by no means exclusive, since the image
also appears at sanctuaries for Hera, Athena,
Apollo, and other divinities. In the imagery of
Homeric epic, the deer stands generically for
the idea of "victim" and is the counterpart of
the lion in an iconographic dualism celebrating

the triumph of nobility and strength over weakness and timidity.

PUBLISHED

Acquisitions (Fogg Art Museum) (1966–1967) 159; 82 (ill.).

Newsletter (Fogg Art Museum) 4:3 (Feb. 1967) fig. 4.

J.-L. Zimmermann, "Bronziers béotiens et cervidés géométriques" *NumAntCl* 19 (1990) 9–29.

NOTES

On the Boston Deer and Fawn: Comstock and Vermeule, *Greek, Etruscan and Roman Bronzes in the Museum of Fine Arts, Boston* 5; Mitten and Doeringer, *Master Bronzes from the Classical World* 41, and no. 24.

On the relationship between animal herds, farmsteads, and the Geometric period sanctuary of Olympia: Heilmeyer, *Frühe Olympische Bronzefiguren* 195–97; on bronze deer figurines on bases at Olympia, 148–51, pl. 87, 253, no. 721.

Deer at Tegea: Voyatzis, *The Early Sanctuary of Athena Alea at Tegea* 140–43; pl. 74–76.

On deer images: Bevan, *Representations of Animals in Sanctuaries of Artemis* 100–114; 389–93 for remains of deer found at sanctuaries.

On the dualism of lions and deer in Homer: Vermeule, *Aspects of Death in Early Greek Art and Poetry* 83–117.

T. A.

87 BELLY-HANDLED AMPHORA

Melian, Cycladic Middle Geometric ca. 750 B.C.

Height 0.71, diameter 0.36.

Ceramic; repaired from fragments, parts of both handles restored, small restorations associated with breaks.

Indiana University Art Museum, Given in Honor of Burton Y. Berry and Herman B. Wells by Thomas T. Solley (79.68).

Photograph by Michael Cavanaugh, Kevin Montague.

See Plate 13.

87

Tall and sober, this elegant amphora reflects the discipline of Attic Middle Geometric style in the spirit of the Cycladic world. The ovoid body rises from a small flaring foot. Handles set above midbelly emphasize the vessel's high center of gravity and taut construction. The slightly concave neck offers a countercurve for the gently rounded shoulder. At the top of the neck a low molding anticipates the transition to a broad horizontal lip.

The neck and the handle zones carry the primary decoration. Between the handles are three sets of compass-drawn concentric circles with starburst centers; dot rosettes fill the interstices between circles. The handle zone is reserved except for stars in the upper corners. Above, a band of alternating vertical strokes and double axes encircles the shoulder. The neck carries a large meander, bordered above and below with the same band of vertical strokes and double axes. Against the overall dark scheme, two groups of narrow reserved bands on the lower body and one on the shoulder warm the tone and prevent too great a contrast between decorative and solid zones.

This decorative system reflects Attic models in overall scheme and individual motifs, providing the general chronological framework for island styles. The bands of double axes between vertical lines entered Attic pottery in Middle Geometric I. In particular the deployment of concentric circles in panels at the handle zone was typical of this shape in Early Geometric, but while Attic amphorae featured two sets of circles, Melian versions began with three, as on the Indiana example. The artist of this vessel neglected to insert the standard panel divider between two of his circle sets.

The belly-handled amphora with double-arc handles was borrowed from the Attic repertoire of shapes. In Protogeometric Athens it was the standard cremation vessel for women; by the end of Early Geometric it was apparently restricted to women of high social rank. The form reached its apogee under the hand of the Dipylon Master in Late Geometric I, epitomized in the artist's finest creation, monumental amphora Athens 804, the most famous of all Geometric pots. Attic influence brought the shape to Melos in Early Geometric, where it immediately became a local specialty. Owing to the incomplete records of Cycladic graves opened early in this century, it is unknown whether the shape signified female burials on Melos; since the local production center seems to have specialized in this shape, it was likely used for both sexes and probably contained cremations, the burial custom of Melos and nearby Kimolos, as it was among the southern Cyclades in Middle Geometric. The export of these impressive amphorae to Thera for cremation use, and to other islands, supports the general picture of

the homogeneous culture in the early eighth-century Cyclades, one that changes by Late Geometric as various distinctive stylistic "schools" develop. One can only wonder whether the local popularity of this vessel was related to its special significance among high-ranking Athenians. If future excavations permit, the Melian belly-handled amphorae offer an important class of material for the study of inter-island economy and the dissemination of rank-related symbols.

UNPUBLISHED

NOTES
On the shape in Attic pottery: Coldstream, *Geometric Greece* 55; Smithson, "The Tomb of a Rich Athenian Lady"; Whitley, *Style and Society in Dark Age Greece* 133–34.

For Cycladic MG: Coldstream, *Greek Geometric Pottery* 167–68; Coldstream, *Geometric Greece* 90–92.

Melian burials: *BSA* 2 (1895–1896) 70; Coldstream, *Geometric Greece* 91.

Parallels: amphora lidded by means of a pyxis, Cahn, *Early Art in Greece* 37–38, no. 108, here called Attic; Munich 6166, Coldstream, *Greek Geometric Pottery* pl. 34m, and Schweitzer, *Greek Geometric Art* pl. 79; Louvre A266, *CVA* Louvre 16, 8–9 with extensive bibliography for the type, pl. 2.1–2.

S. L.

88 HYDRIA

Cretan, Early Orientalizing, ca. 700 B.C.
Height 0.30, base diameter 0.0715, rim diameter 0.077.
Ceramic; rim restored.
University of Missouri–Columbia, Museum of Art and Archaeology (69.118).

Set on a slightly concave base, the ovoid body terminates in a neck constricted in the middle. Two horizontal handles rise at a low angle from the broadest diameter of the body; a vertical handle attaches from the shoulder

88

88

to the neck. The lower body is decorated with three groups of thin horizontals flanked by broad bands and separated by reserve bands. Between the handles the shoulder zone features a horizontal multiple zigzag with a pair of triglyphs at each end framing a smaller metope. The metopes contain on one side a quartered, dotted circle and on the other a lozenge cross. On the front shoulder panel three birds with hatched bodies stand with upswept wings and head and tail lowered to the groundline. Two metopes containing abstract Tree of Life images flank the handle attachment on the back of the shoulder. Horizontal lines, a band of outline leaves, and a chain of blind lozenges subdivide the neck.

This vessel exemplifies Cretan style and at the same time is unparalleled among early Cretan hydriai. The water jug was an early favorite on the island, passing from domestic use to a popular grave gift in the later ninth century. By the end of Late Geometric it had fallen out of fashion. Among the globular

hydriai of Late Geometric and Early Orientalizing, this slender example with a high center of gravity stands out, although the other closed shapes tend to become similarly attenuated at this time. In further contrast to the Missouri vessel, typical late hydriai have handles set lower on the body and often a ring foot.

The restrained style of Late Geometric Crete is typified in this vessel, which betrays nothing of the flamboyant beginnings of Cretan pottery before the arrival of Attic influence. The subdued decorative treatment continues the Middle Geometric dark-ground scheme. Two of the handle-zone motifs, the quartered circle and lozenge cross, were Late Geometric period favorites. More interesting are the three birds with heads oddly lowered to the groundline. Immediately reminiscent of products of the Bird Workshop of Knossos, the creatures on the hydria share with them the raised curving wing, reserved dotted eye, vertical hatching, and carefully drawn beak.

The lack of filling ornament gives these birds a strong presence. Yet this hydria is not a creation of the workshop. Although the rather humorous effect of the birds' pose is in keeping with the conscious individuality of the workshop, the hydria's overall effect of decorative restraint, even monotony, does not fit the exuberance of the Bird Workshop's products. In fact the arrangement of three birds in the panel nearly constitutes a bird file, a common motif in other regional styles, but otherwise unknown in Crete; its appearance here suggests an altogether different influence, perhaps from the Cyclades. A Knossian origin for the hydria is supported by a miniature pithos from Knossos with all-over banding and a similar handle-zone treatment. Finally, the small abstract Trees of Life, inserted almost as an afterthought in panels beside the birds, hint of the transformation soon to overtake this austere style as curvilinear ornamentation, especially plant motifs, arrives from the East.

PUBLISHED

Cahn, *Early Art in Greece* no. 139.
Sale catalogue, Sotheby's (London) November 26, 1968, lot 109.
"Acquisitions 1969" *Muse* 4 (1970) 6, 7.

NOTES

Generally on Cretan Late Geometric and Early Orientalizing styles: Coldstream, *Greek Geometric Pottery* 249–61.
For late hydria shapes: ASAtene 10–12 (1927–1929) 406 fig. 523 from Arkades, 517 fig. 600 in Candia Museum, 579 fig. 624 from Kavousi, 589 fig. 638 from Kavousi; Hall, *Vrokastro* pl. 27; Brock, *Fortetsa* pls. 25, 29.
On the Cretan Bird Workshop: Coldstream, *Greek Geometric Pottery* 246–49; Brock, *Fortetsa* 149.
Miniature pithos from Knossos: CVA Oxford 2, 53, pl. I.7; Boardman, *The Cretan Collection in Oxford* pl. XXXII, 437.

S. L.

89 LEKYTHOS-OINOCHOE

Corinthian, Late Geometric, 750–720 B.C.
Height 0.226, width 0.210, mouth diameter 0.058.

Ceramic; broken and repaired, with minor retouching of paint; large section of the base repaired.
Detroit Institute of Arts, Founders Society Purchase, William H. Murphy Fund (76.97). Previously Charles Seltman Collection.

The flat-bottomed lekythos features thin banding over the lower area of the body up to a dotted lozenge chain and crosshatched triangles on the shoulder. The neck is decorated with alternating dotted lozenge chains, banding, and multiple zigzags. The solid black trefoil lip bears a swastika in a reserve circle on either side. The tall vertical strap handle is horizontally banded. The underside of the base is reserved.

The dramatic geometric shape of this conical oil container is heightened by its simple web of fine brushwork, which detracts little from the potter's art. Although the vessel is heavy-bottomed, the fine banding and delicately slender neck lighten the total effect. In this shape culminates an evolution begun in Middle Geometric in which an Attic form was given a wholly Corinthian identity by broadening the base and lengthening the neck (compare Cumaean lekythos-oinochoe **65**).

The limited repertoire of the almost completely nonfigural Corinthian tradition allowed for a fastidious approach to linear decoration. Typical of Corinthian motifs are the attachment of the horizontal zigzags to the frame by short bars on the apices and the addition of dots to the interstices of lozenge chains. Both of these details add to the overall halftone effect of the surface, in which no single element is permitted to dominate. The sparing use of the swastika in Corinthian painting enters under Attic influence. The swastika's appearance in Attic art as a filling ornament in figured scenes, particularly in proximity to birds and horses, has occasioned discussions of a possible symbolic meaning for the motif. In the austere context of Corinthian art, such an interpretation is especially difficult to support.

89

The Detroit lekythos dates to Late Geometric, near the onset of the Orientalizing fashion that will generate the extremely popular Protocorinthian style and the wave of pottery exports far beyond the Corinthia.

PUBLISHED

J. Chittenden and C. Seltman, *Greek Art: A Commemorative Catalogue of an Exhibition held in 1946 at the Royal Academy Burlington House, London* (London 1947) no. 48, pl. 9.

A. Lane, *Greek Pottery* (London 1948, 1963) 26, pl. 11 b.

Sale catalogue, Sotheby's (London), April 21, 1975, lot 282 (ill.).

Charles Ede Limited, *Corinthian and East Greek Pottery* (September 1976) no. 12.

Catalogue, *Greek Vase-Painting in Midwestern Collections*, no. 2.

EXHIBITED

Greek Vase-Painting in Midwestern Collections, The Art Institute of Chicago, December 1979–February 1980.

NOTES

Compare Coldstream, *Greek Geometric Pottery* pl. 19d, Munich 2284; T. J. Dunbabin, ed., *Perachora* II (Oxford 1962) pl. 9 no. 215; Waldstein, *Argive Heraeum* II, 129, figs. 57–58.

For decorative scheme: A. N. Stillwell and J. L. Benson, *The Potters' Quarter* (Corinth XV, pt. III, Princeton 1984) pl. 6, 94.

S. L.

90 FRAGMENT OF A KRATER

Argive, from the Heraion, Late Geometric II, ca. 725–700 B.C.

Height 0.07, width 0.08.

Ceramic; body fragment; exterior painted with dark brown slip, interior with brown slip, fine buff-colored clay with no inclusions.

Arthur M. Sackler Museum, Harvard University Art Museums, Transfer from the Department of Classics, Harvard University, Gift of George H. Chase (1977.216.1834.1).

The fragment, from the Argive sanctuary to Hera, originally occupied part of the central panel decoration on a deep-bodied krater, which would have had a high flaring lip and a low conical foot. Such krater shapes are among the more popular ceramic forms of Late Geometric Argos and present a large surface that attracted much of the figure drawing of Argive workshops. Two of the commonest subjects are horses, either alone or accompanied by a male figure, and lines of dancing women who hold hands and carry branches between them (see **52–53**).

A barrel-chested horse, lean-bodied and with rigid, tapering legs, is surrounded by the standard geometric decoration for this krater type. These images may be variously identified as simply filling ornament or as the Geometric period artist's representation of real structures and objects that may in turn have underlying social and religious significance. Above the back of the horse, a dotted hook shape is all that remains of the border from the small corner panels that would have filled the rectangular space created by the horse's neck and body. A wheel shape, perhaps signifying a chariot wheel, fills the gap created by the curvature of the horse's neck, and a swastika is painted beneath the forepart of the horse. Stacked chevrons fill the space in front of and behind its legs, and hatched meander hooks stand vertically in front of it. The space beneath its belly is occupied by a fish, with curved linear fins and hatched body. Its eye and body center line are indicated by a dot and line painted in reserve.

Such an arrangement of fish and horse, sometimes with the addition of a male figure known as the horse-leader or master of horses, is uniquely Argive (see Fig. 26). The standard relationship between them as depicted by the Argive artists is too regular to be interpreted as just a simple decorative theme surrounded by filling ornament. The single fish has been interpreted as a determinative of the god

90

Fig. 26. Argive skyphos with man and horses. (Photo courtesy of Deutsches Archäologisches Institut, Athens, neg. Tiryns 1064)

Poseidon. Evidence for this relationship is drawn from an Archaic period bronze fish, found at Amyclae in Laconia, with the word *Pohidanos* (Poseidon) inscribed upon it. Additionally, the fish and horse connection with Poseidon can be drawn from Pausanias' description of the ancient cult picture of Demeter of Phigalia, which he saw on his visit to this Arcadian site. The goddess was depicted as human except for her horse's head; in her right hand she held a dolphin and in her left a bird.

The religious association of fish and horse is also recalled in the *Iliad* (23.307) and the *Homeric Hymn to Poseidon* (22.1–7), in which context Poseidon is seen as a teacher of all aspects of horsemanship and as the sea god, savior of ships, probably responsible for the

abundant supplies of food from the sea for the Argive population. As Poseidon Hippios, he was associated with the fertility and the taming of horses and was celebrated with chariot races and the recipient of horse sacrifices as well. Horses were seen as chthonic creatures of Poseidon and as such were the objects of drowning sacrifices in the freshwater springs that rise from the sea near Argos.

Other interpretations of the scene on this fragment are more pragmatic, viewing these recurring fish and horse representations as referring to the Argolid's well-watered agricultural plains—where horses prospered as symbols of their owner's social and economic status—and to the surrounding seas, rich with fish. The presence of the fish and horse iconography on late Helladic kraters from Ugarit, dating around 1200 B.C., perhaps points to the long-standing tradition of fish, horse, and man as significant in religious rituals late in the Bronze Age, rituals carried down, through tradition and myth, to Late Geometric Argos.

UNPUBLISHED

NOTES

For examples of this krater type, Athens N.M.231 and 877: Coldstream, *Greek Geometric Pottery* pls. 28e, 29d.

For the early excavations of the Argive Heraion: Waldstein, *The Argive Heraeum* II; esp. for vases and fragments, 57–67, 101–18, pls. LVI–LVII.

On Argive Late Geometric pottery: Coldstream, *Geometric Greece* 141–45; Schweitzer, *Greek Geometric Art* 61–63.

On the wheel shape and broken hatched meander: Boardman, "Symbol and Story in Geometric Art" 20–22.

For the fish and horse related to Poseidon and religious ritual: Schweitzer, *Greek Geometric Art* 62–63; S. Langdon, "The Return of the Horse-Leader" 190–93.

For pragmatic interpretation of Argive Geometric as representational: Courbin, *La céramique géométrique de l'Argolide* 495;

Boardman, "Symbol and Story in Geometric Art" 15.

A. J. P.

91 OINOCHOE

Boeotian, Late Geometric, 750–735 B.C.
Height 0.378.
Ceramic; complete, mended from fragments.
Yale University Art Gallery, Gift of Rebecca
Darlington Stoddard, 1913 (1913.52).

Belonging to the early stages of development of the trefoil oinochoe in the Late
Geometric period, this example comprises a
globular body without a foot and with a relatively low broad neck. The decoration features
sets of concentric circles in the main ornament zones, the shoulder and the widest
diameter of the belly. Both circle zones are
bordered top and bottom with horizontal
banding and a continuous zigzag. The neck is
divided into five panels filled with multiple
zigzags and crosshatched lozenges. The lower
body is solid, with a single reserve line, below
an area of thin banding.

Typically Boeotian is the predilection for
compass-drawn concentric circle groups with
a central dot. This motif was likely borrowed
from Euboean and Cycladic pottery by the
eclectic Boeotian painters. Placed in this
example at the greatest circumference of the
swelling belly, the motif is set off to best
advantage, reiterating the three-dimensional
shape beneath. The Attic influence that
strongly guided the development of Boeotian
Late Geometric style is seen in the division
of the neck into square metopes, each treated
differently within a narrow range of motifs.
The dramatic contrast of circular and angular
decoration throughout this vessel exemplifies
the exuberance of the Boeotian regional style.
These large oinochoai seem to have been created for funerary use, as is suggested by the
slightly later versions, which have plastic
snakes on their handles. A comparison of the
Yale oinochoe with the Missouri Attic oinochoe (**33**) offers a revealing distinction
between styles.

PUBLISHED
Auction Drouot (Paris, June 2–4, 1904) 33
pl. 1, 210.
Baur, *Catalogue of the R. D. Stoddard Collec-
tion* 47 no. 52, fig. 11.
Hampe, *Frühe griechische Sagenbilder in
Böotien* 24 V.28.
F. Canciani, "Böotische Vasen aus dem 8. und
7. Jahrhundert" *JdI* 80 (1965) 18–75 at 25
no. 1 (Ruckert reports that the Yale oi-
nochoe is identical with Canciani's 26 no.
3).
Coldstream, *Greek Geometric Pottery* 201
no. 5.
Matheson Burke and Pollitt, *Greek Vases at
Yale* 16 no. 23.
Ruckert, *Frühe Keramik Böotiens* cat. Oi 3 pp.
17, 41–43, 76, pl. I, 2.

NOTES
Parallels: *JdI* 14 (1899) 83, fig. 39; Canciani,
"Böotische Vasen aus dem 8. und 7. Jahrhundert" 67, fig. 19; *CVA* Copenhagen 2,
49, pl. 67.3.
On the date: Coldstream, *Greek Geometric
Pottery* 201, dates this oinochoe to the second stage of a series that begins no earlier
than 740; see also his *Geometric Greece*
201; Ruckert, *Frühe Keramik Böotiens* 17,
dates this vase to 750–735. Coldstream sets
the vase into Kunze's second stage of oinochoe development, while Ruckert attributes it to a first stage.

S. L.

92 HORSE FIGURINE

Laconian, Late Geometric, 750–725 B.C.
Height 0.075, base 0.033 x 0.076.
Bronze; tail broken and mended.
**The Museum of Fine Arts, Houston, gift of
Miss Annette Finnigan (acc: 37.22).**

The Houston horse is a classic example of
Laconian style as defined by horse figurines
from the Laconian sanctuaries of Artemis
Orthia, Athena Chalkioikos, the Menelaion,
and Apollo at Amyklai. Built on a strongly
axial framework, the horse stands sturdily on

91

92

a rectangular base pierced with triangular cut-outs and a projection at the back for the tail attachment. The horse's short, cylindrical trunk links broad shoulders and flanks in a powerfully compact physique. The squared breastbone and short, broad neck reiterate the angularity of the orthogonal structure. Against the tapering conical head pointed ears stand upright. Small projections on the legs indicate knees and hocks. Proportions follow the trend at mid-eighth century to lengthen the legs.

The elegant architecture of the Laconian style is immediately recognizable and constitutes with Corinthian and Argive one of the great influential styles of Geometric sculpture. Widely renowned, as the broad dissemination of their bronze horses demonstrates, the Laconian bronzeworkers led their peers in the perfecting of complicated group sculptures. The famous centaur group in New York, the lion-fighting hero from Samos, and the finest of the chariot groups from Olympia are all Laconian masterpieces. The enigmatic seated figure from the Walters Art Gallery (80) is also probably Laconian.

Although the homeland of this style is assured by the consistency of material excavated in and around Sparta, an irony finds the majority of Laconian horses far from home. In contrast to the thirteen found at Spartan sanctuaries, Zimmermann records at least ninety-four from Olympia and another nineteen from other sites and regions. Among the several thousand bronze animals dedicated at Olympia, Laconian products seem to have dominated the scene from about 775 to 740 B.C., a span that has been linked to the literary tradition of Sparta's role in the organization of the Olympic Games starting in 776 B.C. (a date by no means universally accepted) and the dramatic decline of Laconian offerings explained by the onset of the first Messenian War. Politics may well have played a role in the installation of Laconian bronzeworkers at Olympia, but it has been pointed out that relations with other production centers and sanctuaries prevent the complicated evidence from corresponding so neatly with literary history.

PUBLISHED
Hoffmann, *Ten Centuries That Shaped the West* 146 no. 67.
U. Höckmann, *Antike Bronzen. Staatliche Kunstsammlungen Kassel* (Kassel 1972) 15, under no. 4.
Zimmermann, *Les chevaux* 132 no. 133, pl. 35.

EXHIBITED
Ten Centuries That Shaped the West: Greek and Roman Art in Texas Collections, October 1970–July 1971.

NOTES
On Laconian horse style: Herrmann, "Werkstätten geometrischer Bronzeplastik" 21–24; Heilmeyer, *Frühe Olympische Bronzefiguren* 110–31; Zimmermann, *Les chevaux* 123–75.
Parallels: Zimmermann, *Les chevaux* pl. 31 no. 98, pl. 35 no. 137.
Laconian group sculptures: Schweitzer, *Greek Geometric Art* pls. 182–87; Floren, *Die geometrische und archaische Plastik* I, pl. 5, figs. 1–2.
On the Laconian presence at Olympia: Heilmeyer, *Frühe Olympische Bronzefiguren* 19–24, 115–16; Zimmermann, *Les chevaux* 171–75.

S. L.

93

93 HORSE FIGURINE

Messenian, Late Geometric, 750–730 B.C.
Height 0.10, length 0.08, base 0.072 x 0.042.
Bronze; ears missing, tail bent, surface
corroded.
The Art Museum, Princeton University, Gift
of Frank Jewett Mather, Jr. (y1937.222).

The leggy horse stands on a flat rectangular support decorated with irregular triangular
perforations in three rows. Its slightly bent tail
attaches to a short extension at the back of
the base. A tall straight neck with flattened
mane and a much reduced torso accentuate
the strong vertical accents of the animal's construction. A sinuous contour rises from the
shoulder to the high rump. The long muzzle
ends abruptly in a flat nose, with a horizontal
incision across the end marking the mouth.
The eyes are rendered in relief.
    The origin of the figurine is unknown, but
great majority of Messenian horses come from
Olympia, where the presence of diverse
regional workshops creating votive sculptures
offered a host of new ideas to visiting bronze-
smiths. The animal figurines identified as
Messenian exhibit multiple stylistic sources, as

the Princeton horse demonstrates. Laconian
influence is evident in the form of the support, the figure's short-torsoed proportions,
and the hint of the strong Laconian orthogon-
ality. The set of the rump higher than the
shoulder level is characteristic of Arcadian animal figures. The production of Messenian
horses has been dated to 780–730, with
Laconian influence prevailing to the midcen-
tury, when Arcadian influence replaced it.
Accordingly, since affinities to both regions
are detectable, the Princeton horse may be
dated between 750 and 730 B.C. A closely
similar horse of unknown provenance has
been identified as by the artist of the
present work.

PUBLISHED
Zimmermann, *Les chevaux* 116 no. 45, pl. 26,
    45.

NOTES
On Messenian horse style: Zimmermann, *Les
    chevaux* 114–22.
Similar horses: Ex Müller collection, Christie's
    (London) Catalogue, June 14, 1978, lot 93;
    Zimmermann, *Les chevaux* pl. 26, 46; Voy-
    atzis, *The Early Sanctuary of Athena Alea
    at Tegea* pl. 69 L4.

S. L.

94 HORSE FIGURINE

Argive, Late Geometric, ca. 700 B.C.
Height 0.0625, length 0.067, base 0.047 x
    0.023–0.026.
Bronze; intact.
The Metropolitan Museum of Art, Bequest
    of Walter C. Baker, 1972 (1972.118.55).

    The delicate figure is remarkable among
Geometric bronze horses as much for its lack
of straight lines as for the unique decoration
of its support. Argive horses have been identified by their essentially organic construction.
Contours flow smoothly and forms are
rounded; the inner profile of legs and belly is
often a continuous arc. Although the present
example lacks close parallels, its small, gently

94

rounded head, flattened mane, agile flexed stance, and relatively long trunk are features found among works considered Argive in origin. The unusual drilled eyes occur in a small number of horses at Olympia that are thought to have once been yoked to tiny bronze chariots, but the presence of a stand weighs against such an interpretation for this figure.

Support for an Argive identification comes especially from the base. Incised or hollowed designs on the underside of bases are found among the animals at the Argive Heraion. The Metropolitan horse offers a rare example of a human figural motif as base decoration. Rendered in intaglio, a charioteer, his horse, the chariot, and the vehicle's wheels are all shown separately in the rectangular field, the artist having studiously avoided overlapping any of the elements. This particular scene is unique, and not only in bronzework; even among painted chariot scenes on pottery the artists do not take their conceptual art quite so literally, scattering the chariot parts across the background.

The intaglio-decorated supports in particular suggest that the Geometric bronze animals on bases once functioned as seals. Although the designs in general lack variety, it may be no coincidence that the series of bronze fig-

ures on platform bases stops just when ivory seals come into use and stone seals increase. It may be that the small pictorial fields of Argive and Arcadian bases were influenced by seals, even if the triangular perforations typical of Laconian and Corinthian bronzes served a different function.

PUBLISHED

D. Von Bothmer, *Greek, Etruscan, and Roman Antiquities . . . from the Collection of Walter Cummings Baker, Esq.* (New York 1950) no. 9.

D. Von Bothmer, *Ancient Art from New York Private Collections* (New York 1961) no. 124, pl. 43.

J. Boardman, *Island Gems* (London 1963) 114.

J. Boardman, *Greek Gems and Finger Rings: Early Bronze Age to Late Classical* (London 1970) 134, pl. 207.

Zimmermann, *Les chevaux* 49 no. 132, pl. 1.

NOTES

On Argive horse style: Herrmann, "Werkstätten geometrischer Bronzeplastik" 24–29; Heilmeyer, *Frühe Olympische Bronzefiguren* 54–72; Zimmermann, *Les chevaux* 18–62, esp. 48–50.

On figurine bases as seals: H. Payne, *Perachora I. Architecture, Bronzes, Terracottas* (Oxford 1940) 125; D. Amyx, "Geometric Platform Bronzes" AJA 53 (1949) 147–48; J. Boardman, *Greek Gems and Finger Rings* 110; Heilmeyer, *Frühe Olympische Bronzefiguren* 121; Zimmermann, *Les chevaux* 316–18.

S. L.

95 HORSE FIGURINE

Arcadian, Late Geometric, 750–725 B.C.
Length 0.07.
Bronze, green to brown patina; tips of ears broken off.
Walters Art Gallery, Baltimore (54.2401).

With its front legs extended forward, back legs flexed, and tail raised, the horse figurine has such an active look that Hill characterized

95

it as a "running horse." Related examples show its unstable posture to be typical of this Arcadian type. It stands without a base, its loose, low construction heightened by the simple rolled trunk, legs, and tail that taper to their ends. Anatomical details of the body are confined to articulated knees and hocks, tiny back feet, and roughly indicated genitalia. The head similarly tapers to a rounded muzzle with a concave upper surface and a jawline modeled in a curve up to the ears. In contrast to the smooth trunk, the head shows an interest in texture. The flattened neck and mane are covered in an incised herringbone pattern, the head with a zigzag on either cheek.

This animal style with engraved decoration, found in bulls as well as horses, is noted for its extremely high quality of finish. The problem the animals pose is one of origin. Of the twenty closely similar horses, sixteen come from Olympia, two of which are identical to the Baltimore figurine, and two come from Lousoi. Although Heilmeyer believed all to be of Argive manufacture, their connections with other Arcadian bronzes has won more support for an Arcadian provenance. Recent evidence for bronze production at the site of Lousoi seems to support this attribution. Suggested dates for this horse type have ranged from the ninth century to the seventh. Zimmermann's recent dating of it to the third quarter

of the eighth century is based on considerations of style, in particular the engraved patterns and the subordination of the structure to the profile view.

PUBLISHED
D. K. Hill, "Other Geometric Objects in Baltimore" *AJA* 60 (1956) 37 no. 3, pl. 28, fig. 4.
Bulletin of the Walters Art Gallery 8, 4 (1956).
Zimmermann, *Les chevaux* 93 no. 36, pl. 18.

NOTES
On Arcadian horse style, see **55**.
Closest parallels: Heilmeyer, *Frühe Olympische Bronzefiguren* pl. 16 nos. 109, 110.
Dating: Hill, "Other Geometric Objects in Baltimore" 37; M. Weber, "Eine arkadisch-geometrische Bronzegruppe" *StädelJb* 1 (1967) 8–17; Heilmeyer, *Frühe Olympische Bronzefiguren* 59; Zimmermann, *Les chevaux* 100–101.

S. L.

96 HORSE FIGURINE

Aetolian, Late Geometric, 750–725 B.C.
Height 0.078, length 0.076, base 0.028 x 0.060.
Bronze; intact, surface rough and pitted in places.
Memorial Art Gallery of the University of Rochester, R. T. Miller Fund (54.43). Previously Simkhovitch Collection.

In this attractive figurine individual details conspire to create a rather mannered interpretation of a horse. Although standing with its slightly splayed legs planted firmly on a rectangular plaque with four oval perforations, the animal seems tensed and alert rather than static. With neck arching forward, its trumpet-shaped muzzle is lowered and the tall ears curve forward at the same angle as the neck. Shoulders and hindquarters are approximately the same size. The thin legs are articulated by small projections for knees and hocks.

It is difficult to assign a likely provenance to this little bronze. Clear affinities exist with

96

Corinthian bronze horse production, including the specific forms of the base and the muzzle, the sharp knees, and the cylindrical torso. On the other hand, the ears are longer than most Corinthian examples and, unlike them, are not included in the contour of the mane. The torso rises somewhat to the shoulders instead of maintaining an even horizontality, and the mane is not strongly offset from the shoulder. The figure has accordingly been called Peloponnesian. Most recently, Zimmermann connects it to the Aetolian production area as defined by the style of a small number of horses found at Calydon and Thermon, but known from other sanctuaries as well, such as Olympia, Pherai, Delphi, and Philia. It is unsurprising to find bronze figurine production heavily influenced by Corinthian work, as ties between Corinth and Aetolia are well known.

PUBLISHED
Memorial Art Gallery, Rochester, *Handbook* (1961) 11, ill.
Mitten and Doeringer, *Master Bronzes from the Classical World* 37, no. 17.
Rudolph and Calinescu, eds., *Ancient Art from the V. G. Simkhovitch Collection* 83, no. 57.

Zimmermann, *Les chevaux* 204 no. 10, pl. 45, 10.

EXHIBITED
Master Bronzes from the Classical World, The Fogg Art Museum, Cambridge MA, December 1967–January 1968, City Art Museum of Saint Louis, March–April 1968, The Los Angeles County Museum of Art, May–June 1968.
The Age of Homer, University Museum, University of Pennsylvania, December 1969–March 1970.
Ancient Art from the V. G. Simkhovitch Collection, Indiana University Art Museum, September–December 1987.

NOTES
On Aetolian horse style: Zimmermann, *Les chevaux* 203–17.
Parallels: from Olympia, Berlin Charlottenburg Ol. 6770, W. Lamb, *Greek and Roman Bronzes* (London 1929) 40, fig. 3; Munich 4318, AA (1962) 627–29, fig. 27–28; Zimmermann, *Les chevaux* pl. 45 nos. 8–9.

S. L.

97 HORSE FIGURINE

Allegedly from near Elis, Thessalian, 725–700 B.C.
Height 0.08, base 0.055 x 0.03.
Bronze, greenish patina; breaks on right upper thigh, top of tail, and left hind hoof.
Museum of Fine Arts, Boston, William E. Nickerson Fund, no. 2 (65.1316).

Standing stiff-legged on a rectangular base, the horse represents one of the finest examples of Thessalian style in bronze animal figurines. The short cylindrical trunk connects broad swelling flanks and shoulders above slender legs with pointed hocks. The broad mane rises abruptly from the shoulders in a smooth curve to the tips of the ears. The trumpet muzzle and incised lines at the base of the neck complete the articulation of the head, and the incised decoration is repeated

97

on the lower legs. Triangular perforations in the base create a zigzag effect.

The styles of Thessalian bronze horses have been defined from examples found among the extraordinary number of votive bronzes at two sanctuaries, that of Athena Itonia at Philia and that of Artemis Enodia at Pherai. Said to have come from Elis, the Boston horse might have been destined for Olympia; if so it would be the first of this style that site has yielded. It is among the most mannered of Thessalian figurines. It derives closely from Corinthian horse style in specific details such as base form and treatment of the flanks, and more profoundly in its emphasis on contours rather than on plastic mass. Like the Corinthian horses, the present example exudes a decorative air not only through added surface incisions but also through anatomical exaggerations such as the pointed hocks and flaring muzzle.

Its obvious construction from parts betrays the technique by which this horse was made. The narrow round parts such as trunk and

head were attached to the broad thin flanks and neck cut from wax sheets. The decorative lines on neck and legs were incised after the animal was cast and cooled. Its surface may also have been polished at this stage, as was the case with the finest Thessalian products.

PUBLISHED
C. C. Vermeule, *MFA Annual Report* 1965, 67.
C. C. Vermeule, "Small Sculptures in the Museum of Fine Arts, Boston" *CJ* 62 (1966) 101–2, fig. 8.
Mitten, "The Earliest Greek Sculptures in the Museum" 5 fig. 3, 7.
Comstock and Vermeule, *Greek, Etruscan and Roman Bronzes in the Museum of Fine Arts, Boston* 7 no. 5.
Zimmermann, *Les chevaux* 244 no. 23, 251–52, pls. 58, 79.

NOTES
Thessalian horse style: Zimmermann, *Les chevaux* 242–60.
Horses from Philia and Pherai: Y. Béquignon, *Recherches archéologiques à Phères de Thessalie* (Strasbourg 1937) 67; Kilian, *Fibeln in Thessalien* pls. 86–87; Heilmeyer, *Frühe Olympische Bronzefiguren* 90, fig. 4; F. Johansen, "Graeske Geometriske Bronzer" *MeddNyCG* (1982) 73–98, esp. 79 fig. 8.
S. L.

98 FIGURAL KRATER FRAGMENT

Attic, Late Geometric Ia, 760–750 B.C.
Height ca. 0.13.
Ceramic; wall fragment.
Yale University Art Gallery, Classic Department Transfer (1981.61.271).

The fragment preserves parts of two registers. In the top zone appears the upper part of a fallen helmeted warrior at the left, one arm lying under his head; beside him are swastika and X filling ornaments. A Dipylon warrior, characterized by his massive body shield with reserved rim, stands in the lower zone facing right and holding two spears. Like the figure above, he wears a helmet with a

98

Fig. 27. Fragment of Krater Louvre A519. (Reproduced by permission)

crest that curves behind. Head, spears, and upper body including the right arm and most of the chest area are preserved. In the field are double axes, one dotted, a swastika with angled arms, and two dotted oval ornaments.

Fragments of monumental vases found in the Dipylon cemetery in the nineteenth century were carried off to various European and American museums. Only later, particularly through the efforts of Villard and Kunze, were joins and relationships among fragments from the same vessels discovered. The Yale sherd was published by Villard, who found its precise placement in the great krater fragment Louvre A519 (Fig. 27). This funerary vessel is of critical significance to the history of Greek art, as it preserves the largest extant multifigured battle scene from the Geometric period. It has been estimated that the picture originally involved as many as forty figures.

Better preserved examples of grave-marker kraters show that the section represented in the Louvre and at Yale comes from the back of the vase; the front bore the prothesis scene, showing the dead man lying in state

and surrounded by mourners. On the Louvre and Yale fragments a horrific battle takes place in two registers. The upper zone pictures in bird's-eye view the battlefield strewn with corpses, their disarrayed limbs and trailing fingers contrasting poignantly with the vital heroes engaged in hand-to-hand combat beside them. Individual deaths unfold as vividly here as in the *Iliad* and in fact are remarkably reminiscent of Homer's fascination with wounds. One man is about to lose his head, unless his comrade to the left comes to the rescue in the nick of time; felled by an archer another man topples with an arrow through his head; beyond, a Dipylon warrior crashes from his chariot to the ground, struck in the leg and neck with spears, his great eye staring open in death. The Yale sherd fits at this point, preserving a shieldless warrior fallen headlong beneath the giant with the Dipylon shield; the edge of the shield appears on the Yale fragment just as its fallen man's leg extends onto the Louvre section. He plucks at a spear driven through his waist.

In the lower register a line of Dipylon heroes files to the right, each carrying two spears. Each is also accompanied by a sinuous-necked bird, perhaps the birds of prey that no representation of an epic battle, Near Eastern or Homeric, omitted; they populate the *Iliad* as well. Partially preserved on the left is a man fighting a four-legged figure, certainly an early example of that controversial image the Siamese "Molione twins," which some think is merely an artistic convention for two warriors fighting next to each other. Webster offered the most ingenious explanation for the numerous occurrences of this double figure by connecting it with the aristocratic Athenian Neleid family, supposedly descended from King Nestor of Pylos who counted among his heroic battle deeds the routing of the Aktorione or Molione twins. The appearance of this heroic moment on a grave monument would have served the deceased man and his family well (but see Boardman's objections).

The Yale fragment and its companion in the Louvre were created by an artist nicknamed the Kunze Painter for the scholar who traced the artist's personal traits among fragments in several museums. Specific to the Kunze Painter are the double-rimmed Dipylon shields and the grazing birds of prey; the body attitudes and filling ornaments are shared by many painters of this time. Some five vases and numerous fragments are now associated with this artistic hand. Scholars agree that Louvre A519 was potted and painted at the same time as the famous amphora ascribed to the Dipylon Master, Athens 804 (Fig. 7), but the two artists are made only slightly less anonymous by their popular names. While not intended to suggest a place of work, the conventional attribution of such vase-painters to the "Dipylon Workshop" raises crucial questions that remain unanswered: were these artists teacher and pupils, friends, competitors, working partners, potters as well as painters, women as well as men? The attribution of smaller-figured and nonfigured vases shows the varied nature of their careers and of their clients. Little else is known of the artists who first standardized the human figure and experimented with the expressiveness of the human body.

Schweitzer rightly described these scenes as "thrilling, instantaneous pictures." They break the rules of Geometric art. Except for the line of Dipylon warriors, the artist has eschewed the identical repetition of motifs

that was the essence of Geometric style and given more details than were necessary to convey a generic battle scene. The monumental funerary kraters took Attic art to the brink of narrative expression and stopped. For reasons unknown, the next generation of artists settled into the steady production of formulaic images of prothesis and chariot processions.

PUBLISHED

Villard, *CVA Louvre* 11, 6 fig. 2 (drawing is not accurate).

Davison, *Attic Geometric Workshops* 29, fig. 12a–b.

Coldstream, *Greek Geometric Pottery* 31 no. 17.

Ahlberg, *Fighting on Land and Sea* 16 fig. 7.

NOTES

Discussion and interpretation of Louvre A519: Villard, *CVA Louvre* 11, 6, pl. 5.7–9; Ahlberg, *Fighting on Land and Sea*; Coldstream, *Geometric Greece* 113; J. N. Coldstream, "The Geometric Style: Birth of the Picture" in *Looking at Greek Vases* ed. T. Rasmussen and N. Spivey (Cambridge 1991) 37–56 at 49–51.

Identification of the Dipylon Master and associates: G. Nottbohm, "Der Meister der grossen Dipylon-Amphora in Athen" *JdI* 58 (1943) 1–31; E. Kunze, "Disiecta membra attischer Grabkratere" *ArchEph* (1953–1954) 162–71; E. Kunze, "Bruchstücke attischer Grabkratere" in *Neue Beiträge zur klassischen Altertumswissenschaft: Festschrift zum 60. Geburtstag von Bernard Schweitzer* (Stuttgart 1954); Davison, *Attic Geometric Workshops* 22–31.

Molione twins: T. B. L. Webster, "Homer and Attic Geometric Vases" *BSA* 50 (1955) 38–50; contra, Boardman, "Symbol and Story in Geometric Art" 25–26.

S. L.

99 OINOCHOE WITH FIGURAL SCENE

Attic, Late Geometric IIa, 735–720 B.C.
Height 0.178.

Ceramic; surface worn in places.
**Museum of Fine Arts, Boston, Richard
    Norton Memorial Fund (25.43). From
    Schliemann Collection.**
See Plate 9.

The flat-bottomed oinochoe comprises a
globular body with cylindrical neck rising
abruptly from the sloping shoulder to a broad
trefoil lip. Sets of four hand-drawn concentric
circles around a central rosette decorate the
sides and provide a frame for the figural panel
at the front; three horizontal wavy lines fill
the space below the panel. A water bird is
tucked under the handle at the back of the
vase.

Dotted-circle chains above and on the sides
frame three men involved in an unusual
scene. Rendered entirely in silhouette, two
stand facing each other and clasping their
inner hands above a third, inverted figure.
The standing figure on the left holds an
object, certainly a sword or dagger, in his free
hand. Made smaller to fit his cramped space,
the upside-down man is shown in an inactive
pose with hands against his thighs and toes
pointing upward. Alone of the three, he has a
single eye reserved in his silhouette head. At
his waist is a sword or scabbard.

This oinochoe belongs to a growing number attributed to the Concentric Circle
Group, an Athenian workshop that adapted
from Cypriot tradition the odd decorative system that uses concentric circles on a closed
vessel. For the most part the painter or painters who produced these oinochoai were not
inventive when it came to figure scenes. Most
examples employ the old iconographic stand-
bys of one or two horses tied to a manger or
a tripod and, once, a man standing between
two horses. The present scene is unique not
only to the Concentric Circle Group but to
the corpus of Geometric figural scenes.

The many iconographic signals in this
simple scene have encouraged a variety of
interpretations, from generic battle excerpt to
narrative allusion. Some scholars favor the
interpretation first advanced by Tölle in 1964

99

of an acrobatic dance to parallel Homer's references to dances involving two tumblers
"somersaulting" among the other dancers.
Tölle admits that the painted figure's head-
stand may not correspond precisely to the real
activity but suggests that this image was the
best visual translation at hand for Homer's
phrase. It should be noted that Egyptian and
Minoan artists had no difficulty creating an
unambiguous depiction of the move Homer
describes. Supporters of the acrobat interpretation cite a skyphos from the Kerameikos
with a scene in which two large figures clasp
hands over the head of a smaller one who
holds a branch, an item regularly carried by
dancers.

More plausibly, one can read in this panel a
straightforward fighting scene that owes its
rather humorous appearance to the small field
in which the artist had to fit the requisite elements: opponents in high action, with a fallen

comrade shown in bird's-eye view much as the corpses that litter the battlefields of the great Dipylon kraters (see 98). In favor of this meaning is the smaller figure's pose, with his limbs completely unengaged and his toes pointing heavenward. His unusual reserve eye was a fine touch to contrast the emptiness of death with the "normal" consciousness of the living warriors; the same solution is used by the artist of Louvre krater fragment A519 (see Fig. 27 and 98). The specific event, in which one man has lost his weapon, offers a dramatic tension that must have delighted the drinkers using this wine jug. Without assuming a direct influence of epic upon art, this duel can be compared to the hand-to-hand combats of the *Iliad*, particularly those contests to recover a body. Less conservatively, Brommer has read in the scene the return of Hektor's body to Priam by Achilles, whose sword distinguishes him from the old man, and Hurwit ingeniously suggests the murder of Agamemnon by Aigisthus and Klytemnaestra. Whether the artist had in mind or even knew of that critical episode, at least we can see here the interest in visual detail that will make narrative images possible.

PUBLISHED

A. Fairbanks, *Catalogue of Greek and Etruscan Vases* (Museum of Fine Arts, Boston) I (Cambridge MA 1928) 81, pl. 23 no. 269c.

G. H. Chase, *Greek and Roman Antiquities. A Guide to the Classical Collection* (Boston 1950) 15 fig. 13.

Kübler, *Die Nekropole des 10. bis 8. Jahrhunderts* 179.

H. Marwitz, "Kreis und Figur in der attisch-geometrischen Vasenmalerei" *JdI* (1959) 88 type VIIIc.

C. C. Vermeule, *Greek, Etruscan, and Roman Art* (The Classical Collections of the Museum of Fine Arts, Boston, Boston 1963, 1972) fig. 24.

Coldstream, *Greek Geometric Pottery* 75 no. 12.

Ahlberg, *Fighting on Land and Sea* 79.

Schweitzer, *Greek Geometric Art* 48, 49, pl. 57.

Tölle, *Frühgriechische Reigentänze* 15 no. 11, 63.

Fittschen, *Untersuchungen zum Beginn der Sagensdarstellungen* 22 no. A9.

F. Brommer, *Vasenlisten* 3d ed. (Marburg/Lahn 1973) 330 (Priam and Achilles).

Boreas 2 (1979) 14, n. 38.

Vermeule, *Aspects of Death in Early Greek Art and Poetry* 98 fig. 15.

S. Foltiny in H.-G. Buchholz, S. Foltiny, and O. Höckmann, *Kriegswesen* 2 (*ArchHom* I, E, Göttingen 1980) 246, n. 1486.

Ahlberg-Cornell, "Games, Play and Performance" 66–67, fig. 23.

Rombos, *The Iconography of Attic Late Geometric II Pottery* 283, 345, 383, 492 no. 291, pl. 74b.

NOTES

For the Concentric Circle Group: Marwitz, "Kreis und Figur in der attisch-geometrischen Vasenmalerei"; Coldstream, *Greek Geometric Pottery* 74–76.

For a similar scene on a Protoattic vessel stand in Munich: K. Vierniesel, "Neuerwerbungen. Staatliche Antikensammlungen und Glyptothek" *MüJb* 18 (1967) 241–48, fig. 1.

For the acrobatic interpretation: Tölle, *Frühgriechische Reigentänze* 63; *Iliad* 18.604–5; *Odyssey* 4.18–19; Fittschen, *Untersuchungen zum Beginn der Sagensdarstellungen* 22–23; Schweitzer, *Greek Geometric Art* 49; Rombos, *The Iconography of Attic Late Geometric II Pottery* 283.

Egyptian and Minoan representations of similar dance: Laser, *Sport und Spiel* 73–75, fig. 27.

Kerameikos skyphos inv. 812: Kübler, *Die Nekropole des 10. bis 8. Jahrhunderts* pl. 117.

S. L.

100 MAN WITH BIRD

Subgeometric, early seventh century B.C.
Height 0.049, base 0.098 x 0.039.
Bronze; missing lower section of man's right leg.

100

Sol Rabin Collection, Los Angeles; formerly Leon Pomerance Collection.

On a flat rectangular base, a large bird grasps in its beak the hand of a small dismayed man who, sitting, braces his right leg against the bird and his left hand on the ground in an attempt to extricate himself. The man's large bulbous head has deeply punched eyes, an incised mouth, and projecting ears and nose. He wears a cap with a small peak in front. His body is relatively slight, with simple tubular limbs. Incised lines across his back indicate a belt. Standing on short stocky legs, the bird's triangular body rises to a flattened tail with vertical striations; its long neck strains forward as the man pulls back. The eyes are indented, and the edges of the beak are visible along the man's arm.

Formally, the pair recalls the paratactic group compositions of the late eighth century, such as the deer and dogs from Olympia and the centaur group in New York, which were compositionally conceived in profile. Although incised with greater detail, the geometricized bird reflects various types of bird pendants popular at the end of the eighth century and the beginning of the seventh. The position of the man, seated on the ground with legs drawn up near his body, corresponds with other seated bronze figures, most notably a bronze in the Ashmolean Museum and the series of little helmet-makers hammering away on anvils. Characteristic of Subgeometric sculpture is an uneven interest in a naturalistic rendering of a few anatomical details at the expense of the figure's organic unity, seen here in the overly large head and facial features.

The image of a man-bird tussle is unparalleled in Geometric art, where the theme of a human fighting a wild animal is a well-established heroic emblem. In this small bronze pair the domesticity of the scene, smacking of farmyard foibles, has a mock-heroic air. The scene has been thought to represent Herakles momentarily bested by one of the lethal Stymphalian birds, an interpretation without parallel in Geometric or Archaic art and one that lends an unaccustomed humor to Herakles' trials for an audience that had only just begun to explore this serious subject. Equally unlikely is a comic depiction of a vulture attacking a not-quite-dead hero on a battlefield (compare Fig. 27 for a serious visual reference to the Homeric bird of prey). A more likely interpretation may be the *geranomachy*, the battle of the pygmies against the cranes who attacked them on the birds' return from their seasonal migration out of Scythia. Beginning with Herodotus, ancient writers variously located the pygmies' home in Africa near the source of the Nile, in Asia Minor, or in the Black Sea vicinity. The first Greek depiction of the theme occurs in painting on the foot of the François Vase of about 570 B.C., but already by the eighth century it was sufficiently familiar for book 3 of the *Iliad* to open with a simile comparing raucous Trojans to the cranes. Although Homer's attacking Trojans are rather daunting, artistic interpretations of the geranomachy tend toward parody, a treatment already detectable in the bronze pair.

Earlier than the François Vase, a seventh-century Cypriot jug may depict the myth in a large decorative bird surveying a diminutive and slightly agitated man. A Mycenaean krater from Enkomi carries a similar scene from the Late Bronze Age, with enormous birds threatening people who flee in chariots. Closer in date to the bronze pair is a fragment in the Louvre of a terracotta plaque or sarcophagus rim found at Caesarea (Kayseri) in Cappadocia and dated to the eighth to seventh century B.C. Preserved on the piece is a large human-legged bird attacking a small man who strikes the bird with a stick. As in the other examples the bird appears to have the advantage; it grasps the man's head in its beak.

Most important here is the eastern origin of these representations. Although the existence of mythological reference in Mycenaean art has its skeptics, Near Eastern myth and art provide a rich background, particularly in pitting heroes against fantastic creatures. Ancient writers tended to locate the pygmy-crane myth in the east; Pliny set it in Caria, Stephenos of Byzantium cited a Carian story of pygmies in Thrace, and Strabo placed the myth in the Caucasus. Other Near Eastern myths such as that of the Babylonian Anzu bird also might have been depicted by the

sort of imagery seen in these Cypriot and Cappadocian works.

The style of the bronze group has no easily identifiable locale. Although the man's deep eye indentations and round cap, his loose-jointed body, and the bird's triangular profile are congruent with Subgeometric Peloponnesian bronze figurines, his heavy full chin, the odd curl at this forehead, and the bird's open beak look alien. The quirkiness of the scene recalls the surprising inventions of Cypriot art, but the island's tradition in bronze figurine sculpture offers a feeble background for comparison. Similarly, bronze sculpture in neighboring eastern cultures was too firmly grounded in fixed types with long Bronze Age pedigrees to offer new directions in the Iron Age. The coming together of myth and bronze in fact leads us on surer footing back to Greece.

The bronze man and bird represent the lingering of the Geometric tradition of group sculpture into the seventh century, when in many areas of Greece the individuality of small-scale bronze sculpture was yielding to the influence of Daedalic terracotta style and large-scale sculpture. Based not on real life but on folktale, the pair reflects the beginning of an enduring influence of Homeric poetry on art. This naive image of a pygmy was for the artist and his audience an early attempt to render visible the world beyond their shores.

PUBLISHED
Archaeology 23 (1970) 52.

EXHIBITED
The Age of Homer, University Museum, University of Pennsylvania, December 1969–March 1970.

NOTES
For the Olympia deer and dogs: Schweitzer, *Greek Geometric Art* pl. 190; Heilmeyer, *Frühe Olympische Bronzefiguren* pl. 87, no. 723.
For the centaur group: Schweitzer, *Greek Geometric Art* pl. 185.

For the François Vase: P. E. Arias and M. Hirmer, *A History of Greek Vase Painting* (London 1962) pl. 40.

Cypriot jug: V. Karageorghis, "Une représentation de pygmée et de grue sur une vase cypriote du VIIe siècle avant J.-C." *RA* (1972) 47–52; Karageorghis and Des Gagniers, *La céramique chypriote de style figuré* 105, IX.10.

Mycenaean vase from Enkomi: E. Vermeule and V. Karageorghis, *Mycenaean Pictorial Vase Painting* (Cambridge MA 1982) 16, III.6.

Cappadocian fragment: E. Pottier, "Documents céramiques du Musée du Louvre" in *Recueil Edmond Pottier* (Paris 1937) 147–211 at 197–98, 201–4 and fig. 21.

For ancient authors on the pygmy-crane myth: Pottier, "Documents céramiques" 202–3; E. Wüst, "Pygmaioi" *RE* 23, pt. 2, 2064.

S. L.

101

101 LYRE-PLAYER AND BOY

Cretan, ca. 690–670 B.C.
Height 0.115, base length 0.075.
Bronze, lustrous patina, nearly black; intact; some incrustation within crevices.
The J. Paul Getty Museum (90.AB.6).

A nude male playing a lyre stands next to a smaller figure on a narrow rectangular base, the edge of which is marked with vertical notches. Two holes pierce the base, which was probably attached to a larger support. The size of the figures makes it unlikely they were attached to a cauldron or other vessel; they may have been part of a votive offering. Figures and base are solid-cast in a single unit. The musician holds the lyre with his left hand as he strikes the strings with the *plektron* in his right. His body is schematically rendered, with rubbery limbs, narrow waist, and triangular torso; the massive head is unsupported by a neck. The nose is broad, the mouth a mere slit, and the eyes and ears simple rings. Knees, navel, and nipples are

represented with small circular incisions. Above the prominent genitals, the pubic hair is indicated by an incised triangle with a roughened surface. The man's hair is shaped like a cap or bowl, without sideburns or pendant locks, and rows of braids marked with parallel lines radiate from the crown.

The smaller figure at left has the same kind of hair; he too, then, should be male, and because of his size, a boy. Unlike the musician, he wears a cylindrical belt and a triangular codpiece or loincloth; the latter hangs freely, not extending over the rather prominent buttocks. The vertical incision in the center of the loincloth might be taken for an indication of female sex, but in addition to the identical hairstyles, other points argue against this: the slit is too high, stopping well short of the crotch; nude females are only rarely depicted wearing belts; the pubic area is rendered differently on the man, with the apex of the triangle at the top. It is not anachronistic to assume that a little girl would not have her genitals thus represented. The pellet-like breasts are too small to be considered female; plastic breasts are not the rule on Geometric males, but they do occur, in both bronze and terracotta.

The boy's trunk and legs are lean and nearly cylindrical; the knees are marked by circular incisions. The face is narrower than the musician's, but equally massive in profile. The nose is broader, and the rings around the eyes are marked with parallel incisions representing eyelashes. With his left arm, the boy reaches out to touch the hip of the lyre-player; his boneless right arm curves down like a fishhook. On both figures, the toes and fingers are roughly indicated by incisions. The boy is the more beguiling figure, with a slight but definite smile that animates the whole group.

Groups of any kind are rare in Geometric bronze sculpture, and this example is unique in featuring a musician. The side-by-side composition is used in an earlier, eighth-century group from Syme, in Crete, with a pair of males—one short, one tall—standing on a narrow base, their hands touching. Although crudely modeled, with small, pinched heads, the figures from Syme may be direct ancestors of the Getty pair. Bowl haircuts like those of the Getty figures (albeit with queues in back) appear on Cretan statuettes of the late eighth and early seventh century. A few of these, such as the bronze Apollo from Dreros and a smaller youth from Afrati, are garbed with belt and loincloth, garments with a long history on Crete, where they were among the most distinctive elements of Minoan dress, later reappearing on male figurines in the Daedalic style.

Although lyre-players were frequently depicted by Geometric vase painters and appear on oriental gems from Greek sites, sculptural representations are exceedingly rare; an eighth-century bronze statuette in Brussels, probably Peloponnesian, may be the earliest. Smaller than the Getty figures, but closer in style and feeling, are a seated lyre-player in Heraklion, of the early seventh century, and a very similar example in a private collection (17), probably from the same Cretan workshop. Their four-stringed lyres have rounded soundboards, while the Getty instrument, probably abbreviated by the artist, is squarer and has but two strings. All three lyres, as well as those on Geometric vases, may be equated with the Homeric phorminx, the instrument employed by bards in the *Iliad* and *Odyssey*, which seems to have had fewer strings than the seven-stringed lyres and kitharas of later times.

The Getty group marks the first appearance of the *plektron* in Greek sculpture, perhaps indicating a slightly later date than the seated lyre-players. A seventh-century date is supported by the style of the figures, in which a concern for detail is combined with a softness and rotundity of modeling uncharacteristic of eighth-century bronzes. The pubic hair of the lyre-player is a feature usually not encountered before the early seventh century, and the slight smile and touching gesture of the boy introduce a note of humanity usually lacking in earlier sculptures. Taken together, these elements suggest a date of about 690–670 B.C.

The mouth of the lyre-player is closed, but his head is raised: he is about to sing. Whether the fashioner of the wax model was thinking of a bard spinning an epic tale, or of a local lyrist strumming a tune for the village dancers, we cannot know. But recalling that Homer was said to be blind, and that in book 8 of the *Odyssey* the sightless Phaiakian bard Demodokos was helped to his seat by a herald before moving Odysseus with his song, one could imagine this singer too may be glad of a steadying hand.

PUBLISHED
GettyMusJ 19 (1991) 136–37, no. 8.

NOTES
For bronze and terracotta male figurines with pellet breasts: Naumann, *Subminoische und protogeometrische Bronzeplastik* pl. 28, 1 and pl. 30, 3; W.-D. Heilmeyer, *Frühe Olym-*

pische Tonfiguren (OlForsch VII, Berlin 1972) pl. 27, no. 168, and pl. 34, no. 203.

For the group from Syme (Heraklion inv. 3137): A. Lebessi, "A Sanctuary of Hermes and Aphrodite in Crete" *Expedition* 18, 3 (Spring 1976) 4, no. 4; another bronze male from Syme may have shared his rectangular base with a second figure, now lost: *Ergon* (1981) 69, pl. 114.

For the Apollo from Dreros: P. Blome, *Die figürliche Bildwelt Kretas in der geometrischen und früharchaischen Periode* (Mainz 1982) pl. 4; Beyer, *Die Tempel von Dreros und Prinias* A 154–56, pls. 47 and 51, 4–5.

For the statuette from Afrati: AR (1973–1974) 36–37, fig. 76; A. Lebessi, *Stele: Tomos eis mnemen Nikolaou Kontoleontos* (Athens 1980) 87–95, pls. 25–30.

For Cretan figures with a loincloth: Minoan, J. Mertens, *Greek Art of the Aegean Islands* (New York 1979) 92, no. 46; Subminoan, Naumann, *Subminoische und protogeometrische Bronzeplastik* pl. 1, 2; Protogeometric, Naumann, *Subminoische* pl. 32; Daedalic, *Dädalische Kunst auf Kreta im 7. Jahrhun-*

derts v. Chr. (Mainz 1970) 46–48, pl. 19 and color pl. III.

For the lyre-player in Brussels (inv. R 826): Tölle, *Frühgriechische Reigentänze* no. 27B.

For the lyre-player in Heraklion (inv. 2064), only 5.5 cm. tall: Schweitzer, *Greek Geometric Art* 161, pl. 161; D. Levi, "Arkades" *AsAtene* 10–12 (1927–1929) 541–42, fig. 609.

For Greek stringed instruments: M. Maas and J. M. Snyder, *Stringed Instruments of Ancient Greece* (New Haven and London 1989). For *plektra*: K. Schneider, "Plectrum" *RE*, series 2, 21, pt. 1, 187–89. For music in ancient Greece: Wegner, *Musik und Tanz*; M. Wegner, *Das Musikleben der Griechen* (Berlin 1949); G. Comotti, *Music in Greek and Roman Culture* (Baltimore and London 1989).

Representation of pubic hair: cf. an early seventh-century bronze warrior at Delphi (inv. 3232); Schweitzer, *Greek Geometric Art* 145–46, pls. 174–75.

For the herald helping Demodokos to his seat and later assisting him to the athletic events: *Odyssey* 8.63–70, 104–8.

J. M. P.

FREQUENTLY
CITED SOURCES

For abbreviations see American Journal of Archaeology 95 (1991) 4–16.

The Aegean and the Near East. Studies Presented to Hetty Goldman, ed. S. S. Weinberg. Locust Valley NY 1956.

Ahlberg, G. *Fighting on Land and Sea in Greek Geometric Art* (SkrAth 1, 16). Stockholm 1971.

———. *Prothesis and Ekphora in Greek Geometric Art* (SIMA XXXII). Göteborg 1971.

Ahlberg-Cornell, G. "Games, Play and Performance in Greek Geometric Art: The Kantharos Copenhagen NM727 Reconsidered." *ActaArch* 58 (1987) 55–86.

Ashmead, A. H., and K. M. Phillips, Jr. *Classical Vases: Catalogue of the Classical Collection* (Museum of Art, Rhode Island School of Design). Providence RI 1976.

Baur, P. V. C. *Catalogue of the Rebecca Darlington Stoddard Collection of Greek and Italian Vases in Yale University.* New Haven CT 1922.

Benson, J. L. *Horse, Bird, and Man.* Amherst 1970.

Benton, S. "Evolution of the Tripod-lebes." *BSA* 35 (1934–1935) 74–130.

Betancourt, P. "The Age of Homer." *Expedition* 12, 1 (1969) 2–14.

Bevan, E. *Representations of Animals in Sanctuaries of Artemis and Other Olympian Deities* (BAR S315). Oxford 1986.

Beyer, I. *Die Tempel von Dreros und Prinias A und die Chronologie der kretischen Kunst des 8. und 7. Jhs. v. Chr.* Freiburg 1976.

Blinkenberg, Chr. *Fibules grecques et orientales.* Copenhagen 1926.

Boardman, J. *The Cretan Collection in Oxford. The Dictaean Cave and Iron Age Crete.* Oxford 1961.

———. *The Greeks Overseas.* London 1980.

———. "Symbol and Story in Geometric Art" in W. Moon, ed., *Ancient Greek Art and Iconography* 15–36. Madison 1983.

Boardman, J., and G. Buchner, "Seals from Ischia and the Lyre-Player Group." *JdI* 81 (1966) 1–62.

Bohen, B. *Die geometrischen Pyxiden* (Kerameikos XIII). Berlin 1988.

Borrell, B. *Attisch geometrische Schalen: Eine spätgeometrische Keramikgattung und ihre Beziehungen zum Orient* (Keramikforschungen II). Mainz 1978.

Bouzek, J. *Graeco-Macedonian Bronzes.* Prague 1973.

Brann, E. T. H. *Late Geometric and Protoattic Pottery* (Agora VIII). Princeton 1962.

Brock, J. K. *Fortetsa, Early Greek Tombs Near Knossos* (BSA Supplement 2). Cambridge 1957.

Buchholz, H.-G., G. Jöhrens, and I. Maull. *Jagd und Fischfang* (ArchHom II, J). Göttingen 1973.

Cahn, H. A. *Early Art in Greece: The Cycladic, Minoan, Mycenaean, and Geometric Periods.* Andre Emmerich Gallery New York 1965.

Carter, J. B. "The Beginning of Narrative Art in the Greek Geometric Period." *BSA* 67 (1972) 25–58.

Catling, H. W. *Cypriot Bronzework in the Mycenaean World.* Oxford 1964.

Catling, R. W. V., and I. Lemos, *Lefkandi* II, pt. 1 *The Pottery.* London 1990.

Cesnola, L. P. di. *Cyprus. Its Ancient Cities, Tombs, and Temples.* New York 1878.

———. *A Descriptive Atlas of the Cesnola Collection of Cypriote Antiquities in the Metropoli-*

tan Museum of Art, New York I–III. New York 1885–1903.

Coldstream, J. N. *Geometric Greece*. London 1977.

———. *Greek Geometric Pottery*. London 1968.

Comstock, M. B., and C. C. Vermeule. *Greek, Etruscan and Roman Bronzes in the Museum of Fine Arts, Boston*. Greenwich CT 1971.

Cook, J. M. "Athenian Workshops around 700." *BSA* 42 (1947) 139–55.

Courbin, P. *La céramique géométrique de l'Argolide*. Paris 1966.

Davison, J. *Attic Geometric Workshops* (Yale Classical Studies XVI). New Haven CT 1961.

Dawkins, R. M. *The Sanctuary of Artemis Orthia at Sparta*. London 1929.

Demetriou, A. *Cypro-Aegean Relations in the Early Iron Age* (SIMA LXXXIII). Göteborg 1989.

Desborough, V. R. d'A. *The Greek Dark Ages*. London 1972.

———. *The Last Mycenaeans and Their Successors*. Oxford 1964.

———. *Protogeometric Pottery*. Oxford 1952.

Dörig, J. *Art antique: Collections privées de Suisse romande*. Geneva 1975.

Dothan, T. *The Philistines and Their Material Culture*. New Haven and London 1982.

Dunbabin, T. J. *The Greeks and Their Eastern Neighbors*. London 1957.

Early Greek Cult Practice, ed. R. Hägg, N. Marinatos, G. C. Nordquist (SkrAth 4, 38). Stockholm 1988.

Early Society in Cyprus, ed. E. Peltenburg. Edinburgh 1989.

Fittschen, K. *Untersuchungen zum Beginn der Sagensdarstellungen bei den Griechen*. Berlin 1969.

Floren, J. *Die geometrische und archaische Plastik* (Fuchs, W., and J. Floren, *Die griechische Plastik* I). Munich 1987.

Gjerstad, E. *The Cypro-Geometric, Cypro-Archaic and Cypro-Classical Periods* (Swedish Cyprus Expedition IV, part 2). Stockholm 1948.

Goodison, L. *Death, Women, and the Sun. Symbolism of Regeneration in Early Aegean Religion* (BICS Supplement 53). London 1989.

The Greek Renaissance of the Eighth Century

B.C.: Tradition and Innovation, ed. R. Hägg (SkrAth 4, 30). Stockholm 1983.

Greenhalgh, P. A. L. *Early Greek Warfare. Horsemen and Chariots in the Homeric and Archaic Ages*. Cambridge 1973.

Hahland, W. "Neue Denkmäler des attischen Heroen- und Totenkultes" in W. Müller, ed., *Festschrift für Friedrich Zucker zum 70. Geburtstage* 177–94. Berlin 1954.

Hall, E. *Excavations in Eastern Crete, Vrokastro*. Philadelphia 1914.

Hampe, R. *Frühe griechische Sagenbilder in Böotien*. Athens 1936.

Heilmeyer, W.-D. *Frühe Olympische Bronzefiguren: Die Tiervotive* (OlForsch XII). Berlin 1979.

Herrmann, H.-V. "Werkstätten geometrischer Bronzeplastik." *JdI* 79 (1964) 17–71.

Himmelmann-Wildschütz, N. *Bemerkungen zur geometrischen Plastik*. Berlin 1964.

Hoffmann, H. *Ten Centuries That Shaped the West: Greek and Roman Art in Texas Collections*. Exhibition catalogue. Houston 1971.

Hommes et dieux de la Grèce antique. Exhibition catalogue, Palais des Beaux-Arts, Brussels, ed. K. van Gelder. Brussels 1982.

Hurwit, J. M. *The Art and Culture of Early Greece, 1100–480 B.C.* Ithaca NY 1985.

Iacovou, M. *The Pictorial Pottery of Eleventh Century B.C. Cyprus* (SIMA LXXVIII). Göteborg 1988.

Jacobsthal, P. *Greek Pins and Their Connexions with Europe and Asia*. Oxford 1956.

Karageorghis, V. *Palaepaphos-Skales: An Iron Age Cemetery in Cyprus* (Ausgrabungen in Alt-Paphos auf Cypern III). Konstanz 1983.

Karageorghis, V., and J. Des Gagniers, *La céramique chypriote de style figuré*. Rome 1974. *Supplément*. Rome 1979.

Kearsley, R. *The Pendent Semi-circle Skyphos* (BICS Supplement 44). London 1989.

Kilian, K. *Fibeln in Thessalien von der mykenischen bis zur archaischen Zeit* (Prähistorische Bronzefunde XIV, 2). Munich 1975.

———. "Trachtzubehör der Eisenzeit zwischen Ägäis und Adria." *PZ* 50 (1975) 9–140.

Kilian-Dirlmeier, I. *Anhänger in Griechenland von der mykenischen bis zur spätgeometrischen*

Zeit (Prähistorische Bronzefunde XI, 2).
Munich 1979.

Kozloff, A. P., and D. G. Mitten, eds. *The Gods Delight. The Human Figure in Classical Bronze.* Exhibition catalogue. Cleveland 1988.

Kübler, K. *Die Nekropole des 10. bis 8. Jahrhunderts* (Kerameikos V, 1). Berlin 1954.

Langdon, M. K. *A Sanctuary of Zeus on Mount Hymettos* (Hesperia Supplement XVI). Princeton 1976.

Langdon, S. "From Monkey to Man: The Evolution of a Geometric Sculptural Type." *AJA* 94 (1990) 407–24.

———. "The Return of the Horse-Leader." *AJA* 93 (1989) 185–201.

Laser, S. *Sport und Spiel* (ArchHom III, T). Göttingen 1989.

Lorimer, H. *Homer and the Monuments.* London 1950.

Maass, M. *Die geometrischen Dreifüsse von Olympia* (OlForsch X). Berlin 1978.

Matheson Burke, S., and J. J. Pollitt, *Greek Vases at Yale.* New Yaven CT 1975

Mitten, D. G. *Classical Bronzes: Catalogue of the Classical Collection* (Museum of Art, Rhode Island School of Design). Providence RI 1975.

———. "The Earliest Greek Sculptures in the Museum." *BMFA* 65 (1967) 4–18.

Mitten, D. G., and S. F. Doeringer, eds. *Master Bronzes from the Classical World.* Exhibition catalogue. Greenwich CT 1967.

Moorey, P. R. S., and S. Fleming, "Problems in the Study of the Anthropomorphic Metal Statuary from Syro-Palestine before 330 B.C." *Levant* 16 (1984) 67–90.

Morris, S. P. *Daidalos and the Origins of Greek Art.* Princeton 1992.

Muthmann, F. *Der Granatapfel. Symbol des Lebens in der alten Welt.* Bern 1982.

Myres, J. L. *Handbook of the Cesnola Collection of Antiquities from Cyprus.* New York 1914.

Naumann, U. *Subminoische und protogeometrische Bronzeplastik auf Kreta* (AM Supplement 6). Berlin 1976.

Negbi, O. *Canaanite Gods in Metal. An Archaeological Study of Ancient Syro-Palestinian Figurines.* Tel Aviv 1976.

Neugebauer, K. A. *Staatliche Museen zu Berlin: Katalog der statuarischen Bronzen im Antiquarium. Die minoischen und archaischen griechischen Bronzen.* Berlin 1931.

Niemeyer, H. G., ed. *Phönizier im Westen.* Mainz 1982.

Nilsson, M. P. *The Minoan-Mycenaean Religion and Its Survival in Greek Religion,* 2d ed. Lund 1968.

Philipp, H. *Bronzeschmuck aus Olympia* (OlForsch XIII). Berlin 1981.

Pilali-Papasteriou, A. *Die bronzenen Tierfiguren aus Kreta* (Prähistorische Bronzefunde I, 3). Munich 1985.

Popham, M. R., and L. H. Sackett, *Lefkandi I. The Iron Age: The Settlement* (BSA Supplement 11). Oxford 1979–1980.

Powell, B. B. *Homer and the Origin of the Greek Alphabet.* Cambridge 1991.

Richter, G. M. A. *Handbook of the Greek Collection.* Metropolitan Museum of Art, Cambridge MA 1953.

Rolley, C. *Greek Bronzes.* London 1986.

———. *Monuments figurés, les statuettes de bronze* (FdD V). Paris 1969.

Rombos, Th. *The Iconography of Attic Late Geometric II Pottery* (SIMA-PB 68). Jonsered 1988.

Ruckert, A. *Frühe Keramik Böotiens.* Bern 1976.

Rudolph, W., and A. Calinescu, eds. *Ancient Art from the V. G. Simkhovitch Collection.* Bloomington IN 1988.

Schefold, K. *Die Griechen und ihre Nachbarn.* Berlin 1967.

———. *Meisterwerke griechischer Kunst.* Basel 1960.

Schweitzer, B. *Greek Geometric Art.* New York 1969.

Seeden, H. *The Standing Armed Figurines in the Levant* (Prähistorische Bronzefunde I, 1). Munich 1980.

Smithson, E. L. "The Tomb of a Rich Athenian Lady circa 850 B.C." *Hesperia* 37 (1968) 77–116.

Snodgrass, A. *An Archaeology of Greece.* Berkeley 1987

———. *The Dark Age of Greece.* Edinburgh 1971.

Spartz, E. *Das Wappenbild des Herrn und Herrin der Tiere in der minoisch-mykenischen und frühgriechischen Kunst.* Munich 1962.

Tölle, R. *Frühgriechische Reigentänze.* Waldsassen 1964.

Verlinden, C. *Les statuettes anthropomorphes cré-toises en bronze et en plomb, du IIIe millénaire au VIIe siècle av. J.-C.* Providence RI and Louvain 1984.

Vermeule, E. *Aspects of Death in Early Greek Art and Poetry.* Berkeley, Los Angeles 1979.

———. *Götterkult* (ArchHom III, 5). Göttingen 1974.

Vickers, M. "Some Early Iron Age Bronzes from Macedonia." *APXAIA MAKEDONIA* II (Second International Symposium, August 19–24, 1973) 17–31. Thessaloniki 1977.

Voyatzis, M. E. *The Early Sanctuary of Athena Alea at Tegea and Other Archaic Sanctuaries in Arcadia* (SIMA-PB 97). Göteborg 1990.

Waldstein, C. *The Argive Heraeum* I–II. Boston 1902–1905.

Wegner, M. *Musik und Tanz* (ArchHom III, U). Göttingen 1968.

Whitley, J. *Style and Society in Dark Age Greece.* Cambridge 1991.

Young, R. S. *Late Geometric Graves and a Seventh Century Well in the Agora* (Hesperia Supplement 2). Athens 1939.

Zimmermann, J.-L. *Les chevaux dans l'art géométrique grec.* Mainz 1989.

INDEX
OF CATALOGUED OBJECTS BY COLLECTION

(by entry number)

INDEX
OF NAMES AND TERMS IN THE CATALOGUE

(by entry number)